BIBLE PROPHECY

by
Oliver B. Greene

The Gospel Hour, Inc.
Oliver B. Greene, Director
Box 2024, Greenville, South Carolina 29602

First printing, March 1970—15,000 copies

$9.95

FOREWORD

"The secret things belong unto the Lord our God: *but those things which are revealed belong unto us and to our children for ever . . ."* (Deut. 29:29).

No minister, teacher, or believer will ever understand all of the Bible; but most of us are content to understand *all too little* of what God is willing to reveal to His children. The *secret* things belong unto God, but the things *revealed* belong unto His children; and by comparing Scripture with Scripture and spiritual things with spiritual we can know much concerning prophetic and spiritual truths. The Holy Spirit is the Author of the Word of God, and He dwells in the heart of every believer. The author of *any* book is the best *teacher* of that book, therefore the Holy Spirit reveals the deep things of God to believers who are willing to pay the price in systematic study.

It is true that man cannot lift the veil which hides future events from human eyes, events yet to take place in the program of God. But too many prophecies have already been literally fulfilled for any reasonable person to say that these things happened by chance. They happened according to the plan and program of Almighty God, who writes history in advance.

To shake the foundation of the faith of the true believer, all that Jesus was and did must be explained away—and that is a human impossibility. History confirms the undeniable fact that a Man named Jesus

3

lived, and the Word of God reveals exactly *who He was* and *why He lived, died, and rose again.* Twenty centuries since Bethlehem, the name of Jesus is on the lips of more people than at any time in the history of man.

As we study prophetic truth, we will see that the first coming of Jesus demands His second coming, just as His second coming necessitated the first. He came the first time to redeem the souls of men. He is coming the second time to redeem all creation.

Christ crucified, risen, ascended, and coming again *bodily* must be accepted if the Bible is to be understood and its teaching harmonized. Prophecies already fulfilled in minute detail give absolute proof that prophecies not yet fulfilled *will be* brought to pass at the appointed time in God's program, *exactly as prophesied.*

I trust the Lord will use the simple chapters of this book to enlighten, encourage, and strengthen many Christians—and may unbelievers who read these chapters be born again as they hear the Word of God, the incorruptible seed that brings the new birth. "Faith cometh by hearing, and hearing by the Word of God" (Rom. 10:17).

"The Spirit and the bride say, Come. And let him that heareth say, Come. And let him that is athirst come. And whosoever will, let him take the water of life freely. . . . He which testifieth these things saith, Surely I come quickly. Amen. Even so, COME, LORD JESUS" (Rev. 22:17, 20).

The Author

Contents

BIBLE PROPHECY

Chapter I

Prophecy in Relation to the Sovereign Claims of Almighty God

"Remember the former things of old: for I am God, and there is none else; I am God, and there is none like me, declaring the end from the beginning, and from ancient times the things that are not yet done, saying, My counsel shall stand, and I will do all my pleasure: calling a ravenous bird from the east, the man that executeth my counsel from a far country: yea, I have spoken it, I will also bring it to pass; I have purposed it, I will also do it. Hearken unto me, ye stouthearted, that are far from righteousness: I bring near my righteousness; it shall not be far off, and my salvation shall not tarry: and I will place salvation in Zion for Israel my glory" (Isa. 46:9-13).

No statement like that found in the above passage of Scripture has ever appeared in any book penned by mortal man. The passage recorded here contains divine and supernatural claims, which because of their very nature could be found only in the infallible, living Word of God.

In these tremendous words recorded by the Prophet Isaiah, God declares Himself to be the self-existent One, the uncaused, uncreated, and definitely incomparable One—standing alone in the solitary, divine grandeur of His Eternal Being. Here God reveals

Himself in the wisdom of His omniscience, in the
strength of His omnipotence, and in the eminence of
His omnipresence.   In these inspired words God declares Himself as knowing the end from the beginning,
and that what He has *purposed,* He will *do.*
In God's Holy Word we find history written in
advance—that is, God predetermines history and causes
it to run in the mold of prophecy.   Therefore the
prophets of God, through inspiration, have penned
down world events and divine happenings *centuries*
before they occur.

The holy prophets of God have convincingly demonstrated to every thinking person who reads the Bible
that the Scriptures are verbally inspired, God-breathed,
written under the supervision of the Holy Spirit in the
directing will of our great God.   The prophets have
given undeniable, indisputable, cooperation to the
words of the troubled King Nebuchadnezzar to the
Prophet Daniel who interpreted Nebuchadnezzar's
dream; and the dream interpreted by Daniel swept
across the whole course of the centuries of Gentile
world rule—from beginning to end of that rule.   Then
"the king answered unto Daniel, and said, Of a truth
it is, that your God is a God of gods, and a Lord of
kings, and a revealer of secrets, seeing thou couldest
reveal this secret" (Dan. 2:47).

The words penned by the prophets of God have
definitely and assuredly justified the challenge raised
in Isaiah 41:21-23:   "Produce your cause, saith the
Lord; bring forth your strong reasons, saith the King
of Jacob.   Let them bring them forth, and shew us
what shall happen: let them shew the former things,

what they be, that we may consider them, and know the latter end of them; or declare us things for to come. Shew the things that are to come hereafter, that we may know that ye are gods: yea, do good, or do evil, that we may be dismayed, and behold it together."

No person has ever successfully met the divine challenge recorded here. Many have attempted to assume the role of God's prophet, foretelling events, setting dates—even naming *personalities* as Antichrist and the beast. However, time has pointed out the folly of those who set themselves up as prophets, and time has given undeniable evidence of the delusions and deceptive practices of such so-called "prophets." When the *true prophets of God* spoke, their words came to pass literally as prophesied. The prerogatives of divine prophecy belong only to the omniscient God, for He alone is able to move holy men to speak and to write. He *did* move holy men of old, and through those men God has given us the Old and the New Testament Scriptures.

The Word of God Can Be Trusted

"In hope of eternal life, which God, that *cannot lie,* promised before the world began" (Tit. 1:2).

"That by two immutable things, in which it was *impossible for God to lie,* we might have a strong consolation, who have fled for refuge to lay hold upon the hope set before us" (Heb. 6:18).

The Holy Scripture is God-breathed. Through the Holy Spirit God spoke everlasting truths—things that have literally come to pass and things that are yet

to come to pass. The men who penned our Bible
recognized God as reigning on the throne of His eternal
glory, ruling over the universe and *overruling* in accordance with His *perfect, unerring will* which cannot
be broken. The prophets of God proclaim His sovereignty. They declare that His counsels will stand
and that He will bring to pass that which He has
spoken and all that He has purposed.

The prophets also warn that suffering and shame
will come upon individuals and nations who sin against
God. They declare that God will ultimately triumph
and, through the Lord Jesus Christ, Messiah and King,
He will reign in righteousness over all creation throughout eternity. Events which have occurred (and are
occurring all around us today) prove beyond any shadow of doubt that the Word of God can be trusted, believed, and lived by. Events past and present prove
that the prophetic declarations of all Scripture—both
Old and New Testaments—are positively and unalter-
ably true, for the Word of God cannot be broken.

The Bible is not only up-to-date; it is *far ahead of
date.* It has enabled man to know things that *will*
come to pass long before they have actually occurred.
There is not a single movement of world importance—
yesterday, today, or tomorrow—which is not foretold
in the Word of God through God's prophets, the apostles, and in the words of the Son of God Himself.
They declared that Jesus would be despised and rejected. They foretold that Israel as a nation would
be hated, and that the Lord Jesus Christ, King of the
Jews, would be hated and crucified by His own brethren.

Scientific knowledge being demonstrated today is prophesied in the Word of God—including solemn warning against the dangers of these perilous (yet marvelous) times in which we live. The Old Testament prophets spoke concerning the present world-wide unrest among men and antagonism toward God. They prophesied concerning the spiritual declensions in these terrible days and the increasing apostasy that is all around us, even within the organized *visible* church.

The prophets declared that evil days would grow worse and worse as we come nearer the end of the Church Age (the time of Gentile rule). They foretold the decline of democracy and the rise of dictatorships, with people becoming merchandise of men. Even Jesus Himself prophesied of wars and rumors of wars, distress of nations and perplexities and fears, men's hearts *failing* them for fear.

Things transpiring all around us today declare that the Bible is verbally inspired, God-breathed, and therefore worthy of our acceptance and trust. Truly we *do* have "a more sure word of prophecy" because so many prophecies have been fulfilled as set forth in the Holy Scriptures: "We have also a more sure word of prophecy; whereunto ye do well that ye take heed, as unto a light that shineth in a dark place, until the day dawn, and the day star arise in your hearts: knowing this first, that no prophecy of the Scripture is of any private interpretation. For the prophecy came not in old time by the will of man: but holy men of God spake as they were moved by the Holy Ghost" (II Pet. 1:19-21).

Rest assured, beloved, this world is not as a helpless

iceberg, drifting in a mighty ocean, changing its course as the current and the winds change. It is more like a great ship with a chart, a rudder, a compass, and the Captain on the bridge, following a determined course by His providence—not as the winds blow, but as He determined before the foundation of the world. He "worketh all things after the counsel of His own will" (Eph. 1:11), and makes the wrath of man to praise Him (Psalm 76:10).

It is true that man is allowed to rule *for a season* independently of God—but his rule is characterized by unrest, turmoil, strife, hatred, wars, commotion, confusion, and chaos. In spite of all that man does or attempts to do, God overrules in His sovereign might. He *will* bring order out of chaos, He *will* establish His kingdom of peace on earth and good will toward men. There is a day coming when every tongue will confess that Jesus Christ is Lord, to the glory of God (Phil. 2:11).

Yes, the hand of our sovereign God is in history. He determines the ultimate outcome of all things, and for that very reason prophecy is history written in advance. God made man a free moral agent. Man has the privilege of choosing, therefore man works out his own destiny. But he is not permitted to overthrow God's sovereign decree and God's eternal purpose. God allows man to go along his way as He did in the days of Noah, as He did in the days of Nimrod; but when man has gone far enough, God stops him. I repeat—God is sovereign and He rules in the universe and in all creation. *"Known unto God* are *all His works* from the beginning of the world"

(Acts 15:18).

God and Creation

"In the beginning God created the heaven and the earth" (Gen. 1:1).

"In the beginning was the Word, and the Word was with God, and the Word was God. The same was in the beginning with God. *All things were made by Him; and without Him was not any thing made that was made"* (John 1:1-3).

"God, who at sundry times and in divers manners spake in time past unto the fathers by the prophets, hath in these last days spoken unto us by His Son, whom He hath appointed heir of all things, by whom also He *made the worlds"* (Heb. 1:1,2).

In our text in Isaiah 46, God affirms exclusive claims regarding the creation of this universe and all things therein. God says, *"Remember the former things of old: for I am God,* and there is none else. *I am God, and there is none like me. . . .* My counsel shall stand, and I will do all my pleasure . . . *I have spoken it, I will also bring it to pass. I have purposed it, I will also do it!"*

In other words, God said, *"Look back"*—look back as far as you can see along the pathway of life, as far as history records—and behold how everything of importance has been marked by the wisdom, power, and providence of Almighty God. *Look back*—and remember God's work in creation, when He created the universe from nothing and spoke this world into existence. "He spake, *and it was done.* He commanded, *and it stood fast"* (Psalm 33:9).

Genesis 1:1 and John 1:1-3 give a brief (but truthful and divine) account of creation, perfect in its entirety. Yet man is still searching, attempting to find out how this universe came to be. The *Bible* explains creation— and man has never proved the Bible untrue. God created this universe, but He did not create it a waste. God is perfect, and a perfect God could not create a universe without form and void. "In the beginning" God's works were perfect—as perfect as God Himself. It was after judgment struck the earth that God brought order out of chaos. Imperfection came when the devil (as Lucifer, the shining one) attempted to overthrow God and exalt his throne above the stars. God cast Lucifer out of heaven, and outstanding Bible scholars of the years behind us believe that this was the time when catastrophe struck the earth, causing it to become dark, void, and without form.

Genesis 1:2 would never have been written had not Lucifer attempted to overthrow God and take His throne. The Eden of God was wrecked and ruined through the rebellion of the chief of angels—Lucifer, son of the morning. The account of the fall of Lucifer is clearly recorded by the prophets. In Isaiah 14:12-15 we read:

"How art thou fallen from heaven, O Lucifer, son of the morning! How art thou cut down to the ground, which didst weaken the nations! For thou hast said in thine heart, I will ascend into heaven, I will exalt my throne above the stars of God: I will sit also upon the mount of the congregation, in the sides of the north: I will ascend above the heights of the clouds; I will be like the most High. Yet thou shalt be brought down to hell, to the sides of the pit."

In Ezekiel 28:11-15 we find this record: "Moreover the Word of the Lord came unto me, saying, Son of man, take up a lamentation upon the king of Tyrus, and say unto him, Thus saith the Lord God: Thou sealest up the sum, full of wisdom, and perfect in beauty.   Thou hast been in Eden the garden of God; every precious stone was thy covering, the sardius, topaz, and the diamond, the beryl, the onyx, and the jasper, the sapphire, the emerald, and the carbuncle, and gold: the workmanship of thy tabrets and of thy pipes was prepared in thee in the day that thou wast created.   Thou art the anointed cherub that covereth; and I have set thee so: Thou wast upon the holy mountain of God; thou hast walked up and down in the midst of the stones of fire.   Thou wast perfect in thy ways from the day that thou wast created, till iniquity was found in thee."

So God's perfect earth became "without form, and void; and darkness was upon the face of the deep" (Gen. 1:2)—but that is not the end of the story.   *God spoke.*   He said, "Let there be light!" and there was light (Gen. 1:3).   Then God said, "Let there be a firmament in the midst of the waters"—and it was as God said (Gen. 1:6).   *God kept on speaking* until this wrecked and ruined earth became a beautiful garden instead of a place of chaos and darkness.

God then took dust from the ground and created man—in His own image and after His likeness—and He gave man the authority and rule over every living creature.   When God created woman from the rib of man and gave her to Adam to be his helpmate, He

commanded, "Be fruitful, and multiply, and replenish
the earth, and subdue it: and have dominion over
the fish of the sea, and over the fowl of the air, and
over every living thing that moveth upon the earth"
(Gen. 1:28).

For a season—we do not know how long—man lived
as God instructed him. Then one day Adam disobeyed
God's command and did that which was right in his
own eyes—and by that act of disobedience he plunged
the whole human family into sin and death!

Yes, the Bible makes the acts of creation very definite and clear. *God created this universe and everything in it—including man.* From the earth men dig
gold and silver, and from these precious metals they
design beautiful things; but only God can *create* the
gold and silver.   Man mines the earth for precious
stones and gems, refines them and sets them in orna-
ments; but only God can *create* the gems.   Man uses
things of earth to advance science, civilization, and
standards of living—but man is compelled to use *what
God has created* and placed at his disposal. Evolu-
tionists have tried in vain to banish God from the
universe; but today God lives, and wills, and ordains
according to His eternal plan and purpose. Today, as
in the early days of man's existence, He cries out,
"Remember the former things of old! *for I AM GOD
and there is none else!*"   There is but one true God,
and He refuses to be pushed out of His universe and
crowded out of history by poor, finite man who hates
Him.

God's creative work was accomplished in six days,
"and on the seventh day God ended His work which

He had made; and He rested on the seventh day from all His work which He had made. And God blessed the seventh day, and sanctified it: because that in it He had rested from all His work which God created and made" (Gen. 2:2, 3). But God's rest was soon broken by man's fall into sin and shame, and He began to work again—redemptively, in behalf of fallen man—and He has worked hitherto. The entire history of the human race from Adam until this present hour has been marked by the redeeming energies and the work of the sovereign triune God. He is even now actively engaged in the work of the *new creation*—and one day *all things* will be created new.

"*Remember*"—our God is the God of creation, but He is also the God of different *individuals*. He declared Himself "the God of Abraham, the God of Isaac, and the God of Jacob" (Ex. 3:6, 15). Thus we see that He is also the God of successive generations. Every dispensation has been characterized by the compassion of God toward man—in spite of the fact that every dispensation has been characterized by the failure of sinful man! Each age has affirmed and reaffirmed all the divine claims of God as penned down by His prophets in His Holy Word.

God Is Omniscient

Our text from Isaiah affirms God's exclusive claims to omniscience: "*I am God . . . declaring the end from the beginning, and from ancient times the things that are not yet done.*"

God not only *knows* those "things that are not yet done," He *proves* His omniscience by plainly *declaring*

those things in His Word. Through His prophets He
makes known to us all that will occur until the consummation of time and the beginning of eternity—and
then makes known the new creation which will continue throughout the unending ages. God's prophets
have foretold events that would—and will—occur in
relation to the Church, the elect nation Israel, and the
other nations of earth. Divine prophecy is the fruit
of God's omniscience (which is clearly *proclaimed*
throughout all the Scriptures but is *primarily* seen in
His ability to foretell great events centuries, *even
millenniums,* before they happen). The prophecies from
both the Old and New Testaments which have thus
far been fulfilled have come to pass with such literal
exactness and undeniable accuracy as to silence scoffers
and skeptics.

"From ancient times" God has declared things that
are not yet done, but which surely *will be done* because God cannot lie and His Word cannot be broken.
For example, the Old Testament prophecies relating
to Moab, Edom, Egypt, Assyria, Babylon, Media-
Persia, Greece, Rome, Nineveh, Sodom and Gomorrah
have been so minutely and accurately fulfilled as to
compel critics to be silent. The Old Testament is
filled with prophecies concerning the Lord Jesus Christ,
prophecies given in such detail and fulfilled with such
accuracy that after reading the Old Testament prophecies concerning Messiah, no one could deny that Jesus
was that promised One, "that Prophet" of whom
Moses and others wrote. The coming of Jesus as a
babe in a manger in the city of Bethlehem was so
minutely prophesied and so accurately fulfilled that it

seems impossible that anyone could have missed the Christ, the Messiah who came almost two thousand years ago.

It has been said that the Old Testament is the New Testament infolded and the New Testament is the Old Testament unfolded. Writing to the Hebrew believers, Paul explained: "God, who at sundry times and in divers manners spake in time past unto the fathers by the prophets, hath in these last days spoken unto us by His Son, whom He hath appointed heir of all things, by whom also He made the worlds" (Heb. 1:1, 2). This suggests a process which reaches a climax, the *process* being that in the Old Testament era God spoke "in divers manners" (in divers *portions*). For instance, we might consider how He spoke to various men, and through their inspired pens His words were recorded for our admonition and instruction. The prophecies thus spoken to different men have been literally and minutely fulfilled, further proving the omniscience of the God who created this universe and all things that therein are.

Beginning in Genesis, God revealed to *Adam* the manner of Christ's first coming. He would be the seed of the woman: "And the Lord God said unto the serpent . . . I will put enmity between thee and the woman, and *between thy seed and her seed. It shall bruise thy head, and thou shalt bruise His heel*" (Gen. 3:14, 15).

A little later, God revealed to *Abraham* that Christ would be from the nation of which Abraham would be the head: "Now the Lord had said unto Abram, Get thee out of thy country, and from thy kindred, and

from thy father's house, unto a land that I will shew
thee: and I will make of thee a great nation, and I
will bless thee, and make thy name great; and thou
shalt be a blessing: and I will bless them that bless
thee, and curse him that curseth thee: *and in thee
shall all families of the earth be blessed"* (Gen. 12:1-3).

Still later, God revealed to *Jacob* that the Lord
Jesus Christ would belong to the tribe of Judah: "The
sceptre shall not depart from Judah, nor a lawgiver
from between his feet, until Shiloh come; and unto
Him shall the gathering of the people be" (Gen. 49:10).

To *David* God revealed that Christ would be of the
seed of David, that He would come through the lineage
of David: "When thy days be fulfilled, and thou shalt
sleep with thy fathers, I will set up thy seed after
thee, which shall proceed out of thy bowels, and I will
establish His kingdom.   He shall build an house for
my name, and I will establish the throne of His kingdom for ever" (II Sam. 7:12, 13). Also in Psalm 89:3, 4,
and 29, we read: "I have made a covenant with my
chosen.   I have sworn unto David my servant, Thy
seed will I establish for ever, and build up thy throne
to all generations. . . . His seed also will I make to
endure for ever, and His throne as the days of heav-
en." (See also Luke 1:32, 33.)

To *Micah* God revealed that Christ would be born
in a little obscure village called Bethlehem: "But thou,
Bethlehem Ephratah, though thou be little among the
thousands of Judah, yet *out of thee shall He come
forth unto me that is to be ruler in Israel; whose goings forth have been from of old, from everlasting"*
(Micah 5:2).

To *Malachi* God revealed that Christ would be preceded by a forerunner who would announce His coming and declare Him as King of the Jews: "Behold, I will send my messenger, and he shall prepare the way before me: and the Lord, whom ye seek, shall suddenly come to His temple, even the messenger of the covenant, whom ye delight in: behold, He shall come, saith the Lord of hosts" (Mal. 3:1).

To *Daniel* God made known that the Lord Jesus Christ would appear, and that He would be cut off in death at the end of the sixty-ninth week of the seventy weeks of years determined upon Daniel's people: "Seventy weeks are determined upon thy people and upon thy holy city, to finish the transgression, and to make an end of sins, and to make reconciliation for iniquity, and to bring in everlasting righteousness, and to seal up the vision and prophecy, and to anoint the most Holy. Know therefore and understand, that from the going forth of the commandment to restore and to build Jerusalem unto the Messiah the Prince shall be seven weeks, and threescore and two weeks: the street shall be built again, and the wall, even in troublous times. And after threescore and two weeks shall Messiah be cut off, but not for Himself: and the people of the prince that shall come shall destroy the city and the sanctuary; and the end thereof shall be with a flood, and unto the end of the war desolations are determined" (Dan. 9:24-26).

To *Zechariah* God revealed that Christ would be betrayed by one of His own for the price of a slave— thirty pieces of silver: "And the Lord said unto me, Cast it unto the potter: a goodly price that I was

prised at of them. And I took the thirty pieces of
silver, and cast them to the potter in the house of
the Lord" (Zech. 11:13).

To *Isaiah* it was clearly revealed that Christ would
be wounded for our transgressions, smitten of God;
that He would bear the iniquity of us all; that He
would be numbered with the transgressors, would in-
tercede for His murderers, and would be buried in a
rich man's grave:

"Who hath believed our report? and to whom is the
arm of the Lord revealed? For He shall grow up before Him as a tender plant, and as a root out of a
dry ground: He hath no form nor comeliness; and
when we shall see Him, there is no beauty that we
should desire Him.

"He is despised and rejected of men; a Man of
sorrows, and acquainted with grief: and we hid as it
were our faces from Him; He was despised, and we
esteemed Him not.   Surely He hath borne our griefs,
and carried our sorrows: yet we did esteem Him strick-
en, smitten of God, and afflicted. But He was wounded for our transgressions, He was bruised for our
iniquities: the chastisement of our peace was upon
Him; and with His stripes we are healed.

"All we like sheep have gone astray; we have turned
every one to his own way; and the Lord hath laid on
Him the iniquity of us all. He was oppressed, and
He was afflicted, yet He opened not His mouth: He
is brought as a lamb to the slaughter, and as a sheep
before her shearers is dumb, so He openeth not His
mouth.   He was taken from prison and from judgment:
and who shall declare His generation? for He was cut

off out of the land of the living: for the transgression of my people was He stricken.   And He made His grave with the wicked, and with the rich in His death; because He had done no violence, neither was any deceit in His mouth.

"Yet it pleased the Lord to bruise Him; He hath put Him to grief: when thou shalt make His soul an offering for sin, He shall see His seed, He shall prolong His days, and the pleasure of the Lord shall prosper in His hand.   He shall see of the travail of His soul, and shall be satisfied: by His knowledge shall my righteous Servant justify many; for He shall bear their iniquities.   Therefore will I divide Him a portion with the great, and He shall divide the spoil with the strong; because He hath poured out His soul unto death: and He was numbered with the transgressors; and He bare the sin of many, and made intercession for the transgressors" (Isa. 53:1-12).

To the *Psalmist* God revealed the manner of Christ's death—crucifixion: "For dogs have compassed me: the assembly of the wicked have inclosed me: they pierced my hands and my feet" (Psalm 22:16).

To the Psalmist it was also revealed that Christ would *rise from the dead:* "Thou wilt not leave my soul in hell; neither wilt thou suffer thine Holy One to see corruption.   Thou wilt shew me the path of life: in thy presence is fulness of joy; at thy right hand there are pleasures for evermore" (Psalm 16:10,11).

In these Scriptures—and in scores of others which time and space will not permit me to give—God made known through His prophets His purpose regarding His only begotten Son, and those holy men of old

penned down the message for us. Anyone who really
wants to know the truth concerning the omniscience
of God will find indisputable confirmation of His claim
to omniscience if they will read the prophecies having
to do with the nation Israel—and then read a trust-
worthy, authentic history of the Jews. God wrote the
history of Israel in advance, from the beginning to the
end of that nation, and it is all recorded *in the Word
of God.*

We also see God's omniscience clearly demonstrated
in national and international conditions today. When
we consider the prophecies concerning the end-time of
Gentile nations and compare them with the events
of today, we cannot but see that history being made
today was prophesied and penned down by God's
prophets centuries ago!

God's Claims to Providence

"My counsel shall stand, and I will do all my
pleasure. . . . I have spoken it, I will also bring it to
pass. I have purposed it, I will also do it."

In this part of our text from Isaiah 46, *God claims
providence.* Sovereign in creation, omniscient in government, He is also purposeful in providence. The
hands of His eternal time clock seem to move exceedingly slow at times; but they *do move*—and they move
in the right direction and at the right speed. Furthermore, God's time clock always strikes at the right
hour—the hour of His omniscient appointment. God
is never behind time, He is never ahead of time. Like
the sun, moon, and stars of His own creation, He is
always *exactly ON time.*

In the Word of God we find statements like these: "In the fulness of time . . . In due time . . . it shall come to pass," and "All this was done that it might be fulfilled which was spoken by the prophet." (This latter statement occurs several times in the first three chapters of the Gospel of Matthew.) God always works and performs "in due time," at the right moment—not a moment too soon, not a moment too late. In "the fulness of the time . . . God sent forth His Son" (Gal. 4:4), as prophesied almost four thousand years beforehand. God declared that He *would* send forth His Son, and it was a divine imperative that the Son *come forth!* God in His sovereignty speaks things that are yet centuries ahead, as though the fact were already accomplished. When God declares "It shall come to pass," *it MUST be done.*

God rolled back the waters of the Red Sea and let the children of Israel cross on dry ground—and at the appointed moment the waters closed over Pharaoh and his pursuing army and drowned them all! (Read Exodus 14:21-31.)

God commanded the sun to stand still and Joshua won the battle against the Amorites and their allies. (Read Joshua 10:12-14.)

God put the machinery of the powerful world wide Roman empire in operation leading up to the first advent of His Son—and it is my firm conviction that He has set in motion the machinery of today's nations of earth thus setting the stage for the *second* coming of Jesus and the rebirth of His elect nation Israel. The nations of earth are doing exactly what the prophets foretold would occur just before the second coming of the Lord Jesus Christ, and you may rest assured that God knows *exactly* what is going on in the minds of the rulers of earth. He permits, He allows; but *He also rules* and He has the final word concerning world conditions. At the appointed time He will put a stop to these times of peril and will bring in everlasting righteousness. It is then that this earth will be filled with the knowledge of the Lord as the waters cover the sea. Men will beat their swords into plowshares and their spears into pruning hooks, and will study war no more.

This will not happen until King Jesus sits on the throne of David and reigns in righteousness—and He *will* occupy the throne of David, because God promised, and He will keep His promise! "He shall be great, and shall be called the Son of the Highest: and the Lord God shall give unto Him the throne of His father David: and He shall reign over the house of Jacob for ever; and of His kingdom there shall be no end" (Luke 1:32, 33).

God Chooses the Instruments
Through Whom He Works

"And he (Nebuchadnezzar) was driven from the sons of men; and his heart was made like the beasts, and his dwelling was with the wild asses. They fed him with grass like oxen, and his body was wet with the dew of heaven; till he knew that the most high God ruled in the kingdom of men, and that He appointeth over it whomsoever He will" (Dan. 5:21).

Behind all acts of men we behold the overruling hand of our sovereign God. His *permissions* are many times spoken of as His "givings." The Prophet Daniel, addressing King Nebuchadnezzar, confirmed this. He said to Nebuchadnezzar, "Thou, O king, art a king of kings: *for THE GOD OF HEAVEN hath GIVEN thee a kingdom, power, and strength, and glory"* (Dan. 2:37).

Cyrus, king of Persia, recognized this tremendous truth in his declaration to his subjects regarding the building of God's house. He testified, *"The Lord God of heaven hath GIVEN me all the kingdoms of the earth;* and He hath charged me to build Him an house at Jerusalem, which is in Judah" (Ezra 1:2).

I repeat: *God moves in history.* He writes history in advance; and in due time as appointed by Him the history written in advance *becomes reality.* Men who are powerful in world affairs (like Nimrod and Pharaoh of old, men like Hitler, Stalin, Mussolini and others in this present age) think in their pride and self-will that they are carrying out their own plans; but in reality they are bringing to pass things foretold by the prophets of God centuries ago!

The undermining power of sin is always the cause of decay and destruction in earthly kingdoms. With repeated emphasis the Prophet Jeremiah clearly points this out and declares that Jehovah judges men because of their "evil doings." Listen to the words of the "weeping prophet" as again and again he explains the cause of God's acts against Israel—and against other nations as well:

"... because of the evil of your doings" (Jer. 4:4).

"... because their transgressions are many..." (Jer. 5:6).

". . . because they have not hearkened unto my words . . ." (Jer. 6:19).

". . . because ye have done all these works . . ." (Jer. 7:13).

". . . because we have sinned against the Lord" (Jer. 8:14).

"Because they have forsaken my law . . ." (Jer. 9:13).

". . . because we have forsaken the land . . ." (Jer. 9:19).

". . . because they have hardened their necks . . ." (Jer. 19:15).

". . . because thou hast taught rebellion against the Lord" (Jer. 28:16).

". . . because thy sins were increased" (Jer. 30:14).

". . . because ye have sinned against the Lord . . ." (Jer. 40:3).

"Because of their wickedness which they have committed . . ." (Jer. 44:3).

". . . because of the evil of your doings . . ." (Jer. 44:22).

". . . because of the abominations which ye have committed . . ." (Jer. 44:22).

"Because ye have burned incense . . ." (Jer. 44:23).

". . . because ye have sinned against the Lord . . ." (Jer. 44:23).

As we consider these reasons for God's judgment we see that He judges nations because of their sins and plainly declares, *"Therefore* this evil is come upon you!" If you will study Jeremiah chapter 25 along with Matthew 25:31-46 you will see that nations will be judged in horror, pain, misery, and woe greater than the finite mind of man can conceive. God judges nations *in due time,* and every *individual* will be judged *in eternity.* As we consider the reasons for God's judgment upon the nation of Israel (as pointed out in the foregoing verses from Jeremiah) we can see that the trend is the same today in the nations of earth.

There are certain features which distinguish each and every dispensation. (A "dispensation" is a marked-off period of time—no definite number of years, but a period in which God deals with a specific nation or peoples such as the nation Israel or the Gentile nations.) Each dispensation is clearly marked by seven outstanding features which occur in the following order:

(1) When nations receive increased light (2) the tendency is toward a marked decline of spiritual life and holiness.

(3) Then there gradually comes about union and cooperation between God's people and the world, (4) resulting in a powerful civilization worldly in type and operation.

(5) As these powerful nations move on, there is a parallel development of both good and evil.

(6) Coldness on the part of God's people is sure to follow, for His people *cannot* take part in worldly affairs and escape apostasy.

(7) Finally, God has no alternative but to render judgment!

Thus each dispensation—from the beginning up to and *including* this present hour—parallels increased light with a decline in spiritual life in the organized church. The majority of churches today are worldly because the members of those churches are fellow-shipping with the world. Oh, yes—we have a great and powerful civilization; but it is definitely *worldly* in type. Both good and evil are advancing—i. e., people who are spiritually dedicated are becoming *more* dedicated, while those who are *worldly* are becoming *more* worldly, more like the Laodiceans (Rev. 3:14-17). And because apostasy is all around us, *judgment is imminent!*

We are now living in the sixth dispensation, and the seven characteristics that have marked all other dispensations are definitely with us today. The history of great world powers has always been from bad to worse, not from worse to better as some would have us believe. God's Word clearly teaches that "evil men and seducers shall wax worse and worse, deceiving, and being deceived" (II Tim. 3:13).

The visions God gave Daniel (portraying the times of the Gentiles) clearly illustrate this drifting decline. We see the *golden* kingdom of Babylon with its absolute autocracy immediately followed by the *silver* kingdom of Media-Persia with its outstanding parliament of princes. Then we see the *brass* kingdom of Greece, with its sweeping conquests under the leadership of Alexander the Great and his four powerful generals. This kingdom is followed by the *iron* rule of Rome with its government; and lastly, the *brittle clay* of the powers of the end-time. First gold, then silver, then brass, then iron, and finally *clay*. Thus we note that this great image is top-heavy, and a top-heavy image is sure to crumble.

The same principle is illustrated in Daniel chapter 7.

God gave Daniel a vision in which he saw the mighty, majestic *lion,* followed by a strong and brutal *bear.* The bear in turn was followed by a cunning *leopard,* and the leopard was followed by a hybrid, horned *monstrosity.*

In God's omniscience and providence we see certain great principles illustrated and declared—for instance, He uses one nation to punish another nation, as in Judah's being overcome by mighty Babylon. He then punishes the nation which He uses to punish another nation—Babylon, used of God to punish Judah, was crushed by Media-Persia! So we see that God deals with nations in their corporate capacity *in time,* and not in the *hereafter.* In Joel 3:14 we read, "Multitudes, multitudes in the valley of decision . . . ." These words describe the gathering of the nations, and Christ will *judge* the nations when He comes in His glory.

Our text in Isaiah declares that God reserves *exclusive rights and claims* in His choice of agents and instruments to bring to pass the fulfillment of His Word: "My counsel shall stand, and I will do all my pleasure: calling a ravenous bird from the east, the man that executeth my counsel from a far country." Many Bible scholars believe this *"ravenous bird"* to be Cyrus, spoken of in Isaiah 44:28 as God's "shepherd" and in Isaiah 45:1 as God's "anointed." However, the character of a ravenous bird is certainly not in keeping with the character of God's shepherd and God's anointed. Therefore I firmly believe this "ravenous bird" to be Antichrist, the man of sin, the masterpiece of Satan. He will be "the son of perdition" (the son of the devil). The Apostle Paul gives these enlightening words concerning this personality:

"Now we beseech you, brethren, by the coming of our Lord Jesus Christ, and by our gathering together unto Him, that ye be not soon shaken in mind, or be troubled, neither by spirit, nor by word, nor by letter as from us, as that the day of Christ is at hand. Let no man deceive you by any means: for that day shall not come, except there come *a falling away* first, and that *man of sin* be revealed, *the son of perdition;* who opposeth and exalteth himself above all that is called God, or that is worshipped; so that he as God sitteth in the temple of God, shewing himself that he is God.

"Remember ye not, that, when I was yet with you, I told you these things? And now ye know what withholdeth that he might be revealed in his time. For the mystery of iniquity doth already work: only *He who now letteth will let, until He be taken out of the way.* And then shall *that Wicked* be revealed, whom the Lord shall consume with the spirit of His mouth, and shall destroy with the brightness of His coming: even him, whose coming is after the working of Satan with all power and signs and lying wonders, and with all deceivableness of unrighteousness in them that perish; because they received not the love of the truth, that they might be saved. And for this cause God shall send them strong delusion, that they should believe a lie: that they all might be damned who believed not the truth, but had pleasure in unrighteousness" (II Thess. 2:1-12).

The manifestation of the Antichrist during this Dispensation of Grace is hindered by the restraining power of the Holy Spirit through the body and bride of

Christ, the New Testament Church. Spoken of as *"a ravenous bird from the east,"* this man of sin will come from the east of Palestine and will run his course as the false messiah, and at the end of that course Jesus will personally put him into the lake that burns with fire and brimstone.

This "son of perdition" will be the last world dictator. He will be the beast of Revelation chapter 13. He will run his course and do his devilish deeds as prophesied—but not *because* they were prophesied. On the contrary, they were prophesied because God knew he would do them! There is no escape from the divinely determined course. Under the inspiration of the Holy Ghost the things that will happen through this son of Satan were foretold by God's prophets centuries ago, and they will occur exactly as prophesied.

God is sovereign in His choice of individuals and instruments to carry out His divine will. In the light of John 6:70 and 71 many people have asked why Jesus chose Judas Iscariot as one of the twelve when He clearly declared that He knew what Judas was. He said, "Have not I chosen you twelve, and *one of you is a devil?* He spake of Judas Iscariot the son of Simon: for he it was that should betray Him, being one of the twelve."

Bear in mind that Jesus did not *make* Judas a devil. Just as Satan is a self-made personality, so *Judas* was the product of his own making. He heard the words of Jesus and saw His mighty miracles just as the other apostles did—yet in fulfillment of prophecy he sold the Lord for thirty pieces of silver! However, Christ made

Judas responsible for his act and said of him, "Woe
unto that man by whom the Son of man is betrayed!
*It had been good for that man if he had not been
born*" (Matt. 26:24).

It was by the sovereign act of God that Caesar
Augustus sent forth a decree "that all the world should
be taxed" and every person was forced to return to
"his own city" to pay his taxes (Luke 2:1-3). Behind
the decree was the eternal purpose of Almighty God
concerning the birth of His only begotten Son. Caesar
exercised perfect freedom in *making* his decree, but
God was absolutely sovereign *in that He put the
thought into the mind of the emperor.*

God knows the end in the beginning and He moves
as He wills. With Him, *everything is an ETERNAL
NOW,* and known unto Him are all His works from
the beginning (Acts 15:18).

Paul sets forth the sovereignty of God in his letter
to the Corinthian believers. In I Corinthians 1:26-31
he wrote:

"Ye see your calling, brethren, how that not many
wise men after the flesh, not many mighty, not many
noble, are called: but God hath chosen the foolish
things of the world to confound the wise; and God
hath chosen the weak things of the world to confound
the things which are mighty; and base things of the
world, and things which are despised, hath God chosen, yea, and things which are not, to bring to nought
things that are: that no flesh should glory in His
presence. But of Him are ye in Christ Jesus, who of
God is made unto us wisdom, and righteousness, and
sanctification, and redemption: that, according as

it is written, He that glorieth, let him glory in the Lord!"

In the Old Testament era, God chose Joseph, sold into slavery by his brethren, to prepare a place for the preservation of the heads of the twelve tribes of His elect nation, Israel (Gen. 45:4-8).

He chose a helpless little baby, pulled from the waters of the Nile by a damsel, to deliver His people from the wicked Pharaoh and Egypt and guide them to the promised land (Ex. 2:1-10).

God chose His Man—*the God-man*—to bring His Church into being and give the Gospel of God's saving grace to the nations of the world. It was God who overshadowed Mary in the Person of the Holy Ghost, she conceived, and brought forth the Son of God (Luke 1:26-35).

After the Lord Jesus Christ was born, God chose twelve humble men, fishermen, tax collectors—ordinary, despised Jews—to give Christianity to the world (Matt. 10:1-15).

God chose Israel to transmit and preserve our sacred Scriptures and hand them down to us who read them, love them, and believe them today.

God will again choose Israel to proclaim the Gospel of the kingdom. This Gospel will be preached during the tribulation period, and at the end of that period the Prince of Peace, King of the Jews, will come to establish His kingdom of righteousness in the earth. Son of David after the flesh, He will sit on the throne of David in Jerusalem and reign in righteousness over all creation.

God has not forgotten His elect nation. He has not

cast them aside forever. Man has declared the doom
of the Jew. Dictators have attempted to annihilate
that nation; but this will never be! One day God will
call Israel back into their homeland. They are already
returning there as rapidly as they possibly can, but
after the Rapture they will return from all nations and
from all islands, returning to Palestine by the millions.
In spite of the fact that man has tried to rid the earth
of the Jew and cast him into oblivion, God has shown
that man cannot annihilate God's chosen people! In
the heyday of Hitler's reign, he vowed that he would
not be happy until every Jew was dead—but Hitler
has long been dead and the Jew is still with us. He
will be with us until the end of time, and then he will
be in his own land throughout eternity.

God's Claims to Salvation

"I bring near my righteousness; it shall not be far
off, and my salvation shall not tarry: and I will place
salvation in Zion for Israel my glory."

This reference from our text, penned by Isaiah,
speaks of the final gathering of Israel into their own
land when Jesus returns the second time and stands
upon the Mount of Olives (Zech. 13:6; 14:4; Isa. 66:8;
Rom. 11:26). They will see Him, they will recognize
the scars He bears, and they will then receive Him as
Messiah and King. Isaiah 43:5, 6 also speaks of this
regathering of Israel:

"Fear not: for I am with thee: I will bring thy
seed from the east, and gather thee from the west; I
will say to the north, Give up; and to the south, Keep
not back: bring my sons from far, and my daughters

from the ends of the earth."

Isaiah 43:10-13 declares: "Ye are my witnesses, saith the Lord, and my servant whom I have chosen: that ye may know and believe me, and understand that I am He: before me there was no God formed, neither shall there be after me. *I, even I, am the Lord; AND BESIDE ME THERE IS NO SAVIOUR.* I have declared, and have saved, and I have shewed, when there was no strange god among you: therefore ye are my witnesses, saith the Lord, that *I am God.* Yea, before the day was *I am He;* and there is none that can deliver out of my hand: I will work, and who shall let it?"

God has but one Saviour, He has but one salvation: "For God so loved the world, that *He gave His only begotten Son, that whosoever believeth in Him* should not perish, but have everlasting life" (John 3:16).

"But now the righteousness of God without the law is manifested, being witnessed by the law and the prophets; even the righteousness of God which is by faith of Jesus Christ unto all and upon all them that believe: *for there is no difference: FOR ALL HAVE SINNED, AND COME SHORT OF THE GLO-RY OF GOD;* being justified freely by His grace through the redemption that is in Christ Jesus: whom God hath set forth to be a propitiation through faith in His blood, to declare His righteousness for the remission of sins that are past, through the forbearance of God; to declare, I say, at this time His righteousness: that He might be just, and the Justifier of him which believeth in Jesus.

"Where is boasting then? It is excluded. By what

law? of works? Nay: but by the law of faith. Therefore we conclude that a man is justified by faith without the deeds of the law" (Rom. 3:21-28).

Yes, God has but one Saviour—*His Son, the Lord
Jesus Christ,* who was conceived of the Holy Ghost,
born of a virgin, lived a sinless life, was crucified,
buried, and rose again on the third day, as the Scriptures declared beforehand. He ascended to heaven,
and He will return to receive His own unto Himself,
and to judge the living and the dead.

God has but *one way of salvation*—the way of the
cross. "I must needs go home by the way of the cross
—there's no other way but this!" Christ the *Sin-bearer*
died, the just for the unjust, that He who knew no sin
might bring us to God.

God has but *one Gospel,* and that Gospel is the
power and wisdom of God unto salvation to all who
believe: "Verily, verily, I say unto you, He that heareth my Word, and believeth on Him that sent me,
hath everlasting life, and shall not come into condemnation; but is passed from death unto life" (John
5:24). According to I Corinthians 15:1-4, the Gospel is
the death, burial, and resurrection of the Lord Jesus
Christ *"according to the Scriptures."*

God has but one way of *transformation,* and that
way is effected only by the new birth: "Verily, verily,
I say unto thee, Except a man be born again, he cannot see the kingdom of God. . . . Verily, verily, I say
unto thee, Except a man be born of water and of the
Spirit, he cannot enter into the kingdom of God"
(John 3:3, 5).

Through the new birth man becomes a member of

the family of God, a new creation, partaker of divine nature: "Therefore if any man be in Christ, he is a new creature: old things are passed away; behold, all things are become new" (II Cor. 5:17). "Whereby are given unto us exceeding great and precious promises: that by these ye might be partakers of the divine nature, having escaped the corruption that is in the world through lust" (II Pet. 1:4).

There are skeptics, liberals, and modernists who deny the Gospel of God, the one way of salvation, the one Saviour; but though man may not believe what God has declared, man's unbelief does not alter God's divine and clearly stated facts. To any man, be he minister or layman, who denies any part of the inspired Word of God, the Apostle Paul says, *"What if some did not believe? Shall their unbelief make the faith of God without effect? God forbid! Yea, let God be true, but every man a liar . . ."* (Rom. 3:3, 4).

In these closing days of this Dispensation of Grace, liberals and modernists teach that the way of salvation is not as it used to be in the olden days. They are attempting to bring the Bible "up to date." But beloved, the Word of God has not changed. God has not changed His mind about man nor about His plan of salvation! *Men* have changed—but the Word of God cannot be altered. Jesus Christ is the same—yesterday, today, and forever (Heb. 13:8). *Salvation by faith* is an everlasting and unchanging way!

I would remind you that "there is a way that *seemeth* right unto a *man,* but the end thereof are *the ways of death*" (Prov. 16:25). Jesus declared, *"I am the WAY, the Truth, and the Life: NO MAN cometh unto the*

Father, BUT BY ME" (John 14:6). Modernism cannot change God's changeless Word! and that Word declares that eternal life is received only by faith in the finished work of Jesus, the sacrificial Lamb of God without blemish and without spot. Modernism cannot change the Word of God concerning God's love that caused Him to surrender His Son into the hands of evil men to be crucified for us. As Jesus prayed for those who nailed Him to the cross, so today He calls out to those who deny the Word of God, His virgin birth, and the blood atonement, *"Him that cometh to me I will IN NO WISE cast out"* (John 6:37).

His invitation is still, *"COME UNTO ME, all ye that labour and are heavy laden, and I will give you rest"* (Matt. 11:28).

The prophets, the patriarchs, the apostles—and yes, *the Son of God*—give witness to these exclusive claims and sovereign facts which are *absolute* in the attributes of God's omniscience, omnipotence, omnipresence, and sovereignty. They are absolute in the choice of instruments of God's will and His Word, absolute in the subjects of salvation and in the fulfillment of the prophetic Word of God, from the first verse of Genesis to the last verse in Revelation. Today as never before men make daring and presumptuous attacks against God and against His Word, but *God* will have the *final* word. The nations are raging and the people are imagining a vain thing, but God *will* set His King upon the holy hill of Zion:

"Why do the heathen rage, and the people imagine a vain thing? The kings of the earth set themselves, and the rulers take counsel together, against the Lord, and against His Anointed, saying: Let us break their bands asunder, and cast away their cords from us.

"He that sitteth in the heavens shall laugh: the Lord shall have them in derision. Then shall He speak unto them in His wrath, and vex them in His sore displeasure. Yet have I set my King upon my holy hill of Zion. I will declare the decree: the Lord hath said unto me, Thou art my Son; this day have I begotten thee. Ask of me, and I shall give thee the heathen for thine inheritance, and the uttermost parts of the earth for thy possession. Thou shalt break them with a rod of iron; thou shalt dash them in pieces like a potter's vessel.

"Be wise now therefore, O ye kings: be instructed, ye judges of the earth. Serve the Lord with fear, and rejoice with trembling. Kiss the Son, lest He be angry, and ye perish from the way, when His wrath is kindled but a little. Blessed are all they that put their trust in Him" (Psalm 2:1-12).

All born again, blood-washed children of God stand on these emphatic prophecies, the declarations of God's holy Word; and we wait confidently for the vindication of His Son, the Lord Jesus Christ, and His people. We wait patiently for the glorious appearing of the great God and our Saviour Jesus Christ, who will reign as King of kings and Lord of lords and before whom all nations shall bow and every tongue confess that Jesus Christ is Lord to the honor and glory of God the Father. As a born again believer I trust Him, I believe on Him, and I am patiently waiting for Him. One day *He will come,* and in the words of John the Beloved I personally pray, "Even so, Come, Lord Jesus!"

Chapter II

Christ the Capstone of the Pyramid of Prophecy

"We have also a more sure word of prophecy; whereunto ye do well that ye take heed, as unto a light that shineth in a dark place, until the day dawn, and the day star arise in your hearts" (II Pet. 1:19).

"Wherefore God also hath highly exalted Him, and given Him a name which is above every name: that at the name of Jesus every knee should bow, of things in heaven, and things in earth, and things under the earth; and that every tongue should confess that Jesus Christ is Lord, to the glory of God the Father" (Phil. 2:9-11).

"And behold, two of them went that same day to a village called Emmaus, which was from Jerusalem about threescore furlongs. And they talked together of all these things which had happened. And it came to pass, that, while they communed together and reasoned, Jesus Himself drew near, and went with them. But their eyes were holden that they should not know Him.

"And He said unto them, What manner of communications are these that ye have one to another, as ye walk, and are sad? And the one of them, whose name was Cleopas, answering said unto Him, Art thou only a stranger in Jerusalem, and hast not known the things which are come to pass there in these days? And He said unto them, What things? And they said unto Him, Concerning Jesus of Nazareth, which was a prophet mighty in deed and word before God and all the people: and how the chief priests and our rulers delivered Him to be condemned to death, and have crucified Him. But we trusted that it had been He which should have redeemed Israel: and beside all this, to day is the third day since these things were done. Yea, and certain women also of our company made us astonished, which were early at the sepulchre; and when they found not His body, they came, saying, that they had also seen a vision of angels, which said that He was alive. And certain of them which were with us went to the sepulchre, and found it even so as the women had said: but Him they saw not.

"Then He said unto them, *O fools, and slow of heart to believe all that the prophets have spoken!* Ought not Christ to have suffered these things, and to enter into His glory? And beginning at Moses and all the prophets, He expounded unto them in all the Scriptures the things concerning Himself.

"And they drew nigh unto the village, whither they went: and He made as though He would have gone further. But they constrained Him, saying, Abide with us: for it is toward evening, and the day is far spent. And He went in to tarry with them. And it came to pass, as He sat at meat with them, He took bread, and blessed it, and brake, and gave to them. And their eyes were opened, and they knew Him; and He vanished out of their sight" (Luke 24:13-31).

Christ "is the image of the invisible God, the firstborn of every creature: for *by Him* were all things created, that are in heaven, and that are in earth, visible and invisible, whether they be thrones, or dominions, or principalities, or powers: *all things were created by Him, and for Him: and He is before all things, and by Him all things consist. And He is the head of the body, the Church: who is the beginning, the firstborn from the dead; that in all things He might have the preeminence.* For it pleased the Father that in Him should all fulness dwell" (Col. 1:15-19).

The Lord Jesus Christ is *above all else* in Bible prophecy, and our discussion in this chapter will be based on four simple, easily-understood statements recorded in the verses just given.

First, the declaration made by the Apostle Peter under the inspiration of the Holy Spirit concerning the *certainty and reliability* of prophecy. *All* prophecy is made sure by its fulfillment *in part.* In this present day there is much confusion, bewilderment, perplexity, fear and doubt—all of which is evidence of the darkness which now enshrouds the whole world.   In the words of John the Beloved, "the whole world lieth in wickedness" (or, "in the lap of the Wicked One") (I John 5:19).   Men preach various doctrines and ideas, declaring them to be "Thus saith the Lord" when in reality they are "Thus saith some man or some religious group."

Bible prophecy is a light shining in a dark place— the *only* light that can penetrate the terrible darkness through which we are now passing. *"God is light"* (I John 1:5), and we are assured that this light will

shine until the day dawn, and the Day Star arise in
our hearts.   Christ is *"the true Light,* which lighteth
every man that cometh into the world" (John 1:9).

In Philippians 2:9-11, the second Scripture in our
text, we see the exalted Christ who conquered the
world, the flesh, the devil, death, hell and the grave.
And "when He had by Himself purged our sins" He
ascended back to heaven and "sat down on the right
hand of the Majesty on high" (Heb. 1:3).   He has been
given a name that is above every name.   To Him every
knee shall bow, and every tongue shall confess Him
as Lord to the glory of God the Father—and this, beyond any shadow of doubt, places Christ *above ALL.*

In the passage quoted from Luke 24 we see the risen
Christ teaching two of His disciples as they traveled
from Jerusalem to Emmaus, and the subject of His
teaching was Old Testament prophecy concerning Himself.   Thus Christ Himself was the theme of the lesson,
Christ Himself was the Teacher, two bewildered disciples were the pupils, and the lesson taught by the
Master Teacher was *"Christ ABOVE ALL in prophecy."*

In the passage from Colossians, the Apostle Paul,
under the inspiration of the Holy Spirit, declares that
Christ is to have the preeminence in ALL things; and
since *prophecy is included* in "all things" then Christ
is certainly seen *above all* in prophecy.   This means
that Christ is *the capstone* of the pyramid of Bible
prophecy.   It means that Christ is *the chief theme* of
all Bible prophecy.   All prophecy points to Him, cen-
ters in Him, and revolves around Him.   Christ is the
center and the *circumference* of prophecy.   If Christ

were removed from the Bible, we would have no Bible!

That the Holy Spirit places tremendous emphasis on prophecy is seen from the indisputable fact that practically two-thirds of all Scripture is prophetic—either in type, symbol, or direct statement.

Bible prophecy is twofold in nature: (1) It is descriptive. (2) It is predictive. The prophets were both forthtellers and foretellers—i. e., they forthtold things that had already happened, and they foretold events that were yet to come. They had foresight and they also had insight. Their prophetic words were not the product of human reasoning, but were imparted to them by the Holy Spirit—words that were God-breathed: "For the prophecy came not in old time by the will of man: but holy men of God spake as they were moved by the Holy Ghost" (II Pet. 1:21).

Much that was predictive prophecy when spoken or written by God's prophets has already become history, having happened in minute detail exactly as prophesied; but as we study the Bible we see that more than half of the predictive prophecies concerning the Lord Jesus Christ are *yet to be fulfilled.* Less than fifty percent of the prophecies concerning Him were fulfilled at His first coming and during His earthly ministry, but all such prophecies *will be* literally fulfilled in due time as God has ordained. Known unto God are all of His ways from the beginning, and He is running His program according to His divine schedule of time. "It shall come to pass" are words often spoken by God's prophets, and "that it might be fulfilled" are words often spoken by the Lord Jesus Christ and His disciples, pointing back to prophecies made centuries before. Where the Old Testament Scriptures say "Yea," the New Testament Scriptures proclaim *"Amen!"*

Bible prophecy deals with many things, a few of which we will consider here:

The Jews:—

From God's choosing of Abraham to be the father of the Jewish nation, to the national conversion of the Jews at the beginning of the Millennium (the kingdom of heaven on earth), every movement of Israel's history was foretold in prophecy—not casually penned down, but written in minute detail. It has been (and is being) *fulfilled* in detail, and every word of prophecy concerning Israel will be fulfilled literally to the letter! In the history of the Jewish nation we find times of bondage and times of deliverance. We can follow their wilderness journey and their religious experiences as they come into the land God gave them. We see the coming of their Messiah and their subsequent rejection of Him. We see them being scattered to the four corners of the earth—to every island and among every nation (Lev. 26:33; Psalm 44:11; Jer. 24:9). Then we read the prophecy of their re-gathering into Palestine when a nation will be born in a day (Isa. 66:8) and their King will reign from the throne of David in Jerusalem. All these events are subjects of prophecy— *with Christ above ALL.*

The Gentiles:—

The Gentiles as well as the Jews are subjects of Bible prophecy. The Gentile course among nations in relation to the governments of the world is clearly foretold—how one world power after another will rise and then fall, until the end of the Gentile rule when Gentile power will be crushed by the Stone of Daniel 2:34—the Stone cut out without hands. Isaiah, Ezekiel, Jeremiah, Daniel, Zechariah and others of the Old Testament prophets tell of these events—but again, *Christ is above all* in these prophecies.

The Antichrist:—

Also in Bible prophecy we see the rise and reign of the false messiah. His rule will be both political and religious. Prophecy reveals how he will come to power, the extent of his rule, and how he will be put down. We read many Bible prophecies concerning the Antichrist—*but Christ is still above all,* and believers are commanded to look for *THE Christ,* not for Antichrist!

The Rapture:—

The Rapture of the Church is clearly set forth in prophecy. *Enoch* is a type of the raptured saints, as is *Elijah* who was taken to heaven in a chariot of fire. There is much in prophecy concerning that glorious appearing of the great God and our Saviour Jesus Christ who will come to call His Church to meet Him in the clouds in the air—*and so shall we ever be with the Lord.*

The Great Tribulation:—

Prophecy clearly defines the tribulation period—"the time of Jacob's trouble." This will be a time of woe and misery such as this world has never known. World judgments and world desolations that will come upon the earth during the Great Tribulation are described in

Daniel and in Revelation. Revelation chapters 6
through 19 give a detailed account of the judgments
and desolations that are to come upon the earth during
that time—the last half of Daniel's seventieth week of
prophecy. Yet, even in this prophecy, *Christ is above
all.*

The Millennium:—

After the reign of Antichrist and the destruction that
will come upon his armies, prophecy deals with the
Millennium—that glorious Utopia for which man has
yearned and about which he has planned and dreamed
but has never been able to produce or bring about.
This will be the thousand-year reign of King Jesus
from the throne of David in Jerusalem when He will
reign in righteousness on this earth. Prophecy reveals
the glories and blessings of this thousand years of
peace on earth and good will toward men—and certainly *Christ is above all in this,* as in all other prophecies.

Time and space permitting, there are many other
phases of prophecy that could be named and discussed,
such as the battle of Gog and Magog, the binding of
the beast and the false prophet, the doom of Satan,
the judgment of the living nations, the resurrection of
the righteous, and the consigning of the wicked to the
lake of fire and brimstone. But regardless of how
many phases of prophecy we might discuss, we would
be compelled to close each discussion by proclaiming
"CHRIST ABOVE ALL!"

There are two avenues of prophecy concerning God's
Christ: (1) The prophecy that reveals His coming as a
Babe in the manger—the suffering Servant of Jehovah

God. These prophecies speak of Christ's humiliation and sacrifice at Calvary. (2) The prophecies of Christ's second coming, pointing to His crown of glory, His power and reign from the throne of David in Jerusalem. Failure to see these two lines of prophecy and make proper distinction between them leads to much confusion and misunderstanding. It is from such misinterpretation and confusion that we have the many doctrines and traditions of men concerning the second coming of the Lord Jesus Christ.

The Jews are where they are today because they missed their Messiah. They refused to see prophetic truth, they refused to recognize the crown of thorns as preceding the crown of glory, or the cross as preceding the throne. None of the Old Testament prophets foresaw the Church—a mystery hidden from eternity but revealed to the Apostle Paul.

Anticipations and expectations are seen and felt on every page of the Old Testament Scriptures, and the closing chapters of the Old Testament call for the New Testament. For example, *Malachi* demands the Gospel of Matthew. The Old Testament prophets were definitely expecting Someone. *"Someone is coming!"* was their constant message. They placed the telescope of prophecy to their eyes and looked into the future. Some of the prophets saw things that were very near, others saw things far in the future—and some saw things both near and far distant. *But ALL of God's prophets saw the coming One,* "that Prophet" of whom Moses spoke—Messiah, the King of kings.

Some of the prophets saw Christ's coming in humiliation. Others saw Him coming in revelation and

glory.   Isaiah saw Him wounded, bruised, and chas-
tened.   Some prophesied of His coming in the Incarna-
tion, born of a virgin.   Others prophesied of His glorification and His millennial reign from the throne of
David.   Some saw Him coming to make expiation,
while others saw Him coming for administration, rule,
and deliverance from the tyranny of those who oppressed Israel.   Some prophets saw Him entering the
Holy City in humility, riding on a little donkey.   Others saw Him riding on a great white stallion with the
armies of heaven following Him in splendor and great
glory, going forth conquering and to conquer.   Some
saw Him coming as Abraham's son for the sacrifice at
the altar, while others saw Him coming as David's son
to sit on the throne of David.   But regardless of who
the prophet was or how he saw the One who was to
come, *they all foresaw His coming*—Son of God, King
of kings and Lord of lords!

In these words the Apostle Peter summed up the
ministry of the Old Testament prophets concerning
Christ: "Of which salvation the prophets have inquired and searched diligently, who prophesied of the
grace that should come unto you: searching what, or
what manner of time the Spirit of Christ which was in
them did signify, when it testified beforehand the
sufferings of Christ, and the glory that should follow.
Unto whom it was revealed, that not unto themselves,
but unto us they did minister the things, which are
now reported unto you by them that have preached
the Gospel unto you with the Holy Ghost sent down
from heaven; which things the angels desire to look
into" (I Pet. 1:10-12).

In Romans 8:19 Paul speaks of the lifting of the curse from creation: "For the *earnest expectation* of the creature (creation) waiteth for the manifestation of the sons of God." In the Greek, "earnest expectation" is suggestive of the stretching forth of the hand in expectation of receiving something. The only other place in the New Testament where this expression is used is in Philippians 1:20 where Paul says, "According to my earnest expectation . . . ." The object of attention in this verse is the magnifying of Christ in life and in death, Christ *Himself* being the absorbing object. In Romans 8:19 the object in view is the revealing of the sons of God—a verse bursting forth with expectancy. The Old Testament prophets caused one to stand on tiptoe in expectancy, looking for that One who was to come, the One who would deliver them from bondage and bring glorious liberty. Every detail of the first advent of the Lord Jesus Christ was foretold by the Old Testament prophets; and everything they said *took place literally* just as they declared it.

The supreme wonder and glory of prophecy—yea, the supreme wonder and glory of *the entire Bible* from Genesis through Revelation—is the Son of God, the Lord Jesus Christ. He is the center of prophecy, the center of God's program, past, present, and future. *Christ* is the Bible's *supreme fascination!* Therefore it is impossible to hold to Christ and reject the Bible—and vice versa—it is impossible to hold to the Bible and reject *Christ,* the central *Figure* of the Bible.

True faith in the deity of Christ is married to faith in the verbal inspiration of the Word of God. All types, pictures, and truths in the Bible are so related

to Christ that He alone *explains* the types, pictures,
and truths set forth there—and the explanation is filled
with such perfection of harmony in every detail that
the comments of men are empty and useless. Nothing
can be added to "Thus saith the Lord God Almighty."
The Scriptures are complete in themselves; to add one
word or take away one word is to mar and destroy
the truth of God's Word.

Prophecies Not Yet Fulfilled

Just a little while ago I made the statement that
more than half of the predictive prophecies of the Bible
concerning Christ are as yet unfulfilled. Keep in mind
as we continue our study that the same men who
prophesied of the first coming of Jesus also foretold
His *second* coming; and since they were exactly correct
in what they said about His first advent, why should
we not believe that they were just as accurate in their
prophecies of His second coming?

Next to *salvation,* the doctrine of the second coming
of the Lord Jesus Christ is the greatest subject in the
entire Word of God—and certainly salvation is *vitally
related to* His coming again. His first coming demands
His second coming. In order to complete what He
began in our salvation when He died on the cross at
Calvary He must return and do all the things the
prophets prophesied concerning Him. He came the
first time to redeem us from the *penalty* of sin. He
sits today at the right hand of God the Father to
deliver us from the *power* of sin. He is coming again
to deliver us from the very *presence* of sin. Hebrews
9:23-28 explains:

"It was therefore necessary that the patterns of things in the heavens should be purified with these; but the heavenly things themselves with better sacrifices than these. For Christ is not entered into the holy places made with hands, which are the figures of the true; but into heaven itself, now to appear in the presence of God for us. Nor yet that He should offer Himself often, as the high priest entereth into the holy place every year with blood of others; for then must He often have suffered since the foundation of the world: but now once in the end of the world hath He appeared to put away sin by the sacrifice of Himself. And as it is appointed unto men once to die, but after this the judgment: so Christ was once offered to bear the sins of many; and unto them that look for Him shall He appear the second time without sin unto salvation."

The Word of God places great emphasis on the truth of the second coming of the Lord Jesus Christ—and by His second coming I mean what the *Bible* means, not what "religions" teach nor what men may teach to support their own traditions and ideas. The coming of Christ in the Rapture is imminent—He can come at any second of any minute of any hour of any day. His coming is pre-millennial. His coming is literal, personal, visible, and bodily. He is coming to this earth again just as He was when He was seen by the disciples on the Mount of Olives as He was taken up into the clouds and disappeared from their sight. "And while they looked stedfastly toward heaven as He went up, behold, two men stood by them in white apparel; which also said, *Ye men of Galilee, why stand ye*

*gazing up into heaven? THIS SAME JESUS, which
is taken up from you into heaven, shall so come IN
LIKE MANNER as ye have seen Him go into heaven"*
(Acts 1:10,11).

The Two Stages of Christ's Second Coming

Christ's second coming is *one great event* but it will
be in two stages: (1) *The Rapture*—when the dead in
Christ shall rise and living saints will be translated
and caught up to meet Him in the air. (2) *The Revelation*—when Christ comes with His saints and holy
angels to take His place on the throne of David in
Jerusalem.

The Rapture is clearly described in the following
Scriptures:

I Corinthians 15:51-57: "Behold, I shew you a mystery: We shall not all sleep, but we shall all be
changed, in a moment, in the twinkling of an eye, at
the last trump: for the trumpet shall sound, and the
dead shall be raised incorruptible, and we shall be
changed.   For this corruptible must put on incorruption, and this mortal must put on immortality.   So
when this corruptible shall have put on incorruption,
and this mortal shall have put on immortality, then
shall be brought to pass the saying that is written,
Death is swallowed up in victory. O death, where is
thy sting? O grave, where is thy victory? The sting
of death is sin; and the strength of sin is the law.
But thanks be to God, which giveth us the victory
through our Lord Jesus Christ."

I Thessalonians 4:13-18: "I would not have you to
be ignorant, brethren, concerning them which are

asleep, that ye sorrow not, even as others which have no hope. For if we believe that Jesus died and rose again, even so them also which sleep in Jesus will God bring with Him. For this we say unto you by the Word of the Lord, that we which are alive and remain unto the coming of the Lord shall not prevent them which are asleep. For the Lord Himself shall descend from heaven with a shout, with the voice of the archangel, and with the trump of God: and the dead in Christ shall rise first. Then we which are alive and remain shall be caught up together with them in the clouds, to meet the Lord in the air: and so shall we ever be with the Lord. Wherefore comfort one another with these words."

The Revelation—the second phase of Christ's second coming—is described in the following passages:

Revelation 1:7: "Behold, He cometh with clouds; and every eye shall see Him, and they also which pierced Him: and all kindreds of the earth shall wail because of Him. Even so, Amen."

Revelation 6:12-17: "And I beheld when He had opened the sixth seal, and, lo, there was a great earthquake; and the sun became black as sackcloth of hair, and the moon became as blood; and the stars of heaven fell unto the earth, even as a fig tree casteth her untimely figs, when she is shaken of a mighty wind. And the heaven departed as a scroll when it is rolled together; and every mountain and island were moved out of their places. And the kings of the earth, and the great men, and the rich men, and the chief captains, and the mighty men, and every bondman, and every free man, hid themselves in the dens and in the

rocks of the mountains; and said to the mountains
and rocks, Fall on us, and hide us from the face of
Him that sitteth on the throne, and from the wrath
of the Lamb: for the great day of His wrath is come;
and who shall be able to stand?"

Revelation 19:11-16:   "I saw heaven opened, and
behold a white horse; and He that sat upon him was
called Faithful and True, and in righteousness He doth
judge and make war. His eyes were as a flame of fire,
and on His head were many crowns; and He had a
name written, that no man knew, but He Himself.
And He was clothed with a vesture dipped in blood:
and His name is called The Word of God. And the
armies which were in heaven followed Him upon white
horses, clothed in fine linen, white and clean. And out
of His mouth goeth a sharp sword, that with it He
should smite the nations: and He shall rule them with
a rod of iron: and He treadeth the winepress of the
fierceness and wrath of Almighty God. And He hath
on His vesture and on His thigh a name written,
KING OF KINGS, AND LORD OF LORDS!"

The time *between* the Rapture and the Revelation
will be approximately seven years, and the last half
of that period will be days of such horrible suffering
that if God did not intervene and put a stop to it
there would be no flesh left on earth. Jesus speaks of
that time in Matthew 24:21, 22: "For then shall be
great tribulation, such as was not since the beginning
of the world to this time, no, nor ever shall be. And
except those days should be shortened, there should no
flesh be saved: *but for the elect's* (Israel's) *sake those
days shall be shortened."*

Matthew 25 is a tremendous chapter on the second coming of Christ. In the first part of the chapter He is pictured as a bridegroom—"and at midnight there was a cry made, Behold, the Bridegroom cometh; go ye out to meet Him" (v. 6). In the last part of the chapter we see Him as King—"then shall the King say unto them on His right hand, Come, ye blessed of my Father, inherit the kingdom prepared for you from the foundation of the world" (v. 34).

Events That Demand Christ's Return

Many of the things prophesied in connection with future events cannot be consummated *apart* from His coming. Any failure of the fulfillment of prophecy would declare the Word of God untrue—and this cannot be, because God cannot lie (Tit. 2:1; Heb. 6:18). Not one word of prophecy will fail. All things prophesied will be fulfilled to the letter. Now let us look at some of the things recorded in Scripture that demand the second coming of Jesus:

The Dead In Christ Will Be Raised:—

When Jesus comes in the air and believers are caught up to meet Him, the resurrection of the righteous will take place as recorded in the passages quoted from I Corinthians 15:51-57 and I Thessalonians 4:13-18. It is then that believers will receive glorified bodies like the glorious resurrection body of the Lord Jesus Christ. ". . . we know that, when He shall appear, *we shall be like Him;* for we shall see Him as He is" (I John 3:2). Aside from His second coming we would never receive glorified bodies.

The Great Tribulation: —

This embraces "the time of Jacob's trouble" (the judgment of the Jewish nation) and the world under the reign of Antichrist.

The Consummation of Gentile Rule: —

The times of the Gentiles is minutely described in Revelation chapter 11: "And there was given me a reed like unto a rod: and the angel stood, saying, Rise, and measure the temple of God, and the altar, and them that worship therein. But the court which is without the temple leave out, and measure it not; for it is *given unto the Gentiles:* and the holy city shall they tread under foot forty and two months.

"And I will give power unto my two witnesses, and they shall prophesy a thousand two hundred and three-score days, clothed in sackcloth. These are the two olive trees, and the two candlesticks standing before the God of the earth. And if any man will hurt them, fire proceedeth out of their mouth, and devoureth their enemies: and if any man will hurt them, he must in this manner be killed. These have power to shut heaven, that it rain not in the days of their prophecy: and have power over waters to turn them to blood, and to smite the earth with all plagues, as often as they will.

"And when they shall have finished their testimony, the beast that ascendeth out of the bottomless pit shall make war against them, and shall overcome them, and kill them. And their dead bodies shall lie in the street of the great city, which spiritually is called Sodom and Egypt, where also our Lord was crucified. And they of the people and kindreds and tongues and nations shall see their dead bodies three days and an half, and shall not suffer their dead bodies to be put in graves. And they that dwell upon the earth shall rejoice over them, and make merry, and shall send gifts one to another; because these two prophets tormented them that dwelt on the earth.

"And after three days and an half the Spirit of life from God entered into them, and they stood upon their feet; and great fear fell upon them which saw them. And they heard a great voice from heaven saying unto them, Come up hither. And they ascended up to heaven in a cloud; and their enemies beheld them. And the same hour was there a great earthquake, and the tenth part of the city fell, and in the earthquake were slain of men seven thousand: and the remnant were affrighted, and gave glory to the God of heaven. The second woe is past; and behold, the third woe cometh quickly.

"And the seventh angel sounded; and there were great voices in heaven, saying, The kingdoms of this world are become the kingdoms of our Lord, and of His Christ; and He shall reign for ever and ever" (Rev. 11:1-15).

Here we have the description of the last half of the Great Tribulation, the time when God's two witnesses will prophesy. They will be killed—and then at the appointed time God will display His power by resurrecting them and calling them up to heaven. The declaration will then be made that the kingdoms of this world are become the kingdoms of our Lord and our Christ, and He shall reign forever and ever. This could never occur without the second coming of Jesus.

The Binding of Satan: —

"And I saw an Angel come down from heaven, having the key of the bottomless pit and a great chain in His hand. And He laid hold on the dragon, that old serpent, which is the Devil, and Satan, and bound him a thousand years, and cast him into the bottomless pit, and shut him up, and set a seal upon him, that he should deceive the nations no more, till the thousand years should be fulfilled: and after that he must be loosed a little season" (Rev. 20:1-3). At the beginning of the Kingdom Age, Satan will be placed in the bottomless pit and sealed there for one thousand glorious years—the millennial reign of Christ on earth. This could never come to pass without His second coming.

The Millennial Reign of Christ: —

"After they had held their peace, James answered, saying, Men and brethren, hearken unto me: Simeon hath declared how God at the first did visit the Gentiles, to take out of them a people for His name. And to this agree the words of the prophets; as it is written, *After this I will return, and will build again the tabernacle of David, which is fallen down; and I will build again the ruins thereof, and I will set it up: that the residue of men might seek after the Lord, and all the Gentiles, upon whom my name is called saith the Lord, who doeth all these things.* Known unto God are all His works from the beginning of the world" (Acts 15:13-18).

This passage gives the blueprint of God's plan for

the ages. It is being worked out according to God's blueprint, and will continue until the glorious reign of Christ is a reality. When Jesus comes as King of kings and Lord of lords the Millennium will begin and the Church will reign with Christ in glory for one thousand years. All wickedness will be put down, the curse will be lifted, the devil will be bound and imprisoned in the pit, and universal honor, praise, and adoration will be given to Him to whom all praise is due! All these events—and many more—are prophesied in the Word of God, therefore they *must* come to pass—but not one of them can take place apart from the second coming of the Lord Jesus Christ.

Furthermore, Jesus must return to earth in order to demonstrate the validity of His personal and essential claims, claims spoken not only by the prophets but also by the Lord Jesus Himself during His earthly life. For example, in John 14:2, 3 He told His disciples, "In my Father's house are many mansions. . . . I go to prepare a place *for YOU.* And if I go and prepare a place for you, *I WILL come again, and receive you unto myself;* that where I am, there ye may be also."

The second coming of Jesus is a divine necessity to make good His claim as King of Israel, a truth declared on more than one occasion in the Word of God.

He must return in order to justify the faith of the millions who have exercised faith in Him and who are waiting in Paradise for that glorious morning when all of God's saints will be glorified.

The second coming of Jesus is necessary to complete salvation. His first coming provided perfect

redemption for the soul; but His second coming will
provide redemption for the body and bring to consummation all that He began and all that He *promised
to do* at His return.

The second coming of Jesus is *the hope of all hopes.*
Paul refers to it as *"that blessed hope"* (Tit. 2:13).

The Keystone to the Arch of Truth

Lest someone misunderstand, I would emphasize
that the death of the Lord Jesus Christ on the cross
is the keystone to the arch of truth. If Satan could
have kept Jesus from reaching Calvary, His first coming would have been to no avail. It is not His virgin
birth or His sinless life or His miracles that redeem,
but *the shed blood of the Lamb of God,* the Lamb
without blemish and without spot.

Writing to the believers in Corinth, Paul said, *"I
delivered unto you FIRST OF ALL* that which I also
received, how that *Christ died for our sins* according
to the Scriptures" (I Cor. 15:3). Paul did not mean
this in the sense of being first chronologically, but as
first in importance. The death, burial, and resurrection
of the Lord Jesus Christ "according to the Scriptures"
is first in importance and can never take second place
to any other doctrine. Christ died for our sins, and
"without shedding of blood is *no remission"* (Heb.
9:22). Therefore this doctrine must remain the most
important truth of all.

The precious pearl of Christ's atonement lies in
the casket of truth. Seven facts of history that are
clearly declared in the prophetic Scriptures will illustrate what I mean:

1. The Word of God prophesied how Christ would die: "Dogs have compassed me: the assembly of the wicked have inclosed me: *they pierced my hands and my feet*" (Psalm 22:16). Jesus was "pierced" according to Roman law. He was not stoned to death in accordance with *Jewish* law.

2. Christ was betrayed by a friend: "Yea, mine own familiar friend, in whom I trusted, which did eat of my bread, hath lifted up his heel against me" (Psalm 41:9).

3. He was sold for the price of a slave—thirty pieces of silver: "I said unto them, If ye think good, give me my price; and if not, forbear. So they weighed for my price thirty pieces of silver" (Zech. 11:12).

4. By His death, Christ was to restore that which He took not away: "They that hate me without a cause are more than the hairs of mine head: they that would destroy me, being mine enemies wrongfully, are mighty: then I restored that which I took not away" (Psalm 69:4). Since Jesus bore the sins of all, though He Himself knew no sin, by His death He restored that which He took not away.

5. Christ's sacrifice was freely made, there was no compulsion in it. His readiness to pay sin's penalty is expressed in His own words: "*I delight to do thy will, O my God . . .*" (Psalm 40:8).

6. The extreme debt and the unknowable intensity of Christ's sufferings are heralded forth in the words of sore despair that fell from His lips while He was dying on the cross: "My God, my God, why hast thou forsaken me?" (Psalm 22:1).

7. Christ's absolute identity with the sins of His

people is justly put when He Himself speaks of their
iniquity as His very own: "There is no soundness
in my flesh because of thine anger; neither is there
any rest in my bones *because of MY sin*" (Psalm 38:3).

The cross of Jesus is the substantiation of all prophecy from Genesis through Revelation. We might go a
step further and declare that the cross of Jesus is the
fulfillment of all Scripture, for without Christ and the
cross there would *be* no Scriptures. On the day of
His resurrection Christ Himself reminded the two
disciples on the way to Emmaus that His sufferings
and His glory are the two mighty canals in which
the streams of all truth flow.

Christ is the promised *Seed* of Eden, the fulfillment
of Genesis 3:15.

He is the sheltering *Ark* of Noah.

He is the *Ram* offered in Isaac's stead.

He is the *Passover Lamb* of Exodus.

He is the *perfect Sacrifice* of Leviticus.

He is the life-giving *Serpent* lifted on a pole in
Numbers.

He is the accessible *Refuge* of Deuteronomy.

He is the gracious, compassionate *Saviour* of Joshua.

He is the mighty *Man of valor* of Judges.

He is the kinsman *Redeemer* of Ruth.

He is the *Conqueror* of Samuel.

He is the vigilant *Administrator* of Chronicles.

He is the prayerful *Builder* of Nehemiah.

He is the wise *Leader* of Ezra.

He is the prevailing *Intercessor* in Esther.

He is the delivering *Daysman* of Job 9:33. (A "daysman" is one who stands between two men and lays

a hand on each of them to reconcile them. Jesus, with the hand of God and the hand of man, is *our* Daysman. He can touch both God and man.)

He is the patient *Sufferer* of Psalms.

He is the upright *Son* of Proverbs.

He is the *wise Man* of Ecclesiastes.

He is the attractive *Beloved* of the Song of Solomon.

He is the beautiful *Messenger* of Isaiah.

He is the weeping *Prophet* of Jeremiah.

He is the *glorious One* of Ezekiel.

He is the cut-off *Prince* of Daniel.

He is the refreshing *Dew* of Hosea.

He is the resolute *Judge* of Joel.

He is the *Raiser* of Amos.

He is the satisfying *Physician* of Obadiah.

He is the afflicted *Substitute* of Jonah.

He is the *Caster-away of sins* of Micah 7:19—He casts all our sins "into the depths of the sea."

He is the irresistible *Stronghold* of Nahum.

He is the glad *Singer* of Zephaniah.

He is the faithful *Blesser* of Haggai.

He is the smitten *Shepherd* of Zechariah.

Last, but by no means least, He is the coming *Refiner* of Malachi.

"He which testifieth these things saith, SURELY I COME QUICKLY! Amen. Even so, COME, LORD JESUS!" (Rev. 22:20).

Chapter III

The Bible and Prophecy

"We have also a more sure word of prophecy; where-unto ye do well that ye take heed, as unto a light that shineth in a dark place, until the day dawn, and the day star arise in your hearts: knowing this first, that *no prophecy of the Scripture is of any private interpretation. For the prophecy came not in old time by the will of man: but holy men of God spake as they were moved by the Holy Ghost*" (II Pet. 1:19-21).

"I testify unto every man that heareth the words of the prophecy of this book, If any man shall add unto these things, God shall add unto him the plagues that are written in this book: and if any man shall take away from the words of the book of this prophecy, God shall take away his part out of the book of life, and out of the holy city, and from the things which are written in this book" (Rev. 22:18, 19).

"For ever, O Lord, thy Word is settled in heaven" (Psalm 119:89).

The Bible is not a systematic treatise on morals, science, mathematics, history, theology, or any other subject. The Bible is the Word of God, the revelation of God. It reveals the fall of man, God's way of salvation, and God's foreordained plan and purpose through the ages.

In the Bible we find four predominant *persons:* God

71

the Father, God the Son, God the Holy Spirit—and
Satan.   We also see three specific *places:* heaven,
earth, and hell—in its final state, the lake of fire.
(However, hell and the lake of fire are one and the
same in reality.   *Hell* is the temporary prison of the
spirits of the wicked, and *the lake of fire* will be the
eternal place of damnation at the consummation of
all things.)   In the Bible we see three distinct groups
of people named and dealt with: the *Jew,* the *Gentile,*
and the *Church of God* as named in I Corinthians 10:32.

The Holy Scriptures were given "at sundry times
and in divers manners" (Heb. 1:1,2) over a period of
between 1200 and 1500 years.   Holy men of old—men
called, ordained, and specifically appointed of God—
spake as they were moved by the Holy Ghost.

The Bible contains sixty-six books—thirty-nine in
the Old Testament and twenty-seven in the New.
These books were written by between thirty-five and
forty authors, each of whom was chosen by Almighty
God to pen down the message God gave him.   Among
these authors were *kings* such as David and Solomon;
statesmen such as Daniel and Nehemiah; *priests* such
as Ezra.   There were educated men among the authors
of the holy Scriptures, men like Moses who was learned
in the wisdom of Egypt, and the Apostle Paul who
was a scholar in Jewish law.   But there were others
who were unlearned from the standpoint of formal and
academic education—Amos, a herdsman; Matthew, a
tax collector; Peter, James, and John who were fishermen—spoken of as "unlearned and ignorant men"
(Acts 4:13).

Still other Scriptures were penned under inspiration

by the beloved physician Luke and by such mighty prophets and seers as Isaiah, Ezekiel, Zechariah, and others.

The Bible is not an Asiatic book even though it was written in that part of the world. It was penned on parchment—in the wilderness of Sinai, on the cliffs of Arabia, in the Judaean hills of Palestine, in the courts of the temples, in the schools of the prophets in Bethel and Jericho, in the palace of Shushan in Persia, on the banks of the river Chebar in Babylonia, in the dungeons of Rome—and the book of The Revelation was given to John the Beloved while he was in lonely exile on the Isle of Patmos in the Aegean Sea.

Now let us imagine any other book compiled in like manner as our Bible. Suppose we take sixty-six books written by forty men from different walks of life—statesmen, physicians, scientists, historians, farmers, and various other professions over a period of sixteen centuries—and combine those sixty-six books into one volume. What kind of book would we have? It would be composed of a series of contradictions. Yet the Bible, compiled in such a manner, *contains* no contradictions. It is not a book of ancient history, myths and legends, or religious superstitions. It is a book of continuous, progressive revelation and doctrines.

The judges who wrote in the Scriptures knew more than the patriarchs. The apostles knew more than the prophets because of the light and revelation they received—i. e., the prophets penned down the words of the Old Testament at various times as God spoke to them; but the apostles walked and talked with Jesus.

I would also point out that the Old Testament and
the New Testament are not separate books with the
New *replacing* the Old. They are *two halves of a
completed whole.* In other words, the Old Testament
is the New Testament infolded, and the New Testament
is the Old Testament unfolded. It is impossible for
us to understand the book of Leviticus without the
book of Hebrews. It is impossible to understand Daniel without Revelation. It is impossible to grasp the
meaning of the Passover or the momentous fifty-third
chapter of Isaiah without the four Gospels—Matthew,
Mark, Luke, and John. Just as the first coming of
Christ demands His second coming, so the Old Testament demands the New.

Although the Bible is the revelation of God penned
down by holy men, it is not written in the language
of a superman nor in celestial words. It is written in
words easily understood. The Word of God contains
three kinds of language: (1) figurative, (2) symbolic,
(3) literal.

For examples, the expressions "harden not your
heart" and "let the dead bury their dead" are *figurative* and their meaning is made clear by the context.
Symbolic language is used in describing Nebuchadnezzar's image, Daniel's four wild beasts, and Christ
in the midst of the seven candlesticks in Revelation,
with explanation of the symbolic expressions given
either in the same chapter or in some other book of
the Bible. The rest of the language in the Bible is
literal. We are to read it as we would read any other
book, allow it to say what it says, and allow the Holy
Spirit to enlighten us as He reveals the truth declared.

Man has no right to allegorize or spiritualize the Scriptures. Modernism and liberalism use this false method of interpreting the Word of God, and such practice has led to the beginning of many false religious sects. We are commanded, "Study to shew thyself approved unto God, a workman that needeth not to be ashamed, *rightly dividing* the Word of truth" (II Tim. 2:15).

There are three things we must be very careful to avoid in our study of the Word of God: (1) we must not *misinterpret* the Scriptures, (2) we must not *misapply* the Scriptures, (3) we must not *mislocate* the Scriptures (take Scripture out of its setting). It is sad that "religious" men who are not truly *born again* are not willing to let the Word of God say what it really *says.* They try to make it say what they want to believe and preach. This is due in part to religious training, to religious environment, to religious prejudice, and to a desire to make the Scripture teach some favorite dogma or doctrine in order to build prestige with a specific religious group. There are many ministers (so-called) in pulpits today who would much rather be in the good graces of a denomination than to stand in the grace of Almighty God.

Both the Old and New Testaments contain parables by which a tremendous truth is imparted. The parables Jesus used were a "mystery" form of imparted truth (study Matthew chapter 13). We should understand, however, that "mystery" in the Word of God is not something that cannot be known, but rather something which for a given time or certain dispensation is *hidden,* to be revealed at a later time. For example, Paul said to the Corinthian Christians, "Behold, I shew you a *mystery:* We shall not all sleep, but we shall all be changed" (I Cor. 15:51).

The Rapture of the Church was definitely hidden in the Old Testament era and up to the days of Paul. It was to that apostle that the mystery of the Church was revealed (Eph. 3:3-7), and a mystery made known is no longer a mystery.

The only possible way for man to understand the Word of God is to allow the Holy Spirit to be the Teacher of the Word. Therefore the unbeliever cannot understand the Word of God: "The natural man receiveth not the things of the Spirit of God: for they are foolishness unto him: neither can he know them, because they are spiritually discerned" (I Cor. 2:14). It is by His Spirit that God reveals the truth of the Scriptures to us, "for the Spirit searcheth all things, yea, the deep things of God" (I Cor. 2:10).

Believers possess the Teacher of the Word of God: "Ye have an unction from the Holy One, and ye know all things. . . . The anointing which ye have received of Him abideth in you, and ye need not that any man teach you: but as the same anointing teacheth you of all things, and is truth, and is no lie, and even as it hath taught you, ye shall abide in Him" (I John 2:20, 27). Since the Holy Spirit abides in the heart of every believer, He reveals spiritual truths to us as God would have them taught and not as man might interpret them.

"All Scripture is given by inspiration of God, and is profitable for doctrine, for reproof, for correction, for instruction in righteousness: that the man of God may be perfect, throughly furnished unto all good works" (II Tim. 3:16, 17).

Thus was our Bible written—but what do we mean when we say that the Scriptures are *inspired?* God chose men, and through the Holy Spirit He directed them to pen down the words, laws, doctrines, historical facts, and revelations as God desired to make those truths known to man. To those holy men of His choosing He revealed His will and His plan for the ages. Therefore all Scripture is God-breathed, given of God to holy men as He told them, through the Holy Spirit, just what to write. The Bible does not simply *"contain"* the Word of God—*the Bible IS the Word of God,* and it is *ALL there is OF* the Word of God. (There are no "lost books" as some suggest.) All that God needed to say to men, He has said; and when He gave the book of The Revelation to John the Beloved, the Holy Bible was finished. That which is perfect is come, and we need no further revelation.

God is a Person—therefore God can write and God can speak. The two tables of stone given to Moses on Mount Sinai were *"written with the finger of God"* (Ex. 31:18). God's hand wrote on the wall in the palace of King Belshazzar, pronouncing judgment upon both king and kingdom (Dan. 5:5, 25-31). Over and over again we read of instances when God spoke. For example, "The Lord said unto Moses . . . The Lord spake unto Moses . . . ." (Read Exodus 24:12; 25:1; 30:11.) God talked with Moses on Mount Sinai. He gave Moses the specifications for the tabernacle, its furnishings, the Levitical law, and the order of service *under* the law. God spoke at the baptism of Jesus (Matt. 3:17). He spoke on the Mount of Transfiguration

(Matt. 17:5), and again in John 12:27-30 when the people who heard the voice thought they were hearing thunder, and Jesus said, "This voice came not because of me, but for your sakes."

God not only spoke *directly* to men, He also spoke to men in the Person of the Lord Jesus Christ who was God in flesh: "In the beginning was the Word, and the Word was with God, and the Word was God. The same was in the beginning with God. . . . And the Word was made flesh, and dwelt among us, (and we beheld His glory, the glory as of the only begotten of the Father,) full of grace and truth. . . . No man hath seen God at any time; the only begotten Son, which is in the bosom of the Father, He hath declared Him" (John 1:1-18 in part).

If you will make a careful study of the Gospel of Matthew and the Gospel of John and *underline* the words of Jesus, you will find that three-fifths of the forty-nine chapters in these two Gospels are words spoken by Jesus. In John 12:49, 50 He declared, *"I have not spoken of myself; but the Father which sent me, He gave me a commandment, what I should say, and what I should speak.* And I know that His commandment is life everlasting: whatsoever I speak therefore, even as the Father said unto me, so I speak."

Is ALL of the Bible inspired—every word in every verse of every chapter? Yes! I believe every word in the original parchments was God-breathed and penned down exactly as God gave it. In Matthew 5:17, 18 Jesus said, "Think not that I am come to destroy the law, or the prophets. I am not come to destroy, but to fulfil. For verily I say unto you, *Till heaven and earth pass, one jot or one tittle shall in no wise pass from the law, till all be fulfilled."* When He spoke of "jot" and "tittle" He was referring to the smallest letter (jot) and the smallest mark (tittle) of the Hebrew language. Therefore Jesus taught that the Scriptures were inspired even to the least letter and the least mark written into them!

Someone may ask, "What about the words spoken by the devil and by wicked men? And what about the geological tables, the account of the flood, and other historical events recorded in the Bible? Are these also inspired?" My answer is definitely *"Yes."* The prophets, inspired of God, penned the historical facts. The words of Satan are inspired in that God ordered these words to be written for our admonition and instruction. Anyone who makes a thorough study of the Old Testament and then studies that same period in history with its legends, traditions, and detailed descriptions, will see that the writers of the Old Testament were divinely inspired to record only the things that would shed light on God's plan and purpose in the ages. God's men were instructed what to write and what not to write. There is not one word in our Bible that should not be there, and no word is omitted that should be included. Through the ages —yea, *from everlasting*—God has protected His Word. "For ever, O Lord, thy Word is settled in heaven" (Psalm 119:89) and neither man nor the devil can destroy it.

There is a teaching which declares that the Old Testament writers like Isaiah, Daniel, Moses and others simply wrote according to their *impressions.* Such teaching is definitely of the devil, and the Word of God corrects this error in no uncertain terms. II Peter 1:20 declares "that no prophecy of the Scripture is of any private interpretation." That means that no person has the right to wrest the Scripture to make it say what he *wants* it to say, or interpret the Word to fit his personal belief or his doctrine.

This truth is confirmed in the fact that much of the Scripture penned by the Old Testament prophets was not understood by them. They wrote as they were inspired, but they did not always understand what they wrote. In I Peter 1:10-12 we read, "Of which salvation the prophets have inquired and searched diligently, who prophesied of the grace that should come unto you: searching what, or what manner of time the Spirit of Christ which was in them did signify, when it testified beforehand the sufferings of Christ, and the glory that should follow. Unto whom it was revealed, that not unto themselves, but unto us they did minister the things, which are now reported unto you by them that have preached the Gospel unto you with the Holy Ghost sent down from heaven; which things the angels desire to look into."

There are other statements in the Bible which prove that the men who were chosen of God to pen down His Word did not write according to their own impressions, for God also used instruments who were *not* holy men:

In Numbers 22:38 Balaam said to Balak, "Lo, I am come unto thee: have I now any power at all to say any thing? *The Word that God putteth in my mouth, that shall I speak.*" Also in Numbers 23:26 Balaam said to Balak, "Told not I thee, saying, *All that the Lord speaketh, that I must do?*"

One would not expect *King Saul* to prophesy; yet in I Samuel 10:10 we read, "When they came thither to the hill, behold, a company of prophets met (Saul); *and the Spirit of God came upon him,* and he prophesied among them." (Read also I Samuel 19:23, 24.)

In John 11:49-52 we find words of prophetic truth spoken by the high priest *Caiaphas.* When the chief priests and the Pharisees gathered in council to plot against Jesus, "Caiaphas . . . said unto them, Ye know nothing at all, nor consider that it is expedient for us, *that one man should die for the people, and that the whole nation perish not.* And this spake he not of himself: but being high priest that year, he prophesied that Jesus should die for that nation; and not for that nation only, but that also He should gather together in one the children of God that were scattered abroad."

That the men who penned the Scriptures spoke and wrote the words God gave them is clear from their own statements. When God told Moses to speak to Pharaoh and lead the children of Israel out of bondage in Egypt, Moses offered the excuse that he was not a talented orator. He said, "O my Lord, *I am not eloquent,* neither heretofore, nor since thou hast spoken unto thy servant: but *I am slow of speech, and of a slow tongue.*" Then God said to him, "Who hath made man's mouth? or who maketh the dumb, or deaf, or the seeing, or the blind? Have not I the Lord? *Now therefore GO, and I will be with thy mouth, and teach thee what thou shalt say*" (Ex. 4:10-12).

When God called Jeremiah as a prophet, Jeremiah said, "Ah, Lord God! Behold, I cannot speak: for I am a child." But God said to him, "Say not, I am a child: for thou shalt go to all that I shall send thee, and *whatsoever I command thee thou shalt speak.* Be not afraid of their faces: for I am with thee to deliver thee." And then Jeremiah testifies, *"Then the Lord put forth His hand, and touched my mouth.* And the Lord said unto me, *Behold, I have put MY WORDS in thy mouth"* (Jer. 1:6-9).

Ezekiel, Daniel, and the other Old Testament prophets give testimony to the fact that God spoke to them, and that He told them what to say. In the thirty-nine books of the Old Testament we find more than two thousand such statements as "The Lord spake, saying. . . . The Lord said. . . . Thus saith the Lord." Certainly this is more than sufficient proof of justification for Peter's statement that holy men of God spoke *"as they were moved by the Holy Ghost"* (II Pet. 1:21).

However, as I have previously stated, *Bible revelation* ceased with the book of Revelation. There has been no new revelation from God since He spoke to John on the Isle of Patmos. There are men today who *claim* to have received some new revelation from God, but they are impostors. They are false teachers such as the Apostle Paul warned against in II Corinthians 11:13-15: "For such are false apostles, deceitful workers, transforming themselves into the apostles of Christ. And no marvel; for Satan himself is transformed into an angel of light. Therefore it is no great thing if his ministers also be transformed as the ministers of righteousness; whose end shall be according to their works."

We do have *spiritual illumination,* but that is vastly different from revelation or Bible inspiration. Spiritual illumination is a work of the Holy Spirit in the heart of the believer as He opens the understanding and makes plain the true doctrines of God as set forth in Scripture. Jesus explained this to His disciples in John 16:12-15. He said, "I have yet many things to say unto you, but ye cannot bear them now. Howbeit *when He, the Spirit of truth, is come, He will guide you into ALL truth:* for He shall not speak of Himself; but whatsoever He shall hear, that shall He speak: and He will shew you things to come. He shall glorify me: for *He shall receive of mine, and shall shew it unto you.* All things that the Father hath are mine: therefore said I, that He shall take of mine, and shall shew it unto you."

The work of the Holy Spirit in this Dispensation of Grace is not to impart new revelation to men or inspire men to write or speak as did the prophets and the apostles. The present work of the Holy Spirit is to bring spiritual understanding and illumination to the mind of the believer that we may accept the truth of God and impart that truth to others as we study and rightly divide the Word. It is through the Holy Spirit that the plan and purpose of God in the ages is made known to present day believers as God declared it in the beginning.

Divisions In Bible Prophecy

Prophecies recorded in the Bible automatically divide themselves into three groups:

Past—prophecy that has been literally and minutely

fulfilled.

Present—prophecy that is being fulfilled all around us in this present hour as having to do with the Jews, the nations, the moral and religious character of peoples of the world today.

Future—prophecy clearly set forth in Scripture but also clearly unfulfilled.

The importance of the study of prophecy is clear, because two-thirds of the Scriptures are prophetic—in type, symbol, or direct statement. More than half of the Old Testament prophecies (and almost *all* of the New Testament prophecies) point to events yet future and therefore unfulfilled.

In this day of darkness we need the light of the sure word of prophecy to guide us through these perilous times in which we live. The realization that God has a definite plan and purpose in the ages gives mortal man a desire to live and labor, looking for that glorious hope to which our faith is anchored. "And every man that hath this hope in him purifieth himself . . ." (I John 3:3). God's servants are instructed to "occupy" until Jesus comes (Luke 19:13). Men who are looking for the glorious appearing of the great God and our Saviour Jesus Christ will be *soul-winners,* busy men.

The religious leaders and doctors of the law in Jesus' day missed their Messiah because they were not students of prophecy. They failed to recognize the Lord Jesus Christ because they did not understand the words of the prophets in the Old Testament Scriptures. Likewise, most religious leaders today are in total ignorance concerning the coming of Christ for His Church (and later *with* His Church).

When Jesus joined the disciples on the road to Emmaus on the day of His resurrection, the argument He used to convince them that He was their Messiah was an appeal to prophecy: *"Beginning at Moses and all the prophets, He expounded unto them in all the Scriptures the things concerning Himself"* (Luke 24:27).

It would be interesting to know all the words Jesus spoke to these two disciples as He walked with them toward Emmaus. They were familiar with the Old Testament Scriptures. They were also familiar with the arrest, trial, condemnation, crucifixion, and burial of Jesus of Nazareth—and they were well aware of the rumors that He was no longer in the grave but had risen. Therefore it was not difficult for the risen Christ to take the Old Testament prophecies and show these men that the events of which they had spoken were exactly what the prophets had foretold concerning Messiah. As Jesus outlined the truth concerning the *prophetic* Christ, comparing Him with the *historic* Christ, it is no wonder the hearts of the disciples burned within them as He talked with them and opened their understanding of the Scriptures! (Please read Luke 24:13-32.)

The Scriptures become simple, understandable, and precious when we see Christ in them, for "the testimony of Jesus is the spirit of prophecy" (Rev. 19:10). The spirit and purpose of all prophecy is to testify of Jesus, and since this is true, since Jesus is the capstone of the pyramid of prophecy, too much emphasis *cannot* be placed on the importance of *studying* prophecy.

One hundred and nine of the Old Testament prophecies were fulfilled literally when Jesus came the first time. Of the eight hundred and forty-five quotations from the Old Testament which appear in the New Testament, three hundred and thirty-three speak of Christ. These quotations vary in type and figure, but they all seem meaningless unless we see Christ in them.

There are only five books in the Old Testament which are not quoted in the New—the books of Ruth, Ezra, Nehemiah, Song of Solomon, and Obadiah.

Throughout the Old Testament we find a *double* witness to Jesus—that is, the Old Testament Scriptures speak of His *first* coming and also of His *second* coming. Many times the same prophet speaks of both advents, although he does not always name them in proper order because the Old Testament prophet did not fully understand all that he penned down. Rather, he wrote as God dictated.

This was confusing to the religious leaders of Christ's day. They did not allow the Holy Spirit to reveal the truth and they refused to see that there would be a first and second coming of Jesus. Furthermore, they were expecting a powerful ruler who would set up an earthly kingdom and restore Israel's glory; and since they did not understand the prophecies which declared Christ's sufferings as preceding His glory, they rejected Him. They interpreted the prophecies of the Old Testament as referring to Messiah's coming as King of kings and Lord of lords to set up an earthly kingdom.

The Old Testament prophets did not see the Church Age—the time between the sufferings and the glory of their Messiah; but we who are on this side of Calvary have no excuse for not rightly dividing the prophecies, seeing those that were fulfilled at Christ's first coming and those yet to be fulfilled at His second coming. The Old Testament prophets saw the future as separate *peaks,* but only one *mountain.* They saw the mountain peak of His first coming and they saw His glory, but they did not see the valley of the Day of Grace which lies *between* His first coming and His glory.

The first such mountain peak is made up of the virgin birth of the Son of God, the cross of Calvary, and the glorious Day of Pentecost. Then we see the valley (this Dispensation of Grace), and then the second mountain peak made up of the Rapture of the Church, the coming of Antichrist and, at the end of the Great Tribulation, the revelation of the Lord Jesus Christ, the time of His glorious reign from the throne of David as King of the earth.

Isaiah stands out as one of the greatest prophets of the entire Old Testament era, but even *he* did not fully understand what he wrote when he penned the first two verses of Isaiah chapter 61: "The Spirit of the Lord God is upon me; because the Lord hath anointed me to preach good tidings unto the meek; He hath sent me to bind up the brokenhearted, to proclaim liberty to the captives, and the opening of the prison to them that are bound; to proclaim the acceptable year of the Lord, and the day of vengeance of our God; to comfort all that mourn."

Isaiah did not see the comma that separated *"the acceptable year of the Lord"* from *"the day of vengeance of our God."* Thus Isaiah 61:2 spans centuries, but the prophet did not realize that this period would cover the entire Dispensation of Grace—which, incidentally, has already lasted almost two thousand years.

The Prophet Jeremiah did not see the full import of the words he penned in Jeremiah 23:5, 6: "Behold, the days come, saith the Lord, that I will raise unto David a righteous Branch, and a King shall reign and prosper, and shall execute judgment and justice in the earth.   In His days Judah shall be saved, and Israel shall dwell safely: and this is His name whereby He shall be called: THE LORD OUR RIGHTEOUSNESS."   Jeremiah did not see the comma between *the "righteous Branch"* and *the King who would "reign and prosper."*   The Righteous Branch came almost two thousand years ago, but up to this present hour He has not occupied the throne from which He will one day reign and prosper.

The Old Testament prophets saw the prophetic and kingly work of the Messiah but they did not see the priestly ministry of Christ.   They saw the altar and the throne, but they did not see the Lord's table which was to occupy the time *between* the altar and the throne.

Isaiah prophesied primarily concerning Messiah and the nation Israel, whereas *Jeremiah* prophesied primarily concerning Israel's return to their own land.

Ezekiel also speaks of the restoration of Israel to their own land at which time the temple will be rebuilt and temple worship restored.

Daniel speaks primarily of Gentile world rule and of Antichrist, the final world ruler under Gentile power.

Zechariah wrote mainly of events that will take place when Jesus comes in the Revelation, when He will stand on the Mount of Olives. In Zechariah 11:15-17 we read of the Antichrist. In chapter 14, verses 1 through 3 we read of Armageddon, and in chapter 12 verses 9 through 14 Zechariah clearly tells of the conversion of the nation Israel. In verses 16 through 21 of chapter 14 he tells about the Feast of Tabernacles. However, Zechariah did not see these great events *in chronological order.*

All of the major prophets (and most of the minor prophets) emphasize Christ as King, and the religious leaders when Jesus was born were confused because of this. They were looking for a powerful King, not the humble, sacrificial Lamb described in Isaiah chapter 53.

The Second Coming of Christ

"Let not your heart be troubled: ye believe in God, believe also in me. In my Father's house are many mansions: if it were not so, I would have told you. I go to prepare a place for you. And if I go and prepare a place for you, I will come again, and receive you unto myself; that where I am, there ye may be also. And whither I go ye know, and the way ye know. Thomas saith unto Him, Lord, we know not whither thou goest; and how can we know the way? Jesus saith unto him, I am the way, the truth, and the life: no man cometh unto the Father but by me" (John 14:1-6).

"When they therefore were come together, they asked of Him, saying, Lord, wilt thou at this time restore again the kingdom to Israel? And He said unto them, It is not for you to know the times or the seasons, which the Father hath put in His own power. But ye shall receive power, after that the Holy Ghost is come upon you: and ye shall be witnesses unto me both in Jerusalem, and in all Judaea, and in Samaria, and unto the uttermost part of the earth. And when He had spoken these things, while they beheld, He was taken up; and a cloud received Him out of their sight. And while they looked stedfastly toward heaven as He went up, behold, two men stood by them in white apparel; which also said, Ye men of Galilee, why stand ye gazing up into heaven? This same Jesus, which is taken up from you into heaven, shall so come in like manner as ye have seen Him go into heaven" (Acts 1:6-11).

No fact in history is more clearly, assuredly, and positively established than the fact of Christ's birth almost two thousand years ago. However, since His *first* coming did not fulfill all of the Old Testament prophecies which are *associated with* His coming, it is crystal clear that there must be a *second* coming in order to complete the fulfillment of Old Testament prophecy. Otherwise the Word of God would not be true.

By careful study of the Scriptures we can easily underline the prophecies that were fulfilled when Jesus was *born,* and those which *remain* will be fulfilled when He comes the second time. It is clear in the Scriptures that Christ's first coming was important; but it is not *the complete fulfillment* of all Bible doctrine. It is utterly impossible to understand the Scriptures if we refuse to see the first and second comings of Christ. He came the first time to lay His life down that we might have life and have it more abundantly. His second coming will be as King of kings and Lord of lords to rule over the earth.

Between the fall of Adam and the birth of Jesus we see the altar—pointing *back* to the fall of Adam and *forward* to the coming of the Lamb of God to die on the cross. Between the first and second comings of Christ we see the Lord's table (the communion table) pointing back to Calvary and forward to the second coming of Jesus. The Apostle Paul made this very clear in his first epistle to the Corinthian church. In I Corinthians 11:23-26 he wrote:

"For I have received of the Lord that which also I delivered unto you, That the Lord Jesus the same night in which He was betrayed took bread: and when He had given thanks, He brake it, and said, Take, eat: this is my body, which is broken for you: *this do in remembrance of me.* After the same manner also He took the cup, when He had supped, saying, This cup is the new testament in my blood: this do ye, as oft as ye drink it, in remembrance of me. *For as often as ye eat this bread, and drink this cup, ye do shew the Lord's death TILL HE COME.*"

In his letter to the Hebrew Christians Paul clearly distinguishes between the first and second comings of Christ. In Hebrews 9:24-28 he wrote: "Christ is not entered into the holy places made with hands, which are the figures of the true; but into heaven itself, *now to appear* in the presence of God for us: Nor yet that He should offer Himself often, as the high priest entereth into the holy place every year with blood of others; for then must He often have suffered since the foundation of the world: but now once in the end of the world *hath He appeared* to put away sin by the sacrifice of Himself. And as it is appointed unto men once to die, but after this the judgment: so Christ was once offered to bear the sins of many; and unto them that look for Him *shall He appear the SECOND time* without sin unto salvation."

Writing to the young minister Titus, Paul said, "The grace of God that bringeth salvation hath appeared to all men, teaching us that, denying ungodliness and worldly lusts, we should live soberly, righteously, and godly, in this present world, looking for that blessed hope, and *the glorious APPEARING of the great God and our Saviour Jesus Christ"* (Tit. 2:11-13).

In this passage Paul speaks of the *doctrinal significance* of Christ's appearings.   As a Prophet, He died for our justification.   As God's great High Priest, He lives at the right hand of God to make intercession for us.   He is our Advocate, but He is also our Sanctifier: ". . . Christ Jesus . . . is made unto us wisdom, and righteousness, and *sanctification,* and redemption" (I Cor. 1:30).

When Jesus comes in the Rapture for His Church He will come for our glorification and will give us a body like unto His glorious resurrection body. He died for our *justification,* He lives for our *sanctification,* He is coming again for our *glorification.*

Thus we see that the first and second comings of Christ are not complete in themselves. His first coming demands the second because the first advent did not fulfill all of the prophecies concerning the ministry of Christ on our behalf. His second coming demands the first, because had He not come the first time there could be no second coming, and the first and second comings are necessary to complete the plan of our great salvation. Jesus came the first time to redeem the soul—"Christ died for our sins according to the Scriptures" (I Cor. 15:3). He is coming the second time to redeem the body—and there would be no resurrection of the body if Christ did not come again: "But now is Christ risen from the dead, and become the firstfruits of them that slept. For since by man came death, by man came also the resurrection of the dead. For as in Adam all die, even so in Christ shall all be made alive. But every man in his own order: *Christ the firstfruits; afterward they that are Christ's at His coming"* (I Cor. 15:20-23).

"For the Lord Himself shall descend from heaven with a shout, with the voice of the archangel, and with the trump of God: and the dead in Christ shall rise first: then we which are alive and remain shall be caught up together with them in the clouds, to meet the Lord in the air: and so shall we ever be with the Lord" (I Thess. 4:16, 17).

Theories Concerning the Second Coming of Christ

The majority of professing Christians admit the *fact* of the second coming of Jesus but they do not agree as to the *manner* or *time* of His return. However, all genuinely born again, blood-washed Christians believe that He is coming back to this earth, for the grace of God that saves us also teaches us to look for

Him (Tit. 2:11-13).

It might be well to look at a few of the *theories*
concerning the second coming of the Lord Jesus:

Pentecost:—

One theory is that the second coming of Jesus is
spiritual and that it was fulfilled on the Day of Pentecost; but a study of the Word of God reveals that it
was not the Lord Jesus Christ who came at Pentecost,
but *the Holy Spirit*—and the coming of the Spirit was
conditioned on the absence of the Christ.   To His
disciples He explained, "Nevertheless I tell you the
truth: It is expedient for you that I go away: for *if
I go not away, the Comforter will not come unto you;*
but if I depart, I will send Him unto you" (John 16:7).
So, if the Holy Spirit were only another manifestation
of the Lord Jesus Christ then the Holy Spirit and
Christ would be identical personalities, a teaching
which would nullify and destroy the Holy Trinity of
Father, Son, and Holy Ghost.   Furthermore, if we are
willing to face a clear Bible fact we must admit that
the entire New Testament was written *after* the Day
of Pentecost, and in the books of the New Testament
there are over one hundred and fifty references to the
second coming of Jesus, *all speaking of His coming as
yet future!*   When I speak of Christ's second coming
I am referring to that event in its entirety—one event,
but in two stages.

Furthermore, none of the events prophesied as ac-
companying the second coming (either the Rapture or
the Revelation) occurred on the Day of Pentecost—i. e.,
the bodily resurrection of the dead in Christ, the

translation of the living saints, the binding of Satan, and many, many other things too numerous to mention here. Therefore as we study the Scriptures it becomes increasingly clear that the coming of the Holy Spirit on the Day of Pentecost was *not* the second coming of the Lord Jesus Christ. The two heavenly messengers said to the apostles on the day of the ascension, *"This SAME JESUS,* which is taken up from you into heaven, shall so come in like manner as ye have seen Him go into heaven" (Acts 1:11).

The conversion of a sinner:—

There is also a teaching that the second coming of Jesus occurs when a sinner is converted. This cannot be. When a sinner is converted *the sinner comes to Christ,* not Christ to the sinner. Jesus invited, *"COME UNTO ME,* all ye that labour and are heavy laden, and I will give you rest" (Matt. 11:28). In John 6:37 He promised, "Him that *cometh to me* I will in no wise cast out." The Bible's last invitation to the sinner is recorded in Revelation 22:17: "The Spirit and the bride say, *Come.* And let him that heareth say, *Come.* And let him that is athirst *come.* And whosoever will, let him take the water of life freely."

It is true that the Holy Spirit convicts and draws the sinner to Christ, and then takes up His abode in the heart of the sinner who believes on Jesus; but by no stretch of the imagination can we say that the conversion of a sinner is the second coming of Jesus as described by Himself and the writers in the Scriptures.

The death of a believer:—

Still another theory of the second coming of Jesus

is that the death of a believer is the second coming.
Those who adhere to this teaching base their argument
on John 14:1-6—a passage which is not a funeral text
at all but rather Christ's words of encouragement to
His disciples, assuring them that He would return and
receive them unto Himself. When a believer *dies*, the
spirit immediately passes into eternity. If the death
of a believer were the second coming of Christ then
He must of necessity remain continuously on earth
because believers die every second of every minute of
the day, somewhere around the world! Thus we see
the fallacy of such teaching, for the Lord Jesus Christ
is now seated at the right hand of God the Father,
engaged in His high priestly ministry—and He will not
leave that seat to return to this earth until He comes
for His Church.

Jesus will come *in person* to receive His own (I
Thess. 4:16) but I believe that when a believer dies
the angels accompany the spirit of that believer to
Paradise. When the beggar Lazarus died the angels
carried his spirit to Abraham's bosom (Luke 16:22), and
it seems reasonable that when a born again child of
God departs this life the angels see to it that his spirit
reaches Paradise safely. Jesus does not come for His
children when they die, but *He will come* for the
Church in the Rapture.

Jesus would certainly not have been hypocritical
in teaching His disciples. If His second coming were
death He would have told them, "If I go and prepare
a place for you I will send *death* and *through death*
I will bring you unto myself." But He did not say
that. He said, *"I WILL COME AGAIN, and receive*

you unto myself."

On one occasion Peter asked Jesus, "Lord, what shall *this man* do?" (He was referring to John the Beloved.) Jesus replied, "If I will that he tarry *till I come,* what is that to thee? Follow thou me" (John 21:21, 22). The saying was then spread abroad among the Christians that John the Beloved should not die. Here it is very clear that the disciples did not think of the Lord's second coming as *death.* In their minds there was a great difference between death and His return to take them to be with Him.

Death is the last enemy that will be destroyed (I Cor. 15:26). Death robs the believer of earthly life, of witnessing and joy as he worships and fellowships with the brethren. Death robs the body of its attractiveness. Death is the wages of sin, the result of God's wrath upon sin; but the second coming of Christ is the glorious manifestation of God's love toward His children. The Lord Jesus Christ is the Prince of Life and where *He* is there can be no death. Jesus never conducted a funeral during His earthly ministry. On the contrary He broke up every funeral He attended. When Jesus appears, *death flees.* While He tabernacled among men, no one could remain dead in His presence. He is the resurrection and the life, and His second coming is not death, but resurrection and life. To Martha He declared, "I am the resurrection, and the life. He that believeth in me, though he were dead, yet shall he live: and whosoever liveth and believeth in me shall never die . . ." (John 11:25, 26).

The destruction of Jerusalem:—

Another group of so-called religious leaders and

teachers contend that the destruction of Jerusalem by
Titus the Roman in 70 A. D. was the second coming
of Jesus, but a study of the history of that event will
reveal that Jesus was not present that day. Jerusalem
was destroyed by Roman soldiers, and none of the
things happened that are prophesied to happen at the
second coming of the Lord Jesus Christ. For example—
hear these words from the Prophet Zechariah concerning Christ's coming in the Revelation:

"His feet shall stand in that day upon the Mount
of Olives, which is before Jerusalem on the east, and
the Mount of Olives shall cleave in the midst thereof
toward the east and toward the west, and there shall
be a very great valley; and half of the mountain shall
remove toward the north, and half of it toward the
south. And ye shall flee to the valley of the mountains; for the valley of the mountains shall reach unto
Azal: yea, ye shall flee, like as ye fled from before
the earthquake in the days of Uzziah king of Judah:
and the Lord my God shall come, and all the saints
with thee.

"And it shall come to pass in that day, that the
light shall not be clear, nor dark: but it shall be one
day which shall be known to the Lord, not day, nor
night: but it shall come to pass, that at evening time
it shall be light. And it shall be in that day, that
living waters shall go out from Jerusalem; half of them
toward the former sea, and half of them toward the
hinder sea: in summer and in winter shall it be.

"And the Lord shall be king over all the earth: in
that day shall there be one Lord, and His name one.
All the land shall be turned as a plain from Geba to

Rimmon south of Jerusalem: and it shall be lifted up, and inhabited in her place, from Benjamin's gate unto the place of the first gate, unto the corner gate, and from the tower of Hananeel unto the king's winepresses. And men shall dwell in it, and there shall be no more utter destruction; but Jerusalem shall be safely inhabited" (Zech. 14:4-11).

Then in Ezekiel 47:1-12 we read: "Afterward he brought me again unto the door of the house; and, behold, waters issued out from under the threshold of the house eastward: for the forefront of the house stood toward the east, and the waters came down from under the right side of the house, at the south side of the altar. Then brought he me out of the way of the gate northward, and led me about the way without unto the utter gate by the way that looketh eastward; and, behold, there ran out waters on the right side. And when the man that had the line in his hand went forth eastward, he measured a thousand cubits, and he brought me through the waters; the waters were to the ankles.

"Again he measured a thousand, and brought me through the waters; the waters were to the knees. Again he measured a thousand, and brought me through; the waters were to the loins. Afterward he measured a thousand; and it was a river that I could not pass over: for the waters were risen, waters to swim in, a river that could not be passed over. And he said unto me, Son of man, hast thou seen this? Then he brought me, and caused me to return to the brink of the river.

"Now when I had returned, behold, at the bank of

the river were very many trees on the one side and on the other. Then said he unto me, These waters issue out toward the east country, and go down into the desert, and go into the sea: which being brought forth into the sea, the waters shall be healed. And it shall come to pass, that every thing that liveth, which moveth, whithersoever the rivers shall come, shall live: and there shall be a very great multitude of fish, because these waters shall come thither: for they shall be healed; and every thing shall live whither the river cometh.

"And it shall come to pass, that the fishers shall stand upon it from En-gedi even unto En-eglaim; they shall be a place to spread forth nets; their fish shall be according to their kinds, as the fish of the great sea, exceeding many. But the miry places thereof and the marishes thereof shall not be healed; they shall be given to salt. And by the river upon the bank thereof, on this side and on that side, shall grow all trees for meat, whose leaf shall not fade, neither shall the fruit thereof be consumed: it shall bring forth new fruit according to his months, because their waters they issued out of the sanctuary: and the fruit thereof shall be for meat, and the leaf thereof for medicine."

The purpose of the second coming of Jesus is not to *destroy* Jerusalem, but to restore it and deliver the nation of Israel. According to the Word of God, Jerusalem must be trodden down of the Gentiles until "the times of the Gentiles" are fulfilled. "And then shall they see the Son of man coming in a cloud with power and great glory." (Please read Luke 21:24-28.)

The glorious book of Revelation, written twenty-six

years after the destruction of Jerusalem in 70 A. D.,
speaks again and again of the second coming of Jesus
as still in the future.

The spread of Christianity: —

Still another theory claims that the spread of Christianity is the second coming of Christ, but this, too,
is false. The spread of Christianity is *gradual,* whereas
the Word of God declares that the return of the Lord
will be sudden and as unexpected as the coming of a
thief in the night. Jesus said to His disciples, "As the
lightning cometh out of the east, and shineth even unto the west; so shall also the coming of the Son of
man be. . . . But of that day and hour knoweth no
man, no, not the angels of heaven, but my Father
only. . . . Watch therefore: for ye know not what hour
your Lord doth come. . . . Therefore be ye also ready:
for in such an hour as ye think not the Son of man
cometh" (Matt. 24:27, 36, 42, 44).

I Thessalonians 5:2 tells us "that the day of the
Lord so cometh as a thief in the night," and in Revelation 3:3 we read, "Remember therefore how thou hast
received and heard, and hold fast, and repent. If
therefore thou shalt not watch, I will come on thee as
a thief, and thou shalt not know what hour I will
come upon thee."

The Word of God further teaches that in the revelation of Jesus Christ the world will not be finally *converted,* but on the contrary *sudden destruction* will
come. In I Thessalonians 5:1-3 we read, "Of the times
and the seasons, brethren, ye have no need that I
write unto you. For yourselves know perfectly that

the day of the Lord so cometh as a thief in the night. For when they shall say, Peace and safety; then sudden destruction cometh upon them, as travail upon a woman with child; and they shall not escape."

Then in II Thessalonians 1:7-10 Paul tells us, "To you who are troubled rest with us, when the Lord Jesus shall be revealed from heaven with His mighty angels, in flaming fire taking vengeance on them that know not God, and that obey not the Gospel of our Lord Jesus Christ: who shall be punished with everlasting destruction from the presence of the Lord, and from the glory of His power; when He shall come to be glorified in His saints, and to be admired in all them that believe (because our testimony among you was believed) in that day."

How Will Jesus Come the Second Time?

The Scripture is clear as to *the manner* of Christ's second coming to this earth. First of all, we have the testimony of Jesus Himself. In the Gospel of Matthew He said, "The Son of man shall come in the glory of His Father with His angels; and then He shall reward every man according to his works" (Matt. 16:27).

In Matthew 25:31, 32 Jesus said, "When the Son of man shall come in His glory, and all the holy angels with Him, then shall He sit upon the throne of His glory: and before Him shall be gathered all nations: and He shall separate them one from another, as a shepherd divideth his sheep from the goats."

Reassuring His disciples in John 14:1-3 Jesus said, "Let not your heart be troubled: ye believe in God, believe also in me. In my Father's house are many mansions: if it were not so, I would have told you. I go to prepare a place for you. And if I go and prepare a place for you, I will come again, and receive you unto myself; that where I am, there ye may be also."

Jesus is coming back to this earth bodily, in person —not a spirit, not an angel, not an influence, *but A MAN, the Man Christ Jesus.*

In Acts 1:1-11 Luke tells us that the risen Christ "shewed Himself alive after His passion by many infallible proofs, being seen of (His disciples) forty days, and speaking of the things pertaining to the kingdom of God." He commanded them not to depart from Jerusalem until they were baptized with the Holy Ghost. They would receive power which would enable them to be witnesses for Him *in Jerusalem, and in all Judaea, and in Samaria, and unto the uttermost part of the earth.*

"And when He had spoken these things, while they beheld, He was taken up; and a cloud received Him out of their sight. And while they looked stedfastly toward heaven as He went up, behold, two men stood by them in white apparel; which also said, *Ye men of Galilee, why stand ye gazing up into heaven? THIS SAME JESUS, which is taken up from you into heaven, shall so come IN LIKE MANNER as ye have seen Him go into heaven!"*

Notice: *The SAME JESUS* will return to this earth *in the SAME MANNER* in which He left it. That means that His return will be *visible* and *personal.*

The two men who stood by the disciples assured

them that the same Jesus with whom they had walked and talked and fellowshipped would come again exactly as they had seen Him disappear.

The *Apostle Paul* believed in the personal return of the Lord Jesus Christ. In that glorious passage in I Thessalonians 4:13-18 he declared that *"the Lord HIMSELF"* (bodily) will descend from heaven and will call the Church up to meet Him in the air.

James expected the bodily return of Jesus, and exhorted the brethren to "be patient . . . unto the coming of the Lord" (James 5:7).

Peter believed in the personal return of Jesus. He declared, "We have not followed cunningly devised fables, when we made known unto you the power and coming of our Lord Jesus Christ, but were eyewitnesses of His majesty" (II Pet. 1:16).

Peter was speaking here of his experience on the Mount of Transfiguration (recorded in Matthew 17:1-5) which is a type of the second coming of the Lord Jesus Christ.

Moses on the Mount of Transfiguration is a type of the *resurrection saints.*

Elijah is a type of the *translated saints*—those who will be caught up without dying.

Peter, James, and *John* (who were present that day) are a type of the *Jewish remnant* that shall see Jesus when He comes the second time.

The *powerless disciples* at the foot of the Mount of Transfiguration are a type of the *professed* followers of Jesus who will be left behind in the Rapture, powerless to resist the devil in the day when he rules in the person of Antichrist.

The little book of *Jude* contains only one short chapter but it tells us that Enoch, the seventh from Adam, believed in the personal return of Jesus, saying, "Behold, the Lord cometh with ten thousands of His saints, to execute judgment upon all, and to convince all that are ungodly among them of all their ungodly deeds which they have ungodly committed, and of all their hard speeches which ungodly sinners have spoken against Him" (Jude verses 14 and 15).

Certainly John the Beloved believed in and looked for the bodily return of the Lord. He not only penned the reassuring words of Jesus in John 14:1-6, but also in his first epistle he wrote: "And now, little children, abide in Him; that, *WHEN HE SHALL APPEAR, we may have confidence, and not be ashamed before Him at His coming*" (I John 2:28).

Then in Revelation 1:7 John testified, "Behold, He cometh with clouds; *and every eye shall see Him,* and they also which pierced Him: and all kindreds of the earth shall wail because of Him . . . ." This could mean nothing short of the *personal, bodily return* of Jesus.

Finally, in Revelation 19:11-16, John the Beloved gives this testimony: "I saw heaven opened, and behold a white horse; and He that sat upon him was called Faithful and True, and in righteousness He doth judge and make war. His eyes were as a flame of fire, and on His head were many crowns; and He had a name written, that no man knew, but He Himself. And He was clothed with a vesture dipped in blood: and His name is called The Word of God. And the armies which were in heaven followed Him upon white

horses, clothed in fine linen, white and clean. And
out of His mouth goeth a sharp sword, that with it
He should smite the nations: and He shall rule them
with a rod of iron: and He treadeth the winepress of
the fierceness and wrath of Almighty God. *And He
hath on His vesture and on His thigh a name written,
KING OF KINGS, AND LORD OF LORDS."*

Then in next to the last verse of The Revelation
the beloved disciple gives these words of expectation:
"He which testifieth these things saith, *Surely I come
quickly."* And John prays, *"Even so, COME, LORD
JESUS!"* (Rev. 22:20).

Undoubtedly many church members partake of the
Lord's Supper without fully realizing its meaning; but
each time the bread and the fruit of the vine are offered, those who take part in the communion are testi-
fying that they expect the Lord's return—*"for as often
as ye eat this bread, and drink this cup, ye do shew
the Lord's death TILL HE COME"* (I Cor. 11:26).
The Lord's Supper is not a permanent, eternal ordinance. It is a memorial feast pointing back to Calvary
and pointing forward to the return of Jesus; therefore
it will be discontinued when He comes the second
time.

God gave Paul fourteen epistles, and in these writings the apostle speaks of the second coming of Jesus
thirteen times as often as he speaks of baptism!

In the *Old Testament* there are twenty times as
many references to the second coming of Jesus as there
are references to His first coming, and in the *New
Testament* one verse out of every thirty speaks of the
Lord's second coming. Yet in the face of all this

divine truth there are many people who boldly *deny* the second coming of the Lord Jesus Christ. These are the "scoffers" of whom Peter says, "They are *willingly ignorant*" (II Pet. 3:4, 5).

The Time of Christ's Second Coming

"Of that day and hour knoweth no man, no, not the angels of heaven, but my Father only" (Matt. 24:36).

From these words spoken by Jesus to His disciples we can be sure that no one knows *the exact time* of His second coming; but the Bible has much to say about the time *immediately preceding* His return. Paul wrote of "the times and the seasons" which herald the Lord's second coming. In I Thessalonians 5:1-10 we read:

"Of the times and the seasons, brethren, ye have no need that I write unto you. For yourselves know perfectly that the day of the Lord so cometh as a thief in the night. For when they shall say, Peace and safety; then sudden destruction cometh upon them, as travail upon a woman with child; and they shall not escape.

"But *ye, brethren, are not in darkness, that that day should overtake you as a thief. Ye are all the children of light, and the children of the day: we are not of the night, nor of darkness.* Therefore let us not sleep as do others; but let us watch and be sober. For they that sleep sleep in the night; and they that be drunken are drunken in the night. But let us, who are of the day, be sober, putting on the breastplate of faith and love; and for an helmet, the hope of salva-

tion. For God hath not appointed us to wrath, but to
obtain salvation by our Lord Jesus Christ. Who died
for us, that, whether we wake or sleep, we should live
together with Him."

In the parable of the fig tree Jesus told His disciples, "Now learn a parable of the fig tree: When
his branch is yet tender, and putteth forth leaves,
ye know that summer is nigh: so likewise ye, when
ye shall see all these things, know that it is near, even
at the doors" (Matt. 24:32, 33). When the fig tree puts
forth leaves, those who are familiar with the habits of
the fig tree know that summer is near. We see the
fruit trees begin to bud and bloom and we know spring
is coming—but we cannot name the exact day, the
exact hour or moment, when winter winds will cease
to blow and warm spring breezes will begin to whisper
through the trees. We know there *will be* spring—but
we cannot pinpoint the exact minute it will begin. We
recognize the seasons of the year by changes in temperature, and there are various signs which herald the
coming of spring, summer, fall, and winter. A bit later
in this study we will consider the signs which are all
around us and which definitely point to the imminent
return of the Lord Jesus Christ, just as the budding
of the fig tree points to the soon-coming of summer.

Of these signs, there are some things which must
be fulfilled before Christ comes in Revelation—but
there is not one unfulfilled prophecy to prevent His
coming for His Church at any moment! The signs
around us point to the Revelation, the time when Jesus
will stand on the Mount of Olives and every eye shall
see Him. *Now think, beloved:* The Revelation will

occur seven years after the Rapture; and if present signs point to *The Revelation,* how near the Rapture must be!

The Bible clearly teaches that Jesus must return before the Millennium—the thousand years of peace on earth when Jesus will reign in righteousness as spoken of in Revelation 20:1-6. This extended time of peace on earth and good will toward men is referred to in Scriptures as "the Kingdom," and is described in glorious terms by the prophets. It will be a time when the earth will be blessed with a universal rule of righteousness and peace, when men will beat their swords into plowshares and their spears into pruninghooks. Jesus, Prince of Peace, will occupy the throne of David in Jerusalem and peace will engulf the whole earth.

The structure of the New Testament demands that Christ return to this earth before the Millennium. This is evident for the following reasons:

1. The righteous dead must be raised before the Millennium because they are to reign with Christ during that glorious thousand years. There can be no Millennium until the resurrection of the saints, and there will be no resurrection of the saints until Jesus comes: "For as in Adam all die, even so in Christ shall all be made alive. But every man in his own order: Christ the firstfruits; afterward they that are Christ's at His coming" (I Cor. 15:22, 23). "Blessed and holy is he that hath part in the first resurrection: on such the second death hath no power, but they shall be priests of God and of Christ, and shall reign with Him a thousand years" (Rev. 20:6).

2. The nations must be judged before the Millenni-

um.   Since the Millennium will be a period of one
thousand years of universal righteousness, the tares
must be separated from the wheat before that time of
righteousness and peace on earth, and the separation
of the tares and the wheat will not take place until
Jesus comes the second time.   They will "both grow
together until the harvest," at which time Jesus will
say to His reapers, "Gather ye together first the tares,
and bind them in bundles to burn them: but gather
the wheat into my barn. . . . As therefore the tares are
gathered and burned in the fire; so shall it be in the
end of this world.   The Son of man shall send forth
His angels, and they shall gather out of His kingdom
all things that offend, and them which do iniquity;
and shall cast them into a furnace of fire: there shall
be wailing and gnashing of teeth.   Then shall the
righteous shine forth as the sun in the kingdom of
their Father.   Who hath ears to hear, let him hear"
(Matt. 13:30, 40-43).

3. There can be no Millennium as long as the devil
has his freedom, and certainly we know that Satan is
running rampant today!   But when Jesus comes a
second time He will bind Satan and imprison him for
one thousand years: "And I saw an Angel come down
from heaven, having the key of the bottomless pit and
a great chain in His hand.   And He laid hold on the
dragon, that old serpent, which is the Devil, and Satan, and bound him a thousand years, and cast him
into the bottomless pit, and shut him up, and set a
seal upon him, that he should deceive the nations no
more, till the thousand years should be fulfilled: and
after that he must be loosed a little season" (Rev.

20:1-3).

4. The false messiah, Antichrist, must appear and be put down before the Millennium. His reign will last for approximately seven years. The first three and one-half years will be years of peace, a time of seeming security; and then Antichrist will break his covenant with the Jews and this earth will become a literal hell. At the end of the tribulation period Christ will return and will destroy the Antichrist "with the spirit of His mouth, and . . . with the brightness of His coming" (II Thess. 2:8). The armies of Antichrist will be destroyed, the beast and the false prophet will be cast into the lake of fire (Rev. 19:20), and the Millennium will begin.

5. The Jews must be restored to their own land (Palestine) before the Millennium. They *will be* restored as a nation, and when Jesus comes the second time they will recognize Him as their Messiah. They will fall at His feet and worship Him, a nation will be born in a day, and the Millennium and the kingdom promised to Israel will begin: "Behold, He cometh with clouds; and every eye shall see Him, and they also which pierced Him: and all kindreds of the earth shall wail because of Him . . ." (Rev. 1:7). Please read Ezekiel 36:24-28; Zechariah 12:10; 13:6; 14:1-4.

I repeat for emphasis—Jesus can come for His Church at any moment. There is not one single prophecy that remains to be fulfilled before His coming in the Rapture.

The Rapture

"The Lord Himself shall descend from heaven with

a shout, with the voice of the archangel, and with the trump of God: and the dead in Christ shall rise first: then we which are alive and remain shall be caught up together with them in the clouds, to meet the Lord in the air: and so shall we ever be with the Lord" (I Thess. 4:16, 17).

As I have previously stated, the second coming of Christ will be in two stages, and the words just quoted describe the first stage of His coming—the time when He comes in the air and calls His Church up to meet Him.   In the second stage of His second coming, His feet will stand on the Mount of Olives (Zech. 14:4) and the saints will come with Him to reign with Him on earth.   The time *between* the two stages of His second coming will be approximately seven years (the seventieth week of Daniel's prophecy), during which time Antichrist will reign on earth and the saints will be rewarded for service, their works will be judged, and they will attend the marriage supper of the Lamb.

Our study in the remainder of this chapter will deal with the first stage of Christ's second coming—the time when He comes to call His saints up to meet Him in the clouds in the air.   Some people object to the term *"Rapture"* as used with reference to the Lord's coming for the Church, but the literal meaning of the word is simply "to catch away," and that is exactly what will happen when Christ comes in the Rapture.   He will catch away all believers "in a moment, in the twinkling of an eye, at the last trump: for the trumpet shall sound, and the dead shall be raised incorruptible, and we shall be changed.   For this corruptible must put on incorruption, and this mortal must put on immortality. So when this corruptible shall have put on incorruption, and this mortal shall have put on immortality, then shall be brought to pass the saying that is written, Death is swallowed up in victory!" (I Cor. 15:51-54).

From the passages of Scripture just given, we see that the Rapture will be twofold:

1. The dead in Christ will be raised. (This speaks of the body, not the spirit.) To be absent from the body is to be present with the Lord (II Cor. 5:6, 8; Phil. 1:23). There is no such thing as soul-sleep. When a believer dies, the body returns to dust—*but the spirit returns unto God who gave it* (Eccl. 12:7). The "dead in Christ" are born again believers who have departed this life, whose bodies have returned to dust and whose spirits are resting in Paradise. When the Rapture occurs, Jesus will bring the spirits of the righteous with Him and their bodies will then be resurrected in glorified form to be reunited with their spirits.

2. The living saints will be changed—"in a moment, in the twinkling of an eye"—and together *all saints* will be caught up "to meet the Lord in the air."

Jesus clearly taught the twofold character of the Rapture when He spoke with Martha just before the raising of Lazarus. He said, "I am the resurrection, and the life: he that believeth in me, though he were dead, yet shall he live." (This speaks of the personal resurrection of saints who have died physically. Their bodies will be raised and they will live eternally.) "And whosoever liveth and believeth in me shall never die." (This speaks of believers who will be living when Jesus descends in the air and calls the Church

up to meet Him.   They will be translated, glorified,
but will not see death.) Please read John 11:23-27.

The Apostle Paul emphasizes the twofold character
of the Rapture in I Corinthians chapter 15—the great
chapter on the resurrection.   In verses 51 through 55
he makes known the mystery that "we shall not all
sleep (die), but we shall all be changed, *in a moment,*
in the twinkling of an eye."   When the trumpet of
God sounds, the dead in Christ will be raised *incor-*
ruptible, and the living saints will be changed. Why?
Because "this corruptible must put on *incorruption,*
and this mortal must put on *immortality.* Then shall
be brought to pass the saying that is written, *Death is*
swallowed up in victory!"   Only those who will be
caught up to meet Jesus without dying can shout *"O*
death, where is thy sting?   O grave, where is thy
victory?"

In II Corinthians 5:1-4 Paul made known his heart's
desire to be among those who should not be "unclothed" by death, but clothed with immortality without dying: "We know that if our earthly house of this
tabernacle were dissolved, we have a building of God,
an house not made with hands, eternal in the heavens.
For in this we groan, earnestly desiring to be clothed
upon with our house which is from heaven: if so be
that being clothed we shall not be found naked. For
we that are in this tabernacle (body) do groan, being
burdened: not for that we would be unclothed, but
clothed upon, that mortality might be swallowed up
of life."

To the Philippian believers Paul wrote: "That I
may know Him, and the power of His resurrection, and

the fellowship of His sufferings, being made conformable unto His death; if by any means I might attain unto the resurrection of the dead. Not as though I had already attained, either were already perfect: but I follow after, if that I may apprehend that for which also I am apprehended of Christ Jesus. Brethren, I count not myself to have apprehended: but this one thing I do, forgetting those things which are behind, and reaching forth unto those things which are before, I press toward the mark for the prize of the high calling of God in Christ Jesus" (Phil. 3:10-14).

In other words, Paul would esteem it a marvelous and glorious thing to rise from the dead at the first resurrection when the Rapture occurs, and to be caught up with the changed ones; but he esteemed it a much greater prize if he should be one of those caught up *without dying*. The prize of all prizes for the Christian would be to be living when Jesus comes in the Rapture and calls His Church up to meet Him in the air.

In the passage already quoted from I Corinthians 15 we are clearly told that the Rapture will be over "*in a moment, in the twinkling of an eye*"—and it takes but a fraction of a second to twinkle an eye! The Rapture, therefore, will be a surprise to the masses of mankind. In Revelation 16:15 John the Beloved tells us that Jesus will come "*as a thief.* Blessed is he that watcheth, and keepeth his garments, lest he walk naked, and they see his shame."

In I Thessalonians 5:1, 2 Paul also tells us that Jesus will come as a thief: "But of the times and the seasons, brethren, ye have no need that I write unto you. For yourselves know perfectly that the day of the Lord

so cometh *as a thief in the night.*" I believe Paul is
giving a twofold message in this passage, because in
verse 3 we read, "When they shall say, Peace and
safety; then sudden destruction cometh upon them, as
travail upon a woman with child; *and they shall not
escape.*" The Lord's coming "as a thief in the night"
speaks of the Rapture, but the "sudden destruction"
and the anguish of travail speaks of the Revelation, the
"Day of the Lord" when He comes in judgment.

The Rapture will *definitely* come as a thief in the
night, for Jesus will come when the world is least expecting Him. Only a handful of faithful people were
aware of His *first* coming. The rulers and religious
leaders in Israel (as well as in the Gentile world) knew
nothing of the birth of the Babe who was born King
of the Jews. Likewise, when He comes in the Rapture, the mass of humanity will not be expecting Him.
Only a very small percentage of mankind truly expects
Jesus to return to this earth at any moment, but His
coming is imminent.

A thief comes when least expected, and he does not
announce his coming. He does not come to stay, but
takes what he came for and immediately departs. But
he does not take everything in the house—in fact, he
leaves much more than he takes.

So will it be when Jesus comes in the Rapture. He
will not announce His coming to the world—He will
simply descend in the air and call believers up to meet
Him. He will come expressly for His jewels, the born
again ones; and He will take every born again believer
out of the world. All little babies, all innocent children, and all who have believed on Him unto salvation

will be caught up in the Rapture—but He will leave more than He takes because the masses of humanity today are lost! Hundreds of thousands of church members are lost. They are "religious," but they have never been born again, and only those who have been born of the Spirit and washed in the blood will go in the Rapture. As a thief takes what he came for and then leaves quickly, so Jesus in the Rapture will not come to stay. He will pay a short visit in the air and then immediately return to the heavens above us where the saints will be rewarded for stewardship, and where the marriage supper of the Lamb will take place.

The Rapture will be elective:—

"I tell you, in that night there shall be two men in one bed; the one shall be taken, and the other shall be left. Two women shall be grinding together; the one shall be taken, and the other left. Two men shall be in the field; the one shall be taken, and the other left" (Luke 17:34-36).

"Then shall two be in the field; the one shall be taken, and the other left. Two women shall be grinding at the mill; the one shall be taken, and the other left. Watch therefore: for ye know not what hour your Lord doth come" (Matt. 24:40-42).

When the Rapture occurs, not only will saints be separated from sinners—children of God from children of the devil—but husbands will be separated from wives, children will be separated from parents, brothers will be separated from sisters, and friends will be separated from friends. Two will be sleeping in one bed— one will be taken, the other will be left. Two will be working in the field—one will be taken, the other will be left. Two will be grinding at the mill—one will be taken, the other will be left.

These passages from Luke and Matthew reveal that when the Rapture takes place it will be world-wide. For example, we know that when it is nighttime in America it is daytime in other parts of the world. Therefore while some people are *sleeping,* others are *working.* In the days of Jesus the grinding of the grain was done by women, usually in early morning. Field work, of course, was done during the daylight hours, and at night the people slept. So the Rapture will be instantaneous and world-wide. In some parts of the world it will be early morning. Elsewhere it will be high noon, or evening, or night.

The truth conveyed by our Scripture is that whenever the Rapture occurs and wherever a believer and an unbeliever are together, the believer will be taken, the unbeliever will be left. This will happen so suddenly and silently that those who are sleeping will not miss their companions until they awake in the morning and discover that they are alone in the bed. God's grace takes care of the innocent, therefore innocent little babies will be taken from their cribs and little children will be taken from their beds. The Christian wife will be taken, the unsaved husband will be left— or the Christian husband will be taken and the unbelieving wife will be left.

There will be untold thousands of instances around the world where people are on the job—working in great factories, department stores, hospitals—believer and unbeliever working side by side. The believer will be snatched away, the unbeliever will be left. Perhaps a believer and an unbeliever will be in conversation, discussing salvation. Suddenly the garments of the Christian will fold up on the ground and the unbeliever will be aware that the believer is gone.

Can you imagine what will happen when all born again pilots are removed from the giant passenger liners that are in flight? Think of the bloodshed when all born again drivers are snatched from behind the steeringwheels of automobiles on crowded highways! Imagine the wreckage and unspeakable horror when all born again engineers are taken from trains, when all Christian bus drivers are caught away from their place at the wheel of a loaded bus in transit. I think the human imagination cannot touch the hem of the garment when it comes to picturing the turmoil, chaos, tragedy, and bloodshed that will engulf the world at the time the Rapture occurs!

In Matthew 24:27 Jesus said, "As the *lightning* cometh out of the east, and shineth even unto the west, *so shall also the coming of the Son of man be."* In a moment, in the twinkling of an eye, in the span of a flash of lightning, the Rapture of the Church will take place—and it will be the most startling, world-shaking event of this dispensation! Since believers will be caught up from all over the world at the same time, that part of the world that is not asleep will see the terrible chaos and tragedy which will immediately take place. They will not see the believers depart because their going will be so sudden, but they *will be* aware that loved ones are missing, friends have suddenly been taken away, perhaps even conversations cut short by the instant disappearance of a believer to whom a sinner was talking.

Someone will probably ask, "Will *unbelievers* hear the trumpet of God and the shout of the Lord when the Rapture occurs?" I do not know whether or not the trump of God will be heard by living unbelievers. The dead in Christ will hear the shout, as will the living saints, but we are not told whether or not the unsaved will hear.

In John 12:28, 29 Jesus said, "Father, glorify thy name." Then a voice came from heaven as God said, "I have both glorified it, and will glorify it again." The people who were standing by heard the voice— that is, they heard the sound—but they did not distinguish it as the voice of God. Some said that it thundered, and others said, "An angel spake to Him."

We find another such instance recorded in Acts 9:4-7 when Saul of Tarsus was converted. Jesus spoke to him from heaven and conversed with him, but "the men which journeyed with him stood speechless, *hearing a voice, but seeing no man.*" The Lord's message that day was for Paul alone, and although the men who traveled with him saw the light and heard the voice they did not distinguish the words.

On that glorious resurrection morning the heavens above us will be filled with the spirits of the righteous —the dead in Christ—as they return with Christ in the air to get their glorified bodies. Whether the cemeteries will look like plowed fields or not, I do not know. Whether monuments will be turned over in the church yards, slabs overturned and vaults burst asunder I do not know. The only thing we can know for sure is that the bodies of the saints will be raised literally and literally transformed. Perhaps they will come forth from the sepulchres without disturbing the graves. Christ arose from the dead and His tomb was not disturbed. He left the grave clothes and the napkin from around His face lying in perfect order in the grave. It is true that the angel rolled the stone away, but this was only to show that the tomb was empty. It was for the sake of the disciples and others who visited the tomb that the stone was rolled away, that they might see that the body of Jesus was not there.

Yes, the Rapture will be a startling event and when the people on earth recover from shock and fear they will discover that many of their friends and loved ones are missing. Department stores, banks, manufacturing plants and other professions will be crippled because some of their directors and key personnel will be caught away to meet Jesus in the clouds. People who have heard sermons on the second coming of Jesus will realize what has taken place, but others who know nothing of prophecy and the second coming will be in utter ignorance of what has happened and to them it will be a great mystery.

For a few days after the Rapture, newspapers and radio will be filled with news and pictures relative to the great event which has so suddenly thrown the world into panic and confusion. Television stations will give over their time and efforts to news and discussions about it. But when the excitement dies down and people begin to adjust to a routine, they will settle down and continue in their wickedness. Many will enjoy the money and the profits left by relatives or business associations when the Rapture took place.

The Holy Spirit is the restraining force in the world today, but He will go out of the world with the Church in the Rapture and there will be nothing left on earth to prevent complete degeneration and moral putrification. Sin will run wild, and this earth will become more corrupt than ever before. All manner of crime and iniquity will increase—and this will pave the way for the reign of Antichrist, the devil in flesh. He will come on the scene just after the Rapture. When the Holy Spirit is "taken out of the way . . . then shall *that Wicked* be revealed . . . even him, whose coming is after the working of Satan with all power and signs and lying wonders" (II Thess. 2:7-9); and millions will receive him as messiah.

Although we will discuss this at a later time in our study, I would here sound a solemn warning to any and all who say, "I will get saved immediately after the Rapture, in time to escape hell." If you are one of those dear souls who consistently put off salvation, thinking you will be saved when you are *ready* to be saved or when the Rapture tells you that the end is near, you are indeed treading on dangerous ground! For if you have ever heard the Gospel—even the Gospel given in this message—and you have rejected the grace of God, *you will NOT be saved after the Rapture!* There will be people saved after the Rapture, but they will not be those who have heard the Gospel of the grace of God. There will be millions of heathen —and even some people in "enlightened" America— who have never heard a message on God's saving grace and the simple plan of salvation, and many of these people will be saved after the Rapture when the Gospel of the kingdom is preached. But the Bible is very clear concerning those who have heard *and rejected* the truth. Paul tells us that "because they *received not* the love of the truth, that they might be saved . . . *God shall send them strong delusion, that they should believe a lie:* that they all might be damned who believed not the truth, but had pleasure in unrighteousness" (II Thess. 2:10-12).

Jesus is the *Truth* (John 14:6). Antichrist—the exact opposite of Christ—is *THE Lie.* When Antichrist appears he will perform great miracles and the masses of mankind will follow him. Through his miracles and deception, people will believe and come to trust him, and will follow him as messiah. God will send them strong delusions and they will be eternally damned because they "believed not the Truth, but had pleasure in unrighteousness." This could speak only of those who have heard the Gospel of the grace of God—the truth that sets men free—and rejected that truth!

Who will be taken in the Rapture?

"As the body is one, and hath many members, and all the members of that one body, being many, are one body: *so also is Christ.* For by one Spirit are we all baptized into *one body,* whether we be Jews or Gentiles, whether we be bond or free; and have been all made to drink into one Spirit. *For the body is not one member, but many*" (I Cor. 12:12-14).

Here is Bible proof that the Rapture will not be partial. All born again believers will be caught out when Jesus comes for His Church. The New Testament

Church is the body of Christ. Believers are "members of His body, of His flesh, and of His bones" (Eph. 5:30), and it is inconceivable that the body of Christ should be divided! The split second a person is born of the Spirit he becomes a member of the body of Christ through the miracle of the new birth and the operation of the Holy Spirit. Since all believers are baptized into one body through the baptism of the Spirit, certainly part of that body would not remain asleep in the grave and part be raised in glory and caught up to meet Jesus in the air; nor would some of the living believers be caught up and others left to go through the Great Tribulation. Such doctrine is entirely without scriptural grounds. When Jesus comes in the Rapture, all born again, blood-washed believers will be caught up in the clouds to meet Him in the air. Not one will be left behind.

I realize that there are various and conflicting doctrines being taught on this subject. Some Bible teachers claim that the entire Church will pass through the tribulation period. Others teach that the Church will pass through the first half of the tribulation period, while still other pre-millennialists believe that the Church will be taken out of the world *before* the Great Tribulation. (I personally believe the Scripture teaches this latter interpretation.)

There are some ministers and teachers who use Hebrews 9:28 as a basis for teaching that only those who are really looking for and anxiously expecting the Lord's return will be taken in the Rapture. True, that verse declares that "unto them that *look for Him* shall He appear the second time without sin unto salvation," but this applies to believers who are living when Jesus comes. It certainly does not mean that those who died in the Lord (yet were never taught the blessed hope of the pre-millennial coming of Jesus) will not be raised. The Bible says "the dead in Christ shall rise." It does not say "the dead who were looking for the second coming of Christ." All spiritually minded believers are looking for and expecting the second coming of the Lord Jesus Christ, but when He comes the dead in Christ will be raised, and the living saints will be caught up with them to meet the Lord in the air. Not one believer will be left behind!

On the other hand, not one person will be taken who has not been born of the Spirit and washed in the blood. Regardless of how many churches a person joins or how moral and upright his life may be, God's infallible Word declares, "Except a man be *born again* he cannot see the kingdom of God. . . . Except a man be born of water and of the Spirit, he cannot enter into the kingdom of God" (John 3:3, 5).

Will the Church go through the tribulation?

"God hath not appointed us to wrath, but to obtain salvation by our Lord Jesus Christ, who died for us, that, whether we wake or sleep, we should live together with Him" (I Thess. 5:9, 10).

This passage makes it clear that the Church will not enter or go through any part of the tribulation period. The Great Tribulation is not for the perfecting of the saints and it has nothing to do with the Church. It is "the time of Jacob's trouble" (Jer. 30:7) and will have to do primarily with Israel and God's judgment of that nation. As shown in the verses just given from I Thessalonians, it is God's purpose to keep His Church out of the horrible suffering and woe of the Great Tribulation, for He has not appointed His children to wrath!

In the book of Revelation, John the Beloved was instructed, "Write the things which thou hast seen, and the things which are, and the things which shall be hereafter" (Rev. 1:19). He was then given the messages to the seven churches. (Please read Revelation chapters 2 and 3.)

Then in Revelation 4:1-3 John experienced *in the spirit* what the Church will experience *literally* at the Rapture: "After this I looked, and, behold, a door was opened in heaven: and the first voice which I heard was as it were of a trumpet talking with me; which said, Come up hither, and I will shew thee things which must be hereafter. *And immediately I was in the Spirit:* and, behold, a throne was set in heaven, and one sat on the throne. And He that sat was to look upon like a jasper and a sardine stone: and there was a rainbow round about the throne, in sight like unto an emerald."

These verses portray the catching away of the bride of Christ before the beginning of the tribulation period (which is described in the next several chapters of Revelation). We are now living in the last part of Revelation chapter 3 (verses 7 through 22).

To the church in Philadelphia (the true Church) John was instructed to write: "Because thou hast kept the word of my patience, *I also will keep thee from the hour of temptation, which shall come upon*

all the world, to try them that dwell upon the earth"
(Rev. 3:10).

To the church in Laodicea (the liberals and modernists) John was instructed to write: "I know thy
works, that thou art neither cold nor hot: I would
thou wert cold or hot. So then *because thou art luke-
warm, and neither cold nor hot, I will spue thee out
of my mouth"* (Rev. 3:15, 16).

Thus we see that *the true Church* will be *caught*
out and all others will be *spewed* out. It is absurd
for anyone to teach that the Church will go through
or enter any part of the Great Tribulation.

The confusion concerning who will be taken in
the Rapture—and *when* they will be taken—is largely
due to the fact that prophetic students fail to distinguish between the Rapture (the time when Jesus
comes *for* His saints) and the Revelation (when He
will come *with* His saints). The clear teaching of the
Word of God *demands* the Rapture before the tribulation, because there are many passages of Scripture
which speak of Christ's coming with His saints, and
He cannot come *with* His saints until He first comes
for His saints! Therefore the Rapture must precede
the Revelation—and the Revelation will not be until
the end of the Great Tribulation.

I would now point out seven things which will take
place when the Rapture occurs:

1. *The Lord Jesus will descend from heaven* (I Thess.
4:16). The Word of God clearly declares that Christ
is now in heaven seated at the right hand of God—
"when He had by Himself purged our sins," He "sat
down on the right hand of the Majesty on high" (Heb.

1:3b).   He is seated there because He accomplished
what He came into the world to do.   He endured the
cross, despising its shame but seeing the joy and glory
on the other side (Heb. 12:2).   Mark 16:19 tells us in
very plain language, "So then after the Lord had
spoken unto them, *He was received up into heaven,*
and sat on the right hand of God."   The fact that
He has been received up into heaven shows that He
has thus been acknowledged as the One who has
been accepted by God the Father on our behalf, and
He now sits at the right hand of God to make intercession for us.

Hebrews 4:14 tells us that "we have a great High
Priest that is passed into the heavens, Jesus the Son
of God . . . ."   Since Jesus is passed *into* the heavens,
then He passed *through* the heavens, thus proving
beyond any shadow of doubt that He conquered all
the forces of evil spirits, even the "prince of the power
of the air."   The Prince of Persia hindered God's messenger and kept him from reaching *Daniel* (Dan. 10:13),
but all hell could not stop Jesus.   Therefore He has
been made "*higher* than the heavens" (Heb. 7:26). This
indicates Christ's superiority over all things.   He is
the Exalted One.   God has "highly exalted Him, and
given Him a name which is above every name: that
at the name of Jesus every knee should bow, of things
in heaven, and things in earth, and things under the
earth; and that every tongue should confess that Jesus
Christ is Lord, to the glory of God the Father" (Phil.
2:9-11).

2. The Lord Jesus will descend from heaven "*with
a SHOUT.*"   This will be a *commanding* shout.   It

is used here in the sense that a general would command his armies, as the captain of a galley ship in that day would command his oarsmen, or as a charioteer would command the horses that pulled his chariot. No power on earth or in hell can stay Christ's divine command when with a mighty shout He calls His bride to meet Him in the air. When He stood by the tomb of Lazarus and commanded him to come forth, death and the grave could not hold him: Jesus "cried with a loud voice, *Lazarus, come forth!* And he that was dead came forth, bound hand and foot with graveclothes: and his face was bound about with a napkin. Jesus saith unto them, Loose him, and let him go" (John 11:43, 44). In like manner Christ's command at the Rapture will call the sleeping saints from their graves and living saints will be loosed from mortal bodies that are weakened, diseased, and crippled by sin.

3. Jesus will descend from heaven with a shout and *"with the voice of the archangel."* Rabbinical and Apocryphal writings speak of archangels, and in the Word of God we read of *Michael* the archangel. In Daniel 10:13 he is spoken of as "one of the chief princes," in Daniel 12:1 he is called "the great prince which standeth for the children of thy people (Israel)," and in Revelation 12:7-9 we read, "There was war in heaven: Michael and his angels fought against the dragon; and the dragon fought and his angels, and prevailed not; neither was their place found any more in heaven. And the great dragon was cast out, that old serpent, called the Devil, and Satan, which deceiveth the whole world: he was cast out into the

earth, and his angels were cast out with him."

Michael's position is said to be "one of the chief princes . . . the great prince." His work is to protect God's elect nation Israel, and also to protect the bodies of the saints (Jude 9). This mighty angel also has power to control the forces of evil as they resist the will, the pleasure, and the eternal purpose of Almighty God, as declared in Revelation 12:7, just quoted.

As Jesus hung on the cross He cried with a loud voice, "My God! My God! Why hast thou forsaken me?" (Matt. 27:46). Again from the cross He cried with a loud voice and "yielded up the ghost" (Matt. 27:50). The next time He cries out with a loud voice will be when He calls His saints to meet Him in the clouds in the air.

4. Jesus will descend from heaven *with "the trump of God."* To fully appreciate this, we must go to the Old Testament where we find a most interesting record concerning the trumpet. In Numbers 10:1-10 we read:

"And the Lord spake unto Moses, saying, Make thee two trumpets of silver; of a whole piece shalt thou make them: that thou mayest use them for the calling of the assembly, and for the journeying of the camps. And when they shall blow with them, all the assembly shall assemble themselves to thee at the door of the tabernacle of the congregation. And if they blow but with one trumpet, then the princes, which are heads of the thousands of Israel, shall gather themselves unto thee.

"When ye blow an alarm, then the camps that lie on the east parts shall go forward. When ye blow an alarm the second time, then the camps that lie on the south side shall take their journey: they shall blow an alarm for their journeys. But when the congregation is to be gathered together, ye shall blow, but ye shall not sound an alarm.

"And the sons of Aaron, the priests, shall blow with the trumpets; and they shall be to you for an ordinance for ever throughout your generations. And if ye go to war in your land against the enemy that oppresseth you, then ye shall blow an alarm with the trumpets; and ye shall be remembered before the Lord your God, and ye shall be saved from your enemies.

"Also in the day of your gladness, and in your solemn days, and in the beginnings of your months, ye shall blow with the trumpets over your burnt-offerings, and over the sacrifices of your peace-offerings; that they may be to you for a memorial before your God: I am the Lord your God."

This interesting passage explains the use of two silver trumpets in relation to Israel. The trumpets were to be used for calling the assembly, for the journeyings of the camp, and when the Israelites were confronted by an army of the enemy. When the enemy was approaching the priests were to blow an alarm. Thus the trumpets were blown to gather God's people for worship and also when they were called together for war.

As two trumpets were used in the passage just quoted, so two trumpets are mentioned in connection with the coming of Christ—"the last trump" (at the Rapture) (I Cor. 15:52) and the *seventh* trumpet sounding in judgment (in the Revelation) (Rev. 11:15-19).

As the silver trumpets in the Old Testament era called the people of Israel together to worship, so the trumpet of God will be used to call the saints of God to meet Jesus in the air—our gathering together unto Him. And as the trumpets in the Old Testament were sounded in alarm to gather the Israelites together for war, so the seventh trumpet will be identified with Christ's coming with His saints at the end of the Tribulation period, to judge and make war.

We might also note that when the congregation of God's chosen people were called together for worship there was to be no sound of alarm. So when the Lord Jesus Christ descends in the air for His saints, the sound will not be one of alarm, nor of warfare and judgment. Quietly, secretly, and swiftly, the saints will be gathered together to meet the Lord in the air.

Also, when the trumpet sounded for calling the assembly together (Num. 10:3), the *entire assembly* gathered—not just part of them. Not one was omitted, but all responded to the call. So will it be when the trumpet sounds to call the saints to be with Jesus. His Church will be called in its entirety, not one member will be left behind!

5. *Christ's act:* When the Lord Jesus descends from heaven with a shout, with the voice of the archangel, and with the trumpet of God, the dead in Christ will be raised and the living saints will be transformed. Then together we will all be *caught up* to meet Jesus. So Christ's act is *the catching away of believers.*

The Greek here translated "caught up" indicates a decisive and definite act of divine power which none

can stay, stop, or hinder. In Matthew 11:12 the same
word is rendered *"take it by force."* The same is
true in Acts 23:10 when the chief captain took Paul
"by force" from those who would have destroyed
him. In the Rapture, the truth set forth is as one
being carried away by an irresistible force, as if he
were standing in a field when a tornado struck and
carried him away by the irresistible force of the mighty
wind. The same Greek word is used in Acts 8:39 when
Philip was "caught away" after he had witnessed to
the Ethiopian eunuch, and also in II Corinthians 12:2
and 4 where Paul speaks of being caught up into the
third heaven. No might or power can prevent the
"catching away" of the saints when Jesus calls from
the sky in the Rapture.

6. When Jesus comes in the Rapture the saints will
be caught up into His presence, caught up *in the
clouds to meet Him in the air.* There are two words
here that are especially significant—*"clouds"* and
"meet." When we think of *clouds* we think of the
rain clouds in the heavens just above us—and naturally
so; but in the original Greek text there is no article
("the") and therefore the quotation from I Thessalonians 4:17 reads simply, "We . . . shall be caught up
together with them *in clouds."* I believe the Scripture
teaches that Jesus will descend into the atmospheric
heavens just above us where the clouds are, and that
we will be caught up *into* the clouds; but I believe
our text here also means that *clouds of believers—*
believers in great numbers—will be caught up from
the earth to meet Jesus in the air. Hebrews 12:1 speaks
of "so great *a cloud of witnesses,"* and I believe the

meaning here is the same.

"Meet" is a very precious word in its usage here. It means to go out to meet someone longed for and expected. We go out to meet them and return with them. The same Greek word is used in only two other places in the New Testament. In Matthew 25:1-13 the virgins went forth to meet the Bridegroom and returned with Him to the marriage. In Acts 28:15 the saints from Rome went out to meet Paul at Appii Forum and returned to Rome with him. When we are caught up to meet Jesus in the air we will be rewarded for our stewardship, we will attend the marriage supper of the Lamb, and then we will return with Him to this earth to reign with Him for one thousand glorious years!

7. *We will be satisfied*—and Christ will be satisfied, because *"so shall we ever be with the Lord."* We shall be satisfied when we see Him, never to be separated from Him again. We will be *like* Him, therefore He will be satisfied with us. We will meet Him as a glorious Church, not having spot or wrinkle or any such thing (Eph. 5:27).

"Wherefore COMFORT one another with these words." So closes this marvelous passage from I Thessalonians chapter 4. The Greek word here translated "comfort" can also be rendered *"exhort,"* and it is so translated in Acts 2:40; 11:23; 14:22; 15:32; and 20:2.

The marvelous message of the return of the Lord is given to us to comfort us, to spur us on, to urge us to holy living, to encourage us to present our bodies a living sacrifice and our members as instruments of righteousness to God that He may mold us, draw us nearer to Himself, and rekindle the fires of His love in our hearts. We must occupy and be about the Father's business until Jesus comes again.

"And every man that hath this HOPE in him purifieth himself, even as He is pure" (I John 3:3). This speaks of "that blessed hope, and the glorious appearing of the great God and our Saviour Jesus Christ" (Tit. 2:13). Are YOU prepared to meet Him if He should come today? Are you born again, washed in the blood? If you are not, God grant that you lay this book aside, take your Bible, and read the following Scriptures: John 3:16, 18, 36; 5:24; 6:37; Ephesians 2:8, 9; and Romans 10:9, 10.

Believe what these Scriptures clearly tell you. Then bow upon your knees and surrender your heart and life to Jesus—because in such an hour as ye think not, the Son of man cometh. If you are not prepared for His coming you will be like the five foolish virgins in Matthew chapter 25—you will be left outside, and when you cry out to the Lord to let you enter you will find the door shut. I urge you to be saved and be ready for Jesus, whether He comes today, tomorrow, or years from now. We know He is coming back to earth, and since we cannot know the day or the hour, the only safe way to live is to live each day the way you will *wish you had lived* when Jesus comes again!

Chapter IV

The Judgment Seat of Christ;
The Marriage of the Lamb

The Word of God clearly portrays two events of special significance: (1) the judgment seat of Christ, (2) the marriage of the Lamb.

The Judgment Seat of Christ

Writing to the believers in Corinth Paul speaks of the judgment for believers. In II Corinthians 5:10 he wrote, "We must all appear before the judgment seat of Christ; that every one may receive the things done in his body, according to that he hath done, whether it be good or bad."

To the believers in Rome he wrote, "Why dost thou judge thy brother? or why dost thou set at nought thy brother? for we shall all stand before the judgment seat of Christ" (Rom. 14:10).

The judgment seat of Christ is a serious matter and we need to study it carefully. It is explained in detail in I Corinthians 3:9-15:

"We are labourers together with God: ye are God's husbandry, ye are God's building. According to the grace of God which is given unto me, as a wise masterbuilder, I have laid the foundation, and another buildeth thereon. But let every man take heed how he buildeth thereupon. For other foundation can no man lay than that is laid, which is Jesus Christ.

"Now if any man build upon this foundation gold, silver, precious stones, wood, hay, stubble; every man's work shall be made manifest: for the day shall declare it, because it shall be revealed by fire; and the fire shall try every man's work of what sort it is. *If any man's work abide which he hath built thereupon, he shall receive a reward.   If any man's work shall be burned, he shall suffer loss: but he himself shall be saved; yet so as by fire.*"

Paul uses two Greek words in referring to judgment. In I Corinthians 6:4 he says, "If ye then have judgments of things pertaining to this life . . . ," using the Greek word *kriterion* which means a judgment associated with condemnation.   However in II Corinthians 5:10 and Romans 14:10, speaking of the judgment seat of Christ, he uses the Greek word *bema,* which denotes a raised platform or "reward seat."

Historians tell us that there was a raised platform in the arena where the Grecian athletic games were held in Athens.   The umpire of the arena occupied the platform, and from this place of honor he rewarded the winning contestants.   This is Paul's meaning when he speaks of "the judgment seat of Christ." His use of *bema* suggests dignity, honor, authority, and reward instead of condemnation. Believers will never be condemned—"there is therefore now *no condemnation* to them which are in Christ Jesus" (Rom. 8:1).   Only Christians will appear at the judgment seat of Christ, and the judgment will be of stewardship (of works)—not of the eternal state of the soul. That is decided in this life.

The TIME of the judgment seat of Christ:—

The events described in the passage just quoted from I Corinthians chapter 3 will take place immediately following the Rapture of the Church. This fact is clearly set forth in several Scriptures:

Luke 14:14: "Thou shalt be blessed; for they cannot recompense thee: for *thou shalt be recompensed at the resurrection of the just."* Since the resurrection of believers takes place at the Rapture, it must follow that reward is part of the program and is definitely associated with the resurrection.

I Corinthians 4:5: "Therefore judge nothing before the time, until the Lord come, who both will bring to light the hidden things of darkness, and will make manifest the counsels of the hearts: and then shall every man have praise of God."

II Timothy 4:8: "Henceforth there is laid up for me a crown of righteousness, which the Lord, *the righteous Judge,* shall give me at that day: and not to me only, but unto all them also that love His appearing."

Revelation 22:12: "Behold, I come quickly; and *my reward is with me, to give every man according as his work shall be."*

Thus we see that the rewarding of the saints must take place between the Rapture and the Revelation. Christ will first come *for* His saints, and the Church will be caught out before the Great Tribulation begins. Then at the *end* of the tribulation period when the reign of Antichrist has run its course, He will come *with* His saints; but between the two phases of His second coming the saints will appear before Him to receive their reward for faithful stewardship.

The PLACE of the judgment seat of Christ:—

"The Lord Himself shall descend from heaven with a shout, with the voice of the archangel, and with the trump of God: and the dead in Christ shall rise first: then we which are alive and remain shall be caught up together with them *in the clouds, to meet the Lord IN THE AIR:* and so shall we ever be with the Lord" (I Thess. 4:16, 17).

The judgment of believers will follow the resurrection of the righteous dead and the translation of living saints, and since we will be caught up to meet the Lord in the air, then *in the air* must be the place of the judgment seat of Christ. This is supported by Paul's declaration in II Corinthians 5:1-8:

"For we know that if our earthly house of this tabernacle were dissolved, we have a building of God, an house not made with hands, eternal in the heavens. For in this we groan, earnestly desiring to be clothed upon with our house which is from heaven: if so be that being clothed we shall not be found naked. For we that are in this tabernacle do groan, being burdened: not for that we would be unclothed, but clothed upon, that mortality might be swallowed up of life.

"Now He that hath wrought us for the selfsame thing is God, who also hath given unto us the earnest of the Spirit. Therefore we are always confident, knowing that, *whilst we are at home in the body, we are absent from the Lord:* (for we walk by faith, not by sight:) we are confident, I say, *and willing rather to be absent from the body, and to be present with the Lord."*

Since the event described here will take place in the presence of the Lord and in the sphere of the heavenlies, then it is *in the heavenlies* that we will be judged and rewarded for our labors and faithful stewardship.

As pointed out in II Corinthians 5:10, the Judge who will preside on this occasion will be none other than the Lord Jesus Christ, the Son of God. This is substantiated by the words of Jesus in John 5:22: *"The Father judgeth no man, but hath committed all judgment unto the Son."* Part of the glory and exaltation of Christ is that He has been given the right to manifest divine authority in judgment, and *all judgment* has been committed unto Him.

I previously stated that only born again believers will be present at the judgment seat of Christ. (The wicked will be judged at the Great White Throne judgment described in Revelation 20:11-15.) Only the born again ones could meet the qualifications Paul set forth in the passage just given from II Corinthians 5:1-8 —that is, only believers could have *"an house not made with hands, eternal in the heavens"* (v. 1). Only believers could experience *"mortality . . . swallowed up of life"* (v. 4). Only believers could experience the working of Almighty God *"who hath given unto us the earnest of the Spirit"* (v. 5). Only believers could *"walk by faith, not by sight"* (v. 7), and certainly only believers could be confident that *"to be absent from the body"* is to be *"present with the LORD"!* (v. 8).

The BASIS for the judgment seat of Christ: —

The issue here is not to determine whether those present will be judged saved or lost. The question of salvation will not be considered at that time. Salvation by faith in the finished work of Christ has perfectly and entirely delivered the believer from all judgment insofar as condemnation is concerned. To bring a believer into judgment concerning the sin question (whether for sins committed before or after the new birth, or even for *unconfessed* sin in the life of a believer) would be to deny the words of Jesus when He declared, "It is finished!" Such judgment would deny the efficacy of the death of Christ and nullify the promise of Almighty God when He said, *"Their sins and iniquities will I remember no more"* (Heb. 10:17).

The judgment of sin (as having to do with the believer) was taken care of at Calvary. This is made perfectly clear in I Peter 2:24: "Who *His own self bare our sins* in His own body *on the tree,* that we, being dead to sins, should *live unto righteousness:* by whose stripes ye were healed."

I John 4:17 declares, "Herein is our love made perfect, that we may have boldness in the day of judgment: because as He is, so are we in this world."

When we receive the Lord Jesus Christ by faith, He redeems us — and we are as completely and perfectly redeemed as we will ever be, whether we live for Him ten years, fifty years, or seventy-five years. I am not a hyper-Calvinist, but I declare on the basis of God's Word that the person who is redeemed by the blood of Jesus will never again come into judgment on account of his original sin—his natural or inherited iniquity. *Judicially* the true believer is dead with Christ (Gal. 2:20); therefore he is no longer known or dealt with on the grounds of his natural responsibility as a man.

The natural man has been weighed in the balance and found wanting. There is nothing good in him. He is under condemnation, born in sin and shapen in iniquity—born to a natural heritage of wrath. But when that man becomes a believer his guilt and sin are obliterated by the finished work of the shed blood of the Lord Jesus Christ, Redeemer of our souls. The true believer is justly and completely pardoned for Jesus' sake (Eph. 4:32; I John 2:12).

"Therefore being justified by faith, we have peace with God through our Lord Jesus Christ" (Rom. 5:1). The believer stands justified before God—not because of his own merits, but because of the merits of Jesus. We have His promise, "Whosoever therefore shall confess me before men, him will I confess also before my Father which is in heaven" (Matt. 10:32).

The PURPOSE of the judgment seat of Christ:—

Believers "must all appear before the judgment seat of Christ." Greek authorities tell us that the word here translated *"appear"* should read "be made manifest." Thus the text would read, "We must all *be made manifest."* This points out clearly the purpose of the judgment seat of Christ. It is to make a public manifestation (or revelation) of the essential character of the individual believer as he lives in this life. We will not be judged as a group, nor in classes, but *one by one* and according to individual merit! Each believer will stand to be rewarded for his stewardship and faithful labors.   His *works* ("the things done in his body") will be brought into judgment in order to determine "whether it be *good* or *bad.*" The meaning here is not so much whether the deeds of the believer are ethically or morally *evil,* but rather to determine whether the things done in the body are valuable and worthwhile, or worthless and good for nothing.   James 4:17 declares, "To him that knoweth to do good, *and doeth it not,* to him it is sin."

We notice the believer's works are referred to as *"gold, silver, precious stones"* (valuable things) and *"wood, hay, stubble"* (things which are worthless and unenduring) (I Cor. 3:12). The judgment seat of Christ is not for the purpose of chastening the child of God for his sins, but to reward him for those things done in the name of the Lord, deeds which brought glory to the name of Jesus.   That is the reason Paul said to the Corinthian believers, *"Whether therefore ye eat, or drink, or whatsoever ye do, DO ALL TO THE GLORY OF GOD"* (I Cor. 10:31).

The RESULTS of the judgment seat of Christ: —

According to I Corinthians 3:14, 15 there will be a twofold result of this judgment: (1) "If any man's work *abide* . . . he shall receive a *reward.*   (2) If any man's work shall be *burned,* he shall suffer *loss.*" (This refers to loss of reward, not loss of the soul.) That which determines whether the believer *receives* a reward or *suffers loss* of reward is the trial by fire— "the fire shall try every man's work of what sort it is."

"Is not MY WORD like as a fire? saith the Lord; and like a hammer that breaketh the rock in pieces?" (Jer. 23:29). Jesus said, "He that rejecteth me, and receiveth not my words, hath one that judgeth him: *THE WORD that I have spoken, the same shall judge him* in the last day" (John 12:48).

Thus we see that the judgment of Christians at the judgment seat of Christ will not be an external examination with results based on outward observation. Rather, it will test the inner character and motivation of the believer—a judgment by fire to determine that which can be destroyed and that which is indestructible.

"We are labourers together with God," and we have a choice of building materials at our disposal. *Gold, silver, and precious stones* represent indestructible materials which man appropriates and uses to God's glory. *Wood, hay, and stubble* represent works accomplished by man's efforts and abilities, therefore to the glory of self rather than to the glory of God. That which is wrought by God through the individual (and which is done for God's glory) will stand the fire; but that which the individual accomplishes through his own wisdom and strength (and to the glory of the flesh) will be destroyed. The category into which a believer's work falls cannot be determined by outward observation. It must be put into the crucible of judgment fire in order to prove its true character. We may labor diligently—but if our work is not to the glory of God it will be consumed in the fire of judgment. On the other hand, even a cup of cold water given in the name of Jesus will bring reward. This is the determining factor as to whether or not we receive a reward at the judgment seat of Christ—not *how much* we have accomplished in this life, but *"of what SORT it is."*

All things done in the strength of the flesh and to the glory of self will be disapproved, rejected, and consumed in the fire. The Apostle Paul expressed his own fear of dependence on the flesh when he said, "I keep under my body, and bring it into subjection: lest that by any means, when I have preached to others, *I myself should be a castaway"* (I Cor. 9:27). Paul did not mean that he feared loss of his salvation, but that he would lose his reward because that which he had done might be found unacceptable, good for nothing, and destructible. The Greek word here translated *"castaway"* is *adokimos* and means *disapproved* or *rejected*. It has nothing to do with the redemption of the Spirit, but applies only to works and rewards. Paul declares, under inspiration, that those whose works would be burned *would themselves be saved—* *"yet so as BY FIRE."* In other words, he will be saved as "a brand plucked out of the fire" (Zech. 3:2).

While works of wood, hay, and stubble will be consumed and the believer will suffer loss, there will be a reward for those whose works stand the test of fire. The New Testament names five areas in which specific mention is made concerning the rewards of born again believers whose stewardship is of the right sort. These rewards are listed as *five crowns* which can be earned for faithful stewardship:

1. The *incorruptible* crown: "Know ye not that they which run in a race run all, but one receiveth

the prize? So run, that ye may obtain. And every man that striveth for the mastery is temperate in all things. Now they do it to obtain a corruptible crown; but we an incorruptible" (I Cor. 9:24, 25). This is the crown to be given to believers who faithfully run the race, who crucify every selfish desire in order to win souls and point men to Jesus.

2. The crown of *rejoicing:* "For what is our hope, or joy, or crown of rejoicing? Are not even ye in the presence of our Lord Jesus Christ at His coming? For ye are our glory and joy" (I Thess. 2:19, 20). This is the soul-winner's crown, and it may be earned by every born again believer who faithfully witnesses to the saving grace of God and leads souls to Jesus.

3. The crown of *life:* "Blessed is the man that endureth temptation: for when he is tried, he shall receive the crown of life, which the Lord hath promised to them that love Him" (James 1:12). This crown is for those believers who endure trials, tribulations, and severe suffering—yes, even unto death (Rev. 2:8-11).

4. The crown of *righteousness:* "Henceforth there is laid up for me a crown of righteousness, which the Lord, the righteous Judge, shall give me at that day: and not to me only, but unto all them also that love His appearing" (II Tim. 4:8). This crown is for believers who love the appearing of Christ, who anxiously wait and look forward to the day when He will return for His saints.

5. The crown of *glory:* "When the Chief Shepherd shall appear, ye shall receive a crown of glory that fadeth not away" (I Pet. 5:4). This is the pastor's crown and will be given to the ministers who faithfully

feed the flock of God.

The victors' crowns are ours, crowns to lay at the feet of Jesus when we crown Him Lord of all; but the *kingly crown* belongs to Him alone. In Revelation 4:10, 11 the elders are seen casting their crowns before the throne in an act of worship, praise, and adoration.

The Scripture clearly teaches that the believer has been redeemed that he may bring glory and honor to God: "What? Know ye not that your body is the temple of the Holy Ghost which is in you, which ye have of God, and ye are not your own? For YE ARE BOUGHT WITH A PRICE: therefore glorify God in your body, and in your spirit, which are God's" (I Cor. 6:19, 20). This is the eternal destiny of the born again believer. We will crown Jesus Lord of all and we will lay our crowns at His feet, but this will not complete the act of glorification on the part of believers toward God. We will *continue* to glorify Him throughout eternity.

There will be *degrees* of reward received at the judgment seat of Christ. The greater our faithfulness to the Lord Jesus Christ while we live here on earth, the greater our reward when we stand before Him— and it seems that the greater the reward, the greater will be our capacity to glorify God in eternity. However, there will be no personal sense of lack in the believer in heaven. Each and every believer will enjoy heaven to the limit of his ability to do so.

In many passages in the Word of God the reward for faithful stewardship is associated with brightness and shining. For example, Daniel 12:3 tells us, "They that be wise shall shine as the brightness of the firmament; and they that turn many to righteousness as the stars for ever and ever." In Matthew 13:43 Jesus said, "Then shall the righteous shine forth as the sun in the kingdom of their Father. Who hath ears to hear, let him hear."

Then in I Corinthians chapter 15, verses 40, 41, and 49, we read: "There are also celestial bodies, and bodies terrestrial: but the glory of the celestial is one, and the glory of the terrestrial is another. There is one glory of the sun, and another glory of the moon, and another glory of the stars: for one star differeth from another star in glory. . . . And as we have borne the image of the earthy, we shall also bear the image of the heavenly."

The return of Jesus in the Rapture is the blessed hope of the Church; but with its *heavenly privileges* the second coming also brings *holy responsibilities.* Even as thoughts of the Rapture cause us to rejoice, thoughts of the judgment seat of Christ should cause us to shudder because "the terror of the Lord" is connected with that event: *"Knowing therefore THE TERROR OF THE LORD, we persuade men . . ."* (II Cor. 5:11).

This judgment will be severe. "The Lord shall judge His people" (Heb. 10:30) and the works of all believers will be fully revealed by fire (I Cor. 3:13). Some will suffer loss, they will see their entire life's works burned although they themselves will be saved— "yet so as by fire" (I Cor. 3:15). John the Beloved warns, "Look to yourselves, that we lose not *those things which we have wrought,* but that we receive a full reward" (II John 8). John also exhorts us to abide in Christ, "that, when He shall appear, we may have confidence, and not be ashamed before Him at His coming" (I John 2:28).

In Colossians 3:23-25 Paul warns that believers who do wrong shall not escape from their wrongdoing: "Whatsoever ye do, do it heartily, as to the Lord, and not unto men; knowing that of the Lord ye shall receive the reward of the inheritance: for ye serve the Lord Christ. *But he that doeth wrong shall receive for the wrong which he hath done: AND THERE IS NO RESPECT OF PERSONS.*"

To speak of the judgment seat of Christ as gain or loss seems scarcely to do justice to such extremely serious statements as are contained in the various Scriptures we have just given. The Holy Spirit has inspired the serious words of warning to impress upon us the vital necessity of practical holiness and faithful living, the presenting of our bodies as living sacrifices to the glory of God.

FAITHFULNESS is the standard by which we will be judged when we stand before the judgment seat of Christ: "Let a man so account of us, as of the ministers of Christ, and stewards of the mysteries of God. Moreover it is required in stewards, that a man be found faithful. But with me it is a very small thing that I should be judged of you, or of man's judgment: yea, I judge not mine own self. For I know nothing by myself; yet am I not hereby justified: but He that judgeth me is the Lord. *Therefore judge nothing before the time, until the Lord come, who both will bring to light THE HIDDEN THINGS OF DARKNESS, and will make manifest THE COUNSELS*

OF THE HEARTS: and then shall every man have praise of God" (I Cor. 4:1-5).

We will be judged for the sum total of our life, the product of our development as a born again believer— not only for deeds done, but for deeds we should have done and failed to do, for *"to him that knoweth to do good, and doeth it not, to him it is SIN"* (James 4:17). The Righteous Judge will take note of the most inward elements—the impulses, motives, and counsels of the heart, the secrets of the soul—and will judge not so much according to what we actually attain, but according to what we *attempted to attain* to the glory of God. To the faithful He will say, "Well done, thou good and faithful servant: thou hast been faithful over a few things, I will make thee ruler over many things. Enter thou into the joy of thy Lord" (Matt. 25:21, 23).

In Hebrews 4:13 we read, "Neither is there *any creature* that is not manifest in His sight; but *all things are naked and opened unto the eyes of Him with whom we have to do!"* This is indeed a sobering statement. The Righteous Judge not only knows our deeds, He knows the thoughts and intents of our hearts. The hidden things will be brought to light at the judgment seat of Christ, and each individual will receive his due reward without respect to persons:

"For God is not unrighteous to forget your work and labour of love, which ye have shewed toward His name, in that ye have ministered to the saints, and do minister. And we desire that every one of you do shew the same diligence to the full assurance of hope unto the end: that ye be not slothful, but followers of them who through faith and patience inherit the promises" (Heb. 6:10-12).

"It is written, *BE YE HOLY; FOR I AM HOLY.* And if ye call on the Father, who *without respect of persons judgeth according to every man's work,* pass the time of your sojourning here in fear" (I Pet. 1:16, 17).

Redemption from sin depends on belief in the shed blood and finished work of Jesus, whereas rewards depend entirely on our faithfulness to God in all that we do. Exercising true faith in the Lamb of God, we become sons and receive the life of God. After we become born sons, as faithful servants we will receive rewards. He who is appointed Judge of all things declares, *"Behold, I come quickly; and MY REWARD IS WITH ME, to give every man according as his work shall be!"* (Rev. 22:12).

We must be careful to distinguish between the judgment seat of Christ, the judgment of the nations, and the Great White Throne judgment. As we have already discussed, *the judgment seat of Christ* will follow immediately after the Rapture and only Christians will be present. It is not to be decided there whether a person is saved or lost, but whether or not a reward is to be given for faithful stewardship on earth.

The *judgment of the nations* (set forth in Matthew 25:31-46) will take place at the end of the Great Tribulation, at the beginning of the millennial reign of Christ, and the nations will be judged according to their treatment of the Jews during the tribulation period.

The *Great White Throne judgment* will be at the consummation of all things, after the millennial reign of Christ, after the battle of Gog and Magog, and it is described in Revelation 20:11-15. We will discuss all of these subjects later in our study.

All born again believers will spend eternity with Jesus in the Pearly White City, but there will be different degrees of glory and splendor, as described in I Corinthians 15:40-42. The Word of God clearly teaches that there will be great and small vessels, but *all* vessels will be *filled*. There will be degrees of glory but no difference (or degrees) in happiness.

The faithful will be specially crowned, specially rewarded, and the Church will then attend the marriage supper of the Lamb:

"I heard as it were the voice of a great multitude, and as the voice of many waters, and as the voice of mighty thunderings, saying, Alleluia: for the Lord God omnipotent reigneth. Let us be glad and rejoice, and give honour to Him: for the marriage of the Lamb is come, and His wife hath made herself ready. And to her was granted that she should be arrayed in fine linen, clean and white: for the fine linen is the righteousness of saints.

"And he saith unto me, Write, Blessed are they which are called unto the marriage supper of the Lamb. And he saith unto me, These are the true sayings of God" (Rev. 19:6-9).

The marriage of the Lamb climaxes simultaneously with the great day in which the Lord God will punish the hosts of wicked ones and the ungodly kings and rulers of the earth: "And it shall come to pass in that day, that the Lord shall punish the host of the high ones that are on high, and the kings of the earth upon the earth" (Isa. 24:21).

At the climax of the judgment of the kings of the earth, God will give the great kingdom of power and glory to His "little flock," as promised in Luke 12:32: "Fear not, little flock; for it is your Father's good pleasure to give you the kingdom."

In Revelation 20:4, John the Beloved saw and recorded the following: "I saw thrones, and they sat upon them, and judgment was given unto them: and I saw the souls of them that were beheaded for the witness of Jesus, and for the Word of God, and which had not worshipped the beast, neither his image, neither had received his mark upon their foreheads, or in their hands; and they lived and reigned with Christ a thousand years!"

Daniel also saw the saints of the most high God receive the kingdom prepared for them: *"The saints of the most High shall take the kingdom, and possess the kingdom for ever, even for ever and ever.*   Then I would know the truth of the fourth beast, which was diverse from all the others, exceeding dreadful, whose teeth were of iron, and his nails of brass; which devoured, brake in pieces, and stamped the residue with his feet; and of the ten horns that were in his head, and of the other which came up, and before whom three fell; even of that horn that had eyes, and a mouth that spake very great things, whose look was more stout than his fellows.   I beheld, and the same horn made war with the saints, and prevailed against them; *until the Ancient of days came, and judgment* was given to the saints of the most High; and the time came that the saints possessed the kingdom" (Dan. 7:18-22).

Those who, at the judgment seat of Christ, have been counted faithful and worthy will be made rulers in the eternal kingdom of heaven.

There is one body, Christ is the head of that body, and each believer is a member of that body.   Therefore *the inheritance is all ONE*—i. e., the individual will not be glorified before the body.   The individual will have a portion therein, but all believers *together as one body* are a royal family and a kingdom.   Paul speaks of "giving thanks unto the Father, which hath made us meet to be *partakers of the inheritance of the saints in light*" (Col. 1:12).   Jesus has made us "kings and priests unto God and His Father; to Him be glory and dominion for ever and ever.   Amen" (Rev. 1:6).

In Revelation 5:8-10 we read: "When He had taken the book, the four beasts and four and twenty elders fell down before the Lamb, having every one of them harps, and golden vials full of odours, which are the prayers of saints.   And they sung a new song, saying, Thou art worthy to take the book, and to open the seals thereof: for thou wast slain, and hast redeemed us to God by thy blood out of every kindred, and tongue, and people, and nation; *and hast made us unto our God KINGS AND PRIESTS: and we shall reign on the earth!*"

Individuals are declared priests and kings in the royal realm—and *we will reign*—but the whole of the body is superior to the individual.   There is but one

Individual whom God honors and glorifies, and that is the Lamb of God. The individual believer is set in his place by the Lord Jesus Christ, and will glorify God in his capacity as part of the bride, the body of Christ.

"Known unto God are all His works from the beginning of the world" (Acts 15:18), and His goal is not only the salvation of the individual believer but the glorifying of the whole royal community; not only individual blessedness and joy, but the kingdom of God (Matt. 6:10). Even now God's universal state is under the government of *angels* (as described in Daniel 10:13-20) and in the eternity ahead of us a company of *glorified saints* will reign as kings and priests, with Christ at the head of the kingdom. Paul speaks of this in I Corinthians 6:2, 3: "Do ye not know that the saints shall judge the world? and if the world shall be judged by you, are ye unworthy to judge the smallest matters? Know ye not that we shall judge angels? How much more things that pertain to this life?"

In Revelation 3:21 Jesus promised, "To him that overcometh will I grant to sit with me in my throne, even as I also overcame, and am set down with my Father in His throne."

Luke 12:37 records these precious words of Jesus: *"BLESSED are those servants, whom the Lord when He cometh shall find WATCHING!* Verily I say unto you, that He shall gird Himself, and make them to sit down to meat, and will come forth and serve them."

The Marriage of the Lamb

"Let us be glad and rejoice, and give honour to Him: for the marriage of the Lamb is come, and His wife hath made herself ready. And to her was granted that she should be arrayed in fine linen, clean and white: for the fine linen is the righteousness of saints. And he saith unto me, Write, Blessed are they which are called unto the marriage supper of the Lamb. And he saith unto me, These are the true sayings of God" (Rev. 19:7-9).

There are many passages in the New Testament which present Christ and His Church as the Bridegroom and the bride. For instance, in John 3:29 John the Baptist said, "He that hath the bride is the Bridegroom: but the friend of the Bridegroom, which standeth and heareth Him, rejoiceth greatly because of the Bridegroom's voice . . . ."

In Romans 7:4 the Apostle Paul explains, "Wherefore, my brethren, ye also are become dead to the law by the body of Christ; that ye should be married to Another, even to Him who is raised from the dead . . . ."

To the Corinthian believers Paul wrote, "I am jealous over you with godly jealousy: for I have espoused you to one husband, that I may present you as a chaste virgin to Christ" (II Cor. 11:2).

In Ephesians 5:23-32 we see Christ and the Church as an example to husband and wife: "For the husband is the head of the wife, even as Christ is the head of the Church: and He is the Saviour of the body. Therefore as the Church is subject unto Christ, so let the wives be to their own husbands in every thing. Husbands, love your wives, even as Christ also loved the Church, and gave Himself for it; that He might sanctify and cleanse it with the washing of water by the

Word, that He might present it to Himself a glorious
Church, not having spot, or wrinkle, or any such thing;
but that it should be holy and without blemish. So
ought men to love their wives as their own bodies. He
that loveth his wife loveth himself. For no man ever
yet hated his own flesh; but nourisheth and cherisheth
it, even as the Lord the Church: for we are members
of His body, of His flesh, and of His bones. For this
cause shall a man leave his father and mother, and
shall be joined unto his wife, and they two shall be
one flesh. *This is a great mystery: BUT I SPEAK
CONCERNING CHRIST AND THE CHURCH.*"

When Jesus comes in the Rapture He will appear
as a Bridegroom to take His bride unto Himself, and
the relationship that was pledged between Christ and
the Church will be consummated—i. e., the two will
become one. This great and grand event is the consummation of joy to Christ as man. It is not said to
be the marriage of *the bride,* but "the marriage of
THE LAMB" (Rev. 19:7). *It is HIS joy, not ours,*
that is especially in view.

The TIME of the marriage of the Lamb:—

The marriage of the Lamb and the marriage supper
(of which no details are given) take place in heaven
on the eve of the Lord's return in the Revelation. In
the Word of God these events are revealed as taking
place between the translation of the Church and the
Revelation of Christ when He returns to earth *with
His Church.*

Notice Revelation 19:7, 8 states that "the marriage
of the Lamb is come, and His wife hath made herself

ready.   And to her was granted that she should be arrayed in fine linen, clean and white: for the fine linen is *the righteousness of saints.''* This could refer only to those things which have been accepted at the judgment seat of Christ, therefore the marriage itself must occur between the time when our works are judged and the time when the King of kings will reign from the throne of David and the bride will reign with Him.

The PLACE of the marriage of the Lamb: —

Since the marriage follows immediately after the judgment seat of Christ, it will undoubtedly take place in heaven.   It is from heaven that the Church will return with Christ when He comes in the Revelation (Rev. 19:14), therefore the marriage of the Lamb must take place there.   Certainly no *other* place would be fit for such a glorious wedding and such a glorious people as will be married to the Bridegroom.   He will "change our vile body, that it may be fashioned like unto His glorious body, according to the working whereby He is able even to subdue all things unto Himself'' (Phil. 3:21).

The marriage of the Lamb involves the true Church, made up of all born again, blood-washed believers— from the one hundred and twenty in the upper room on the Day of Pentecost up to and including the last person born again before the Rapture occurs.   *All believers* will participate in the marriage.

Old Testament Saints: —

The resurrection of the Old Testament saints will take place at the Rapture when the Lord Jesus Christ

returns in the air for His bride. I Thessalonians 4:14
tells us, ". . . even so *them also which sleep in Jesus*
will God bring with Him." Certainly those who "sleep
in Jesus" include the Old Testament saints. They were
saved by faith in the coming Messiah (looking *forward*
to Calvary) just as *we* are saved by faith looking *back*
to Calvary.

When Christ died, He descended into the Paradise
side of hell in the heart of the earth. "For as Jonas
was three days and three nights in the whale's belly;
so shall the Son of man be three days and three nights
in the heart of the earth" (Matt. 12:40).

In Ephesians 4:8-10 the Apostle Paul explains,
"Wherefore He saith, *When He ascended up on high,*
He led captivity captive, and gave gifts unto men.
(Now that He ascended, what is it but that *He also*
descended first into the lower parts of the earth? He
that descended is the same also that ascended up far
above all heavens, that He might fill all things.)"

Then in I Peter 3:18, 19 we read, "For Christ also
hath once suffered for sins, the just for the unjust,
that He might bring us to God, being put to death in
the flesh, but quickened by the Spirit: by which also
He went and preached unto the spirits in prison."

When Christ rose from the dead He brought the Old
Testament saints with Him and carried them to the
Paradise above—"when He ascended up on high, He
led captivity captive." Some of the Old Testament
saints have already received their new bodies. They
came out of their graves at the resurrection of Jesus
more than nineteen hundred years ago (Matt. 27:53).
At the Rapture, the rest of the Old Testament saints

will be raised and caught up to meet the Lord in the air.   They will not be part of the bride, they will be *friends of the Bridegroom;* and as such they will enjoy a deeper and dearer character of blessedness and joy than would be theirs if they were friends of the *bride.*

John the Baptist was martyred before the Church was formed, but he will no doubt be one of the most honored guests at the marriage supper in the sky.   The Old Testament saints will constitute the large company of guests who will be rejoicing in Christ's presence and at the sound of His voice.

In addition to the Church and the Old Testament saints, still another group will be added to the saints of the first resurrection.   This will be the tribulation saints.

Isaiah 26:19-21 tells us, "Thy dead men shall live, together with my dead body shall they arise.   Awake and sing, ye that dwell in dust: for thy dew is as the dew of herbs, and the earth shall cast out the dead.   Come, my people, enter thou into thy chambers, and shut thy doors about thee: hide thyself as it were for a little moment, until the indignation be overpast.   For, behold, the Lord cometh out of His place to punish the inhabitants of the earth for their iniquity: the earth also shall disclose her blood, and shall no more cover her slain."

But Revelation 20:4-6 makes it clear that those who are saved during the Great Tribulation will not be resurrected until the Revelation: "I saw thrones, and they sat upon them, and judgment was given unto them: and I saw the souls of them that were beheaded for the witness of Jesus, and for the Word of God, and which had not worshipped the beast, neither his image, neither had received his mark upon their foreheads, or in their hands; and they lived and reigned with Christ a thousand years. But the rest of the dead lived not again until the thousand years were finished. This is the first resurrection. Blessed and holy is he that hath part in the first resurrection: on such the second death hath no power, but they shall be priests of God and of Christ, and shall reign with Him a thousand years."

Thus we see that the martyred saints of the Great Tribulation are part of the first resurrection; but since they will not be raised until the end of the tribulation period they cannot be participants in the marriage of the Lamb. But we see them in Revelation 7:14-17 before the throne of God, in perfect peace awaiting the end of the tribulation and the martyrdom of their fellow servants, when Jesus Christ will take vengeance on their enemies and deliver them.

The Bible clearly teaches that the Church will already have been translated, resurrected, cleansed, and presented to the Son at the time of the marriage supper. (See Ephesians 5:26, 27.) At that time the Church will have become the object through which the eternal glory of God will be forever manifest to all creation. This present age, this Day of Grace, will witness the development and the completion of God's program and purpose in taking out "a people for His name" (Acts 15:14).

The Lamb

"Blessed are they which are called unto the marriage

supper of the Lamb" (Rev. 19:9). It is exceedingly interesting to study the marriage supper—those who will participate, those who will be invited, where and when the supper will be held; but the Bridegroom is the most interesting study of all. He will be the fairest of all the multi-millions and billions who will attend the marriage supper. We note especially the title used in speaking of Him in connection with the wedding and the supper—He will come to His wedding as "THE LAMB."

There are more than seven hundred titles ascribed to Jesus in the Word of God, and we cannot but ask why the Holy Spirit chose *"The Lamb"* as the name to be used in contracting Christ's eternal marriage to His bride. The wedding announcement *could* have read "Blessed are they which are called to the marriage of *the Creator,"* for certainly *Christ IS the Creator.* "All things were made by Him, and without Him was not anything made that was made" (John 1:3). Hebrews 1:2 declares that *the worlds* were made by Him. Christ was before the world was, when this universe was nothing but empty, limitless space inhabited only by God the Father, God the Son, and God the Holy Spirit. This Divine Person who at the marriage supper is called "the Lamb" was present in the bosom of God "in the beginning" (John 1:1, 2, 14). He spoke—and it was done. He commanded—and it stood fast. This universe was spoken into existence by this "Lamb." He flung the worlds from His finger-tips, He put the seas in their places, He molded the hills and the valleys, He planted the trees and painted the deserts and plains. Yes, Christ is truly the Creator.

In the fulness of time this same Personality was born of woman, and still another time came when He wrought another work—a work that outshines all other works as the sun outshines the moon! When He created the universe *He spoke—and it was done;* but in His *NEW creation* it was not possible for even the triune God to speak and the work be done. It was necessary that God take upon Himself the form of man, and in a body of flesh come to this earth to live as man lives, to be tempted in all points as man is tempted, and (at the appointed time) surrender to His enemies to be nailed to a Roman cross. The Lamb of God—yes, very God in flesh—had to *die* in order to bring about His new creation, the New Testament Church. He suffered and died that men might have eternal life, life abundant; and the day is not far distant when this Creator of heaven and earth, this Christ of God who took a body of humiliation in order to make the supreme sacrifice for the sins of mankind, will be married to His blood-bought, blood-washed bride, *His NEW CREATION!* ("If any man be in Christ, he is *a new creature:* old things are passed away; behold, all things are become new"—II Cor. 5:17.)

Christ stands as the crown and the climax of *all creative power,* but it was as *the Lamb,* not as the Creator, that He purchased His bride with His own precious blood. Therefore we read, "Blessed are they which are called unto *the marriage supper of the LAMB."*

Again, the wedding announcement could have read, "Blessed are they which are called to the marriage supper of *the LORD,"* for *Christ IS Lord.* He is to be married to His bride, chosen from every tribe and tongue, kindred and nation, every individual who has believed on the name of Jesus and confessed *His lordship* through this Dispensation of Grace. But it was not as Lord that He died on the cross to purchase His bride. Therefore the marriage invitation reads, ". . . the marriage supper of *the LAMB.*"

The announcement could also have read, "Blessed are they which are called unto *the marriage supper of the KING,*" for Christ is King of kings and Lord of lords—King eternal. He will take unto Himself the queen eternal, the Church of the living God, to sit with Him and reign with Him forever. But it was as the sacrificial Lamb, not as King, that He purchased His bride by the sacrifice of Himself. Therefore those who are entitled to attend the marriage supper are invited in the name of *the LAMB*—the title given to the heavenly Bridegroom in the hour of His great glory and eternal joy when He takes His bride to sit with Him upon the throne and reign with Him throughout all eternity.

You see, although the Lord Jesus Christ is the Creator, one day Satan stepped into the Garden of Eden and in a moment of temptation he hurled this world into darkness, pain, and misery. Since that day the whole creation has groaned and travailed in pain, waiting for that glorious day when Christ will call His bride, *His new creation,* to be with Him in glory. The only way God could redeem what Adam sold out to the devil was to provide a spotless Redeemer, sinless Lamb of God, who would pay the full redemption price to buy back what Adam lost in the fall.

It is also true that Christ is Lord of lords—but what good is the title to those who will not allow Him to *be* Lord? Satan stole the allegiance of Adam and Eve, and through their disobedience all men are sinners. Therefore the Lord of lords had to find a way by a divine act of His own whereby He could bring back man's allegiance so that man might bow before Him and worship Him as everlasting Lord. Only as the Lamb, offering Himself in eternal sacrifice, could He bring back that which Adam sold in the Garden of Eden.

Christ was born "King of the Jews"—and certainly He is King of kings—but what good is that royal title if the devil occupies the throne of the hearts of men and rules in the kingdoms of the earth? Only those who accept the sacrifice of the Lamb are subjects of the King. Therefore the King of kings had to find a way to regain the kingdoms Adam sold to Satan, He had to find a way to reign in the hearts of men. He found this way in the *Lamb,* dying on the cross of Calvary.

What God demanded, only God could provide. Therefore without the aid of man and completely within Himself He found a way to redeem this poor, crushed, groaning, travailing creation: *"By GRACE are ye saved through faith; and that not of yourselves: it is the GIFT of God: not of works, lest any man should boast"* (Eph. 2:8, 9). He found a way to break man's rebellious heart and make him willing to bow at the feet of Jesus and confess Him as Lord of lords. He found a way whereby the kingdoms of this world will one day become the kingdom of God, ruled over

by Him who is King of kings.   The day that WAY
was opened to man was the day Jesus left the bosom
of the Father and through the miracle of the virgin
birth was born of the Virgin Mary.   It was the day
when the Creator died for man whom He had created.
It was the day when the Lord of lords became the
Lamb of God and gave Himself in sacrifice for the
sin of the world.   It was the day when the King of
kings became a subject and willingly submitted to
wicked hands that led Him to Calvary and nailed
Him to the cross.

In I Peter 1:18-20 the Word of God tells us, "Ye
know that ye were not redeemed with corruptible
things, as silver and gold, from your vain conversation
received by tradition from your fathers; but with the
precious blood of Christ, *as of A LAMB* without blemish and without spot: who verily was foreordained
before the foundation of the world, but was manifest
in these last times for you."   Here Peter tells us that
the title "Lamb of God" has belonged to the Lord
Jesus Christ *since before the foundation of the world!*
Yes, He was the Lamb of God before He was the
Creator, Lord of lords and King of kings.

Throughout the Old Testament we see *types* of
the Lamb of God.   The covering God provided for
Adam and Eve in the Garden of Eden was a type
of the sacrifice of the Lamb who would one day fulfill *all* types and shadows.   God clothed Adam and
Eve in the skins of innocent animals, slain that they
might be covered—and I personally believe these little
animals were lambs.   The innocent *Lamb of God* was
slain that mankind might have a covering for sin.

(Read Genesis 3:1-21.)

The offering of Isaac (Genesis 22:1-14) is a type of Christ. Abraham said, "My son, God will provide Himself a Lamb for a burnt-offering" (v. 8), and God *did* provide HIMSELF *THE Lamb!*

In Israel's darkest hour of doom and despair in Egypt, God's people were instructed to take a lamb, slay it, and sprinkle its blood on either side and on the top of the door—"and when I see the blood I will pass over you" (Ex. 12:13). Yes, the blood on the doorposts in Egypt pointed to the shed blood of the Lamb of God—"Christ our passover is sacrificed for us" (I Cor. 5:7).

In that tremendous fifty-third chapter of Isaiah we see Christ, the suffering Saviour, presented as the Lamb upon whom God laid "the iniquity of us all." Who can read verse 6 in that passage without seeing the altar and the sacrificial Lamb laid thereon?

But we are not living in the hour of types and shadows today. *The type has been fulfilled,* the Lamb of God took our sins and nailed them to the cross, and by His stripes we are healed. From Genesis through Malachi we see Christ the Lamb of God—and it was with that title that John the Baptist presented Him when first Jesus came on the scene of His public ministry: ". . . John seeth Jesus coming unto him, and saith, *Behold THE LAMB OF GOD, which taketh away the sin of the world*" (John 1:29).

In the book of Revelation, the last book in our Bible, it is extremely interesting to read and underline the verses where the Lord Jesus Christ is called *the Lamb of God.* In fact, in Revelation He is called "the Lamb of God" more often than in all other books of the Bible combined.

In Revelation chapter 5 John the Beloved "wept much because no man was found worthy to open and to read the book, neither to look thereon." Then one of the elders said to him, "Weep not: behold, the Lion of the tribe of Juda, the Root of David, hath prevailed to open the book, and to loose the seven seals thereof." Then John looked—but instead of beholding the Lion of the tribe of Juda he saw "*a LAMB as it had been slain.*" (Read Revelation 5:1-7.)

In Revelation 6:15-17 we read of "the kings of the earth, and the great men, and the rich men, and the chief captains, and the mighty men, and every bond-man, and every free man" who were hiding in the dens and in the rocks of the mountains, begging the mountains and rocks to fall on them and hide them "from the face of Him that sitteth on the throne, *and from the wrath of THE LAMB:* for the great day of His wrath is come; and who shall be able to stand?"

Revelation chapter 21 describes the new heaven, the new earth, and the Pearly White City where the saints will dwell. In verses 22 and 23 we are told that there is "no temple therein: for the Lord God Almighty and *the Lamb* are the temple of it. And the city had no need of the sun, neither of the moon, to shine in it: for the glory of God did lighten it, and *THE LAMB is the light thereof!*"

Christ will come to His wedding as a Lamb. You see, it is "the Lamb" with whom believers fall in love. We do not fall in love with a Creator, a Lord,

or a King—but with the Lamb dying on a cross that
we might live.   Do you remember the day you were
saved? Do you remember the message you heard? the
words that broke your heart? I will never forget the
night I was saved.   The minister preached on the
wages of sin—but that is not what brought me to
accept salvation.   He closed the message by empha-
sizing the gift of God—eternal life through Jesus Christ
our Lord.   He presented Him on the cross, dying
in my stead—*and when I saw the Lamb of God I fell
in love with HIM.*

As I prepare this message I have been saved for
thirty-seven years, but I still clearly remember the
Lamb of God as I saw Him that night in my mind
and heart, dying for me, looking with love and compassion toward a world lost in sin.   I received Him
by faith as the Lamb of God, Saviour of sinners.   One
day He is coming for me, He will catch away His
Church, His bride, and we will be married to Him.
We will be perfectly at home in His presence because
we are His and He is ours.   We will sing the song
of Moses and the Lamb. I am looking forward to that
glorious day when I will see the Lamb who saved
me, the time when I will sit with Him at the marriage supper.   May God hasten that day and hour
when we will see the face of Him who died that we
might be saved.   Blessed indeed are they who are
called to the marriage supper of the LAMB!

Chapter V

Will the Church Go Through the Great Tribulation?

"God hath not appointed us to wrath, but to obtain salvation by our Lord Jesus Christ" (I Thess. 5:9).

"Because thou hast kept the word of my patience, *I also will keep thee from the hour of temptation,* which shall come upon all the world, to try them that dwell upon the earth" (Rev. 3:10).

These two verses of Scripture declare that believers will be kept from the wrath (or temptation) that will come upon the whole world. Paul assures us that God has not appointed His children to *"wrath"*—and "wrath" here speaks of *tribulation.*

"Salvation" in this verse from I Thessalonians does not only refer to the redemption of the soul from the *penalty* of sin, but to *the fulness* of salvation—soul, spirit, and body redeemed from sin and the curse. We are *redeemed* when we believe on Jesus, but our salvation will not be full and complete until the resurrection of the body, when Jesus comes in the Rapture and we receive our glorified bodies.

"The word of my patience" in Revelation 3:10 is *the Word of God.* Here we have God's promise that because we have *kept His Word* He will keep us "from the hour of temptation" (meaning the Great Tribulation period) "which shall come upon all the world, to try

them that dwell upon the earth."

Now the Bible does not speak of born again, blood-washed believers as *earth-dwellers!* Our citizenship is in heaven, we sit together in heavenly places in Christ Jesus, we are hid with Christ in God. Therefore we, the believers who make up the New Testament Church, are not earth-dwellers. We are pilgrims and strangers on earth, traveling toward that city not made with hands, eternal in the heavens.

When the Bible speaks of *"those who dwell upon the earth"* it refers to people who are *earthly,* not spiritual—those who are sons of Satan rather than sons of *God.* If you will make a careful study of the book of Revelation you will see that this particular class of people is mentioned over and over again. They have refused the Gospel and the heavenly calling, they have chosen to be earthlings and follow the things of the flesh. Thus we understand that "them which dwell upon the earth" speaks of *unregenerated* people, those who have not accepted the spiritual life and believed in the shed blood and finished work of the Lamb of God. It is upon them that this "hour of temptation"—or tribulation—will come. But we who are members of the New Testament Church, the body of Christ, will not enter or go through any part of the Great Tribulation.

As we go into a deeper and more extensive study of this subject we will look into the Word of God, compare Scripture with Scripture and spiritual things with spiritual, allowing the Holy Spirit to enlighten us as we search God's precious Word.

First of all, we must have a clear, Bible under-

standing of the term *"tribulation."* It is evident from
the Word of God that during this present age the
Church will have trials and tribulations. Jesus said,
"In the world *ye shall have tribulation:* but be of
good cheer. *I have OVERCOME the world"* (John
16:33). The Apostle Paul, God's minister to the Church,
warned, "Yea, and *all that will live godly in Christ
Jesus* shall suffer persecution" (II Tim. 3:12).

But—according to the Scriptures the Great Tribulation period is "the time of *Jacob's* trouble," not the
time of the *believers'* trouble, not the time of the
Church's trouble; and that time will not—yea, cannot—
begin until after the parenthetic period (the Church
Age or the Day of Grace) that comes between Daniel's
sixty-ninth and seventieth weeks of prophecy.

From beginning to end of the Church Age God
makes no distinction between Jew and Gentile. During
this Dispensation of Grace "there is neither Jew nor
Greek, there is neither bond nor free" (Gal. 3:28). We
are all *ONE in Christ.* "For He is our peace, who
hath made both one, and hath broken down the middle
wall of partition between us; having abolished in His
flesh the enmity, even the law of commandments
contained in ordinances; for *to make in Himself of
twain ONE NEW MAN*, so making peace" (Eph.
2:14, 15). Jesus has broken down the middle wall of
partition and *now* we who were "aliens from the com-
monwealth of Israel, and strangers from the covenants
of promise, having no hope, and without God in the
world" (Eph. 2:12) are invited into the family of God.

It will be when the Church is removed from the
earth that God will again recognize the nation Israel

in a special covenant relationship with Himself. God made a perpetual covenant with Abraham, Isaac, Jacob, and David, and this covenant has not been annulled. Therefore *after the Church is taken out of the world* God will again turn to His elect nation, and it is then that the time of final trial will begin. Israel will go through the "time of Jacob's trouble" which will be a period of tribulation such as this world has never known.

In Deuteronomy 4:26, 27 we find the first reference to the hour of testing for the nation Israel:

"I call heaven and earth to witness against you this day, that ye shall soon utterly perish from off the land whereunto ye go over Jordan to possess it; ye shall not prolong your days upon it, but shall utterly be destroyed. And the Lord shall scatter you among the nations, and ye shall be left few in number among the heathen, whither the Lord shall lead you."

These verses are part of the message Moses delivered to Israel on the plains of Moab shortly before the end of his responsibility as God's appointed leader of that nation, and the words he spoke were the words God had given him. He warned Israel that because of their sin, because they had violated God's holy law, judgment would come upon them and they would be scattered. This particular dispersion took place after the destruction of Jerusalem in 70 A. D. when Titus the Roman with his armies overran that city and laid it waste.

Certainly we know that since that day the nation Israel has not turned to God to know and worship Him *as God,* nor have they yet been restored to their own land in the blessings God promised Abraham. The nation Israel still exists, and millions of Jews have returned to Palestine. However this is not a *spiritual* return as it will be when they see Jesus as He stands on the Mount of Olives in His return to reign on earth.

Then in Deuteronomy 4:29-31 we read, "But if from thence thou shalt seek the Lord thy God, thou shalt find Him, if thou seek Him with all thy heart and with all thy soul. When thou art in tribulation, and all these things are come upon thee, even *in the latter days,* if thou turn to the Lord thy God, and shalt be obedient unto His voice . . . He will not forsake thee, neither destroy thee, nor forget the covenant of thy fathers which He sware unto them."

This part of God's message to Israel has not yet been fulfilled. The returning of Israel to her own land is to take place when *tribulation* comes upon them *"in the LATTER DAYS."* I am sure someone will quickly say that the Jew and the nation of Israel have *been* in tribulation for centuries, and that is true; but you will note that our present Scripture speaks *specifically* of tribulation and things that will come upon Israel "in the LATTER days"—that is, in the days just before the beginning of the eternity of eternities. This reference is not to the age-long trials and tribulations, persecutions and prejudices through which the Jews and their nation have passed, but to *a definite, fixed period* of testing and tribulation *in the latter days.*

BUT—"If thou turn to the Lord thy God . . . He will not forsake thee . . . *nor forget THE COVENANT OF THY FATHERS which He sware unto them!"*

Although the nation Israel has sinned, rebelled against
God, and *forfeited everything* based on the *Mosaic*
covenant, God has not forgotten His covenant with
Abraham—a perpetual covenant of pure grace. It will
not be broken. God will restore the nation of Israel.

Moses spoke of the definite period of tribulation,
linking it with "the latter days." *The time of Jacob's
trouble* will come upon Israel immediately after the
Rapture of the Church. The false messiah will appear
—a subject which we will discuss at length later in
our study—and he will make a covenant with the
Jewish people. But at the appointed time he will
break that covenant and the Jews will suffer as they
have never suffered since Israel became a nation!

The Time Of Jacob's Trouble

"The word that came to Jeremiah from the Lord,
saying, Thus speaketh the Lord God of Israel, saying,
Write thee all the words that I have spoken unto thee
in a book. For, lo, the days come, saith the Lord,
that I will bring again the captivity of my people
Israel and Judah, saith the Lord: and I will cause
them to return to the land that I gave to their fathers,
and they shall possess it. And these are the words
that the Lord spake concerning Israel and concerning
Judah. For thus saith the Lord: We have heard a
voice of trembling, of fear, and not of peace.

"Ask ye now, and see whether a man doth travail
with child? Wherefore do I see every man with his
hands on his loins, as a woman in travail, and all
faces are turned into paleness? *Alas! for that day is
great, so that none is like it: it is even THE TIME*

OF JACOB'S TROUBLE, but he shall be saved out of it. For it shall come to pass in that day, saith the Lord of hosts, that I will break his yoke from off thy neck, and will burst thy bonds, and strangers shall no more serve themselves of him: but they shall serve the Lord their God, and David their king, whom I will raise up unto them.

"Therefore fear thou not, O my servant Jacob, saith the Lord; neither be dismayed, O Israel: for, lo, I will save thee from afar, and thy seed from the land of their captivity; and Jacob shall return, and shall be in rest, and be quiet, and none shall make him afraid. For I am with thee, saith the Lord, to save thee: though I make a full end of all nations whither I have scattered thee, yet will I not make a full end of thee: but I will correct thee in measure, and will not leave thee altogether unpunished.

"For thus saith the Lord, Thy bruise is incurable, and thy wound is grievous. There is none to plead thy cause, that thou mayest be bound up: thou hast no healing medicines. All thy lovers have forgotten thee; they seek thee not; for I have wounded thee with the wound of an enemy, with the chastisement of a cruel one, for the multitude of thine iniquity; because thy sins were increased. Why criest thou for thine affliction? Thy sorrow is incurable for the multitude of thine iniquity: because thy sins were increased, I have done these things unto thee.

"Therefore all they that devour thee shall be devoured; and all thine adversaries, every one of them, shall go into captivity; and they that spoil thee shall be a spoil, and all that prey upon thee will I give for a prey. For I will restore health unto thee, and I will heal thee of thy wounds, saith the Lord; because they called thee an Outcast, saying, This is Zion, whom no man seeketh after.

"Thus saith the Lord: Behold, I will bring again the captivity of Jacob's tents, and have mercy on his dwellingplaces; and the city shall be builded upon her own heap, and the palace shall remain after the manner thereof. And out of them shall proceed thanksgiving and the voice of them that make merry: and I will multiply them, and they shall not be few; I will also glorify them, and they shall not be small. Their children also shall be as aforetime, and their congregation shall be established before me, and I will punish all that oppress them.

"And their nobles shall be of themselves, and their governor shall proceed from the midst of them; and I will cause him to draw near, and he shall approach unto me: for who is this that engaged his heart to approach unto me? saith the Lord.

"And ye shall be my people, and I will be your God. Behold, the whirlwind of the Lord goeth forth with fury, a continuing whirlwind: it shall fall with pain upon the head of the wicked. The fierce anger of the Lord shall not return, until He have done it, and until He have performed the intents of His heart: *in the latter days* ye shall consider it" (Jer. 30:1-24).

Please also read Jeremiah chapter 31 in connection with this, for these two chapters give a summary of the nation Israel in the tribulation period, the time of Jacob's trouble—*"but he shall be saved out of it."* Why? Verse 3 of chapter 31 answers: "The Lord hath appeared of old . . . saying, *Yea, I have loved thee with an everlasting love:* therefore with lovingkindness have I drawn thee!"

In these passages we see that it is *Israel,* not the Church, that is to suffer great tribulation. God will bring His elect nation back from the four corners of the earth and will establish them in their own land.

Isaiah 13:6-9 is another passage which clearly identifies the people and the land that will play the leading role in *the time of Jacob's trouble* in the latter days:

"Howl ye; for the day of the Lord is at hand; it shall come as a destruction from the Almighty. Therefore shall all hands be faint, and every man's heart shall melt: and they shall be afraid: pangs and sorrows shall take hold of them; they shall be in pain as a woman that travaileth: they shall be amazed one at another; their faces shall be as flames. Behold, the day of the Lord cometh, cruel both with wrath and fierce anger, to lay the land desolate: and He shall destroy the sinners thereof out of it!"

"The LAND" in this passage is the land of Palestine. Throughout the Old Testament Scriptures when the prophets of God spoke of "the land" they were speaking of the promised land, Palestine, the land of God's people.

"He shall destroy the SINNERS out of it." During the Great Tribulation the Jewish remnant will turn to the Lord, the sinners will be destroyed out of it, and their spirits will drop into everlasting damnation. But notice also the supernatural things that will take place at the time of Jacob's trouble:

"The stars of heaven and the constellations thereof

shall not give their light: the sun shall be darkened
in his going forth, and the moon shall not cause her
light to shine. And I will punish the world for their
evil, and the wicked for their iniquity; and I will
cause the arrogancy of the proud to cease, and will lay
low the haughtiness of the terrible. I will make a man
more precious than fine gold; even a man than the
golden wedge of Ophir. Therefore I will shake the
heavens, and the earth shall remove out of her place,
in the wrath of the Lord of hosts, and in the day of
His fierce anger" (Isa. 13:10-13).

This passage describes what God will do to the
proud, ungodly civilization which will be left behind
when the Rapture takes place—the same civilization
that boasted of its self-sufficiency, its lack of need for
God, even declaring that God is dead and many other
damnable heresies of liberalism and modernism!

Apostate Israel will be sorely tried—but the Gentiles
will also suffer, because we note that God will punish
the wicked people of *the world.* That takes in all who
will be practicing evil—Gentiles as well as Jews.

John the Beloved saw a similar occasion when, on
the Isle of Patmos, he was given God's last revelation
to man. When the sixth seal is opened after the appearing of Antichrist there will be a time of horror
such as this world has never seen or imagined:

"And I beheld when He had opened the sixth seal,
and, lo, there was a great earthquake; and the sun
became black as sackcloth of hair, and the moon became as blood; and the stars of heaven fell unto the
earth, even as a fig tree casteth her untimely figs,
when she is shaken of a mighty wind. And the heaven

departed as a scroll when it is rolled together; and every mountain and island were moved out of their places. And the kings of the earth, and the great men, and the rich men, and the chief captains, and the mighty men, and every bondman, and every free man, hid themselves in the dens and in the rocks of the mountains; and said to the mountains and rocks, Fall on us, and hide us from the face of Him that sitteth on the throne, and from the wrath of the Lamb: for the great day of His wrath is come; and who shall be able to stand?" (Rev. 6:12-17).

The Scripture makes it crystal clear that when the Rapture takes place there will be no such supernatural changes as are described in the passages just quoted. When the sun refuses to shine, when the moon "becomes as blood" (Rev. 6:12) and the stars fall, when the mountains and islands are moved and the ocean turns to blood, the Church will be with Jesus in the sky. Certainly such things will not take place before the bride of Christ is taken out of the earth!

In Isaiah 17:4-11 we find another vivid picture of Israel's apostasy and Jehovah's dealing with that nation:

"In that day it shall come to pass, that the glory of Jacob shall be made thin, and the fatness of his flesh shall wax lean. And it shall be as when the harvestman gathereth the corn, and reapeth the ears with his arm; and it shall be as he that gathereth ears in the valley of Rephaim. Yet gleaning grapes shall be left in it, as the shaking of an olive tree, two or three berries in the top of the uppermost bough, four or five in the outmost fruitful branches thereof, saith the

Lord God of Israel.

"At that day shall a man look to his Maker, and
his eyes shall have respect to the Holy One of Israel.
And he shall not look to the altars, the work of his
hands, neither shall respect that which his fingers
have made, either the groves, or the images. In that
day shall his strong cities be as a forsaken bough, and
an uppermost branch, which they left because of the
children of Israel: and there shall be desolation.

"Because thou hast forgotten the God of thy salvation, and hast not been mindful of the rock of thy
strength, therefore shalt thou plant pleasant plants,
and shalt set it with strange slips. In the day shalt
thou make thy plant to grow, and in the morning shalt
thou make thy seed to flourish: but the harvest shall
be a heap in the day of grief and of desperate sorrow."

When Jesus walked on earth, Palestine was an
abundantly fruitful land; but when the Jews rejected
their Messiah and nailed Him to a cross instead of
crowning Him King, not only were the *people* dispersed
but the *land* was also cursed. Desert replaced fruitful
plains, and until recently the land of Palestine remained a desert where goats and sheep grazed on what
little grass and vegetation grew there. In these closing
days of this Age of Grace, Israel has been recognized
as a nation and the Jews who have returned to Palestine are planting and cultivating the land, and it is
again becoming fruitful and productive.

This, as seen in the passage just quoted from Isaiah,
is the definite fulfillment of prophecy. Because the
people forgot God and turned from Him, the land
would become desolate. Then it would be set *"with*

strange slips"—that is, plants from strange lands would be brought in to replace the plants that were taken away when the land was cursed. This is exactly what has been going on for several years in Palestine. The majority of the land there has been given to the Jew, the nation Israel. Trees, shrubs, and plants have been brought in from every nation in the world, and the country is becoming a garden spot again.

Bible believing Christians look at present day Israel in the light of the prophetic Word. We see the Jews returning to their own land, we see the land flourishing and the people prospering—but little do those people realize that the greatest blood bath in the history of Israel is still in the future! They are yet to pass through the Great Tribulation with such suffering as they have never before endured. Then, at the designated moment, their Messiah will appear on the Mount of Olives. They will see and recognize Him, they will receive Him, the nation will be born in a day and God will fulfill *in detail* every promise He made to Abraham. This will all take place *after* the Rapture of the Church.

A Faithful Remnant

"I say then, Hath God cast away His people? God forbid. For I also am an Israelite, of the seed of Abraham, of the tribe of Benjamin. God hath not cast away His people which He foreknew. Wot ye not what the Scripture saith of Elias? how he maketh intercession to God against Israel, saying:

"Lord, they have killed thy prophets, and digged down thine altars; and I am left alone, and they seek

my life. But what saith the answer of God unto him?
I have reserved to myself seven thousand men, who
have not bowed the knee to the image of Baal. Even
so then at this present time also there is a remnant
according to the election of grace. And if by grace,
then is it no more of works: otherwise grace is no
more grace. But if it be of works, then is it no more
grace: otherwise work is no more work" (Rom. 11:1-6).

Here the Apostle Paul points out that Israel is
blinded—but only until the times of the Gentiles be
fulfilled. God has not cast away His people, He will
turn again to Israel. In the history of Israel, a *remnant* is always seen—a *spiritual* Israel within *national*
Israel. God assured Elijah that there were yet seven
thousand men who had not bowed the knee to Baal
(I Kings 19:18).

In the days of Isaiah there was a very small Jewish
remnant, and God spared the nation because of that
remnant (Isa. 1:9).

In times of captivity the Jewish remnant appeared
in men like Ezekiel, Daniel, Shadrach, Meshach, Abednego, and Mordecai. At the end of the seventy years
of captivity in Babylon it was the *remnant* that returned home under the leadership of Ezra and Nehemiah.

When Jesus came as a Babe in a manger there was
a very small remnant of believing Jews—among them
Simeon and Anna—who looked for redemption in Jerusalem (Luke 2:38).

During this Church Age the remnant is made up
of born again, believing Jews, as Paul declared in
verse 5 of the passage just quoted from Romans chapter

11—"even so then at *this present time* also there is *a remnant according to the election of grace.*"

However, the chief interest in the present Jewish remnant is definitely *prophetic*. During the Great Tribulation a remnant out of Israel will turn to their Messiah and will become His witnesses after the Rapture of the Church (Rev. 7:3-8). Many of these faithful witnesses will be killed (Rev. 6:9-11), although some of them will be spared to enter the Millennium (Zech. 12:6—13:9). Many of the Psalms profess prophetically the joys and sorrows of the Israelites who will go through the tribulation period.

Ezekiel 20:33-38 also speaks of the future judgment of Israel: "As I live, saith the Lord God, surely with a mighty hand, and with a stretched out arm, and with fury poured out, will I rule over you: and I will bring you out from the people, and will gather you out of the countries wherein ye are scattered, with a mighty hand, and with a stretched out arm, and with fury poured out. And I will bring you into the wilderness of the people, and there will I plead with you face to face. Like as I pleaded with your fathers in the wilderness of the land of Egypt, so will I plead with you, saith the Lord God. And I will cause you to pass under the rod, and I will bring you into the bond of the covenant: and I will purge out from among you the rebels, and them that transgress against me. I will bring them forth out of the country where they sojourn, and they shall not enter into the land of Israel: and ye shall know that I am the Lord."

In this passage Ezekiel clearly tells us *why* God

will allow this time of horrible suffering and trouble. It will be *a time of judgment* against the people who have rebelled against Him. He will cause them to "pass under the rod"—the Shepherd's rod—and He will separate the true remnant (true Israel) from the counterfeit Israel. The remnant He will own as His flock, all others will be cast out.

Daniel, like many other Old Testament prophets, did not understand many of the things God gave him to pen down. In Daniel 12:8, 9 he said, *"I heard—but I understood not. Then said I, O my Lord, what shall be the end of these things?"* The Lord replied, "Go thy way, Daniel: for the words are *closed up and sealed* till the time of the end." Today it has been given to God's men to understand these prophecies of Daniel whereas in earlier years they were not understood because it was not the appointed time.

In Daniel 12:1 we read: "And at that time shall Michael stand up, the great prince which standeth for the children of thy people: and there shall be a time of trouble, such as never was since there was a nation even to that same time: and at that time thy people shall be delivered, every one that shall be found written in the book."

Michael the archangel is especially mentioned in connection with God's elect nation Israel. Daniel here prophesies of *"a time of trouble"* such as has not been "since there *was* a nation." And what will be the result of this time of trouble, this tribulation period? We find the answer in Matthew 24:22:

"Except those days should be shortened, there should no flesh be saved: but *for the elect's sake* those days shall be shortened." In this verse the *"elect"* is the nation Israel.

The Great Tribulation
Has Nothing To Do With the Church

The Scriptures which describe the Great Tribulation speak of Israel (Jacob), and *the Church* is not once named:

In Jeremiah 30:6, 7 it is called "the time of *Jacob's* trouble" and is compared in its suffering to the pain and anguish of a woman travailing in childbirth.

In Ezekiel 20:37 the tribulation period is spoken of as a time when *Israel* will be made to pass under the rod of God.

In Ezekiel 22:18-22 we note that it is *Israel,* not the Church, that will be cast into God's melting pot to be melted and refined in the fires of God's wrath, as precious metals are melted and refined.

In Malachi 3:2, 3 it is *Israel* who will go through the fire for purification, and again in Zechariah 13:9 it is God's people (Israel) who will pass through the fire to be refined as silver and gold are refined.

From these clear Bible statements it is evident that the Great Tribulation is something that has to do with the Jews, with the nation Israel. It is a judgment through which they must pass in a refining process to prepare them for the blessings that lie ahead for God's chosen people.

Indirectly, of course, the Gentiles will be affected by the tribulation period, but *the Church* will not be affected by it because the Church will be caught out of the world before that great and terrible day of the

Lord.

The New Testament contains two descriptions of the Great Tribulation.   Matthew 24:9-22 records the words of Jesus concerning that time of suffering and terrible anguish, and Revelation 6:1 through 19:21 also tells what John saw and penned down concerning that time.   I trust you will turn to these passages in your Bible and read them, for time and space will not permit quoting them here.   Certainly the words in Matthew 24 are graphic enough to challenge human imagination, and John records his vision of the various judgments which will come upon the earth under the seals, the trumpets, and the vials of wrath.   These things will occur literally upon this earth—primarily in Palestine and surrounding areas—during that indescribably horrible period which will come after the Church is caught out of this earth.

Comparing Spiritual Things With Spiritual

"As it is written, Eye hath not seen, nor ear heard, neither have entered into the heart of man, the things which God hath prepared for them that love Him.   But God hath revealed them unto us by His Spirit: for the Spirit searcheth all things, yea, the deep things of God.   For what man knoweth the things of a man, save the spirit of man which is in him?   Even so the things of God knoweth no man, but the Spirit of God.

"Now we have received, not the spirit of the world, but the Spirit which is of God; that we might know the things that are freely given to us of God.   Which things also we speak, not in the words which man's wisdom teacheth, but which the Holy Ghost teacheth;

comparing spiritual things with spiritual. But the natural man receiveth not the things of the Spirit of God: for they are foolishness unto him: neither can he know them, because they are spiritually discerned" (I Cor. 2:9-14).

God's true ministers do not speak words taught by man's wisdom, but words taught by the Holy Ghost, comparing spiritual things with spiritual and comparing scriptural truths with scriptural truths. There is no passage in the Bible so vague or mysterious but what another passage or verse sheds light on it. Therefore, if we do a little spiritual "comparing" we will see that many of the doctrines being taught concerning the Church and the tribulation period do not rightly divide the Word of Truth.

Some ministers and teachers believe that the Church will go through the tribulation period. They say that Christ's coming for the Church will take place at the same time as His setting up His kingdom to reign right here on earth; but if we compare Scriptures having to do with the translation of the Church, and those passages relating to the setting up of the kingdom, we will see that it would be utterly impossible for these two events to occur simultaneously.

There is no Scripture having to do with the establishing of the kingdom that has one word to say about believers being translated from this earth or caught up to meet Jesus in the air. For instance, in Matthew 25:31-41 we read, "When the Son of man shall come in His glory, and all the holy angels with Him, then shall He sit upon the throne of His glory: and before Him shall be gathered all nations: and He shall separate them one from another, as a shepherd divideth his sheep from the goats: and He shall set the sheep on His right hand, but the goats on the left. Then shall the King say unto them on His right hand, Come, ye blessed of my Father, inherit the kingdom prepared for you from the foundation of the world. . . . Then shall He say also unto them on the left hand, Depart from me, ye cursed, into everlasting fire, prepared for the devil and his angels."

Now if we analyze this familiar passage of Scripture we will see some very clear, understandable, and obvious *facts:*

Jesus will come in His glory, accompanied by myriads of holy angels. There will be both saved and unsaved people on earth at that time, and all the nations will be gathered before the Lord of glory— here on earth, not in the air. He will set up His throne and separate the sheep from the goats—the righteous from the unrighteous. But you will notice that the "sheep" nations are not caught up into the clouds or translated from the earth. They simply *enter the kingdom,* while the "goat" nations are taken away and cast into everlasting fire. It is important for us to see that when Jesus comes to set up His kingdom there is no translation—i. e., no one is caught up into the air to enter heaven. Those who enter the kingdom go into the Millennium *in their natural bodies.*

The little book of Jude contains only one chapter, but verses 14 and 15 of that chapter are dedicated to the second coming of the Lord Jesus Christ:

"And Enoch also, the seventh from Adam, prophesied of these, saying, Behold, the Lord cometh with ten thousands of His saints, to execute judgment upon all, and to convince all that are ungodly among them of all their ungodly deeds which they have ungodly committed, and of all their hard speeches which ungodly sinners have spoken against Him."

We note that in this short but tremendous passage there is no mention of anyone being translated or caught up into heaven. When Jesus comes "with ten thousands of His saints" He will come to judge, to convince the ungodly of their ungodly deeds and words. *After* the judgment He will set up the kingdom, the *righteous* will enter the kingdom, and the *ungodly* will be cast into hell.

Revelation 19:11-16 is also a marvelous and enlightening passage on the second coming of Christ and the sequence of events immediately following:

"I saw heaven opened, and behold a white horse; and He that sat upon him was called Faithful and True, and in righteousness He doth judge and make war. His eyes were as a flame of fire, and on His head were many crowns; and He had a name written, that no man knew, but He Himself. And He was clothed with a vesture dipped in blood: and His name is called The Word of God. And the armies which were in heaven followed Him upon white horses, clothed in fine linen, white and clean. And out of His mouth goeth a sharp sword, that with it He should smite the nations: and He shall rule them with a rod of iron: and He treadeth the winepress of the fierceness and wrath of Almighty God. And He hath on His vesture and on His thigh a name written,

KING OF KINGS, AND LORD OF LORDS."
Note the sequence of events described here: John
sees heaven opened. A white horse appears, ridden
by One whose name is *"Faithful and True."* In
righteousness He judges and makes war. His eyes
are as flaming fire, there are many crowns on His
head, He has a name written on His vesture, and His
clothing is dipped in blood. *His name is THE WORD
OF GOD*—so we know that He can be none other
than the Lord Jesus Christ.

The armies which were in heaven follow Him on
white horses, and these armies, too, are clothed in
white linen. In verse 8 of that same chapter we are
told that this white linen is "the righteousness of
the saints," which tells us that this takes place after
the marriage of the Lamb, after the judgment seat
of Christ. So this is the Church appearing *and returning to earth* with Christ.

Then verse 15 tells us, "Out of His mouth goeth
a sharp sword." He smites the nations, He rules them
with a rod of iron, and He treads the winepress of
the wrath of Almighty God. This is the tribulation
period, and at the end of that period when all the
wicked are cast into the winepress and judged, He
will be *King of kings and Lord of lords.* Therefore,
this is the time when Jesus comes to set up His kingdom and reign with His bride here on earth for one
thousand glorious years.

In verses 17 through 21 of Revelation chapter 19 we
read the description of the awful destruction of the
wicked. The beast and the false prophet are cast
alive into the lake burning with brimstone and the

wicked are slain. The birds and the beasts are called to come and eat the flesh of kings, captains, mighty men, bond and free, small and great.

Then in chapter 20 of Revelation a mighty Angel comes down from heaven, "having the key of the bottomless pit and a great chain in His hand." This mighty Angel lays hold on the dragon, the devil, binds him for a thousand years, places him in the bottomless pit and seals him there (verses 1-3).

Verses 4 through 6 of chapter 20 give the account of the resurrection of those who will be beheaded during the tribulation period and they, together with the Church and all the righteous, are with Jesus. "Blessed and holy is he that hath part in the first resurrection: on such the second death hath no power, but they shall be priests of God and of Christ, and shall reign with Him a thousand years!"

Looking at these passages from Revelation which so vividly describe the returning of Jesus with His saints, we see the Lord Jesus Christ coming to set up His kingdom—but we are again aware that no one is translated into heaven. On the contrary, the saints are *returning* to earth with the Bridegroom. They have already been caught up into heaven and are now ready to reign with the King of kings. There is no part of even *one verse* in the Bible that suggests that the Church will enter or go through one day of the tribulation period. The Church will be removed from this earth before the appearing of Antichrist.

Consider this: At the time of the flood, not one drop of water fell until Noah and his family were safely in the ark and God had shut them in. Then the rains fell and the wicked were destroyed.

Lot was a backslider, but the Bible tells us that he was a *"just* man," a righteous man (II Pet. 2:7,8). And in Genesis 19:22 the heavenly messengers confessed that God could not destroy the city of Sodom until Lot was *outside* that city—and they took him by the hand and led him out. Then and only then did God rain fire and brimstone on that wicked city.

Now I ask you: Do you think God loves the bride of His only begotten Son *any less* than He loved Noah and Lot? I think not! God loves the Church, and you can rest assured that not one moment of the Great Tribulation will occur on this earth until the Church is safe with Jesus up above the storm.

Rapture Before Revelation— Translation Before Tribulation

"Let not your heart be troubled: ye believe in God, believe also in me. In my Father's house are many mansions: if it were not so, I would have told you. I go to prepare a place for you. And if I go and prepare a place for you, I will come again, and receive you unto myself; that where I am, there ye may be also" (John 14:1-3).

The first mention of the Rapture (the translation of believers) is found in these wonderful words that fell from the lips of Jesus the night before He was crucified. He had told His disciples that He would go to Jerusalem where He would be arrested, tried, condemned, and crucified. Then He reassured their troubled hearts with the promise to return for them and take them to the place He would prepare for them.

What an outstanding revelation this must have been to the disciples! They were expecting Christ to establish His kingdom on earth, occupy the throne of David, and deliver Israel from the tyranny of Rome. In their study of the Old Testament prophecies they did not separate His first and second comings. They did not see the crown of thorns before the crown of glory, nor the cross before the throne. They anticipated that Christ would at His first advent set up His kingdom, free Israel from their oppressors, and bring in the glorious period of righteousness and peace on earth spoken of so many times in the Old Testament Scriptures.

Today we know that there is a long, unmeasured period between the first and second comings of Christ, but the Old Testament did not reveal this period of grace, the Church Age. The disciples did not understand that the *second* coming—not the first—would introduce the millennial kingdom; and because they did not understand the difference between the first and second comings they could not understand His words of promise to return and take them to heaven. They expected to stay right here on earth and share the glorious kingdom described in the Old Testament Scriptures.

Please notice in this first mention of the translation of believers Jesus made it clear that He was going to *the Father's house* where there were already "many mansions," but He would *prepare* a place for those for whom He would return. He is in heaven now.

He has been there since He ascended from the Mount of Olives nearly two thousand years ago, and He will descend into the air to call believers up to meet Him before He returns to this earth to set up His kingdom.

Even after Christ's resurrection the disciples still expected Him to set up the kingdom and reign from the throne of David. Acts 1:3 tells us that Jesus, *the risen Lord,* "shewed Himself alive after His passion by many infallible proofs, being seen of (the disciples) forty days, and speaking of the things pertaining to the kingdom of God." He then instructed them to remain in Jerusalem until they should be "baptized with the Holy Ghost not many days hence" (Acts 1:5). It was then that they asked Him, "Lord, wilt thou *at this time RESTORE AGAIN THE KINGDOM TO ISRAEL?*" He answered them, "It is not for you to know the times or the seasons, which the Father hath put in His own power" (Acts 1:6, 7). So you see the disciples never fully understood, even after the resurrection of Jesus, that He would not set up an earthly kingdom until His *second coming.*

It is extremely important for us to understand that according to the words of Jesus believers will go to heaven *to be with Him* when He comes in the Rapture, and then when He comes to set up the kingdom believers will come with Him *from heaven* and will reign with Him during the Millennium. So if the purpose of Christ's coming is to take believers from earth to heaven, it would certainly be foolish to say that He will *come for the saints* on His way to earth to establish His millennial kingdom! The two events are assuredly and decidedly different. He will come *for* the saints in the Rapture, and He will come *with* the saints in the Revelation to set up the kingdom on earth.   The two phases of the second coming are approximately seven years apart.

I Corinthians 15:51, 52 is another important Scripture which has to do with the translation before the tribulation:

"Behold, I shew you a mystery: We shall not all sleep, but we shall all be changed, in a moment, in the twinkling of an eye, at the last trump: for the trumpet shall sound, and the dead shall be raised incorruptible, and we shall be changed."

Please study all of this fifteenth chapter of I Corinthians in connection with the two verses I have given you here.   In the first part of the chapter Paul gives the definition of the Gospel by which we are saved— the death, burial, and resurrection of Jesus "according to the Scriptures."   He points out that Christ was seen by many witnesses after His resurrection, including more than five hundred brethren who saw Him at one time.   The doctrine of the bodily resurrection is proclaimed as definitely essential to saving faith, for if Christ did *not* rise from the dead our *faith* is vain, our *preaching* is vain, *and we have no hope!*

Paul then explains *the divine necessity* of the bodily resurrection.   Our mortal bodies are not suited to heaven or eternity.   We must *die,* or we must be *changed,* for flesh and blood cannot inherit heaven. Having established this pattern of death and resurrection as normal and necessary, Paul declares one exception—at the last trumpet, when the dead in Christ will be raised and living saints will be translated into their glorified bodies without experiencing death. This will occur "in a moment, in the twinkling of an eye . . . for the trumpet shall sound, and the dead shall be raised incorruptible, and we shall be changed."

This clear, concise, understandable statement is one of the positive proofs of a pre-tribulation Rapture. It also shows that there *must* be a period of time between Christ's coming for His Church and His coming to establish His kingdom on earth, for after the Church is taken out of the world there must be an entire generation of righteous people raised up to populate the millennial earth.

Scriptural proof for this is found in Isaiah 65:20-25:

"There shall be no more thence an infant of days, nor an old man that hath not filled his days: for the child shall die an hundred years old; but the sinner being an hundred years old shall be accursed. And they shall build houses, and inhabit them; and they shall plant vineyards, and eat the fruit of them. They shall not build, and another inhabit; they shall not plant, and another eat: for as the days of a tree are the days of my people, and mine elect shall long enjoy the work of their hands. They shall not labour in vain, nor bring forth for trouble; for they are the seed of the blessed of the Lord, and their offspring with them. And it shall come to pass, that before they call, I will answer; and while they are yet speaking, I will hear. The wolf and the lamb shall feed together, and the lion shall eat straw like the bullock: and dust shall be the serpent's meat. They shall not hurt nor destroy in all my holy mountain, saith the Lord."

In the first part of that chapter the Prophet Isaiah discusses the new heaven and the new earth; then beginning with verse 20 he discusses the millennial earth.   These statements certainly could not be made about people in resurrection bodies nor about people who have been translated into heavenly or spiritual bodies.   In the millennial earth people will live in their *natural bodies,* they will enter the Millennium in their natural bodies, and they will live out *their span of life* in their natural bodies.

We find a similar statement in Zechariah 8:5: "The streets of the city shall be full of boys and girls playing in the streets thereof."   This will occur during the Millennium.   Children will be born during that time, and parents who, through the tribulation period, refuse to receive the mark of the beast will enter the kingdom when the Lord Jesus divides the "sheep" from the "goats."

Post-millennialists and others try to discredit the pre-millennial view of the second coming on the basis of I Corinthians 15:52 where reference is made to "the last trump," but this last trump of God has no relation whatsoever to the trumpets that sound in Revelation.   The trumpet in I Corinthians 15:52 calls the sleeping bodies of the saints to come forth from the grave and announces the translation of living saints, whereas the trumpets in Revelation have to do with the judgment of unbelievers and are described in a totally different context.   There are many trumpets in Scripture, and it is foolish to put them all together and try to prove that all trumpets mean the same thing. "The last trump" concludes the Church Age, but has nothing to do with the trumpets of judgment in Revelation. The time when the dead in Christ are raised and living saints are caught up will be a time of victory—the blessed hope and the glorious appearing of Jesus; it will not be a time of judgment and suffering.

I suppose the most important Scripture concerning the Rapture before the Revelation is found in Paul's letter to the believers in Thessalonica. These were new Christians, young in the faith, and while they had been instructed in prophetic truth, they did not fully understand about their loved ones who had died in the Lord. Therefore Paul gave them clear, understandable instruction, assuring them that they should not be sorrowful as were others who had no hope. They believed that Jesus was coming for them before the time of trouble and suffering, but they were concerned about their loved ones who had departed this life. Therefore Paul assured them that their loved ones would be raised from the dead even before the living saints were changed, and together they would be caught up to meet Jesus in the clouds.

"For the Lord Himself shall descend from heaven with a shout, with the voice of the archangel, and with the trump of God: and *the dead in Christ shall rise FIRST.* Then we which are alive and remain shall be caught up together with them in the clouds, to meet the Lord in the air; *and so shall we ever be with the Lord. WHEREFORE COMFORT ONE ANOTHER WITH THESE WORDS*" (I Thess. 4:16-18).

These words bring comfort that no other doctrine in the Word of God can bring! I ask you: *What comfort* would the message of the second coming bring if Jesus were not coming until after the tribulation? If we must go through the horrible time described in the Word of God as "the time of Jacob's trouble" how could Paul say, *"COMFORT one another with these words"*?

In I Thessalonians 5:1-11 Paul continues his message to the Christians at Thessalonica, and in verses 1 and 2 we read: "Of the times and the seasons, brethren, ye have no need that I write unto you. For yourselves know perfectly that the day of the Lord so cometh as a thief in the night."

Bible scholars have differences of opinion concerning this passage. Some say that "the day of the Lord" will begin with the thousand-year reign of Christ, and others believe that "the day of the Lord" will begin immediately after the Rapture of the Church. Personally, I believe that when the Day of Grace *climaxes,* "the day of the Lord" will *begin.*

The *day of the Lord* includes the second coming— that is, the tribulation and the Millennium up to "the day of God" which begins at the close of the Millennium. Today we are in the Day of Grace. The Day of Grace has been *since Pentecost* and it will end when Jesus comes for His Church in the Rapture, because the Holy Spirit will be taken out with the Church.

This does not mean that grace will terminate completely when Jesus comes for the Church. It simply means that the *DAY of Grace* will terminate, the day when grace is supremely revealed and manifested as it has been revealed and manifested since the Day of Pentecost. As soon as this Day of Grace comes to a climax, "the day of the Lord" will begin, when God will punish sin and pour out horrible judgment on the wicked and ungodly.

Then at the climax of the tribulation, Jesus will come and destroy Antichrist. The beast and the false prophet will be put in the pit, and in the Battle of Armageddon the wicked will be destroyed from the face of the earth and their spirits will plunge into hellfire. Then the Millennium will begin; and for one thousand years Christ will exercise absolute and supreme rule over the entire earth.

When the Millennium ends, the new heaven and the new earth will begin. Then will be the fulfillment of the day Peter speaks of: "Looking for and hasting unto the coming of the day of God, wherein the heavens being on fire shall be dissolved, and the elements shall melt with fervent heat. Nevertheless we, according to His promise, look for new heavens and a new earth, wherein dwelleth righteousness" (II Pet. 3:12, 13).

"The day of God" is another expression for eternity —the eternity of eternities which will begin when time is no more.

So in the Word of God we see three periods: the Day of Grace (which has been running its course since the Day of Pentecost and will continue until the Rapture); the day of the Lord (which will begin at the Rapture and continue through the Millennium); and at the close of the Millennium will be the day of God

—the *eternal day.*

The Thessalonian believers wanted to know when they would see their departed loved ones again, when they would be raised. In the discussion, Paul turns from the Rapture to the day of the Lord without any break whatsoever. Why? Simply because the Rapture brings the Day of Grace to a climax and ushers in the day of the Lord.

In the strict sense of Bible prophecy there are no signs pointing to the Rapture of the Church. The signs point to the time when Jesus will come to set up His kingdom. The coming of Christ to begin His rule over the earth is preceded by *many* signs. Matthew chapter 24 lists many of them, and many, many other signs are given in Revelation chapters 4 through 19. But *the Rapture* will be "as a thief in the night."

Those who hold to the belief that the Church will go through the tribulation teach that believers will not feel the wrath of God during that time as sinners will feel it. This would be impossible, because God's wrath and judgments which will be poured out on this earth could not be poured out without Christians feeling the horror, pain, and misery of those judgments. There will be wars, famines, earthquakes, and all kinds of supernatural destruction and judgment; and when those terrible judgments of destruction are poured out upon this world they will certainly not be poured out on a specific class of people, but on *the inhabitants of the earth.* The very nature of the wrath of God in the tribulation teaches that none will escape.

Tens of thousands will be put to death because

they refuse to worship the beast and receive his mark. If any survive they will do so by hiding in the mountains and caves, living from the streams and fields. Most of those who refuse to worship the beast and receive his mark will be killed. But believers are not appointed unto wrath, therefore they need not *fear* the day of wrath. When the horrible tribulation period breaks out upon this earth under the reign of Antichrist, the Church will be at rest with Jesus in the clouds in the air.

What comfort to know that we are not appointed to wrath. We are not looking for Antichrist, but for THE Christ! We are not looking for the tribulation, but for the Rapture. We are not looking for a day of darkness, but for that blessed hope and the glorious appearing of our great God and our Saviour, Jesus Christ. I say with John the Beloved, "Even so, Come, Lord Jesus!"

Chapter VI

The Person of the Antichrist

"I am come in my Father's name, and ye receive me not: if another shall come in his own name, him ye will receive" (John 5:43).

"Now we beseech you, brethren, by the coming of our Lord Jesus Christ, and by our gathering together unto Him, that ye be not soon shaken in mind, or be troubled, neither by spirit, nor by word, nor by letter as from us, as that the day of Christ is at hand. Let no man deceive you by any means: for that day shall not come, except there come a falling away first, and that man of sin be revealed, the son of perdition; who opposeth and exalteth himself above all that is called God, or that is worshipped; so that he as God sitteth in the temple of God, shewing himself that he is God.

"Remember ye not, that, when I was yet with you, I told you these things? And now ye know what withholdeth that he might be revealed in his time. For the mystery of iniquity doth already work: only He who now letteth will let, until He be taken out of the way. And then shall that Wicked be revealed, whom the Lord shall consume with the spirit of His mouth, and shall destroy with the brightness of His coming: even him, whose coming is after the working of Satan with all power and signs and lying wonders, and with all deceivableness of unrighteousness in them that perish; because they received not the love of the truth, that they might be saved. And for this cause God shall send them strong delusion, that they should believe a lie: that they all might be damned who believed not the truth, but had pleasure in unrighteousness" (II Thess. 2:1-12).

The ultimate goal of Christianity is the Lord Jesus Christ, God's only Son. The end of Christendom is the false messiah, the Antichrist. He will be *a person* just as truly as the Lord Jesus Christ is a Person. He will be the son of the devil (the devil incarnate) just as Jesus is the Son of God (God incarnate).

The Bible teaches clearly that the *goal* of history is not the *product* of history. The kingdom of God does not reach its ultimate through gradual growth, but through world-wide collapse and catastrophe under the rule of Antichrist. He will be the last world dictator.

According to the Word of God this world is not going to get better. In Matthew 24:12 we read, "Because *iniquity shall abound,* the love of many shall wax cold." Paul warns us, "Evil men and seducers shall wax *worse and worse,* deceiving, and being deceived" (II Tim. 3:13). So we see that lawlessness will take the upper hand, evil men and seducers will wax worse and worse, and instead of world conditions becoming better they will go from bad to worse!

In Luke 18:8 Jesus asked, "When the Son of man cometh, shall He find faith on the earth?" He also testified that just before His return to this earth the days of Noah will be repeated: "As the days of Noe were, so shall also the coming of the Son of man be. For as in the days that were before the flood they were eating and drinking, marrying and giving in marriage, until the day that Noe entered into the ark, and knew not until the flood came, and took them all away; so shall also the coming of the Son of man be" (Matt. 24:37-39).

In Noah's day only eight souls were saved from the flood. If you will do a little comparative checking percentage-wise I think you will agree that we have almost reached that point today. When you count the real, born again, God-fearing, spiritually minded Christians in your neighborhood I think you will find the percentage is almost as low as that of the days of Noah.

Jesus also said, "As it was in the days of *Lot*—they did eat, they drank, they bought, they sold, they planted, they builded; but the same day that Lot went out of Sodom it rained fire and brimstone from heaven, and destroyed them all. Even thus shall it be in the day when the Son of man is revealed" (Luke 17:28-30). If you will read the account of the destruction of Sodom as recorded in Genesis chapter 19 you will see that *only three people*—Lot and his two daughters—escaped the fate of that wicked city!

They teach error who say that the world will grow better and better until finally the preaching of the Gospel will convert the world and bring in the kingdom. They are wrongly dividing the Word of Truth. The Church was not put here to convert the world, but *to call out a people for Jesus' name;* and that is what the Church has been doing for almost two thousand years!

The Word of God does not teach that the Gospel will Christianize the world with the result of the entire civilization being saved. On the contrary the Word teaches that *as the end of time approaches* there will be increasing enmity toward God to the point that civilization will *totally reject* Christianity and the old-time grace of God! Christ has not delayed His coming because the world is not yet *good* enough or *spiritual* enough for His return, but because the world has not yet reached that final point of unbelief and wickedness. The following Scriptures prove this to be true:

"This know also, that in the last days perilous times shall come. For men shall be lovers of their own selves, covetous, boasters, proud, blasphemers, disobedient to parents, unthankful, unholy, without natural affection, trucebreakers, false accusers, incontinent, fierce, despisers of those that are good, traitors, heady, highminded, lovers of pleasures more than lovers of God" (II Tim. 3:1-4).

"For the time will come when they will not endure sound doctrine; but after their own lusts shall they heap to themselves teachers, having itching ears; and they shall turn away their ears from the truth, and shall be turned unto fables" (II Tim. 4:3, 4).

". . . there shall come in the last days scoffers, walking after their own lusts, and saying, Where is the promise of His coming? for since the fathers fell asleep, all things continue as they were from the beginning of the creation" (II Pet. 3:3, 4).

"Now the Spirit speaketh expressly, that in the latter times some shall depart from the faith, giving heed to seducing spirits, and doctrines of devils; speaking lies in hypocrisy; having their conscience seared with a hot iron; forbidding to marry, and commanding to abstain from meats, which God hath created to be received with thanksgiving of them which believe and know the truth" (I Tim. 4:1-3).

As we study the Word of God we discover a basic principle of divine government, and that basic principle is that all things—the good and the evil—must climax (or reach fulness), and this will lead to more horrible, more severe judgment. In Matthew 13:30, speaking of the tares growing with the wheat, Jesus said, "Let both grow together until the harvest: and in the time of harvest I will say to the reapers, Gather ye together first the tares, and bind them in bundles to burn them: but gather the wheat into my barn."

Then in Revelation 14:15-18 we read, "Another angel came out of the temple, crying with a loud voice to Him that sat on the cloud, Thrust in thy sickle, and reap: for the time is come for thee to reap; for the harvest of the earth is ripe. And He that sat on the cloud thrust in His sickle on the earth; and the earth was reaped. And another angel came out of the temple which is in heaven, he also having a sharp sickle. And another angel came out from the altar, which had power over fire; and cried with a loud cry to him that had the sharp sickle, saying, Thrust in thy sharp sickle, and gather the clusters of the vine of the earth; for her grapes are fully ripe."

In our text for this discussion Paul said, "Let no man deceive you by any means: for that day shall not come, except there come a falling away first, and that man of sin be revealed, the son of perdition; who opposeth and exalteth himself above all that is called God, or that is worshipped; so that he as God sitteth in the temple of God, shewing himself that he is God. . . . And then shall that Wicked be revealed, whom the Lord shall consume with the spirit of His mouth, and shall destroy with the brightness of His coming" (II Thess. 2:3, 4, 8).

The Lord Jesus will win the victory. He will triumph over evil. It may seem that the devil is winning the battle today, and that Christianity is on the losing side—but not so! Remember, it is not by *reconciliation* but by *intensifying* the conflict between good and evil that the victory will be brought about; not by the *glorification* of human development but by its *collapse.* It is true that we have more means of spreading the Gospel today than at any other time since God created Adam. It is equally true that *the mind of man* has developed to a degree never before known in the history of the human race. But man is *glorifying himself,* and the Bible emphatically declares that the wisdom of man is foolishness to God (I Cor. 3:19).

Therefore the ultimate victory will not be when God makes an agreement with civilization, but when God shatters civilization by shattering the kingdoms of the world. The Stone of Daniel 2:34, 35 will crush the wicked kingdoms of earth when Jesus comes to set up His kingdom: Daniel saw "a Stone . . . cut out without hands, which smote the image upon his feet that were of iron and clay, and brake them to pieces. Then was the iron, the clay, the brass, the silver, and the gold, broken to pieces together, and became like the chaff of the summer threshingfloors; and the wind carried them away, that no place was found for them: and the Stone that smote the image became a great mountain, and filled the whole earth!"

In Revelation 19:11-21 John the Beloved wrote: "I saw heaven opened, and behold a white horse; and He that sat upon him was called Faithful and True, and in righteousness He doth judge and make war. His eyes were as a flame of fire, and on His head were many crowns; and He had a name written that no man knew, but He Himself. And He was clothed with a vesture dipped in blood: and His name is called The Word of God.

"And the armies which were in heaven followed Him upon white horses, clothed in fine linen, white and clean. And out of His mouth goeth a sharp sword, that with it He should smite the nations: and He shall rule them with a rod of iron: and He treadeth the winepress of the fierceness and wrath of Almighty God. And He hath on His vesture and on His thigh a name written, KING OF KINGS, AND LORD OF LORDS.

"And I saw an angel standing in the sun; and he cried with a loud voice, saying to all the fowls that fly in the midst of heaven, Come and gather yourselves together unto the supper of the great God; that ye may eat the flesh of kings, and the flesh of captains, and the flesh of mighty men, and the flesh of horses, and of them that sit on them, and the flesh of all men, both free and bond, both small and great.

"And I saw the beast, and the kings of the earth, and their armies, gathered together to make war against

Him that sat on the horse, and against His army. And
the beast was taken, and with him the false prophet
that wrought miracles before him, with which he deceived them that had received the mark of the beast,
and them that worshipped his image. These both
were cast alive into a lake of fire burning with brimstone. And the remnant were slain with the sword of
Him that sat upon the horse, which sword proceeded
out of His mouth: and all the fowls were filled with
their flesh."

Let us face a fact that becomes clear as we study
the Scriptures—and then *look around us* today: Under
the leadership of the mighty Nimrod, man decided to
build a tower to heaven; but God thrust down the
tower and scattered the people abroad "upon the face
of all the earth" (Gen. 11:1-9). Today man is again
attempting to invade God's heaven—not by way of
the cross, but by the wisdom of man; and Revelation
chapter 18 gives the record of the end of the civilization that is ruling today in religion and world affairs.
The heights of heaven are not to be reached through
the wisdom of man, and one day God will destroy the
mighty "tower" that is being constructed today, just
as He destroyed Nimrod's tower.

Man today is searching for a *superman,* a political
leader who can bring about world peace and the great
Utopia about which men have talked and dreamed for
centuries. According to the testimony of the Word of
God, after the Rapture occurs and all believers are
taken out of this earth, a leader *will* come on the
scene and will head up a system of civilization which
will seem to fulfill the longing that has been in the

heart of man through the ages. This mighty ruler will be a genius for world-wide organization. He is described in Revelation 13:1-10:

"And I stood upon the sand of the sea, and saw a beast rise up out of the sea, having seven heads and ten horns, and upon his horns ten crowns, and upon his heads the name of blasphemy. And the beast which I saw was like unto a leopard, and his feet were as the feet of a bear, and his mouth as the mouth of a lion: and the dragon gave him his power, and his seat, and great authority. And I saw one of his heads as it were wounded to death; and his deadly wound was healed: and all the world wondered after the beast. And they worshipped the dragon which gave power unto the beast: and they worshipped the beast, saying, Who is like unto the beast? Who is able to make war with him?

"And there was given unto him a mouth speaking great things and blasphemies; and power was given unto him to continue forty and two months. And he opened his mouth in blasphemy against God, to blaspheme His name, and His tabernacle, and them that dwell in heaven. And it was given unto him to make war with the saints, and to overcome them: and power was given him over all kindreds, and tongues, and nations. And all that dwell upon the earth shall worship him, whose names are not written in the book of life of the Lamb slain from the foundation of the world.

"If any man have an ear, let him hear. He that leadeth into captivity shall go into captivity: he that killeth with the sword must be killed with the sword.

Here is the patience and the faith of the saints."

Revelation 6:1, 2 speaks of the Antichrist (identical with the beast of Revelation 13:11-18): "I saw when the Lamb opened one of the seals, and I heard, as it were the noise of thunder, one of the four beasts saying, Come and see. And I saw, and behold a white horse: *and he that sat on him had a bow; and a crown was given unto him: and he went forth conquering, and to conquer.*"

These verses have often been interpreted as applying to Christ, but this is error. *The Christ* is seen in Revelation 19:11-16, and the *Antichrist* is counterfeit—*a copy* of the true Christ. Therefore he, too, will ride a white horse—and you will notice he will come on the scene offering peace, for he "had *a bow*" but no arrows. A crown will be given to him and he will conquer *without bloodshed.* He will then counsel the nations and for a season it will *seem* that world peace has become a reality.

This ruler will have power to inflame men with enthusiasm and, announcing that he is God, he will go forth and by diplomacy he will bring about unity; but the peace and unity he brings will be counterfeit and false. This superhuman personality will be none other than the devil incarnate—the master deceiver, the father of lies; and in the middle of the tribulation period the counterfeit peace will come to an abrupt end and all hell will break loose on earth. The red horse of war, the pale horse of famine, and the black horse of death will come on the scene and so horrible will be the slaughter and destruction that without the overruling of Almighty God there would be no life left on earth! But for Israel's sake God will intervene and will cut short the reign of Antichrist.

When this false messiah sits in the temple announcing that he is God, men will actually worship him *as God*. They will build a magnificent image in his honor, and with his supernatural power he will make the image talk. But the sovereign God of heaven and earth will not allow such blasphemy to go on. Jeremiah declared, *"Thus saith the Lord:* Cursed be the man that trusteth in man, and maketh flesh his arm, and whose heart departeth from the Lord" (Jer. 17:5).

Jehovah God will not give His honor to another, nor will He give His praise to dust-begotten rebels. In Isaiah 42:8 we read, "I am the LORD: that is my name: and my glory will I not give to another, neither my praise to graven images." In answer to the challenge of the Antichrist, God will send His Son back to this earth (Acts 3:20, 21), and God's Christ will destroy the Antichrist "with the spirit of His mouth, and . . . with the brightness of His coming" (II Thess. 2:8). He will come "in flaming fire taking vengeance on them that know not God, and that obey not the Gospel of our Lord Jesus Christ" (II Thess. 1:8).

In these Scriptures we see the closing of the civilization that will reach its zenith under the leadership of the devil incarnate. The *summit of civilization* will become the closing drama of history, and in the red sunset of blood we will see the judgment of Almighty God poured out upon the Antichrist and all who choose to follow him. As the hand of God wrote on Belshazzar's palace wall, "Thou art weighed in the balances, and art found wanting" (Dan. 5:27), so it is

written over civilization today! We are headed for a
judgment such as this world has never known!

Contrast: The Christ — The Antichrist

I think it would be most helpful and extremely interesting to note the contrasts between God's Christ
and the Antichrist as given in various portions of God's
Word:

God's Christ "came down *from heaven*" (John 6:38).
The Antichrist will ascend "out of *the bottomless pit*"
(Rev. 11:7).

The true Christ came *in His "Father's name"* (John
5:43).   Antichrist will "come *in his own name*" (also
John 5:43).

The Christ, Son of the sovereign God, "*humbled*
Himself, and became obedient unto death, even the
death of the cross" (Phil. 2:8).   Antichrist, son of the
devil, will *exalt himself* "above all that is called God,
or that is worshipped . . ." (II Thess. 2:4).

The Christ was "despised and rejected of men"
(Isa. 53:3, also Luke 23:18).   Antichrist will be admired,
wondered after, and worshipped (Rev. 13:13, 14).

The Christ came into the world to do His Father's
will (John 6:38).   Antichrist will do *his OWN will*, he
will exalt and magnify himself (Dan. 11:36).

The Christ came "*to seek and to save* that which
was lost" (Luke 19:10).   Antichrist will come to destroy, "and he shall destroy wonderfully, and shall
prosper, and practise, and shall destroy the mighty and
the holy people" (Dan. 8:24).

The Christ is "the Good Shepherd," and "the Good
Shepherd giveth His life for the sheep" (John 10:11).

The Antichrist will be "the idol shepherd that leaveth the flock." He will not "seek the young one, nor heal that that is broken, nor feed that that standeth still: but he shall eat the flesh of the fat, and tear their claws in pieces" (Zech. 11:16, 17).

The Christ is "the true vine," and God the Father is the husbandman (John 15:1). Antichrist will be "the vine of the earth" (Rev. 14:18, 19).

The Christ is "the Truth," the Truth that makes men free (John 14:6; 8:32). Antichrist will be "the Lie" (II Thess. 2:11). ". . . there is no truth in him. When he speaketh a lie, he speaketh of his own: for he is a liar, and the father of it" (John 8:44).

Christ is "the Holy One of God" (Mark 1:24). Antichrist will be "that Wicked," the lawless one (II Thess. 2:8).

Christ was the sinless One. He was "without sin" (Heb. 4:15), He "knew no sin" (II Cor. 5:21). Antichrist will be *the "man of sin"* (II Thess. 2:3).

The Christ, virgin-born, is the only begotten Son of God (Luke 1:35). Antichrist will be "the son of perdition," the son of the devil (II Thess. 2:3).

The Christ, conceived of the Holy Ghost and born of the Virgin Mary, is "the mystery of godliness: God was manifest in the flesh, justified in the Spirit, seen of angels, preached unto the Gentiles, believed on in the world, received up into glory" (I Tim. 3:16). Antichrist will be "the mystery of iniquity"—Satan manifest in the flesh (II Thess. 2:7).

The Christ, only begotten Son of God, has been exalted and given "a name which is above every name: that at the name of Jesus every knee should bow, of

things in heaven, and things in earth, and things under
the earth; and that every tongue should confess that
Jesus Christ is Lord, to the glory of God the Father"
(Phil. 2:9-11).   Antichrist, son of perdition, will "be
brought down to hell, to the sides of the pit" (Isa.
14:15).   He will be "cast alive into a lake of fire burning with brimstone" (Rev. 19:20).

Names of the Antichrist

The title "Antichrist" is found only in the writings
of John. We find it used five times in his epistles. He
speaks of the *person* of Antichrist—that is, "Ye have
heard that *Antichrist* shall come" (I John 2:18). This
is the same person referred to by Paul as "the man of
sin . . . the son of perdition . . . that Wicked."   He is
also the person of whom Daniel speaks as "the little
horn . . . the king of fierce countenance" (Dan. 7:8;
8:23), and he is the "beast" of Revelation chapter
13:11-18.   This Antichrist will be the last world dictator.

But John also speaks of "antichrists" (plural).   In
I John 2:18 he says "even now are there *many* antichrists."   In I John 4:3 he speaks of *the "spirit* of
Antichrist."   There have been antichrists in the world
ever since the days of the apostles, and they will remain until the Church is taken out. The *spirit* of Antichrist is at work in the world today.   But after the
Rapture THE Antichrist, the Man of Sin, will appear.

Antichrist Will Be a Personality

Some people teach that the Antichrist will be a
"system."   It is true that he will be the *head* of a

system, but he will also be *a person,* a world dictator. As an individual he will be the personal head of world government and he will give power to the world political leaders. He will also be the head of the world system of religion, the leaders of a human revolt against Almighty God.

The *spirit* of Antichrist is present in the world today, but as the complete exhibition of the closing history of man, Antichrist will appear in a body just as God's Christ appeared in a body. The universality of the spirit of Antichrist certainly does not exclude the fact of the individual, and the fact of the individual Antichrist does not exclude the spirit (or movement) of Antichrist. Jesus Himself declared to the Jews, "I am come in my Father's name, and ye receive me not. If *another* shall come in *his own name,* him ye will receive" (John 5:43). Here, *"I AM"* speaks of God's Messiah, the Christ. *"Another"* speaks of the *devil's* messiah, the Antichrist—and he will be an individual just as Christ is an individual.

Mark 13:14 offers further proof that Antichrist will be *a person:* "When ye shall see the *abomination of desolation,* spoken of by Daniel the prophet, standing where it ought not . . . then let them that be in Judaea flee to the mountains." The *"abomination of desolation"* is definitely and plainly connected with the anti-Christian period which follows immediately after the Rapture of the Church. Authorities on the Greek language tell us the striking fact that the Greek noun here translated *"abomination"* is of the neuter gender, while its dependent participle (*"standing"*) is of the masculine gender. This proves that "the abomination of desolation" is not an image made of stone or metal, but *a person,* standing in the holy temple of Almighty God and profaning the sanctuary by his presence. Paul verifies the fact that this will come to pass when the Man of Sin stands in the holy place announcing that he is God and demanding divine worship for himself (II Thess. 2:3, 4).

II Thessalonians 2:9 also tells us that the Antichrist will be a person, for Paul speaks of him as "him whose coming is after the working of Satan with all power and signs and lying wonders." Here we see that the Antichrist as an individual will have *his* coming, just as *Jesus* as an individual will come in the Rapture. Christ came—and will come again—*bodily.* So will the Antichrist come in person as a man, and he will be visibly revealed (II Thess. 2:8), just as God's Christ will be revealed when every eye shall see Him and all the kindreds of the earth shall wail because of Him (Rev. 1:7).

Prophecies Concerning the Coming of Antichrist

Isaiah 11:4: "With righteousness shall (Christ) judge the poor, and reprove with equity for the meek of the earth: and He shall smite the earth with the rod of His mouth, and *with the breath of His lips shall He slay the WICKED.*"

The Hebrew word here translated *"wicked"* is in the singular, therefore it could not refer to wicked persons in general nor to the wicked who will be destroyed everlastingly in the lake of fire. It must, then, refer to a *person,* someone who is unusual and outstanding. We note that Isaiah's expression strikingly resembles the inspired words of the Apostle Paul in II Thessalonians 2:8—"then shall *THAT WICKED* be revealed, whom the Lord shall consume *with the spirit of His mouth,* and shall destroy with the brightness of His coming."

We know that the same Spirit who spoke to Isaiah and inspired him to pen the book of prophecy that bears his name also spoke to the Apostle Paul. Thus Isaiah and Paul, centuries apart, wrote of *the same person*—the Antichrist, the devil incarnate. So among other things that God's Christ will do, He will slay "THE WICKED."

Daniel 7:1-7—(the beast vision of Daniel): "In the first year of Belshazzar king of Babylon Daniel had a dream and visions of his head upon his bed: then he wrote the dream, and told the sum of the matters. Daniel spake and said, I saw in my vision by night, and, behold, the four winds of the heaven strove upon the great sea. And four great beasts came up from the sea, diverse one from another."

(The world-empire of Nebuchadnezzar): "The first was like a lion, and had eagle's wings: I beheld till the wings thereof were plucked, and it was lifted up from the earth, and made stand upon the feet as a man, and a man's heart was given to it."

(The world-empire of Media-Persia): "And behold another beast, a second, like to a bear, and it raised up itself on one side, and it had three ribs in the mouth of it between the teeth of it: and they said thus unto it, Arise, devour much flesh."

(The world-empire of Greece under Alexander): "After this I beheld, and lo another, like a leopard, which had upon the back of it four wings of a fowl; the beast had also four heads; and dominion was given to it."

(The Roman world-empire): "After this I saw in the night visions, and behold a fourth beast, dreadful and terrible, and strong exceedingly; and it had great iron teeth. It devoured and brake in pieces, and stamped the residue with the feet of it: and it was diverse from all the beasts that were before it; and it had ten horns."

The vision God gave Daniel was the vision of the end of the Gentile world. We note here that the fourth beast (the iron kingdom of Daniel 2) will have ten horns, each horn representing a king. So there will be ten kings: "And the ten horns which thou sawest are ten kings, which have received no kingdom as yet; but receive power as kings one hour with the beast" (Rev. 17:12).

These ten kings correspond to the ten toes of the great image in Daniel 2, the part of the image that represents the Gentile world; and among the ten horns which represent ten kings a "little horn" rises. The little horn represents a king, and this king so completely subdues three of the ten kings that the separate identity of their kingdoms is totally destroyed.

The "little horn" is "the king of fierce countenance" typified by that other king of fierce countenance, Antiochus Epiphanes (Dan. 8:23-25). The "little horn" also typifies "the prince that shall come" (Dan. 9:26, 27), and *"the king"* who shall do *"according to his will,"* the king who will *"exalt and magnify himself above every god."* (Please read Daniel 11:36-45.)

The "little horn" also typifies "the abomination" of Daniel 12:11 and Matthew 24:15, "the man of sin" of II Thessalonians 2:3, 4, and the beast of Revelation 13:11-18. These personalities are one and the same person.

The "little horn" of Daniel 7:8 had "eyes like the eyes of a man, and *a mouth speaking GREAT THINGS.*" Daniel was told that this little horn was a king who would arise—an unusual, extraordinary person of remarkable intelligence and possessing great powers. He would have the gift of oratory—his mouth would speak great things. He would also be audacious, arrogant, proud, he would seek to change "times and laws," and God's people (Israel) were to be "given into his hand until a time and times and the dividing of time"—which means three and one-half years. This is clearly set forth in Daniel 7:23-26:

". . . The fourth beast shall be the fourth kingdom upon earth, which shall be diverse from all kingdoms, and shall devour the whole earth, and shall tread it down, and break it in pieces. And the ten horns out of this kingdom are ten kings that shall arise: and another shall rise after them; and he shall be diverse from the first, and he shall subdue three kings. And he shall speak great words against the most High, and shall wear out the saints of the most High, and think to change times and laws: and they shall be given into his hand until a time and times and the dividing of time. But the judgment shall sit, and they shall take away his dominion, to consume and to destroy it unto the end."

Later, God gave Daniel another vision in which he

saw a ram and a he-goat contesting for supremacy:

"In the third year of the reign of king Belshazzar a
vision appeared unto me, even unto me Daniel, after
that which appeared unto me at the first. And I saw
in a vision; and it came to pass, when I saw, that I
was at Shushan in the palace, which is in the province
of Elam; and I saw in a vision, and I was by the
river of Ulai.

"Then I lifted up mine eyes, and saw, and, behold,
there stood before the river a ram which had two
horns: and the two horns were high; but one was
higher than the other, and the higher came up last. I
saw the ram pushing westward, and northward, and
southward; so that no beasts might stand before him,
neither was there any that could deliver out of his
hand; but he did according to his will, and became
great.

"And as I was considering, behold, an he goat came
from the west on the face of the whole earth, and
touched not the ground: and the goat had a notable
horn between his eyes. And he came to the ram that
had two horns, which I had seen standing before the
river, and ran unto him in the fury of his power. And
I saw him come close unto the ram, and he was moved
with choler against him, and smote the ram, and
brake his two horns: and there was no power in the
ram to stand before him, but he cast him down to the
ground, and stamped upon him: and there was none
that could deliver the ram out of his hand.

"Therefore the he goat waxed very great: and when
he was strong, the great horn was broken; and for it
came up four notable ones toward the four winds of

heaven. And out of one of them came forth a little horn, which waxed exceeding great, toward the south, and toward the east, and toward the pleasant land. And it waxed great, even to the host of heaven; and it cast down some of the host and of the stars to the ground, and stamped upon them.

"Yea, he magnified himself even to the prince of the host, and by him the daily sacrifice was taken away, and the place of his sanctuary was cast down. And an host was given him against the daily sacrifice by reason of transgression, and it cast down the truth to the ground; and it practised, and prospered.

"Then I heard one saint speaking, and another saint said unto that certain saint which spake, How long shall be the vision concerning the daily sacrifice, and the transgression of desolation, to give both the sanctuary and the host to be trodden under foot? And he said unto me, Unto two thousand and three hundred days; then shall the sanctuary be cleansed.

"And it came to pass, when I, even I Daniel, had seen the vision, and sought for the meaning, then, behold, there stood before me as the appearance of a man. And I heard a man's voice between the banks of Ulai, which called, and said, Gabriel, make this man to understand the vision. So he came near where I stood: and when he came, I was afraid, and fell upon my face: but he said unto me, Understand, O son of man: for at the time of the end shall be the vision.

"Now as he was speaking with me, I was in a deep sleep on my face toward the ground: but he touched me, and set me upright. And he said, Behold, I will

make thee know what shall be in the last end of the
indignation: for at the time appointed the end shall
be.   The ram which thou sawest having two horns are
the kings of Media and Persia. And the rough goat is
the king of Grecia: and the great horn that is between
his eyes is the first king.

"Now that being broken, whereas four stood up for
it, four kingdoms shall stand up out of the nation,
but not in his power.   And in the latter time of their
kingdom, when the transgressors are come to the full,
a king of fierce countenance, and understanding dark
sentences, shall stand up.   And his power shall be
mighty, but not by his own power: and he shall destroy wonderfully, and shall prosper, and practise, and
shall destroy the mighty and the holy people.   And
through his policy also he shall cause craft to prosper
in his hand; and he shall magnify himself in his heart,
and by peace shall destroy many: he shall also stand
up against the Prince of princes; but he shall be broken
without hand.   And the vision of the evening and the
morning which was told is true: wherefore shut thou
up the vision; for it shall be for many days.

"And I Daniel fainted, and was sick certain days;
afterward I rose up, and did the king's business; and
I was astonished at the vision, but none understood
it" (Dan. 8:1-27).

We note in this chapter that the he-goat had a
"notable horn" between his eyes. This notable horn
was broken, and in its place *four* notable horns appeared.   Then out of one of the four horns appeared a
"little horn," and the little horn "waxed exceeding
great—toward the south, and toward the east, and

toward the pleasant land" (the land of Palestine).

Having waxed great, the little horn cast down "some of the host (of heaven) and . . . some of the stars to the ground, and stamped upon them." Furthermore the little horn "magnified himself even to *the Prince of the host"* — and "the Prince of the host" is none other than the Lord God (Joshua 5:13-15; I Sam. 17:45). The *"little horn"* of whom Daniel spoke will be the Man of Sin, the Antichrist. He will take away the daily sacrifice, and "the place of the sanctuary" (God's temple) he will cast down.

Daniel sought for the meaning of his great vision, and he was told that the mighty ram stood for the kingdoms of Media and Persia, the powerful he-goat represented the kingdom of Greece, the four horns represented four kings, and the *little horn* represented the "king of fierce countenance" who would understand "dark sentences," and who would also magnify himself and his power. Yet the power of the king of fierce countenance will not be *his own power.* He will be the devil incarnate and his power will be of the devil. He will "destroy wonderfully," whatever he does will prosper, he will practice wickedness such as has never been known in the history of mankind. He will destroy "the holy people" (the people of Israel), and no one will be able to buy or sell without the mark of the beast (Rev. 13:17). He will even stand against *"the Prince of princes,"* but you will notice in Daniel 8:25 that this "king of fierce countenance" will be *"broken without hand."* No king on this earth has ever stood against the Prince of princes (the Lord Jesus Christ), but the Antichrist, the devil incarnate,

Daniel's "king of fierce countenance," will take his stand against the Lord of hosts.

That he will be "broken without hand" means that he will be supernaturally destroyed. His kingdom will be broken to pieces by Daniel's "Stone cut out without hands, which smote the image upon his feet that were of iron and clay, and brake them to pieces" (Dan. 2:34). "And in the days of these kings shall the God of heaven set up a kingdom, which shall never be destroyed: and the kingdom shall not be left to other people, but it shall break in pieces and consume all these kingdoms, and it shall stand forever" (Dan. 2:44). Antichrist himself will be destroyed by the brightness of the coming of Jesus (II Thess. 2:8) and will be cast alive into the lake that burns with fire and brimstone (Rev. 19:20).

Some Bible teachers maintain that the "little horn" of Daniel's vision was fulfilled in the wicked King Antiochus Epiphanes, king of Syria; but they overlook the clear fact that while Antiochus Epiphanes destroyed Palestine, raised up an idol altar and sacrificed the flesh of swine (an abomination to the Jews), he did not at all fit the description of *the little horn* of Daniel's prophecy. In the first place, Antiochus Epiphanes did not compare with the personality of the little horn in Satanic power and hatred. Also, the "abomination of desolation" spoken of by Daniel is to appear in the last half of Daniel's seventieth week of his seventy weeks of prophecy. Therefore this means that the "abomination of desolation" will appear in the last half of the tribulation period, and this is yet to come upon the earth.

Jesus Himself spoke of the fulfillment of Daniel's prophecy as yet future, so Antiochus Epiphanes could not have been the fulfillment of Daniel 8:9-13. This powerful, wicked king has yet to appear.

It was revealed to Daniel that that *"little horn"* would come out of the four horns that took the place of the *great horn* on the head of the he-goat; but Daniel needed further light as to *which* of the horns the *little horn* replaced. From secular history we now know that the great horn of Daniel's vision represented Alexander the Great; and also from history we know that the four horns which took the place of the great horn represent the four kingdoms into which Alexander's kingdom was divided at his death—the kingdoms of Egypt, Macedonia, Thrace, and Syria (which included Assyria). In time, these four kingdoms were absorbed and swallowed up into *the fourth world kingdom*—the mighty Roman empire.

Fifteen years after Daniel's vision of the ram and the he-goat, God gave him still another vision, recorded in Daniel chapter 11. In this vision Daniel saw *two kings*—the "king of the north" and the "king of the south." The *king of the north* was the king of Syria, and since his character and conduct are described as being very similar to the character and conduct of the "little horn" of Daniel's former vision, some Bible scholars believe that the Antichrist will come from Syria.

Certainly we know that *Antichrist IS coming*, and it is altogether possible that he will come out of the Syrian division of the kingdom of Alexander the Great. Thus he would be a Syrian Jew. It is very unlikely that the Jews would accept a Gentile as their Messiah, and from God's Word we know that they *will* accept this false messiah. So it seems reasonable that he will be a Jew from the standpoint of the flesh, but this would not prevent his also being a Roman citizen and a king in the revived Roman empire. *Saul of Tarsus* was a free-born Roman citizen (Acts 22:25-28), but he was also a thoroughbred Jew. So the Antichrist could be a Jew and a Roman citizen at the same time.

The Apostle Paul also prophesied concerning the Antichrist. In II Thessalonians 2:3-12 he wrote:

"Let no man deceive you by any means: for that day shall not come, except there come a falling away first, and that man of sin be revealed, the son of perdition; who opposeth and exalteth himself above all that is called God, or that is worshipped; so that he as God sitteth in the temple of God, shewing himself that he is God.

"Remember ye not, that, when I was yet with you, I told you these things? And now ye know what withholdeth that he might be revealed in his time. For the mystery of iniquity doth already work: only He who now letteth will let, until He be taken out of the way. And then shall *that Wicked* be revealed, whom the Lord shall consume with the spirit of His mouth, and shall destroy with the brightness of His coming: even him, whose coming is after the working of Satan with all power and signs and lying wonders, and with all deceivableness of unrighteousness in them that perish; because they received not the love of the truth, that they might be saved.

"And for this cause God shall send them strong

delusion, that they should believe a lie: that they all might be damned who believed not the truth, but had pleasure in unrighteousness."

Paul speaks of Antichrist as *"the son of perdition,"* and the name is not without significance. It is used only twice in the entire Bible—here in Paul's letter to the Thessalonians in speaking of Antichrist, and in John 17:12 where Jesus speaks of *Judas Iscariot* as "the son of perdition." Judas was the only man ever to be called by that name, and it is only natural for us to wonder why Jesus thus referred to him. We find the answer to that question in John 6:70, 71 where Jesus said to His disciples, "Have not I chosen you twelve, and one of you is *a devil?* (He spake of Judas Iscariot the son of Simon: for he it was that should betray Him, being one of the twelve.)"

In the Greek, the article "a" is not used. Therefore Jesus actually said, "one of you is *devil."* The Greek word used here is *"diabolus,"* and it is not used in connection with any other person. Thus, in the words of Jesus, Judas Iscariot was the devil incarnate, and this explains why the Lord called him "the son of perdition."

Since Judas Iscariot is called "the son of perdition" and the Antichrist is called "the son of perdition," will *Judas* be the Antichrist when he appears after the Rapture? In Revelation 11:7 we read, "When they shall have finished their testimony, the beast that ascendeth out of the bottomless pit shall make war against them, and shall overcome them, and kill them." This verse refers to God's two witnesses who will testify during the last half of the tribulation period, and

they will be slain by the Antichrist. Now note that
this beast in our verse from Revelation will ascend out
of the bottomless pit, the abyss—and the question
arises, *How did he get INTO the abyss?*

Acts 1:25 tells us that when Judas committed suicide
after he sold Jesus for thirty pieces of silver, *he went
"to his own place."* This is not said of any other
person! The *rich man* died and in hell he lifted up
his eyes—but the Scripture does not say that hell was
the rich man's "own place." In the same passage
from Luke 16 the beggar Lazarus died and the angels
carried him into Abraham's bosom—but the Scripture
does not say that this was "his own place." *Only
Judas Iscariot* is said to have gone to his own place
when he died. *And where was that place?*

In Matthew 25:41 we are told that *hell* was prepared
"for the devil and his angels," so in reality hell could
be referred to as the devil's *"own place"* since it was
created for him, for his angels—and of course everyone
who chooses to serve the devil in this life must spend
eternity in hell with him. When Judas died, he went
"to his own place." Now notice this verse from Revelation:

"The beast that thou sawest *was,* and *is not;* and
shall ascend out of the bottomless pit, and go *into
perdition:* and they that dwell on the earth shall
wonder, whose names were not written in the book of
life from the foundation of the world, when they behold the beast that was, and is not, and yet is" (Rev.
17:8).

Since this is the same beast who will slay the two
witnesses we know that he is the Antichrist. And we

notice four things about him: (1) He *was*. (2) He *is not*. (3) He will *ascend out of* the bottomless pit. (4) He will go *into perdition!* When God gave these words to John on the Isle of Patmos, *the beast WAS NOT*; but he *HAD BEEN on earth*, and John was clearly told that this beast *WOULD BE on earth again*. And when he returns to earth he will do so by ascending up from the abyss, the bottomless pit. This is proof positive that the Antichrist has been on this earth, and when he comes in the future he will come from below, not from above. By contrast, *THE Christ* came from heaven when He came the first time, He ascended back to heaven, and when He comes back to this earth He will again come from heaven.

Now if Antichrist has been on this earth before (and *he has*), the question naturally arises, *When* was he here? Since Judas was, according to the words of Jesus, *the devil* (and Antichrist will be *the son* of the devil), it stands to reason that the time when Antichrist appeared on earth in days gone by was when he appeared as a member of the disciple band in the person of Judas Iscariot! When Judas was here on earth, he *was*. When he went out and hanged himself and went to his own place, he *was NOT*. When he returns from the bottomless pit after the Rapture of the Church, he *will be* again, right here on earth in the person of Antichrist.

I do not ask others to accept what I have just declared on the grounds of the Scriptures I have given, but in my own heart *I believe it!* It has nothing to do with your salvation or mine, but it does constitute a most interesting study and insofar as I am personally

concerned I believe that Judas Iscariot was the devil
incarnate and that he will return to this earth as the
Antichrist, the Man of Sin, "son of perdition"! He
will not be called "Judas," but will be called by some
or all of the many names given to him in Scripture.
I further believe that the same spirit that dwelt in
Judas was in *other men before Judas*—men like Pharaoh—who were forerunners (or types) of the devil in
flesh, types of the Antichrist.

I would like for us to look at one other statement
in the passage previously quoted from Paul's second
letter to the Thessalonians: "For the *mystery of iniquity* doth already work . . ." (II Thess. 2:7). Since
Christ is "the mystery of *godliness*" (I Tim. 3:16), *God
in flesh,* then Antichrist (exactly the opposite of God's
Christ) will be "the mystery of *iniquity,*" the *devil*
in flesh.

Now *how* was God manifest in the flesh? The Holy
Spirit overshadowed Mary, she conceived in her womb,
and the Son of God was born (Luke 1:35). Just as
Christ was the Son of God, Antichrist will be "the son
of perdition," the son of the devil. And as Christ was
born of a virgin, I believe the Antichrist will be born
of a *very wicked* woman, probably a harlot, and he
will be conceived by the spirit of Satan!

A Comparison Between John's Beast and Daniel's Fourth Beast

"The beast that thou sawest was, and is not; and
shall ascend out of the bottomless pit, and go into
perdition: and they that dwell on the earth shall
wonder, whose names were not written in the book of

life from the foundation of the world, when they behold the beast that was, and is not, and yet is. And here is the mind which hath wisdom. The seven heads are seven mountains, on which the woman sitteth. And there are seven kings: five are fallen, and one is, and the other is not yet come; and when he cometh, he must continue a short space. And the beast that was, and is not, even he is the eighth, and is of the seven, and goeth into perdition. And the ten horns which thou sawest are ten kings, which have received no kingdom as yet; but receive power as kings one hour with the beast. These have one mind, and shall give their power and strength unto the beast" (Rev. 17:8-13).

"After this I saw in the night visions, and behold a fourth beast, dreadful and terrible, and strong exceedingly; and it had great iron teeth: it devoured and brake in pieces, and stamped the residue with the feet of it: and it was diverse from all the beasts that were before it; and it had ten horns" (Dan. 7:7).

We find that both of these beasts came up out of the sea and were utterly unlike any beast ever heard of. Daniel's beast was dreadful, terrible, and exceedingly strong, and it had teeth of iron and nails of brass. The beast John saw was like a leopard. It had feet like a bear, but its mouth was like the mouth of a lion. As in the case of Daniel's beast, John's beast also represented a kingdom on this earth—the kingdom of the Roman empire.

The characteristics of Daniel's beast describe the *old* Roman empire, and the characteristics of *John's* beast describe the *revived* Roman empire, the Rome which will again come into power. Certainly the old

Roman empire (which was in power at the time of
Christ's earthly ministry) was like a beast—strong and
powerful like a beast with iron teeth and nails of brass.
From the description of the beast John saw, the revived Roman empire will also have the characteristics
of a beast, as seen in the leopard-like body, feet like
the feet of a bear, and a mouth like the king of beasts,
the lion.

These two beasts each had ten horns, representing
ten kings, which correspond to the ten toes of Nebuchadnezzar's image. In the revived Roman empire
these ten kings will come into power just before "the
Stone cut out without hands" destroys them. The
Stone kingdom (which is the millennial kingdom of the
Lord Jesus Christ) will supplant the ten separate kingdoms (federated kingdoms).

Then we note a difference in the beast John saw
and the beast of Daniel's vision: While they each had
ten horns, John's beast had seven heads while Daniel's
beast had only *one* head. Also, among the ten horns
on Daniel's beast there came up a little horn; but this
little horn is not seen in the midst of the ten horns
of the beast John saw.

The little horn of Daniel's vision plucks three of the
ten horns and destroys all three of them, taking their
kingdoms away. John does not mention this at all.
The anti-Christian character of the beast Daniel saw
is seen in its little horn, the conduct of which corresponds with not just a part but the whole of the
beast John saw—and for the same length of time:
"time and times, and the dividing of time," which is
exactly forty and two months.

It is clear in the light of God's Word that Daniel and John saw the same beast. Daniel's beast represents the powerful Roman empire as it existed from 30 B. C. until—as a kingdom—it *ceased* to exist. In 364 A. D. as the result of an ecclesiastical schism in the empire, it was divided into the eastern and western divisions, suffering loss of national life and loss of power as a world ruler. However, Rome has never lost its religious existence, influence, or power. It continues even today in the Greek and Roman churches, and Roman law is still a controlling power in laws throughout the world.

In the two descriptions of this beast there is a dual meaning: The beast represents both the revived Roman empire and the world dictator (the Antichrist) who will be at the head of that mighty empire. In Revelation 13:1 the revived Roman empire is seen coming "out of the sea," and this reference is to *the sea of NATIONS*. The Antichrist comes up out of the abyss. It cannot be said that the Roman empire of John's day "was—and is not," for in the day when John the Beloved lived, the Roman empire was at the height of its power. Nor can it be said of that empire that it will ascend out of the abyss and go into perdition. Such language would be used only of a person. Therefore we must distinguish between the *body* of the beast, and its heads and horns. The body of the beast was as a leopard, with feet like a bear and mouth like a lion. This shows that the revived Roman empire in its last days will include all of the characteristics of the first three beasts seen by Daniel in his vision— the lion (which represents Babylon), the bear (repre-

senting Medo-Persia), and the leopard (representing
Greece).

In Revelation chapter 13 the beast coming out of
the sea has seven heads and ten horns, and on the
horns are crowns. This represents the Roman empire
at the zenith of its power, when it will have all of its
heads; and the ten kings who head up the ten federated kingdoms will have received their crowns and
be in full power.

The beast in Revelation 17, coming up out of the
pit, has seven heads and ten horns, but no crowns.
So the ten kings represented by the ten horns on the
beast from the abyss have not yet received their kingdoms and their crowns. This shows that the beast of
Revelation 17 definitely typifies the Antichrist at the
beginning of the tribulation period. At this stage "the
woman"—the mother of harlots in Revelation 17:5—is
seen *riding* the beast. This woman is not pagan Rome
alone. She is the mother of every "ism" and false
religion that has been born since Cain thought he
could satisfy God with an offering of his own choosing.
But the fact that the woman is not seen *until* Revelation chapter 17 proves that she rides the beast from the
very beginning of the tribulation period, for the woman
represents the religious power of Rome which comes
into ecclesiastical power immediately after the true
Church of God is raptured to meet Jesus in the air.

During the wars that will precede the rise of Antichrist, the nations that will then be found in the
boundary lines of the old Roman empire will form a
federated alliance for mutual protection and power.
There will be ten of these nations (which are repre-

sented by the ten horns of the beast). No doubt the
Roman ecclesiastical system will play a very prominent
part in the proceedings at that time.

The woman will be rewarded by the restoring to her
of political power, and this union of church and state
will give the church full control (as shown by the
woman riding the beast). She *controls* the beast because she is *riding* it. She *dominates* the beast because she is *seated upon it*. But when the ten kings
receive the kingdoms and are crowned with power they
will "hate the whore (the woman) and shall make her
desolate and naked, and shall eat her flesh, and burn
her with fire" (Rev. 17:16).

In Revelation 17:9 we are told that the seven heads
of the beast are seven mountains. This identifies the
Roman empire, the place typified by the beast. Verse
10 in that chapter tells us that the seven heads represent seven kings—"*five* are fallen, and *one* is, and *the
other* is not yet come; and when he cometh, he must
continue a short space."

This shows us that in the days of John the Beloved,
five of these kings had already fallen, one was then in
power (the emperor of Rome), and the last (and seventh) was yet to come. John does not tell us who the
five kings were. The *sixth* king (who was on the
throne in John's day) banished him to the Isle of Patmos. Revelation 13:3 tells us that one of the seven
heads (kings) received a "deadly wound," and while
we are not told *which king* this is, the inference is
that it is the last, or seventh. In Revelation 17:11 he
is called "the beast that was, and is not, even he is
the eighth, and is of the seven, and goeth into per-

dition."

In Revelation 13:3 we read, "I saw one of his heads as it were wounded to death; and his deadly wound was healed: *and all the world wondered after the beast."* In the fifth century after the birth of Christ, the head of the great Roman empire was wounded unto death. The monster empire of Rome was killed. Parts of it have existed ever since, but the real head died. Now the beast is that head raised to life again, consisting of ten federated kingdoms. A Roman emperor rules again, and the whole world wonders at the great miracle of the revived Roman empire.

John Describes the Beasts of the End Time— Political and Religious Dictators

"And I stood upon the sand of the sea, and saw *a beast rise up out of the sea,* having seven heads and ten horns, and upon his horns ten crowns, and upon his heads the name of blasphemy. And the beast which I saw was like unto a leopard, and his feet were as the feet of a bear, and his mouth as the mouth of a lion: and the dragon gave him his power, and his seat, and great authority. AND I SAW ONE OF HIS HEADS AS IT WERE WOUNDED TO DEATH; AND HIS DEADLY WOUND WAS HEALED: AND ALL THE WORLD WONDERED AFTER THE BEAST.

"And they worshipped the dragon which gave power unto the beast: and they worshipped the beast, saying, Who is like unto the beast? Who is able to make war with him? And there was given unto him a mouth speaking great things and blasphemies; and power was given unto him to continue forty and two months.   And he opened his mouth in blasphemy against God, to blaspheme His name, and His tabernacle, and them that dwell in heaven.

"And it was given unto him to make war with the saints, and to overcome them: and power was given him over all kindreds, and tongues, and nations.   And all that dwell upon the earth shall worship him, whose names are not written in the book of life of the Lamb slain from the foundation of the world.   If any man have an ear, let him hear.   He that leadeth into captivity shall go into captivity: he that killeth with the sword must be killed with the sword.   Here is the patience and the faith of the saints.

"And I beheld *another beast coming up out of the earth;* and he had two horns like a lamb, and he spake as a dragon.   And he exerciseth all the power of the first beast before him, and causeth the earth and them which dwell therein to worship the first beast, whose deadly wound was healed.   And HE DOETH GREAT WONDERS, so that he MAKETH FIRE COME DOWN FROM HEAVEN ON THE EARTH in the sight of men, and DECEIVETH them that dwell on the earth BY THE MEANS OF THOSE MIRACLES WHICH HE HAD POWER TO DO in the sight of the beast; *saying to them that dwell on the earth, that they should MAKE AN IMAGE TO THE BEAST, WHICH HAD THE WOUND BY A SWORD, AND DID LIVE.*

"AND HE HAD POWER TO GIVE LIFE UNTO THE IMAGE OF THE BEAST, THAT THE IMAGE OF THE BEAST SHOULD BOTH SPEAK, AND CAUSE THAT AS MANY AS WOULD NOT WOR-

SHIP THE IMAGE OF THE BEAST SHOULD BE KILLED. And he causeth all, both small and great, rich and poor, free and bond, to receive a mark in their right hand, or in their foreheads: and that no man might buy or sell, save he that had the mark, or the name of the beast, or the number of his name. Here is wisdom. Let him that hath understanding count the number of the beast: for it is the number of a man; and *his number is Six hundred three score and six"* (Rev. 13:1-18).

In secular and sacred history combined no such person as described in verses 11 through 18 has ever appeared on earth. Such a person is almost inconceivable—but *he will appear,* and he will be the Antichrist, the devil incarnate.

His reign will be for approximately seven years, as given in Daniel 9:27: "And he shall confirm the covenant with many for one week: and in the midst of the week he shall cause the sacrifice and the oblation to cease, and for the overspreading of abominations he shall make it desolate, even until the consummation, and that determined shall be poured upon the desolate."

The Doom of Antichrist

At the climax of the reign of Antichrist, the armies of the ten federated nations under his rule will gather in the valley of Megiddo just outside Jerusalem to the north, where many bloody battles were fought in ancient days. This powerful allied army of the federated kingdoms, under the leadership of Antichrist, will gather around the city of Jerusalem to besiege the city in a last attempt to destroy the nation of Israel (Zech. 14:2). But the Lord Jesus Christ, the true Messiah, will come to the rescue, leading the armies of heaven (Rev. 19:11-16).

The Jews will see Christ descend from heaven and stand on the Mount of Olives. They will see the scars in His hands and they will recognize Him as Messiah. They will receive Him, and a nation will be born in a day. They will then go into the kingdom promised to Abraham and the patriarchs, and Jesus will reign over that kingdom for one thousand glorious years!

The following chapters from *Zechariah* describe the scene as the beast and his armies besiege Jerusalem, also the *victory* won by the Lord Jesus Christ, and the setting up of the kingdom:

CHAPTER 12

The Siege of Jerusalem by the Beast and His Armies
"The burden of the Word of the Lord for Israel, saith the Lord, which stretcheth forth the heavens, and layeth the foundation of the earth, and formeth the spirit of man within him. Behold, I will make Jerusalem a cup of trembling unto all the people round about, when they shall be in the siege both against Judah and against Jerusalem. And in that day will I make Jerusalem a burdensome stone for all people: all that burden themselves with it shall be cut in pieces, though all the people of the earth be gathered together against it."

The Siege: Judah Strengthened;
the Lord's Deliverance
"In that day, saith the Lord, I will smite every horse with astonishment, and his rider with madness:

and I will open mine eyes upon the house of Judah, and will smite every horse of the people with blindness. And the governors of Judah shall say in their hearts, The inhabitants of Jerusalem shall be my strength in the Lord of hosts their God.

"In that day will I make the governors of Judah like an hearth of fire among the wood, and like a torch of fire in a sheaf; and they shall devour all the people round about, on the right hand and on the left: and Jerusalem shall be inhabited again in her own place, even in Jerusalem. The Lord also shall save the tents of Judah first, that the glory of the house of David and the glory of the inhabitants of Jerusalem do not magnify themselves against Judah.

"In that day shall the Lord defend the inhabitants of Jerusalem; and he that is feeble among them at that day shall be as David; and the house of David shall be as God, as the angel of the Lord before them. And it shall come to pass in that day, that I will seek to destroy all the nations that come against Jerusalem."

The Spirit Poured Out: the Pierced One
Revealed to the Delivered Remnant

"And I will pour upon the house of David, and upon the inhabitants of Jerusalem, the spirit of grace and of supplications: and they shall look upon me whom they have pierced, and they shall mourn for Him, as one mourneth for his only son, and shall be in bitterness for Him, as one that is in bitterness for his firstborn."

The Repentance of the Remnant

"In that day shall there be a great mourning in Jerusalem, as the mourning of Hadadrimmon in the valley of Megiddon. And the land shall mourn, every family apart; the family of the house of David apart, and their wives apart; the family of the house of Nathan apart, and their wives apart; the family of the house of Levi apart, and their wives apart; the family of Shimei apart, and their wives apart; all the families that remain, every family apart, and their wives apart."

CHAPTER 13

The Repentant Remnant Pointed to the Cross
"In that day there shall be a fountain opened to the house of David and to the inhabitants of Jerusalem for sin and for uncleanness."

Idols and False Prophets Cease
"And it shall come to pass in that day, saith the Lord of hosts, that I will cut off the names of the idols out of the land, and they shall no more be remembered: and also I will cause the prophets and the unclean spirit to pass out of the land. And it shall come to pass, that when any shall yet prophesy, then his father and his mother that begat him shall say unto him, Thou shalt not live; for thou speakest lies in the name of the Lord: and his father and his mother that begat him shall thrust him through when he prophesieth.

"And it shall come to pass in that day, that the prophets shall be ashamed every one of his vision, when he hath prophesied; neither shall they wear a rough garment to deceive: but he shall say, I am no prophet, I am an husbandman; for man taught me to keep cattle from my youth."

The Preaching to Israel After the Return of the Lord
"And one shall say unto Him, What are these

wounds in thine hands? Then He shall answer, Those
with which I was wounded in the house of my friends.
Awake, O sword, against my shepherd, and against the
man that is my fellow, saith the Lord of hosts: smite
the shepherd, and the sheep shall be scattered: and I
will turn mine hand upon the little ones."

Result of the Gentile Invasion Under the Beast

"And it shall come to pass, that in all the land,
saith the Lord, two parts therein shall be cut off and
die; but the third shall be left therein. And I will
bring the third part through the fire, and will refine
them as silver is refined, and will try them as gold is
tried: they shall call on my name, and I will hear
them: I will say, It is my people: and they shall say,
The Lord is my God."

CHAPTER 14

Armageddon

"Behold, the day of the Lord cometh, and thy spoil
shall be divided in the midst of thee. For I will gather all nations against Jerusalem to battle; and the city
shall be taken, and the houses rifled, and the women
ravished; and half of the city shall go forth into captivity, and the residue of the people shall not be cut
off from the city. Then shall the Lord go forth, and
fight against those nations, as when He fought in the
day of battle."

The Visible Return in Glory:
Physical Changes in Palestine

"And His feet shall stand in that day upon the
mount of Olives, which is before Jerusalem on the east,
and the mount of Olives shall cleave in the midst

thereof toward the east and toward the west, and there shall be a very great valley; and half of the mountain shall remove toward the north, and half of it toward the south. And ye shall flee to the valley of the mountains; for the valley of the mountains shall reach unto Azal: yea, ye shall flee, like as ye fled from before the earthquake in the days of Uzziah king of Judah: and the Lord my God shall come, and all the saints with thee.

"And it shall come to pass in that day, that the light shall not be clear, nor dark: but it shall be one day which shall be known to the Lord, not day, nor night: but it shall come to pass, that at evening time it shall be light."

The River of the Sanctuary

"And it shall be in that day, that living waters shall go out from Jerusalem; half of them toward the former sea, and half of them toward the hinder sea: in summer and in winter shall it be."

The Kingdom Set Up On the Earth

"And the Lord shall be King over all the earth: in that day shall there be one Lord, and His name one. All the land shall be turned as a plain from Geba to Rimmon south of Jerusalem: and it shall be lifted up, and inhabited in her place, from Benjamin's gate unto the place of the first gate, unto the corner gate, and from the tower of Hananeel unto the king's winepresses. And men shall dwell in it, and there shall be no more utter destruction; but Jerusalem shall be safely inhabited.

"And this shall be the plague wherewith the Lord will smite all the people that have fought against

Jerusalem: Their flesh shall consume away while they stand upon their feet, and their eyes shall consume away in their holes, and their tongue shall consume away in their mouth. And it shall come to pass in that day, that a great tumult from the Lord shall be among them; and they shall lay hold every one on the hand of his neighbour, and his hand shall rise up against the hand of his neighbour. And Judah also shall fight at Jerusalem; and the wealth of all the heathen round about shall be gathered together, gold, and silver, and apparel, in great abundance. And so shall be the plague of the horse, of the mule, of the camel, and of the ass, and of all the beasts that shall be in these tents, as this plague."

The Worship and Spirituality of the Kingdom

"And it shall come to pass, that every one that is left of all the nations which came against Jerusalem shall even go up from year to year to worship the King, the Lord of hosts, and to keep the feast of tabernacles. And it shall be, that whoso will not come up of all the families of the earth unto Jerusalem to worship the King, the Lord of hosts, even upon them shall be no rain. And if the family of Egypt go not up, and come not, that have no rain; there shall be the plague, wherewith the Lord will smite the heathen that come not up to keep the feast of tabernacles.

"This shall be the punishment of Egypt, and the punishment of all nations that come not up to keep the feast of tabernacles. In that day shall there be upon the bells of the horses, HOLINESS UNTO THE LORD; and the pots in the Lord's house shall be like the bowls before the altar. Yea, every pot in Jerusalem and in Judah shall be holiness unto the Lord of hosts: and all they that sacrifice shall come and take of them, and seethe therein: and in that day there shall be no more the Canaanite in the house of the Lord of hosts."

John the Beloved gives a moving account of the *end* of the battle of Armageddon and the doom of the beast and the false prophet:

"And I saw an angel standing in the sun; and he cried with a loud voice, saying to all the fowls that fly in the midst of heaven, Come and gather yourselves together unto the supper of the great God; that ye may eat the flesh of kings, and the flesh of captains, and the flesh of mighty men, and the flesh of horses, and of them that sit on them, and the flesh of all men, both free and bond, both small and great.

"And I saw the beast, and the kings of the earth, and their armies, gathered together to make war against Him that sat on the horse, and against His army. And the beast was taken, and with him the false prophet that wrought miracles before him, with which he deceived them that had received the mark of the beast, and them that worshipped his image.   These both were cast alive into a lake of fire burning with brimstone.

"And the remnant were slain with the sword of Him that sat upon the horse, which sword proceeded out of His mouth: and all the fowls were filled with their flesh" (Rev. 19:17-21).

The Satanic Trinity

Our God is ONE GOD manifest in three Persons—Father, Son, and Holy Spirit.   Although we do not

understand the Holy Trinity, it is plainly declared in
the Word of God. In Matthew 3:16, 17 we read, "And
Jesus, when He was baptized, went up straightway out
of the water: and, lo, the heavens were opened unto
Him, and He saw the Spirit of God descending like a
dove, and lighting upon Him: and lo a voice from
heaven, saying, This is my beloved Son, in whom I am
well pleased."

The Trinity is plainly evident in this passage—Jesus
standing in the water, the Holy Spirit resting upon
Him in the form of a dove, and at the same time the
voice of God the Father speaking from heaven.

The devil is the master counterfeiter, and he has
counterfeited everything good and true that God has
put on this earth. Jesus said, "I will build my Church"
(Matt. 16:18), and the Church He is building is the
true Church. But Antichrist will have a church, and
immediately after the Rapture his church will take
over. Revelation 2:9 speaks of it as *"the synagogue of
Satan."* (See also Revelation 3:9.)

When Jesus walked among men he chose His disciples. Today He calls ministers to preach the Gospel,
just as He called the Apostle Paul and separated him
unto the Gospel. But Satan also has ministers, and
just as surely as *God* has ordained ministers today, the
devil has ordained ministers. Paul tells us, "Such
are false apostles, deceitful workers, transforming themselves into the apostles of Christ. And no marvel; for
Satan himself is transformed into an angel of light.
Therefore it is no great thing if his ministers also be
transformed as the ministers of righteousness; whose
end shall be according to their works" (II Cor. 11:13-15).

The Lord Jesus Christ will have a bride—the Church of the living God will be the bride of Christ (Eph. 5:25-27).

Antichrist, the devil in flesh, will also have a bride —the harlot of Revelation 17:1-16.

Before Jesus left His disciples, He instituted the Lord's Supper: "The cup of blessing which we bless, is it not the communion of the blood of Christ? The bread which we break, is it not the communion of the body of Christ?" (I Cor. 10:16). We observe the Lord's Supper in memory of Him until He comes again (I Cor. 11:25, 26).

The false messiah, Antichrist, also has a cup—the "cup of devils," and the Apostle Paul warns, "Ye cannot be partakers of the Lord's table, and of the table of devils" (I Cor. 10:21).

The Lord Jesus Christ, God in flesh, born of a virgin, had an earthly ministry which lasted approximately three and one-half years.

Antichrist will reign in terror for approximately three and one-half years during the last half of the tribulation period.

Just as God is one God manifest in three Persons— Father, Son, and Holy Spirit—so there is a Satanic trinity made up of three persons: The dragon (which is the devil or anti-God), the beast (the Antichrist), and the false prophet (the anti-Spirit). All three are mentioned in the book of Revelation:

"There appeared another wonder in heaven; and behold a great red dragon, having seven heads and ten horns, and seven crowns upon his heads. And his tail drew the third part of the stars of heaven, and did cast them to the earth: and the dragon stood before the woman which was ready to be delivered, for to devour her child as soon as it was born. . . . And when the dragon saw that he was cast unto the earth, he persecuted the woman which brought forth the man child" (Rev. 12:3, 4, 13). In these verses we see Satan, the dragon.

Antichrist, son of the devil, is mentioned in Revelation chapter 13, and since we have already studied that chapter I will not give you the text here. I do suggest that you read it again. Jesus was the greatest worker of miracles the world has ever seen. Antichrist will also be a great miracle worker.

The false prophet (the false spirit) is mentioned three times in Revelation. In Revelation 16:13 we read, "I saw three unclean spirits like frogs come out of the mouth of the dragon, and out of the mouth of the beast, and out of the mouth of *the false prophet.*" In Revelation 19:20, the false prophet along with the beast is "cast alive into a lake of fire burning with brimstone." And in Revelation 20:10 "the devil that deceived them was cast into the lake of fire and brimstone, where the beast and *the false prophet* are, and shall be tormented day and night for ever and ever."

Satan has imitated and counterfeited everything Divine, and in this last quotation given from Revelation we see that the Satanic trinity—the devil, the beast, and the false prophet—are consigned to the lake of fire and brimstone forever.

Chapter VII

The Day of the Lord—
the Great Tribulation Period

"When ye therefore shall see the abomination of desolation, spoken of by Daniel the prophet, stand in the holy place, (whoso readeth, let him understand:) then let them which be in Judaea flee into the mountains. Let him which is on the housetop not come down to take any thing out of his house: neither let him which is in the field return back to take his clothes. And woe unto them that are with child, and to them that give suck in those days!

"But pray ye that your flight be not in the winter, neither on the sabbath day: for then shall be great tribulation, such as was not since the beginning of the world to this time, no, nor ever shall be. And except those days should be shortened, there should no flesh be saved: but for the elect's sake those days shall be shortened.

"Then if any man shall say unto you, Lo, here is Christ, or there; believe it not. For there shall arise false Christs, and false prophets, and shall shew great signs and wonders; insomuch that, if it were possible, they shall deceive the very elect. Behold, I have told before. Wherefore if they shall say unto you, Behold, He is in the desert; go not forth: behold, He is in the secret chambers; believe it not" (Matt. 24:15-26).

253

One of the major lines of prophecy throughout both the Old and New Testaments is the prophetic truth having to do with "the Day of the Lord." The term *"Day of the Lord"* is found in the following passages: Isaiah 2:12; 13:6, 9; Ezekiel 13:5; 30:3; Joel 1:15; 2:1, 11, 31; 3:14; Amos 5:18, 20; Zephaniah 1:7, 14; Zechariah 14:1; Malachi 4:5; Acts 2:20; I Thessalonians 5:2; II Peter 3:10. This same period is also spoken of as "that day . . . the day . . . the great day." These three expressions occur more than seventy-five times in the Old Testament and the frequence with which they occur is evidence of their importance in prophetic Scriptures.

Bible scholars of the past have disagreed on the time area within the Day of the Lord. Some believe that time period begins with the Rapture, others contend that it begins at the Revelation when Jesus returns with His Church to execute judgment upon the ungodly. I personally believe that the Day of the Lord includes the Great Tribulation and will run through the cleansing of the heavens by fire, the time when the heavens will be prepared for the creation of all things new. This has nothing to do with our salvation by grace through faith in the finished work of Christ, but one thing is clear: The Day of the Lord will be the time when the judgments of God will be poured out upon this earth. We see this very clearly in Zephaniah 1:14-18:

"The great day of the Lord is near, it is near, and hasteth greatly, even the voice of the day of the Lord: the mighty man shall cry there bitterly. That day is a day of wrath, a day of trouble and distress, a day of

wasteness and desolation, a day of darkness and gloominess, a day of clouds and thick darkness, a day of
the trumpet and alarm against the fenced cities, and
against the high towers. And I will bring distress
upon men, that they shall walk like blind men, because they have sinned against the Lord: and their
blood shall be poured out as dust, and their flesh as
the dung. Neither their silver nor their gold shall be
able to deliver them in the day of the Lord's wrath;
but the whole land shall be devoured by the fire of
His jealousy: for He shall make even a speedy rid-
dance of all them that dwell in the land."

The judgment of "that great day" includes not only
judgments upon the nation Israel and upon the nations
associated with Israel in the earth during the reign of
Antichrist, but also extends over a period of time prior
to the second advent of Christ. Therefore *the Day of
the Lord* must include the time of the Great Tribulation:

"Behold, the day of the Lord cometh, and thy spoil
shall be divided in the midst of thee. For I will
gather all nations against Jerusalem to battle; and the
city shall be taken, and the houses rifled, and the
women ravished; and half of the city shall go forth
into captivity, and the residue of the people shall not
be cut off from the city. Then shall the Lord go forth,
and fight against those nations, as when He fought in
the day of battle. And His feet shall stand in that
day upon the mount of Olives, which is before Jerusalem on the east, and the mount of Olives shall cleave
in the midst thereof toward the east and toward the
west, and there shall be a very great valley; and half

of the mountain shall remove toward the north, and half of it toward the south" (Zech. 14:1-4).

II Peter 3:10 gives authority for including the entire millennial age within this period of the Day of the Lord:

"The day of the Lord will come as a thief in the night, in the which the heavens shall pass away with a great noise, and the elements shall melt with fervent heat, the earth also and the works that are therein shall be burned up." This does not happen until after the Millennium, and out of this purification of the heavens and earth will emerge a new heaven and a new earth:

"Seeing then that all these things shall be dissolved, what manner of persons ought ye to be in all holy conversation and godliness, looking for and hasting unto the coming of the day of God, wherein the heavens being on fire shall be dissolved, and the elements shall melt with fervent heat? Nevertheless we, according to His promise, *look for new heavens and a new earth,* wherein dwelleth righteousness. Wherefore, beloved, seeing that ye look for such things, be diligent that ye may be found of Him in peace, without spot, and blameless" (II Pet. 3:11-14).

Events of the Day of the Lord

The Day of the Lord will include the following events:

The federation of nations which will combine to make up the old Roman empire (Daniel chapters 2 and 7).

The rise of the *political ruler* of the revived Roman

empire, the ruler who will make a covenant with the people of Israel back in their own land (Dan. 9:27; Rev. 13:1-10).

The formulation of the false religious system under the leadership of the beast who is a member of the Satanic trinity (Rev. 13:11-18).

The pouring out of the judgments under the seals, described in Revelation chapter 6.

The separation of the 144,000 Jewish missionaries who will preach the Gospel of the kingdom to every creature on earth who has not heard the Gospel of the grace of God (Rev. chapter 7).

The trumpet judgments outlined in Revelation chapters 8 through 11.

The time when God's two witnesses will testify in Jerusalem as recorded in Revelation chapter 11.

The persecution of the nation Israel (Rev. chapter 12).

The pouring out of the judgments described in Revelation chapter 16.

The overthrowing of the false "professing" church, the church of Antichrist, symbolized by the harlot (Rev. chapters 17 and 18).

The momentous events of the battle of Armageddon (Ezek. chapters 38 and 39; Rev. chapter 16; 19:17-21).

The time when the Gospel of the kingdom will be proclaimed to every tribe, nation, and kindred (Matt. 24:14).

The return of the Lord in glory with His holy angels, approximately seven years after the Rapture (Matt. 24:29, 30).

The resurrection of the tribulation saints (Rev. 20:4).

The Church and the Old Testament saints will already have been raised, but at the end of the tribulation period those who will be martyred by the Satanic trinity will be raised.

The destruction of the beast, the armies of the beast, and the false prophet (Rev. 19:17-21).

The judgment of the nations (Matt. 25:31-46).

The re-gathering of the *nation* of Israel in their own land (Ezek. 37:1-14).

The judgment of *living* Israel (Ezek. 20:33-38).

The *restoration* of Israel (Amos 9:15).

The binding of Satan (Rev. 20:1-3).

The events of the thousand-year reign of Christ here on earth with His bride, the New Testament Church, and the final revolt of Satan at the end of the Millennium (Rev. 20:6-10).

The Great White Throne judgment (Rev. 20:11-15).

The renovation of the earth by fire, the time when the elements will melt with fervent heat and the heavens will actually explode (II Pet. 3:10-13).

These are a few of the many, many things that will occur during the Day of the Lord—which includes "the time of Jacob's trouble . . . the Great Tribulation . . . Daniel's seventieth week." These and many related subjects must be dealt with as we study *"the Day of the Lord."*

The Day of the Lord — The Day of Christ

Many believers confuse the Day of the Lord with the Day of Christ. They are closely related but they are not identical. When we compare Isaiah 2:12 and Revelation 19:11-21 with II Thessalonians 2:2 we readily see that "the day of Christ" and "the Day of the Lord" are definitely two different events.

The Day of Christ relates entirely to the reward and blessing of the children of God at His coming. The Day of the Lord is connected entirely with judgment poured out on the ungodly.

The Day of Christ has to do with the redeemed and their rewards. The Day of the Lord has to do with unbelievers, those who have rejected Christ and therefore automatically fall under the judgment and wrath of Almighty God.

"The Day of the Lord" is an expression from the Old Testament and has to do with Christ's universal dealing with the ungodly in judgment in preparation for His eternal kingdom. The Day of Christ is an expression found in the New Testament and has to do with the second coming of the Lord Jesus Christ in the Rapture, to catch away His Church and reward His children just prior to His return to reign in the Millennium (at which time the Church will reign with Him).

"Day" in the Word of God is not necessarily *a* *"time" word*. II Peter 3:8 tells us, ". . . one day is with the Lord as a thousand years, and a thousand years as one day." A *"day"* in Scripture is not necessarily a fixed time as we know our days of twenty-four hours. It may be for the events which occur within *any* period of time. Paul so used the term when writing to the believers in Corinth when he spoke of *"the day of salvation"* (II Cor. 6:2).

Failing to understand that the term "day" is not necessarily a "time" word, some teachers and commentators have thought that the Day of the Lord and the Day of Christ must be two definite periods of time, whereas each of these "days" actually represents an *event,* not necessarily separate *periods of time.*

The second coming of Jesus is *one event* but it will be in *two stages.* He will come for the Church and will remove His bride from this earth before judgment falls in the tribulation period. Certainly the Lord loves His Church as much as Jehovah God loved Lot, and even though Lot was living in a backslidden condition he was removed from Sodom before God rained fire from heaven to destroy that wicked city. (Read Genesis chapter 19.)

The Day of Christ and the Day of the Lord may fall within the same time period, but two different programs are in view. In I Corinthians 1:8 the Apostle Paul speaks of *"the day of our Lord Jesus Christ"* to show us that Christ is related to both of these "days" since He is "both *Lord* and *Christ"* (Acts 2:36).

The Fact of the Tribulation

In the passage from Matthew chapter 24, given at the beginning of this chapter, Jesus speaks of *"great tribulation,* such as was not since the beginning of the world . . . no, nor ever shall be." This will be a time of such suffering and wholesale slaughter that "except those days should be shortened, there should no flesh be saved: but for the elect's sake *(for the sake of Israel)* those days shall be shortened" (Matt. 24:21, 22).

The words of Jesus do not stand alone in declaring the *fact* of the Great Tribulation. That period is mentioned in many prophecies in both the Old and New Testaments. It would be impossible to give all of these passages at this time, but we will consider enough of them to show beyond any shadow of doubt that there is a time coming when this world will see such tribulation as has never been known on earth before, nor will ever be known again.

Prophecies having to do with the Great Tribulation begin early in the Old Testament and continue through the New Testament, even to the very end of Revelation. One of the first statements concerning the tribulation which will befall Israel is mentioned by Moses in Deuteronomy 4:30, 31:

"When thou art in tribulation, and all these things are come upon thee, even in the latter days, if thou turn to the Lord thy God, and shalt be obedient unto His voice; (for the Lord thy God is a merciful God;) He will not forsake thee, neither destroy thee, nor forget the covenant of thy fathers which He sware unto them."

The following passages in Isaiah speak of the time of terrible tribulation and suffering when the Lord will arise and shake the earth:

Isaiah 2:19: "They shall go into the holes of the rocks, and into the caves of the earth, for fear of the Lord, and for the glory of His majesty, when He ariseth to shake terribly the earth."

Isaiah 24:1-6: "Behold, the Lord maketh the earth empty, and maketh it waste, and turneth it upside down, and scattereth abroad the inhabitants thereof. And it shall be, as with the people, so with the priest; as with the servant, so with his master; as with the maid, so with her mistress; as with the buyer, so with the seller; as with the lender, so with the borrower;

as with the taker of usury, so with the giver of usury to him.

"The land shall be utterly emptied, and utterly spoiled: for the Lord hath spoken this word. The earth mourneth and fadeth away, the world languisheth and fadeth away, the haughty people of the earth do languish. The earth also is defiled under the inhabitants thereof; because they have transgressed the laws, changed the ordinance, broken the everlasting covenant. Therefore hath the curse devoured the earth, and they that dwell therein are desolate: therefore the inhabitants of the earth are burned, and few men left."

Isaiah 24:19-21: "The earth is utterly broken down, the earth is clean dissolved, the earth is moved exceedingly. The earth shall reel to and fro like a drunkard, and shall be removed like a cottage; and the transgression thereof shall be heavy upon it; and it shall fall, and not rise again. And it shall come to pass in that day, that the Lord shall punish the host of the high ones that are on high, and the kings of the earth upon the earth."

Isaiah 26:20,21: "Come, my people, enter thou into thy chambers, and shut thy doors about thee: hide thyself as it were for a little moment, until the indignation be overpast. For, behold, the Lord cometh out of His place to punish the inhabitants of the earth for their iniquity: the earth also shall disclose her blood, and shall no more cover her slain."

Jeremiah, the weeping prophet, speaks of the time of great tribulation, the time of Jacob's trouble, as suffering comparable to the travail of a woman in childbirth: "These are the words that the Lord spake concerning Israel and concerning Judah. For thus saith the Lord: We have heard a voice of trembling, of fear, and not of peace. Ask ye now, and see whether a man doth travail with child? Wherefore do I see every man with his hands on his loins, as a woman in travail, and all faces are turned into paleness? Alas! for that day is great, so that none is like it: it is even the time of Jacob's trouble, but he shall be saved out of it" (Jer. 30:4-7).

The Prophet Ezekiel speaks of the Great Tribulation as the time when the nation Israel shall "pass under the rod": "And I will bring you out from the people, and will gather you out of the countries wherein ye are scattered, with a mighty hand, and with a stretched out arm, and with fury poured out. And I will bring you into the wilderness of the people, and there will I plead with you face to face. Like as I pleaded with your fathers in the wilderness of the land of Egypt, so will I plead with you, saith the Lord God. And I will cause you to pass under the rod, and I will bring you into the bond of the covenant: and I will purge out from among you the rebels, and them that transgress against me: I will bring them forth out of the country where they sojourn, and they shall not enter into the land of Israel: and ye shall know that I am the Lord" (Ezek. 20:34-38).

Again Ezekiel speaks of the nation Israel as being put in the melting pot to be refined as gold is refined: "Therefore thus saith the Lord God: Because ye are all become dross, behold, therefore I will gather you into the midst of Jerusalem. As they gather silver, and brass, and iron, and lead, and tin, into the midst of the furnace, to blow the fire upon it, to melt it; so will I gather you in mine anger and in my fury, and I will leave you there, and melt you. Yea, I will gather you, and blow upon you in the fire of my wrath, and ye shall be melted in the midst thereof. As silver is melted in the midst of the furnace, so shall ye be melted in the midst thereof; and ye shall know that I the Lord have poured out my fury upon you" (Ezek. 22:19-22).

In Zechariah 13:9 we read, "I will bring the third part through the fire, and will refine them as silver is refined, and will try them as gold is tried: they shall call on my name, and I will hear them: I will say, It is my people: and they shall say, The Lord is my God."

The Prophet Daniel speaks of the Great Tribulation as a time of trouble for his own people, the Jews: "At that time shall Michael stand up, the great prince which standeth for the children of thy people: and there shall be a time of trouble, such as never was since there was a nation even to that same time: and at that time thy people shall be delivered, every one that shall be found written in the book" (Dan. 12:1).

From these Scriptures we learn that the Great Tribulation period has to do primarily with the Jewish people. It is a judgment through which the Jews must pass in a refining process to prepare them and make them fit to again receive the blessings of God's chosen people. The Gentiles will be *indirectly* affected by the Great Tribulation, but the Church will be caught out before that great and terrible day of the Lord.

Joel speaks of the day when the Almighty will come

in destruction. In Joel 1:15 we read, "Alas for the day! for the day of the Lord is at hand, and as a destruction from the Almighty shall it come." Joel 2:1, 2 declares, "Blow ye the trumpet in Zion, and sound an alarm in my holy mountain: let all the inhabitants of the land tremble: for the day of the Lord cometh, for it is nigh at hand; a day of darkness and of gloominess, a day of clouds and of thick darkness, as the morning spread upon the mountains: a great people and a strong; there hath not been ever the like, neither shall be any more after it, even to the years of many generations."

The Prophet Amos declares woe unto all who desire the day of the Lord, and describes it as a day of very great darkness: "Woe unto you that desire the day of the Lord! to what end is it for you? The day of the Lord is darkness, and not light. As if a man did flee from a lion, and a bear met him; or went into the house, and leaned his hand on the wall, and a serpent bit him. Shall not the day of the Lord be darkness, and not light? even very dark, and no brightness in it?" (Amos 5:18-20).

There are also many Scriptures in the *New* Testament which set forth the truth concerning the Great Tribulation. We will look at a few of them here:

In Matthew 24:21, 22 we have already seen that Jesus described the tribulation period as so severe that there would be no flesh saved if God did not intervene.

Luke 21:25, 26 also speaks of that terrible day of the Lord: "There shall be signs in the sun, and in the moon, and in the stars; and upon the earth distress of nations, with perplexity; the sea and the waves roaring;

men's hearts failing them for fear, and for looking after those things which are coming on the earth: for the powers of heaven shall be shaken."

In I Thessalonians 5:3 Paul says of that day, "When they shall say, Peace and safety; then sudden destruction cometh upon them, as travail upon a woman with child; and they shall not escape."

To the church at Philadelphia John the Beloved was instructed to write: "Because thou hast kept the word of my patience, I also will keep thee from the hour of temptation (tribulation) which shall come upon all the world, to try them that dwell upon the earth" (Rev. 3:10).

In Revelation 6:15-17 John again declares that horrible day when kings and mighty men will see Jesus coming, and they will cry for the rocks and the mountains to fall on them and hide them from His wrath:

"And the kings of the earth, and the great men, and the rich men, and the chief captains, and the mighty men, and every bondman, and every free man, hid themselves in the dens and in the rocks of the mountains; and said to the mountains and rocks, Fall on us, and hide us from the face of Him that sitteth on the throne, and from the wrath of the Lamb: for the great day of His wrath is come; and who shall be able to stand?"

As we read and study these Scriptures we see that the nature—the very character—of the Great Tribulation (the Day of the Lord) is a time of great wrath. Time and space will not permit me to give you the text of the following Scriptures, but please read them carefully.   They each make declarations concerning the

Day of the Lord:

A day of *wrath:* Zephaniah 1:15-18; I Thessalonians 1:10; 5:9; Revelation 6:16, 17; 11:18; 14:10-19; 15:1-7; 16:19.

A day of *judgment:* Revelation 14:7; 15:4; 16:5; 19:2.

A day of *indignation:* Isaiah 26:20, 21; 34:1-3.

A day of *trial:* Revelation 3:10.

A day of *trouble:* Jeremiah 30:7; Zephaniah 1:14, 15; Daniel 12:1.

A day of *destruction:* Joel 1:15; I Thessalonians 5:3.

A day of *darkness:* Joel 2:2; Amos 5:18; Zephaniah 1:14-18.

A day of *desolation:* Daniel 9:27; Zephaniah 1:14, 15.

A day of *overturning:* Isaiah 24:1-4.

A day of *punishment:* Isaiah 24:20, 21.

Nowhere in the entire Bible can a passage be found which will alleviate to any degree the severity of this time of terrible suffering and misery, wrath and judgment that will come upon the earth in the Day of the Lord!

The Source of Wrath Poured Out In the Day of Tribulation

The Great Tribulation period is not the *devil's* wrath being directed against the saints because they reject the Antichrist, nor is it a time when the wrath of *man* will be spent on Satan. It is a time when the wrath of *God* will be poured out on the inhabitants of the earth.

It is true that during the tribulation period the wrath of Satan will be hurled against the nation Israel, as set forth in Revelation 12:12-17. It is also true that

Satan's puppet, the beast, in his animosity against the saints of God will *declare war* on the saints (Rev. 13:7). These things Satan will be *allowed* to do. But this is only a *small part* of the outpouring of wrath in that day. God is almighty, Satan cannot move apart from God's permission, and when he has gone as far as he is *permitted* to go, *God will stop him.*

The Word of God proves beyond any shadow of doubt that it is *God's wrath* that will be visited upon the people of earth in the Great Tribulation period:

Isaiah 24:1: "Behold, *the LORD* maketh the earth empty . . . ."

Isaiah 26:21: "Behold, *the LORD* cometh out of His place to punish the inhabitants of the earth for their iniquity . . . ."

Joel 1:15: ". . . as a destruction from *the ALMIGHTY* shall it (the Day of the Lord) come."

Zephaniah 1:18: "Neither their silver nor their gold shall be able to deliver them in the day of *the LORD'S* wrath."

Revelation 6:16: ". . . hide us . . . from the wrath of *the LAMB.*"

Revelation 11:17, 18: ". . . O Lord God Almighty . . . the nations were angry, and *THY wrath* is come . . . ."

Revelation 14:7: "Fear God, and give glory to Him; for the hour of *HIS judgment* is come . . . ."

Revelation 14:10: "The same shall drink of the wine of the wrath *of GOD,* which is poured out without mixture into the cup *of HIS indignation* . . . ."

Revelation 14:19: "The angel thrust in his sickle into the earth, and gathered the vine of the earth, and cast it into the great winepress of *the wrath of GOD.*"

Revelation 15:4: "Who shall not fear thee, O LORD . . . ? . . . for *THY judgments* are made manifest."

Revelation 15:7: "One of the four beasts gave unto the seven angels seven golden vials full of *the wrath of GOD* . . . ."

Revelation 16:1: "I heard a great voice out of the temple saying to the seven angels, Go your ways, and pour out the vials of *the wrath of GOD* upon the earth!"

Revelation 16:7: "Even so, *LORD GOD ALMIGHTY*, true and righteous are *THY judgments.*"

Revelation 16:19: ". . . Babylon came in remembrance *before GOD*, to give unto her the cup of the wine of the fierceness of *HIS wrath.*"

Certainly these Scriptures show that the time of Jacob's trouble (the Great Tribulation period) is peculiarly the time when God Almighty will pour out His wrath and judgment upon the earth. He may use *men,* He may allow *Satan* to be used, for the execution of God's will; but the wrath which will be poured out upon the earth is the wrath of *God* and the tribulation is *from God.* Also, this period will differ from all preceding tribulation periods that have fallen upon this earth. It will differ *in intensity,* and in the very *nature* of the tribulation, because it will be *GOD'S wrath* falling.

The Purpose of the Great Tribulation

Since God is a God of *love,* what is the *purpose* of the tribulation period? Yes, *"God IS love"* (I John 4:8); but He is also *"a consuming fire"* (Heb. 12:29). God is longsuffering, not willing that any should perish;

but it is equally true that He will not acquit the wicked (Nah. 1:3), and He is "angry with the wicked every day" (Psalm 7:11). "The wicked shall be turned into hell, and all the nations that forget God" (Psalm 9:17).

The divine purpose of the Great Tribulation is twofold:

The PRIMARY purpose of that time of judgment is to prepare God's elect nation Israel for her Messiah. Jeremiah 30:7 makes it clear that this time of suffering and trouble has particular reference to Israel: "Alas! for that day is great, so that none is like it: it is even *the time of Jacob's trouble,* but he shall be saved out of it."

While the Great Tribulation will affect the entire earth and all peoples of earth at that time, it will be *primarily Jewish.* This clear fact is borne out in the following Scriptures: Deuteronomy 4:30; Jeremiah 30:7; Ezekiel 20:37; Daniel 12:1; Zechariah 13:8, 9.

In His Olivet discourse *Jesus* also declared that the tribulation period is primarily Jewish:

"Then shall they deliver you up to be afflicted, and shall kill you: and ye shall be hated of all nations for my name's sake. And then shall many be offended, and shall betray one another, and shall hate one another. And many false prophets shall rise, and shall deceive many. And because iniquity shall abound, the love of many shall wax cold. But he that shall endure unto the end, the same shall be saved. And this Gospel of the kingdom shall be preached in all the world for a witness unto all nations; and then shall the end come. . . . For there shall arise false Christs, and false prophets, and shall shew great signs and wonders; insomuch that, if it were possible, they shall deceive the very elect. Behold, I have told you before. Wherefore if they shall say unto you, Behold, He is in the desert; go not forth: behold, He is in the secret chambers; believe it not" (Matt. 24:9-14, 24-26).

John the Beloved also declares that the tribulation period is primarily Jewish. In Revelation 7:4 we read:

"I heard the number of them which were sealed: and there were sealed an hundred and forty and four thousand of all the tribes of *the children of Israel.*"

Then in Revelation 12:1, 2, 17 we read: "There appeared a great wonder in heaven; a woman clothed with the sun, and the moon under her feet, and upon her head a crown of twelve stars: and she being with child cried, travailing in birth, and pained to be delivered. . . . And the dragon was wroth with the woman, and went to make war with the remnant of her seed, which keep the commandments of God, and have the testimony of Jesus Christ." (Please read the *entire twelfth chapter* of Revelation.)

In the Scripture, the *Sabbath* . . . the *temple* . . . the *holy place* . . . the land of *Judaea* . . . the holy city *Jerusalem* . . . the twelve *tribes of Israel* . . . the covenant with *the beast* . . . the *sanctuary, sacrifice,* and *oblation of the temple ritual* all refer specifically to the nation Israel. This furnishes emphatic proof that the Great Tribulation period is primarily a time when God will deal with His ancient chosen people prior to their entrance into the promised kingdom. They *will* enter the kingdom, and they *will* accept their Messiah when He returns and stands on the Mount of Olives:

"His feet shall stand in that day upon the mount of Olives, which is before Jerusalem on the east, and the mount of Olives shall cleave in the midst thereof toward the east and toward the west, and there shall be a very great valley; and half of the mountain shall remove toward the north, and half of it toward the south" (Zech. 14:4).

The many Old Testament prophecies yet to be fulfilled for Israel indicate the future time when Jehovah God will again deal specifically with His chosen nation. (In connection with this please study Deuteronomy 30:1-6 and Jeremiah 30:8-10.)

During the suffering and tribulation, a multitude of Jews will be converted and will enter into the millennial blessings when Jesus comes to set up His kingdom on earth. The good news of the coming King will be preached "in all the world for a witness unto all nations" (Matt. 24:14). John the Baptist announced the coming of the King—and of the kingdom; but the Jews rejected John's message and crucified their King. However, when the 144,000 Jewish missionaries preach the Gospel of the kingdom during the tribulation, a great multitude will be saved—"a great multitude, which no man could number, of all nations, and kindreds, and people, and tongues" (Rev. 7:9). These will come out of the Great Tribulation, and will enter into the glorious kingdom right here on this earth.

The SECONDARY purpose of the Great Tribulation is to pour out God's judgment on unbelieving men and nations. Our God is a God of love. He is longsuffering, tender, compassionate—not willing that *any* should perish. But men have rejected Him and refused to receive His only begotten Son, leaving Him no alternative. Judgment *must* come, and Revelation 3:10 tells us that the tribulation period will be world-wide. It will reach all nations.

The following Scriptures also show that God will judge the nations of the earth because of their godlessness and because they rejected the Lord Jesus Christ:

Jeremiah 25:32, 33: "Thus saith the Lord of hosts, Behold, evil shall go forth from nation to nation, and a great whirlwind shall be raised up from the coasts of the earth. And the slain of the Lord shall be at that day from one end of the earth even unto the other end of the earth: they shall not be lamented, neither gathered, nor buried; they shall be dung upon the ground."

Isaiah 26:21: "Behold, the Lord cometh out of His place to punish the inhabitants of the earth for their iniquity: the earth also shall disclose her blood, and shall no more cover her slain."

II Thessalonians 2:10-12 tells us that because people refused to receive the truth of God and be saved, God will send them "strong delusion, that they should believe a lie: that they all might be damned who believed not the truth, but had pleasure in unrighteousness."

The nations of earth have been deceived by the false teaching of the Satanic system—the "harlot" system of Antichrist and the false prophet (Rev. 14:8). At the time of the tribulation, the nations will have followed the false prophet in worshipping the beast (Rev. 13:11-18), and because of their godlessness they must be judged. This horrible judgment will come from God and will be poured out on the kings of the earth, on great men, rich men, chief captains, mighty men, and on men both bond and free (Rev. 6:15). No one will escape who has rejected the message of salvation by grace through faith. Revelation 16:9 tells us that "men were scorched with great heat, and blasphemed the name of God . . . and they *repented not* to give Him glory."

Since God's kingdom and Christ's reign of righteousness is about to begin on earth, the judgment of wicked men is a divine necessity, a divine step in God's program to bring about the time when the earth will be filled with the knowledge of God as the waters now cover the sea. Then will be the time when men will beat their swords into plowshares, their spears into pruning hooks, and they will study war no more. Then —and only then—will peace come to this earth, with good will among men. This can never be until God judges His enemies and puts down wickedness to the ends of the earth.

Can We Pinpoint the Time of the Great Tribulation?

In order to understand the time elements having to do with the tribulation period it is necessary to study the prophecy of Daniel's seventy weeks where Israel's future is outlined. This we find in Daniel 9:24-27:

"Seventy weeks are determined upon thy people and upon thy holy city, to finish the transgression, and to make an end of sins, and to make reconciliation for iniquity, and to bring in everlasting righteousness, and to seal up the vision and prophecy, and to anoint the most Holy. Know therefore and understand, that from the going forth of the commandment to restore and to build Jerusalem unto the Messiah the Prince shall be seven weeks, and threescore and two weeks. The street shall be built again, and the wall, even in troublous times.

"And after threescore and two weeks shall Messiah be cut off, but not for Himself: and the people of the prince that shall come shall destroy the city and the sanctuary; and the end thereof shall be with a flood, and unto the end of the war desolations are determined. And he shall confirm the covenant with many for one week: and in the midst of the week he shall cause the sacrifice and the oblation to cease, and for the overspreading of abominations he shall make it desolate, even until the consummation, and that determined shall be poured upon the desolate."

This passage is explained in detail in my commentary on the book of *DANIEL*. Gabriel reveals to Daniel that a period seven times as long as the one mentioned by Jeremiah (which he has just been studying) is yet to pass before God's plan for Israel will be consummated.

In many ways, the vision of the seventy weeks is the most important revelation in all Scripture because it gives the interpretation of prophetic chronology. It is the key that unlocks the Scriptures of truth, and it discloses that the seventy weeks cover the period when the Jews are dwelling in their own land. It has nothing to do with the period of time when the Jews are *not* in their land. It does not cover *this* dispensation— the period of their dispersion—but it will again take up their history when they return to their own land immediately after the Rapture, when the decree is given to restore and rebuild Jerusalem.

Verse 24 reveals that the purpose of the seventy weeks is *sixfold:*

1. To finish the transgression.
2. To make an end of sin.
3. To make reconciliation for iniquity.
4. To bring in everlasting righteousness.
5. To seal up the vision and prophecy.
6. To anoint the most Holy.

As explained in my commentary on the book of *Daniel,* the Hebrew words translated "seventy weeks" in our authorized King James version of the Bible read *"seventy sevens."* The word "week" is used because we have no word in the English language that is the exact equivalent of the Hebrew word which signifies *seven,* and the translators of our King James version used "week" instead of "sevens." Thus, the vision Daniel saw was really seventy SEVENS.

In the Word of God we find the law of sevens—both in this world and in the spirit world. We read that God created the earth and all things therein in six days and rested on the *seventh* day. All through the Scripture, seven is a basic number. Our week is a week of seven days. The Scripture speaks of the week of *weeks,* the week of *months,* the week of *years,* and the week of *weeks of years.*

In Revelation we read of seven churches, seven seals, seven trumpets, seven personages, seven vials, seven dooms and seven *new things.* Seven is God's perfect number. It is made up of the divine number of *three* (Father, Son, and Holy Spirit) and the number of the earth, which is *four:* Spring, Summer, Autumn, Winter; North, South, East, and West. The earth is the Lord's and the fulness thereof, God is the Creator of heaven and earth and all things therein; therefore, the Trinity plus the number of the earth make *seven—* God's number for perfection.

The Key to Bible Understanding

Spiritual truths are not discovered by human wisdom or through human understanding. God cannot be explained in a test tube in the laboratory. Paul explains, "But as it is written, Eye hath not seen, nor ear heard, neither have entered into the heart of man, the things which God hath prepared for them that love Him. But God hath revealed them unto us by His SPIRIT: for the Spirit searcheth all things, yea, the deep things of God. For what man knoweth the things of a man, save the spirit of man which is in him? Even so the things of God knoweth no man, but *the Spirit of God.* Now we have received, not the spirit of the world, but the Spirit which is of God; that we might know the things that are freely given to us of God" (I Cor. 2:9-12).

Now notice the tremendous truth and revelation in verse 13 of this same passage: *"Which things also we speak, not in the words which man's wisdom teacheth, but which the Holy Ghost teacheth; comparing spiritual things with spiritual."* This is the key to spiritual understanding. The reason the Bible is a riddle instead of a revelation to many church people is that they have never been born of the Spirit. The natural man cannot receive the things of the Spirit of God. They are foolishness to him. Neither can he know them, because they are spiritually discerned (verse 14).

It is true that we will never know ALL there is to know about the Bible; but we can *believe* it because it is God's Word, verbally inspired—the mind of God, the wisdom of God, yea, *very God* (John 1:1). However, by studying and rightly dividing the Word of truth, by comparing Scripture with Scripture and spiritual things with spiritual, we can understand much— yes, we can understand ALL that God would have us to know about His Word and coming events while we are in this body of flesh. We could not *endure* the real depth of spiritual truths—such knowledge is too glorious, too marvelous, for flesh to understand. God *reveals* all that we *need* to know. It is *impossible* for us to know some of the things that have to do with the Almighty and divine dealings.

God has, in the language of man, a *plan,* a timetable. We are faced with "the law of sevens." Does it not seem reasonable that there is a time element set forth in this law? And if God deals in "the law of sevens," is it not reasonable that He is making known His plan and His purpose as having to do with this earth and man during these days in which we live and in the days that lie ahead?

The disciples asked of Jesus, "Lord, wilt thou at this time restore again the kingdom to Israel?" For forty days the risen Lord walked and talked with His disciples, instructing them in things pertaining to the kingdom of God. According to His custom (Luke 24:27, 32, 44, 45) He had probably been instructing them directly out of the Scriptures. But one point He had not touched upon was that time when He would restore the kingdom to Israel, and Himself sit on the throne of David in Jerusalem.

The disciples questioned Him concerning this earthly kingdom which was to be set up. Jesus answered that the time of the kingdom on earth (at which time He would sit on the throne of David and reign) was God's secret. No man knows the day or the hour. God has the times and the seasons set according to His sovereign will (Matt. 24:36, 42, 44; 25:13).

Notice the words of Jesus in Acts 1:6, 7. He pointed out to the disciples that it was not for them to know "the times and the seasons" which are in God's plan for the ages. That plan must and *will* run according to the foreknowledge of Him who planned it, and all hell cannot stop the program of the sovereign God of heaven and earth.

In Genesis 3:15 God promised the seed of the woman, and Paul declares, "When the fulness of the time was come, God sent forth His Son, made of a woman, made under the law, to redeem them that were under the law, that we might receive the adoption of sons" (Gal. 4:4, 5).

If you are familiar with the years preceding and following the birth of Jesus, you know that all hell allied together to prevent His birth. There is a literal stream of blood flowing from Genesis through Malachi; and when Jesus was born and His birth was announced, King Herod had all the babies under three years of age slaughtered in an attempt to destroy the seed of the woman. Jesus came at the God-appointed time— "the *fulness* of the time." Everything moves on schedule in heaven, in earth, and throughout the universal systems, all of which were created by God and for Him.

In studying the Old Testament we learn that, according to the prophecies already fulfilled, nothing has failed; all has been accomplished on time and according to schedule in spite of "principalities and powers and rulers of wickedness in high places." If everything in the past has been accomplished and fulfilled according to schedule, why should we not expect all *future events* prophetically set forth in Scripture to be fulfilled with the same accuracy?

In studying prophecy we read of hours, weeks, months, and years. We also read of "time, times, and an half time." If we are to understand the meaning of these terms we must interpret them according to the scriptural rule for Bible interpretation. Notice these enlightening words: "After the number of the days in which ye searched the land, even FORTY DAYS, each day for a year, shall ye bear your iniquities, even FORTY YEARS, and ye shall know my breach of promise" (Num. 14:34). Certainly we know this judgment was literally fulfilled to the very day and hour. God's chosen people wandered in the wilderness for exactly forty years—a year for each and every day the spies spent in searching out the land of Canaan: "And when thou hast accomplished them, lie again on thy right side, and thou shalt bear the iniquity of the house of Judah forty days: I have appointed thee each day for a year" (Ezek. 4:6).

The divine scale for measuring prophetic time is "A DAY STANDS FOR A YEAR." When we see this, the mist begins to disappear; and when we apply this divine scale to the seventy weeks we find that *seventy weeks add up to 490 years:* "That from the going forth of the commandment to restore and to build Jerusalem unto Messiah the Prince shall be seven weeks, and threescore and two weeks." What do we have here? *Seven plus threescore and two.* ONE score is 20; threescore is 60; plus two makes 62. Seven plus 62 adds up to 69 weeks—or, according to the prophetic scale, *483 years.* But there is one week missing, and we will point out later why this is true.

The Starting Point of the Seventy Weeks

In the interpretation of this important and well known prophecy, Gabriel gave Daniel not only the *starting* point, but the *stopping place* as well. The starting point dates from the giving of the commandment to *restore and build Jerusalem,* and from then unto "Messiah the Prince" shall be 69 sevens—or 69 *weeks*—divided in the twenty-fourth verse as 7 *weeks and 62 weeks.* Bible scholars have not agreed as to the date that marks the starting point of the "seventy weeks."

There were four decrees given concerning the restoration of Jerusalem and the rebuilding of the temple, and all four decrees were issued after the Babylonian captivity.

The First Decree:

This was given by King Cyrus in 536 B. C. (Ezra 1:1-4). II Chronicles 36:22, 23 is another passage which confirms this proclamation: "Now in the first year of

Cyrus king of Persia, that the Word of the Lord spoken by the mouth of Jeremiah might be accomplished, the Lord stirred up the spirit of Cyrus king of Persia, that he made a proclamation throughout all his kingdom, and put it also in writing, saying, Thus saith Cyrus king of Persia, All the kingdoms of the earth hath the Lord God of heaven given me; and He hath charged me to build Him an *house in Jerusalem,* which is in Judah. Who is there among you of all His people? The Lord his God be with him, and let him go up."

In these passages not one word is said about restoring and rebuilding the city of Jerusalem. All that is mentioned in this proclamation is the house of the Lord—the temple.

Cyrus was a heathen king and we might well ask what prompted him to make his decree. Could it be that Daniel had read Jeremiah 25:11-14 to him? Or perhaps Isaiah 44:28: "That saith of Cyrus, He is my shepherd, and shall perform all my pleasure: even saying to Jerusalem, Thou shalt be built; and to the temple, Thy foundation shall be laid." Did Daniel *ask* Cyrus to free his people, or remind him that the 70 years of their prophesied captivity were almost ended? Could it be that the Holy Spirit used this tremendous prophecy to soften the heart of the king and lead him to grant freedom to the Jews and allow them to return to Jerusalem to rebuild their temple? He even allowed them to carry back to their temple the gold and silver vessels which Nebuchadnezzar had confiscated when he overran Jerusalem.

We know that as a result of the decree issued by Cyrus, approximately 50,000 Israelite captives returned to Jerusalem:

"The whole congregation together was forty and two thousand three hundred and threescore, beside their servants and their maids, of whom there were seven thousand three hundred thirty and seven: and there were among them two hundred singing men and singing women" (Ezra 2:64, 65). They set up an altar; they renewed their offerings, their feasts, their sacrifices— and they began to rebuild their temple; but the work dragged because of many, many adversaries.

The Second Decree:

In 519 B. C., after the Jews appealed to King Darius, he issued a decree to make a search in the king's treasure house in Babylon. The search was made—and revealed the decree that had been given by Cyrus. The decree given by Darius was therefore simply a renewing of that issued by Cyrus—but penalties were attached. Notice in the Scripture that nothing is said of the city—just the temple:

"Then the prophets, Haggai the prophet, and Zechariah the son of Iddo, prophesied unto the Jews that were in Judah and Jerusalem in the name of the God of Israel, even unto them. Then rose up Zerubbabel the son of Shealtiel, and Jeshua the son of Jozadak, and began to *build the house of God* which is at Jerusalem: and with them were the prophets of God helping them.

"At the same time came to them Tatnai, governor on this side the river, and Shethar-boznai, and their companions, and said thus unto them, Who hath commanded you to build this house, and to make up this

wall? Then said we unto them after this manner,
What are the names of the men that make this building? But the eye of their God was upon the elders of
the Jews, that they could not cause them to cease, till
the matter came to Darius: and then they returned
answer by letter concerning this matter.

"The copy of the letter that Tatnai, governor on this
side the river, and Shethar-boznai, and his companions
the Apharsachites, which were on this side the river,
sent unto Darius the king: They sent a letter unto him,
wherein was written thus: Unto Darius the king, all
peace. Be it known unto the king, that we went into
the province of Judea, to the house of the great God,
which is builded with great stones, and timber is laid
in the walls, and this work goeth fast on, and prosper-
eth in their hands. Then asked we those elders, and
said unto them thus, Who commanded you to build this
house, and to make up these walls? We asked their
names also, to certify thee, that we might write the
names of the men that were the chief of them. And
thus they returned us answer, saying, We are the servants of the God of heaven and earth, and build the
house that was builded these many years ago, which a
great king of Israel builded and set up. But after that
our fathers had provoked the God of heaven unto
wrath, He gave them into the hand of Nebuchadnezzar
the king of Babylon, the Chaldean, who destroyed this
house, and carried the people away into Babylon.

"But in the first year of Cyrus the king of Babylon
the same king Cyrus made a decree to build this house
of God. And the vessels also of gold and silver of the
house of God, which Nebuchadnezzar took out of the

temple that was in Jerusalem, and brought them into
the temple of Babylon, those did Cyrus the king take
out of the temple of Babylon, and they were delivered
unto one, whose name was Sheshbazzar, whom he had
made governor; and said unto him, Take these vessels,
go, carry them into the temple that is in Jerusalem,
and let the house of God be builded in his place. Then
came the same Sheshbazzar, and laid the foundation of
the house of God which is in Jerusalem: and since
that time even until now hath it been in building, and
yet *it is not finished.* Now therefore, if it seem good
to the king, let there be search made in the king's
treasure house, which is there at Babylon, whether it
be so, that a decree was made of Cyrus the king to
build this house of God at Jerusalem, and let the king
send his pleasure to us concerning this matter.

"Then Darius the king made a decree, and search
was made in the house of the rolls, where the treasures
were laid up in Babylon. And there was found at
Achmetha, in the palace that is in the province of the
Medes, a roll, and therein was a record thus written:

"In the first year of Cyrus the king the same Cyrus
the king made a decree concerning the house of God at
Jerusalem, *Let the house be builded,* the place where
they offered sacrifices, and let the foundations thereof
be strongly laid; the height thereof threescore cubits,
and the breadth thereof threescore cubits; with three
rows of great stones, and a row of new timber: and let
the expenses be given out of the king's house: And
also let the golden and silver vessels of the house of
God, which Nebuchadnezzar took forth out of the temple which is at Jerusalem, and brought unto Babylon,

be restored, and brought again unto the temple which is at Jerusalem, every one to his place, and place them in the house of God.

"Now therefore, Tatnai governor beyond the river, Shethar-boznai, and your companions the Apharsachites, which are beyond the river, be ye far from thence: Let the work of this house of God alone; let the governor of the Jews and the elders of the Jews build this house of God in his place. Moreover I make a decree what ye shall do to the elders of these Jews for the building of this house of God: that of the king's goods, even of the tribute beyond the river, forthwith expenses be given unto these men, that they be not hindered. And that which they have need of, both young bullocks, and rams, and lambs, for the burnt-offerings of the God of heaven, wheat, salt, wine, and oil, according to the appointment of the priests which are at Jerusalem, let it be given them day by day without fail: That they may offer sacrifices of sweet savours unto the God of heaven, and pray for the life of the king, and of his sons.

"Also I have made a decree, that whosoever shall alter this word, let timber be pulled down from his house, and being set up, let him be hanged thereon; and let his house be made a dunghill for this. And the God that hath caused His name to dwell there destroy all kings and people, that shall put to their hand to alter and to destroy this house of God which is at Jerusalem. I Darius have made a decree; let it be done with speed" (Ezra 5:1—6:12).

The Third Decree:

In 458 B. C. Artaxerxes king of Persia gave Ezra a

letter granting him permission to go to Jerusalem and take priests and Levites with him. Ezra was given authority to collect gold and silver, purchase bullocks, rams, and lambs for offerings in the temple; and, should it become necessary, draw on the king's treasury for "whatsoever more shall be needful" for the house of God:

"Now this is the copy of the letter that the king Artaxerxes gave unto Ezra the priest, the scribe, even a scribe of the words of the commandments of the Lord, and of His statutes to Israel. Artaxerxes, king of kings, unto Ezra the priest, a scribe of the law of the God of heaven, perfect peace, and at such a time. I make a decree, that all they of the people of Israel, and of his priests and Levites, in my realm, which are minded of their own freewill to go up to Jerusalem, go with thee. Forasmuch as thou art sent of the king, and of his seven counsellors, to enquire concerning Judah and Jerusalem, according to the law of thy God which is in thine hand; and to carry the silver and gold, which the king and his counsellors have freely offered unto the God of Israel, whose habitation is in Jerusalem, and all the silver and gold that thou canst find in all the province of Babylon, with the freewill offering of the people, and of the priests, offering willingly for the house of their God which is in Jerusalem: That thou mayest buy speedily with this money bullocks, rams, lambs, with their meat-offerings and their drink-offerings, and offer them upon the altar of the house of your God which is in Jerusalem. And whatsoever shall seem good to thee, and to thy brethren, to do with the rest of the silver and the gold, that do after the will of

your God.   The vessels also that are given thee for the
service of the house of thy God, those deliver thou before the God of Jerusalem.   And whatsoever more shall
be needful for the house of thy God, which thou shalt
have occasion to bestow, bestow it out of the king's
treasure house.   And I, even I Artaxerxes the king, do
make a decree to all the treasurers which are beyond
the river, that whatsoever Ezra the priest, the scribe of
the law of the God of heaven, shall require of you, it
be done speedily, unto an hundred talents of silver, and
to an hundred measures of wheat, and to an hundred
baths of wine, and to an hundred baths of oil, and salt
without prescribing how much" (Ezra 7:11-22).

There is nothing in this decree concerning the restoration of the Holy City Jerusalem.

The Fourth Decree:

In 445 B. C. in the twentieth year of the reign of
Artaxerxes Longimanus, Nehemiah appeared before the
king with a sad heart.   His countenance told the king
that something was drastically wrong and that Nehemiah was a man under a heavy burden and much
sorrow.   The king asked him, "Why is thy countenance
sad, seeing thou art not sick?   This is nothing else but
sorrow of heart" (Neh. 2:2).   Nehemiah made his request known to the king and asked permission to return
to Jerusalem to rebuild it.   He said to the king, ". . .
Why should not my countenance be sad, *when the city,*
the place of my fathers' sepulchres, lieth waste, and
the gates thereof are consumed with fire?" (Neh. 2:3).

When Nehemiah made this statement to the king,
he inquired how long the prophet desired to be away,

and just what he wanted the king to do concerning the rebuilding of the city of Jerusalem. Nehemiah was allowed to return to the Holy City—and his mission was not only *religious;* it was also *political* in the eyes of the enemies of the Jews. Such outsiders as Sanballat and Tobiah opposed the mission, saying that the building of the walls and restoration of the city would be an act of rebellion and a danger to the king's empire.

Nehemiah and the group who returned with him repaired the walls in fifty-two days (Neh. 6:15), but it took *twelve years* to complete the rebuilding and restoration of the city of Jerusalem, to re-establish the law and ordinances of worship in the temple. Nehemiah's rebuilding of the wall and the city is definitely a fulfillment of the prophecy in Daniel 9:25: "*. . . The street shall be built again, and the wall, even in troublous times.*"

Nehemiah's mission was not only to re-establish Jerusalem as a city of worship (the city of the temple) but as a political capital also—the capital of the Jewish nation:

"And it came to pass in the month Nisan, in the twentieth year of Artaxerxes the king, that wine was before him: and I took up the wine, and gave it unto the king. Now I had not been beforetime sad in his presence. Wherefore the king said unto me, Why is thy countenance sad, seeing thou art not sick? This is nothing else but sorrow of heart. Then I was very sore afraid, and said unto the king, Let the king live for ever: why should not my countenance be sad, when the city, the place of my fathers' sepulchres, lieth waste, and the gates thereof are consumed with fire?

Then the king said unto me, For what dost thou make request?   So I prayed to the God of heaven. And I said unto the king, If it please the king, and if thy servant have found favour in thy sight, that thou wouldest send me unto Judah, unto the city of my fathers' sepulchres, that I may build it.

"And the king said unto me, (the queen also sitting by him,) For how long shall thy journey be? and when wilt thou return?   So it pleased the king to send me; and I set him a time. Moreover I said unto the king, If it please the king, let letters be given me to the governors beyond the river, that they may convey me over till I come into Judah; and a letter unto Asaph the keeper of the king's forest, that he may give me timber to make beams for the gates of the palace which appertained to the house, and for the wall of the city, and for the house that I shall enter into. And the king granted me, according to the good hand of my God upon me.

"Then I came to the governors beyond the river, and gave them the king's letters. Now the king had sent captains of the army and horsemen with me. When Sanballat the Horonite, and Tobiah the servant, the Ammonite, heard of it, it grieved them exceedingly that there was come a man to seek the welfare of the children of Israel. So I came to Jerusalem, and was there three days.

"And I arose in the night, I and some few men with me; neither told I any man what my God had put in my heart to do at Jerusalem: neither was there any beast with me, save the beast that I rode upon. And I went out by night by the gate of the valley, even before the dragon well, and to the dung port, and viewed the walls of Jerusalem, which were broken down, and the gates thereof were consumed with fire.

"Then I went on to the gate of the fountain, and to the king's pool: but there was no place for the beast that was under me to pass. Then went I up in the night by the brook, and viewed the wall, and turned back, and entered by the gate of the valley, and so returned. And the rulers knew not whither I went, or what I did; neither had I as yet told it to the Jews, nor to the priests, nor to the nobles, nor to the rulers, nor to the rest that did the work.

"Then said I unto them, Ye see the distress that we are in, how Jerusalem lieth waste, and the gates thereof are burned with fire: come, and let us build up the wall of Jerusalem, that we be no more a reproach. Then I told them of the hand of my God which was good upon me; as also the king's words that he had spoken unto me. And they said, Let us rise up and build. So they strengthened their hands for this good work. But when Sanballat the Horonite, and Tobiah the servant, the Ammonite, and Geshem the Arabian, heard it, they laughed us to scorn, and despised us, and said, What is this thing that ye do? Will ye rebel against the king? Then answered I them, and said unto them, The God of heaven, He will prosper us; therefore we His servants will arise and build: but ye have no portion, nor right, nor memorial, in Jerusalem" (Neh. 2:1-20).

In the second chapter of Nehemiah there is no decree in words, but the king undoubtedly gave the prophet some form of document or letters giving him the authority to *repair the walls and rebuild the city—* for had not Nehemiah had some form of legal document, those who opposed the restoration of the Holy City would certainly have stopped him from repairing the walls. The decree given to Nehemiah by Artaxerxes is the only one which has to do with rebuilding the city; therefore, it must be the same decree referred to by Gabriel as having to do with the beginning of the seventy weeks of prophecy.

By using literal arithmetic, it will be found that the yardstick of 483 years (7 weeks and 62 weeks—69 weeks) will not fit into any of these spaces. We can see that the decree of Cyrus in 536 B. C. could not have been the starting point of the seventy weeks, because according to the scale of *a day representing a year,* counting from the time Cyrus issued his decree until "Messiah the Prince," the time would have run out in 53 B. C.— 49 years before the birth of Christ (which Bible authorities agree was 4 B. C.).

Then, if we should take the second decree (given by King Darius in 519 B. C.) the 483 years of the 69 weeks would have run out in 36 B. C., 32 years before the birth of Christ.

If we should take the third decree (given by Artaxerxes in 458 B. C.) the 69 weeks of years—483 years —would run OVER to the year 25 A. D.—29 years AFTER the birth of Christ.

If we take the fourth decree (given by Artaxerxes in 445 B. C.) the 483 years would carry us to 38 A. D., which would be *after the crucifixion of Christ.*

We have seen four suggested beginning points of the 69 weeks. Now let us consider points of *ending* for those weeks. Certainly we know that "Messiah the Prince" (Dan. 9:25) refers to the Lord Jesus Christ—it could mean none other; but what particular period or event in the life of the Lord Jesus does the prophecy point out? Does it refer to His birth? His baptism? His triumphal entry? or to some other incident?

According to authorities, the life of Jesus on earth was 33 years. Was the birth of Christ the point where the 69 weeks climaxed? Many Bible scholars teach that the birth of Christ was the termination of the 69 weeks of prophecy. Remember, it was Gabriel who announced the 69 weeks to Daniel, and it was the same Gabriel who announced to Mary that she would be the mother of *Messiah the Prince:* "And the angel said unto her, Fear not, Mary: for thou hast found favour with God. And, behold, thou shalt conceive in thy womb, and bring forth a son, and shalt call His name JESUS. He shall be great, and shall be called the Son of the Highest: and the Lord God shall give unto Him the throne of His father David: And He shall reign over the house of Jacob for ever; and of His kingdom there shall be no end" (Luke 1:30-33).

It is true that Gabriel did not, in so many words, tell Mary that Jesus was *Messiah the Prince,* but he did announce to her that Jesus would have the throne of David—and He was born a *prince of the house of David.* The wise men in Matthew 2:1, 2 referred to Jesus as King, in John 18:33-37 Pilate asked Him if He were a king, and He was crucified *"King of the Jews."* Yet He was never crowned king, He never occupied the throne of David; but He was a *Prince,* a prince is a king in the making—and a king must be a prince in the house of his father before he is crowned king. To date Jesus has not been crowned King, He has not received His kingdom; but *He will be crowned King,* He will sit on the throne of His father David in Jerusalem and reign over this earth during the Millennium. Jesus is now our High Priest; He is at the right hand of God making intercession for believers (Heb. 1:1-3; I Tim. 2:5).

In the fulness of time Jesus came, born of a virgin, born Jesus the Saviour—born to die on the cross to satisfy the holiness of God and make possible the salvation of sinners in that His death made it possible for God the Father to be just, and yet justify the ungodly on the merit of the shed blood of His Son. Jesus was not King while here upon this earth—He was *Saviour.* He came, born of a woman, born under the law—not to reign, but to *redeem* those who were under the law (Gal. 4:4).

After the custom of the law, Jesus went with His parents to the temple at the age of twelve; but with that one exception His first public appearance was at the age of thirty when He came to John to be baptized in Jordan. John knew who He was and refused to baptize Him, saying, "I have need to be baptized of thee, and comest thou to me?" But Jesus said, "Suffer it to be so now: for thus it becometh us to fulfil all righteousness" (Matt. 3:13-17 in part). John baptized Jesus, "and, lo, the heavens were opened unto Him, and He saw the Spirit of God descending like a dove and lighting upon Him." Jesus was anointed by the Holy Ghost. ("Messiah" means "anointed One.")

When Jesus was baptized, God the Father announced, *"This is my beloved Son, in whom I am well pleased."* He did not announce, "This is my King who shall reign over all the earth." God the Father—sovereign God—knows the end in the beginning; He knows all that will occur *between* the beginning and the ending. Jesus was to wear the crown of thorns before He was to wear a crown as King of kings and reign over the earth. The baptism of Jesus announced His entrance into His public ministry, which ministry announced the kingdom; but the Jews rejected the kingdom. They cried out, "We will not have this Man to reign over us! Give us Barabbas! Crucify the Christ! Let His blood be upon us, and upon our children!"

The third outstanding event in the life of Jesus here on earth was His *triumphal entry* into the Holy City. Christ was omniscient, knowing all things. He knew who He was, He knew why He came into the world. He said, "I came not to be ministered unto, but to minister, and to give my life a ransom for many. No man taketh my life from me—I lay it down of myself. I have come that they might have life and have it more abundantly."

Jesus knew that His crucifixion was near, and that He was soon to be "cut off" (Dan. 9:26). His messiahship must be publicly declared and publicly recognized before He was nailed to the cross. He therefore set the stage and took the proper steps toward the public declaration of His messiahship:

"Rejoice greatly, O daughter of Zion; shout, O daughter of Jerusalem: behold, thy King cometh unto thee: He is just, and having salvation; lowly, and riding upon an ass, and upon a colt the foal of an ass" (Zech. 9:9).

At the time of the yearly Passover, people flocked to the city by the hundreds. On that memorable day Jesus descended the Mount of Olives, riding upon an ass, "the foal of an ass" (as was prophesied centuries before). The people shouted, *"Hosanna to the Son of David: Blessed is He that cometh in the name of the Lord!"*

Since Jesus was omniscient (He was God in flesh), why did He permit the people to refer to Him as King of Israel when He knew that in a few days He would be nailed to a cross, to die the most shameful death any criminal could die in His day? The answer is simple: *To fulfill the Word of God.* Jesus not only allowed it—He encouraged it and set the stage for it. He instructed His disciples to bring a donkey which they would find tied at the entrance to the city (Matt. 21:1-3; Luke 19:28-40). He even told them what to say if the owners of the donkey asked why they were taking him. They were to answer, "The Master hath need of him."

As the people shouted, *"Hosanna! Blessed be the King that cometh in the name of the Lord!"* the Pharisees said to Jesus, "Master, rebuke thy disciples." Jesus answered, "I tell you that, *if these should hold their peace, THE STONES WOULD IMMEDIATELY CRY OUT!"* (Luke 19:40).

Earlier in the ministry of Jesus this same crowd had attempted to force Him to become their King. They would have crowned Him by force, but He rejected their attempt. Now He is consenting and contributing to it. He accepted their calling Him King and gave aid in bringing it about, thus proving that the triumphal entry certainly had prophetic significance. The people spread their garments in His path, strewed His way with palm branches and cried, "Hosanna!" Jesus did not allow this just in order to put Himself in the limelight, to put on a "dress parade" or to make the headlines. This was definitely a fulfillment of prophecy.

Many Bible scholars agree (and so does this author) that *the triumphal entry* is the end of Daniel's 69th week and marks *the point of the coming of Messiah the Prince.* It was the only time in His earthly ministry when Jesus assumed the attitude of a king. Those who *accepted* Him as King accepted Him as *Messiah the Prince,* and there is no reason why the prophecies recorded in Zechariah 9:9 and Daniel 9:25 should not refer to this event.

The first time Jesus rode into Jerusalem He was riding on an humble little donkey as prophesied in Zechariah 9:9. When He comes to Jerusalem a second time, He will be riding on a magnificent white stallion and He will be followed by the armies of heaven riding on white horses (Rev. 19:11-16). When He rides into Jerusalem from the air, followed by His armies on white horses, that will mark *the end of the 70th week* of Daniel's prophecy—the end of the reign of Antichrist, the time when Jesus will *destroy the armies of Antichrist* and annihilate the enemies of God's chosen people, Israel.

It seems reasonable that when Jesus rode into Jerusalem on a little colt, His humble entry into the Holy

City should mark the ending of the 69 weeks of troublesome times; and when He comes with the armies of heaven as recorded in Revelation 19, this tremendous event will mark the climax of the reign of the false messiah, Antichrist.

Scripture's Calendar

How many days are in a year according to the Scriptures? The answer is found in Genesis 7:11-24 and 8:3, 4:

"In the six hundredth year of Noah's life, in the second month, the seventeenth day of the month, the same day were all the fountains of the great deep broken up, and the windows of heaven were opened" (Gen. 7:11).

"And the waters prevailed upon the earth an hundred and fifty days" (Gen. 7:24).

"And the ark rested *in the seventh month, on the seventeenth day of the month,* upon the mountains of Ararat" (Gen. 8:4).

Here is what we have in these verses: The waters were upon the earth for 150 days. According to Genesis 7:11 the flood began in the second month, the seventeenth day of that month; and according to Genesis 8:4 the ark rested the seventh month, the seventeenth day. From the seventeenth day of the second month to the seventeenth day of the seventh month is exactly five months; and five months of 30 days each add up to 150 days. According to Genesis 7:24, *the waters prevailed upon the earth for 150 days.* Thus, the calendar of Scripture gives us a month of 30 days, a year of 360 days.

It is true that in our day we use a year of 365¼ days; but according to Genesis, God determines time by 30 days to the month, 360 days to the year. So in prophetical chronology we use the calendar year of 360 days, and we have learned that God measures prophetic time *a day for a year*. Therefore, 30 days to a month would apply to 30 years—(7 weeks plus 62 weeks would be 483 years)—and by reckoning from the edict granted by Artaxerxes in 445 B. C. as the starting point of the 69 weeks, and the triumphal entry as the climax of the 69 weeks, we have the 483 years represented by the 69 weeks pointed out in Daniel 9:25, plus 6 to 8 years not accounted for.

So it seems that there is a small gap between the seven weeks and the sixty-two weeks, in which there are years not accounted for, just as there is a gap between the sixty-ninth and the seventieth weeks.

One Bible scholar says: "In order to show that in sacred history and prophecy it is no unusual thing to skip years during which God's people are not especially concerned, it may be helpful to look at other dates.

"In I Kings 6:1 it is stated that it was in the four hundred and eightieth year after the children of Israel came out of Egypt that Solomon began building the temple. If we will take the chronological Bible dates and follow them through from the Exodus to the fourth year of Solomon, we will find it is 611 years, or 131 years more than what is stated in I Kings 6:1. But by carefully going through the book of Judges and taking out the years when Israel was under the domination of foreign kings, and adding to it the 20-year period in I Samuel when the ark was out of its accustomed place, we will find that they amount to just exactly 131 years.

1. In Judges 3:8 we learn that the children of Israel served Chushan-rishathaim *eight years.*

2. Judges 3:12-14 tells us that they were in servitude to the Moabites for a period of *eighteen years.*

3. In Judges 4:2, 3 we learn that Israel was in servitude to the Canaanites for *twenty years.*

4. In Judges 6:1 they served the Midianites for *seven years.*

5. In Judges 10:7, 8 they were in servitude to the Philistines for *eighteen years.*

6. In Judges 13:1 we read, 'And the children of Israel did evil again in the sight of the Lord; and the Lord delivered them into the hands of the Philistines *forty years.'*

7. In I Samuel 7:2 the ark was out of its accustomed place.

"So it seems evident that the 480 years of I Kings 6:1 is a sacred cycle in which the years of foreign domination are not counted."

Sir Robert Anderson, a converted English lawyer, worked out the problem in his book called *The Coming Prince,* and used the date 445 as the one to coincide with the prediction of Daniel 9:25. He shows that according to Jewish reckoning, the 483 years would involve a total of 173,880 days. I quote from his book:

"The 1st Nisan in the twentieth year of Artaxerxes (the edict to rebuild Jerusalem) was 14th March, B. C. 445.

"The 10th Nisan in Passion Week (Christ's entry into Jerusalem) was 6th April, A. D. 32.

"The intervening period was 476 years and 24 days (the days being reckoned inclusively, as required by the language of the prophecy, and in accordance with the Jewish practice).

"But 476 x 365 equals—	173,740 days
Add (14th March to 6th April, both inclusive)—	24 days
Add for leap years—	116 days
	173,880 days

"And 69 weeks of prophetic years of 360 days (or 69 x 7 x 360) equals 173,880 days.

"It may be well to offer here two explanatory remarks. First: in reckoning years from B. C. to A. D., one year must always be omitted; for it is obvious, ex. gr., that from B. C. 1 to A. D. 1 was not TWO years, but one year. B. C. 1 ought to be described as B. C. 0, and it is so reckoned by astronomers."

Regardless of whose calculations we use, there seems to be a year or two difference. We can count on one thing, however: The Bible is not wrong and *God's calculations* are not wrong. Any error that may occur is in profane chronology or could easily be in the time space not counted in God's timetable between the "7 weeks and the 62 weeks." The fact is, however, the difference in time in the calculations we have given is so small as to indicate that the "69 weeks" cover the time between the edict of Artaxerxes in B. C. 445 and the triumphal entry of Jesus into Jerusalem.

Then we read, "And after threescore and two weeks shall Messiah be cut off, but not for Himself: and the people of the prince that shall come shall destroy the city and the sanctuary; and the end thereof shall be with a flood, and unto the end of the war desolations are determined" (Dan. 9:26). We know that shortly after Jesus rode into Jerusalem on the little donkey, He was nailed to the cross. *He was "cut off."*

Now this is the question to which we must find an answer: *Is there a time-space between the 69th and 70th weeks of Daniel's seventy weeks of prophecy?* The only place to find the answer is in the textbook of the Christian, the Word of God.

Daniel 9:26 clearly tells us that between the 69th and 70th weeks, Messiah the Prince (the Lord Jesus Christ) should be cut off. *That was fulfilled in the crucifixion of the Lord Jesus on Golgotha.*

In the second place, Daniel 9:26 tells us that Jerusalem and the temple will be destroyed: *This occurred in 70 A. D.* when Titus the Roman overran the city, butchered 5,000,000 Jews and left not one stone upon another.

In the third place, we learn in this verse that after the destruction of the Holy City, there will be a long period of wars and rumors of wars, which period Jesus spoke of as *the times of the Gentiles:* "Jerusalem shall be trodden down of the Gentiles until the times of the Gentiles be fulfilled" (Luke 21:24). We are still in *the times of the Gentiles* and Gentile rulers still dominate world power throughout the earth. It is true that *the fig tree* (Israel) is budding and putting forth leaves, and by that sign we know that summer is near.   Certainly we are living in the closing days of this age of grace— the period of time between the 69th and 70th weeks of Daniel's prophecy.

The Olivet Discourse recorded in Matthew 24, Mark 13, and Luke 21 is the key to the interpretation of Daniel 9:26, 27.   In Matthew 24, the disciples came to Jesus and showed Him the buildings of the temple—tremendous buildings of stone; and Jesus said to them, "Verily I say unto you, There shall not be left here one stone upon another, that shall not be thrown down." This literally happened in 70 A. D.   *Every stone was thrown down and the city was utterly destroyed.*

Later, on the Mount of Olives, the disciples asked Jesus, "Tell us, when shall these things be? and what shall be the sign of thy coming, AND OF THE END OF THE WORLD?"

In reply, Jesus gave the disciples a list of things that will take place before His coming again.   He warned, "Take heed that no man deceive you.   For many shall come in my name, saying, I am Christ; and shall deceive many."   This is the age of religious deception.

There will be "wars and rumours of wars."   These things must come to pass—"but the end is not yet. For nation shall rise against nation, and kingdom against kingdom: and there shall be famines, and pestilences, and earthquakes, in divers places. *All these are the beginning of sorrows.*   Then shall they deliver you (the Jews) up to be afflicted, and shall kill you; and ye shall be hated of all nations for my name's sake." *(We are living in that hour of which Jesus spoke.   Jews have been butchered by the millions in recent years.)*

"And then shall many be offended, and shall betray one another, and shall hate one another. And many false prophets shall rise, and shall deceive many. And because iniquity shall abound, the love of many shall wax cold. . . . And this Gospel of the Kingdom shall be preached in all the world for a witness unto all nations; *AND THEN SHALL THE END COME*" (Matt. 24:1-14 in part).

The "END" is the time when Jesus will return—not FOR the Church in the Rapture, but WITH the Church in the Revelation—to destroy Antichrist. Notice in the very next verse: "When ye therefore shall see the abomination of desolation, spoken of by Daniel the prophet, stand in the holy place, (whoso readeth, let him understand:) Then let them which be in Judaea flee into the mountains" (verse 15).

Here Jesus specifically names four things: (1) Daniel; (2) the "abomination of desolation"; (3) the temple; (4) Judaea. In other words, He points out a specific place and specific events that will transpire just before all hell breaks out on earth, and these things will occur in the middle of the *seventieth week*. After three and one-half years of peace, Antichrist will break his covenant with the Jews and make one last, desperate attempt to annihilate Israel from the face of the earth.

The following verses describe *the Revelation*—not the Rapture. Then in verses 32 and 33 of the same chapter, Jesus gives the parable of the fig tree—and the fig tree is definitely Judah. (Study Jeremiah 24 in connection with this.) In this parable we are clearly instructed, "So likewise ye, when ye shall see all these things, know that (the Revelation) is near, even at the doors."

In the true sense of the word, there are no *"signs"* of the Rapture; the signs given point to the Revelation —the time when Jesus will come in judgment to make His enemies His footstool. The Rapture is the time when Jesus will come to make up His jewels. At that time He will come as a thief in the night, and in a moment, "in the twinkling of an eye," all believers will be translated to meet the Lord in the clouds in the air. Daniel's seventieth week separates the Rapture from the Revelation. The Rapture will take place before the *beginning* of the reign of Antichrist; the Revelation will come *at the close* of the reign of Antichrist. *There is definitely a time space between the 69th and 70th weeks of Daniel, and that space has already run through more than 1900 years.*

We clearly see from the Scriptures we have studied in detail that *Daniel's seventieth week* (as described in Daniel 9:24-27), *the Olivet discourse* (given by Jesus and recorded in Matthew 24:1-35), and *the revelation given to John* on the Isle of Patmos (the message contained in the seals, the trumpets and the vials—Rev. 6:1— 18:24), all cover exactly the same period. This period has to do with the Jews here on earth. It has no reference whatsoever to the Church of the living God. We of the Church will not be here when these events take place; we will be with Jesus at the marriage supper in the sky, being rewarded for our stewardship.

God gave Daniel the blueprint of the seventieth week. In the Olivet discourse, Jesus gave His disciples a much *fuller* picture of Daniel's seventieth week. John the Beloved, in exile, was given a minutely detailed report on Daniel's seventieth week, and what Daniel said in *one verse,* John enlarged to a grand total of thirteen tremendous chapters!

This proves to me beyond the shadow of a doubt that the Bible is not the product of man, but that it is God's infallible, verbally inspired Word. There was no need for Daniel to write 13 chapters describing the Great Tribulation period; there was no need for Jesus to give the disciples 13 chapters in Matthew; but in this day and hour there IS a drastic need for the preaching of these 13 chapters that describe the judgment which will fall upon this earth immediately following the Rapture of the Church, when the Antichrist will reign supreme and blood will run like water in the streets.

The Second Coming of Christ

In studying the book of Daniel we must keep in mind the fact that the book has to do with *"the times of the Gentiles."* Therefore the visions of Daniel cover the entire period of that time. The dream of Nebuchadnezzar (the first vision recorded in Daniel) covers the whole time of the Gentiles, and the image IN the vision was not to be totally destroyed until the Stone cut out of the mountain without hands destroyed the colossal kingdom of Babylon. This will take place at the second coming of Jesus Christ. He is the Stone that will crumble, crush, and grind Babylon into powder.

The beast visions seen by Daniel cover the entire "times of the Gentiles," even to the end when the counterfeit Christ (the "little horn") will be destroyed.

This will take place at the time when Christ comes as described by Jude, with tens of thousands of His saints.

Is the vision of the seventy weeks (seventy sevens) an exception to all other visions in the book of Daniel? Do the seventy weeks extend only to the *first* coming—the *birth of Christ?* And does the seventy-week period end with the destruction of Jerusalem? It stands to reason that the vision of the seventy weeks also covers the entire period of the "times of the Gentiles." The visions of Daniel are not separated; they are one and the same—each adding light and understanding to the others. Therefore, the visions in Daniel—from the beginning of the book to the end—cover the entire period known as "the times of the Gentiles," and this period has already lasted for more than 25 centuries.

It is perhaps a few years—a few weeks, months, days, or even moments—until the Rapture; and then the reign of Antichrist will bring *the times of the Gentiles* to a climax. Jehovah God gave Daniel these visions by way of instructing him as to what would take place concerning the Jews and the Holy City of Jerusalem, until the transgressions of the Jews were finished. Their transgressions are *not yet finished,* and they are still scattered all over the world. It is true that the fig tree is now budding, but the Jews are still hated above all peoples of earth, and by no means are they all back in their own land. Only a percentage of them have returned. Daniel learned through these visions that his people would be scattered all over the world and would be trodden down of the Gentiles until *the times of the Gentiles* shall come to an end. The seventy weeks are distinctly Jewish; they concern the dealings of God with His chosen nation and people, and have nothing whatsoever to do with the Church.

It is very significant that Daniel, in one great leap, moves from "the cutting off" of the Prince (the crucifixion of Christ) *all the way to the destruction of Jerusalem* —which we know happened in 70 A. D. when Titus overran and destroyed the city; and then he moves on from the destruction of Jerusalem in 70 A. D. to the Antichrist (verse 27) and his covenant with the Jews for three and one-half years. This will take place immediately after the Rapture, so we see that in these two verses (26 and 27) Daniel covers a period of more than 1900 years thus far.

The Church had no place in the prophecy concerning Daniel's people and city.   Daniel did not see the Church.   He knew nothing of the Church, and the period of time from the crucifixion to the Rapture was completely blank to him.   The mystery of the Church was not revealed to Daniel (nor to any of the Old Testament prophets).   It was revealed to the Apostle Paul at the appointed time.   The gap between Daniel's 69th and 70th weeks is as wide as the Dispensation of the Church—the period of time in which we now are, and which is rapidly headed toward the climax—the end of the Dispensation of Grace.

In Daniel's seventy weeks of prophecy we have seen that 69 weeks (483 years according to the prophetic scale of a day representing a year) have elapsed, and they closed with the triumphal entry of Jesus into Jerusalem.   It is true that Jerusalem was not destroyed until 70 A. D., but the sentence was passed when the

Jews crucified Jesus.

As Jesus looked out over Jerusalem and wept, He said, "O Jerusalem, Jerusalem, which killest the prophets, and stonest them that are sent unto thee; how often would I have gathered thy children together, as a hen doth gather her brood under her wings, and ye would not! Behold, *your house is left unto you desolate:* and verily I say unto you, Ye shall not see me, until the time come when ye shall say, Blessed is He that cometh in the name of the Lord" (Luke 13:34, 35).

Notice the words, ". . . *Your house IS left unto you desolate."* Jesus did not say, "Your house WILL BE left desolate at some future date." Titus did not destroy the city of Jerusalem until 70 A. D., and these words were spoken in 33 A. D.; but at that very moment the Jews had crossed God's deadline and sentence had been passed! God does not always pay off on Saturday night—but He always pays *for sure.*

We clearly see that 483 years of Daniel's seventy weeks have already passed. Only one week of years remains to be fulfilled. For 1900 years the Jews have been scattered to the ends of the earth and to every island of the sea; but they have never been assimilated by other nations. They have kept their identity: *anywhere, under any circumstance, Jews are clearly recognized as Jews.* They have never lost their national peculiarities; they are the same today as when Jesus walked upon this earth. Everything that has ever happened to the Jews and to their land of Palestine was prophesied and is clearly laid down in God's Word:

"For the children of Israel shall abide many days without a king, and without a prince, and without a sacrifice, and without an image, and without an ephod, and without teraphim: Afterward shall the children of Israel return, and seek the Lord their God, and David their king; and shall fear the Lord and His goodness in the latter days" (Hos. 3:4,5).

There are teachers and preachers today who would have us believe that God has cast away His people, but He has not: Paul says, "I say then, Hath God cast away His people? God forbid. For I also am an Israelite, of the seed of Abraham, of the tribe of Benjamin. God hath not cast away His people which He foreknew. Wot ye not what the Scripture saith of Elias? how he maketh intercession to God against Israel ... For I would not, brethren, that ye should be ignorant of this mystery, lest ye should be wise in your own conceits; that *blindness IN PART is happened to Israel, until the fulness of the Gentiles be come in*" (Rom. 11:1,2,25).

God has preserved His people, and in the latter days they will return to their own land. They are returning in this very hour just as rapidly as they can possibly return to the new state of Israel. In May 1948 the fig tree began to bud. The buds are swelling, the leaves are growing. The stage is now set and one day Israel will be restored to their land. Time will not permit me to give the text of all these Scriptures, but please read and study Jeremiah 30:10, 11; 16:14, 15; 24:6. Then study Isaiah 11:11, 12; 43:5-7; Amos 9:14, 15. These Scriptures given to us by God's holy prophets prove beyond the shadow of a doubt that the Jews will be restored to their own land—*as a nation,* not just a handful of them. To the student of God's Word it is crystal-clear that the Jew is God's timepiece in relation to prophecy; and as far as the Jew is concerned, God's timeclock stopped at the end of the 69th week of Daniel's seventy weeks of prophecy. It stopped when the Jews crucified the Lord of glory:

"Ye men of Israel, hear these words: Jesus of Nazareth, a Man approved of God among you by miracles and wonders and signs, which God did by Him in the midst of you, as ye yourselves also know: Him, being delivered by the determinate counsel and foreknowledge of God, ye have taken, and by wicked hands have crucified and slain" (Acts 2:22, 23).

The Period Between the 69th and 70th Weeks

"And after threescore and two weeks shall Messiah be cut off, but not for Himself: and the people of the prince that shall come shall destroy the city and the sanctuary; and the end thereof shall be with a flood, and unto the end of the war desolations are determined" (Dan. 9:26).

Four things are named in this verse that will occur between the 69th and the ending of the 70th week:

1. Messiah, the Lord Jesus Christ, should be "cut off—but not for Himself."

2. The Holy City and the temple of God will be destroyed.

3. A prince will come who will destroy the city and the sanctuary.

4. Palestine, the home of Israel, will be desolate until the consummation of the seventy weeks, which will end in the second coming of Christ in the Revelation with tens of thousands of His saints to destroy the desolator, the Man of Sin, the Antichrist.

Messiah WAS cut off, Jesus DID die—but not for Himself. He died for others. He bore our sins on the tree in His own body: "Who His own self bare our sins in His own body on the tree, that we, being dead to sins, should live unto righteousness: by whose stripes ye were healed" (I Pet. 2:24).

Gabriel announced to Mary that her Son Jesus would sit on the throne of His father David—but instead of receiving the kingdom and reigning from the throne of David, Jesus was rejected, denied, arrested, and crucified.   He was "cut off" for no reason of His own. There was no guile in Him, He was spotless, not one of His enemies could convince Him of sin. False witnesses were called to *lie,* in order that He might be condemned and sentenced to die on the cross.

Jesus (whom they thought would be the Saviour of Israel, the great King to lead them to victory over the Romans) displayed none of the earthly glories and dignities to which Israel's promised Messiah was entitled, according to the prophecies of the Old Testament. Jesus of Nazareth was not crowned with a king's crown— He was crowned with a crown of thorns. He did not sit on a throne—He was nailed to a cross. But the fact that *He would be cut off* was prophesied by Daniel centuries before it happened.

History teaches that soon after the Jews rejected their Messiah and requested Barabbas in His stead, God refused to recognize them any longer as a nation, and the temple was no longer recognized as God's house. Jesus said, *"It is written, My house shall be called the house of prayer; but ye have made it a den of thieves"* (Matt. 21:13). And from that time forward, Jesus no longer recognized the temple as God's house. He said, "Behold, your house is left unto you desolate (meaning *God-forsaken)"* (Matt. 23:38).

Jesus sat on the Mount of Olives overlooking the city He so loved and over which He wept, and foretold the destruction of that city and its inhabitants: "And they shall fall by the edge of the sword, and shall be led away captive into all nations: and Jerusalem shall be trodden down of the Gentiles, until *the times of the Gentiles* be fulfilled" (Luke 21:24). We know that in 70 A. D. the city was leveled and millions of Jews were slaughtered.

It is clearly set forth in Daniel 9:26 that "the prince that shall come" (Antichrist, not the Lord Jesus Christ) shall arise after the Rapture of the Church, when the Roman empire will be revived and the ten kings ally themselves for one purpose, and the "little horn" rises out of the revived Roman empire. The Antichrist (the little horn), the last Gentile ruler, is described in Daniel 7:8, 24, 25 and various other verses.

We must not forget in the study of Daniel that his prophecy has to do with "the times of the Gentiles," and its purpose is to disclose in *the "little horn"* the last great Gentile world ruler—*the Antichrist.*

The prophecy of the seventy weeks *of necessity* includes this prince who will arise in the end time and will rule over this earth in the latter days. The prince referred to in verse 26 is "the king of fierce countenance," the devil in flesh—*Antichrist.*

Also in this verse we learn that Palestine and the Holy City will be desolated until the consummation of the seventy weeks, at which time the Lord Jesus will come and destroy the desolator and restore the land. There will then be peace on earth and good will toward men.

From Deuteronomy 8:7-9 we learn that when the children of Israel moved into the land of Palestine under Joshua, they found it a land flowing with milk and honey and "all manner of fruits":

"For the Lord thy God bringeth thee into a good land, a land of brooks of water, of fountains and depths that spring out of valleys and hills; a land of wheat, and barley, and vines, and fig trees, and pomegranates; a land of oil olive, and honey; a land wherein thou shalt eat bread without scarceness, thou shalt not lack any thing in it; a land whose stones are iron, and out of whose hills thou mayest dig brass."

The soil in Palestine brought forth abundantly and will do so again during the Millennium. This land of milk and honey continued as long as God's people obeyed His laws and kept His sabbaths; but God warned Israel that if they did not obey Him, if they turned to other gods, He would punish them. He would shut up the heavens and the fields would not yield a harvest:

"And it shall come to pass, if ye shall hearken diligently unto my commandments which I command you this day, to love the Lord your God, and to serve Him with all your heart and with all your soul, that I will give you the rain of your land in his due season, the first rain and the latter rain, that thou mayest gather in thy corn, and thy wine, and thine oil. And I will send grass in thy fields for thy cattle, that thou mayest eat and be full. Take heed to yourselves, that your heart be not deceived, and ye turn aside, and serve other gods, and worship them; and then the Lord's wrath be kindled against you, and He shut up the heaven, that there be no rain, and that the land yield not her fruit; and lest ye perish quickly from off the good land which the Lord giveth you" (Deut. 11:13-17).

It is true that the Jews who are now in Israel are working miracles through *irrigation* of the land—but only to a small degree compared to the time when Jesus will *restore* the land to the descendants of Abraham: "The wilderness and the solitary place shall be glad for them; and *the desert shall rejoice, and blossom as the rose*" (Isaiah 35:1).

"Instead of the thorn shall come up the fir tree, and instead of the brier shall come up the myrtle tree: and it shall be to the Lord for a name, for an everlasting sign that shall not be cut off" (Isaiah 55:13).

"Then shall the earth yield her increase; and God, even our own God, shall bless us" (Psalm 67:6).

"And the floors shall be full of wheat, and the fats shall overflow with wine and oil. And I will restore to you the years that the locust hath eaten, the cankerworm, and the caterpiller, and the palmerworm, my great army which I sent among you. And ye shall eat in plenty, and be satisfied, and praise the name of the Lord your God, that hath dealt wondrously with you: and my people shall never be ashamed" (Joel 2:24-26).

From the Scriptures we have considered under each of these four headings, we see that of these things prophesied in Daniel 9:26 (to occur after the 69th week), *two* have been fulfilled, one is *now in the process* of fulfillment, and the fourth is definitely future: this is the appearing of the prince—the Antichrist:

"And he (Antichrist) shall confirm the covenant with many for one week: and in the midst of the week he shall cause the sacrifice and the oblation to cease, and for the overspreading of abominations he shall make it desolate, even until the consummation, and that determined shall be poured upon the desolate" (verse 27).

Some will suggest that the personal pronoun in this verse refers to the Prince of princes, the Lord Jesus—but not so. The covenant of Christ is *everlasting:*

"Now the God of peace, that brought again from the dead our Lord Jesus, that great Shepherd of the sheep, through the blood of the *everlasting covenant*" (Heb. 13:20).

By contrast, the Antichrist—the same personage who rides out on a white horse, bearing a bow (the symbol of peace) in Revelation 6:2—will *bring* peace for about three and one-half years; and then *he will break the covenant* "in the midst of the week," and all hell will be loosed here upon earth. Here is the picture:

The Jews will be gathered back in their own land, and they will become a great nation. In Jeremiah 16:14, 15; 30:10, 11, Amos 9:14, 15, and Isaiah 43:5-7 we read concerning the great nation that will be revived in the land of Palestine. When the Rapture takes place and the Church is taken out of the earth, every born again person will be gone. The Antichrist will then offer peace to the Jews in their own land. He will permit them to build their temple; and, of course, when he offers them this covenant of peace and permits them to rebuild their temple and set up their worship, they will receive it gladly. (While on a missionary tour in Palestine, I heard that the Jews already have the stones cut, ready to build their temple when they possess the land where the Mosque of Omar now stands—the very spot where Solomon's temple once stood.)

They will enjoy peace for a space of three and one-half years, and then in the midst of the week the Antichrist will break the covenant, take away the freedom he has given Israel, and if Jesus did not intervene and shorten those days there would not be one person left alive!

But God has always had a faithful remnant—and He always will. In I Kings 19:18 we read of the seven thousand who had not bowed their knees to Baal, and in Revelation 7:2-10 we read of the 144,000 sealed in their foreheads with the seal of God. These 144,000 are all children of Israel, and the devil cannot kill them. They will live through the reign of terror and will lead many to believe in the coming kingdom. There will be a great number converted under their preaching—a great host that no man can number.

A New Covenant

After the reign of terror and the destruction of the Antichrist and his armies, there will be *a new covenant*. When Jesus comes in the Revelation with His saints, there will be a great national repentance on the part of Israel and they will see Messiah the King. They will recognize Him by the scars in His hands and they will fall at His feet to worship:

"Behold, the days will come, saith the Lord, that I will make a new covenant with the house of Israel, and

with the house of Judah: Not according to the covenant that I made with their fathers in the day that I
took them by the hand to bring them out of the land
of Egypt; which my covenant they brake, although I
was an husband unto them, saith the Lord: But this
shall be the covenant that I will make with the house
of Israel: After those days, saith the Lord, I will put
my law in their inward parts, and write it in their
hearts; and will be their God, and they shall be my
people. And they shall teach no more every man his
neighbour, and every man his brother, saying, Know
the Lord: for they shall all know me, from the least of
them unto the greatest of them, saith the Lord: for I
will forgive their iniquity, and I will remember their
sin no more" (Jer. 31:31-34).

In Hebrews 8:7-13 Paul gives the same truth. Please
study this passage carefully in connection with that
just quoted from Jeremiah. Paul here declares the
promise of the new covenant, and makes it very clear
that this is for the Jews, not for the Church. The
Church will share in it, in that we will reign with
Christ; but the NEW covenant is definitely to the seed
of Abraham, and it will be made with the Jews when
they repent nationally and accept Christ as King. Their
sins and iniquities will be forgiven and put away, God
will again be their God, and Jesus will reign from the
throne of David in the Holy City, Jerusalem.

The Character of the Tribulation

The tribulation period will last for seven years
(minus a few days, because the days will be shortened).
As to the *severity* of the tribulation period, it will be

divided into two parts of three and one-half years each. The last three and one-half years will be a time of extreme severity, and it is this period that is known as *the Great Tribulation.*

When God gave Daniel the seventy weeks of prophecy He did not reveal to the prophet what was to happen during the *seventieth* week. On the contrary, God commanded Daniel to seal the book: "Thou, O Daniel, *shut up the words, and seal the book, even to the time of the end:* many shall run to and fro, and knowledge shall be increased. . . .

"I heard, but I understood not. Then said I, O my Lord, what shall be the end of these things? And He said, *Go thy way, Daniel, for the words are closed up and sealed till the time of the end*" (Dan. 12:4, 8, 9). All Daniel knew was that the context of the book referred to "the time of trouble" which should come upon his people Israel "at the time of the end." Not the end of *time,* but *the time of the END*—that is, God's dealing with Israel in the end time.

However, what the sealed book contained is no longer a mystery. God did not reveal to *Daniel* the interpretation of what he penned down, but He *did* reveal to John the Beloved what will take place during the last half of Daniel's seventieth week of prophecy. The seven-sealed book of the Revelation reveals what Daniel was commanded to seal up. So if we would know what will happen during the tribulation, all we need do is study the book of Revelation, beginning with chapter 6 and continuing through chapter 19, verse 21.

In Revelation 5:1-5 John saw the seven-sealed book

"in the right hand of Him that sat on the throne," and
he "wept much because no man was found worthy to
open and to read the book, neither to look thereon." (I
personally believe this book contained the message
God did not reveal to Daniel. Daniel could not have
understood it, but it was revealed to John the Beloved.)

Then one of the elders said to John, "Weep not: behold, the Lion of the tribe of Juda, the Root of David,
hath prevailed to open the book, and to loose the sev-
en seals thereof." Of course the "Lion of the tribe of
Juda, the Root of David" is none other than the Lord
Jesus Christ.

Then in verse 6, John looked and saw "a Lamb as it
had been slain, having seven horns and seven eyes,
which are the seven Spirits of God sent forth into all
the earth." In verse 7 and on to the end of chapter 6,
the Lamb took the book and the hosts of heaven rendered due praise and exaltation to Him. "And every
creature which is in heaven, and on the earth, and
under the earth, and such as are in the sea, and all
that are in them, heard I saying, Blessing, and honour,
and glory, and power, be unto Him that sitteth upon
the throne, and unto the Lamb for ever and ever"
(v. 13).

The first seal removed: —

"And I saw when the Lamb opened one of the seals,
and I heard, as it were the noise of thunder, one of the
four beasts saying, Come and see. And I saw, and
behold a white horse: and he that sat on him had a
bow; and a crown was given unto him: and he went
forth conquering, and to conquer" (Rev. 6:1, 2).

It is sometimes mistakenly taught that the rider of this white horse is the Lord Jesus Christ—but not so. Immediately after the Rapture, the Antichrist will appear. As the false (or counterfeit) messiah he will imitate the true Messiah in every way possible. In Revelation 19:11-16 the Rider of the white horse IS *the true Christ,* the King of kings; but in our present passage the rider is the *Antichrist,* "the prince that shall come" (Dan. 9:26). Thus we see that Antichrist will appear at the *beginning* of the tribulation period, not in the middle of it as is sometimes taught.

Now notice the last part of verse 2: This rider carries "*a bow*"—no arrows, just a bow. "And a crown was given unto him: and he went forth *conquering, and to conquer.*" He will conquer with a bow, not with the deadly part of that weapon—the arrow. He will conquer without bloodshed, through flattery and vain promises. He will make a covenant with the people of Israel, and he will extend great promises to *all peoples.* Remember, when the Rapture occurs the earth will be filled with turmoil, confusion, and chaos. Coming on the scene at that time, the Antichrist will offer a solution to those problems. The people (the masses) will accept his solution and his promises, and for the first three and one-half years of the tribulation period a *false peace* will prevail. So great will be the appeal of the Antichrist that when he sits in the temple announcing himself as God the people will *worship* him as God.

The second seal removed: —

"And when He had opened the second seal, I heard the second beast say, Come and see. And there went

out another horse that was red: and power was given
to him that sat thereon to take peace from the earth,
and that they should kill one another: and there was
given unto him a great sword" (Rev. 6:3, 4).

The symbolism here is clear: As the *white* horse
denoted peaceful victory, the *red* horse denotes slaughter and rivers of blood (Isa. 63:2; Rev. 12:3). The horse
is *red,* and red is the color of blood. The rider does
not carry a bow minus arrows. He carries *"a great
sword,"* and the sword is the symbol of war. To this
rider is given power "to take peace from the earth"—
so the three and one-half years of false peace are
brought to an abrupt end and this earth will become a
literal hell! It is given to the rider of the red horse to
stir up angry passions in men "that they should kill
one another." This conqueror is a *bloody* conqueror,
and blood will run like rivers!

The third seal removed: —

"And when He had opened the third seal, I heard
the third beast say, Come and see. And I beheld, and
lo a black horse; and he that sat on him had a pair
of balances in his hand. And I heard a voice in the
midst of the four beasts say, A measure of wheat for a
penny, and three measures of barley for a penny; and
see thou hurt not the oil and the wine" (Rev. 6:5, 6).

As in Zechariah 6:2, a *black* horse follows the *red.*
This is the black horse of famine. The rider holds a
pair of scales in his hand, and a voice cries out, "A
measure of wheat for a penny . . . three measures of
barley for a penny!" When all able-bodied men are
called to war (as will be true in that hour) fields will

be neglected and untilled, food will become scarce, and there will be such famine in the earth as has never before been known. Food will be closely rationed and prices will be unbelievably high! In Jesus' day a "penny" was not as our one-cent money is today. A penny was a day's wages for a soldier or a laboring man (Matt. 20:2). So it is clear that during the last half of the Great Tribulation there will be much suffering and death from hunger as famine rides the black horse.

The fourth seal removed:—

"And when He had opened the fourth seal, I heard the voice of the fourth beast say, Come and see. And I looked, and behold a pale horse: and his name that sat on him was Death, and Hell followed with him. And power was given unto them over the fourth part of the earth, to kill with sword, and with hunger, and with death, and with the beasts of the earth" (Rev. 6:7, 8).

The pale horse of DEATH! Yes, the rider of this horse is named, "and *Hell* followed with him!" These two—Death and Hell—are the custodians of the bodies and souls of men butchered during these terrible days. At the close of the thousand-year reign of Christ they will give up their prisoners and they themselves will be cast into the lake that burns with fire and brimstone (Rev. 20:13, 14).

The fifth seal removed:—

"And when He had opened the fifth seal, I saw under the altar the souls of them that were slain for the Word of God, and for the testimony which they held: and they cried with a loud voice, saying, How

long, O Lord, holy and true, dost thou not judge and
avenge our blood on them that dwell on the earth?
And white robes were given unto every one of them;
and it was said unto them, that they should rest yet
for a little season, until their fellowservants also and
their brethren, that should be killed as they were,
should be fulfilled" (Rev. 6:9-11).

In this passage, John saw under the altar the souls
of martyrs, but not martyrs of the ages past who will
be raised and taken up with the Church. These are
the souls of those saints who will be killed during the
reign of Antichrist. They overcame "by the blood of
the Lamb, and by the word of their testimony; and
they loved not their lives unto the death" (Rev. 12:11).
After the Church is raptured, the preaching of the Gospel of the kingdom will be resumed (Matt. 24:14). The
144,000 Jewish missionaries will announce that the
King of kings is preparing to set up His reign. Of
course this message will be antagonistic and distasteful
to the Antichrist and his followers, and he will set in
motion a persecution so great that if God did not intervene "there should no flesh be saved" (Matt. 24:22).
It is the souls of those who are martyred under this
persecution that John saw under the altar.

You will notice that these martyrs who seal their
testimony with their life's blood are not praying as
Jesus prayed, "Father, forgive them, for they know not
what they do" (Luke 23:34). They are not praying as
Stephen prayed, "Lord, lay not this sin to their charge"
(Acts 7:60). The change of dispensation changes the
character of Jehovah's dealings with ungodly men.
Law was the principle on which God dealt with wicked

men in the Old Testament era. *Grace* is the principle on which He deals with men in this present dispensation. But in our passage in Revelation, *GRACE is past!* and the souls of these martyrs are praying, "How long, O Lord . . . dost thou not judge and avenge our blood on them that dwell on the earth?"

The sixth seal removed:—

"And I beheld when He had opened the sixth seal, and, lo, there was a great earthquake; and the sun became black as sackcloth of hair, and the moon became as blood; and the stars of heaven fell unto the earth, even as a fig tree casteth her untimely figs, when she is shaken of a mighty wind" (Rev. 6:12, 13).

Here we note *great physical changes* occurring, changes which will actually take place during the last half of the tribulation period. The prophet Joel foresaw these changes and recorded them in the book that bears his name: "I will shew wonders in the heavens and in the earth, blood, and fire, and pillars of smoke. The sun shall be turned into darkness, and the moon into blood, before the great and the terrible day of the Lord come" (Joel 2:30, 31).

Isaiah saw the same changes and prophesied, "Behold, the day of the Lord cometh, cruel both with wrath and fierce anger, to lay the land desolate: and He shall destroy the sinners thereof out of it. For the stars of heaven and the constellations thereof shall not give their light: the sun shall be darkened in his going forth, and the moon shall not cause her light to shine. And I will punish the world for their evil, and the wicked for their iniquity; and I will cause the

arrogancy of the proud to cease, and will lay low the
haughtiness of the terrible" (Isa. 13:9-11).

Then will be a time of horror such as has never
been since God created Adam, or ever will be again—
and beloved, I believe *exactly* what this Scripture says!
When the sixth seal is broken the earth will go into
convulsions. The sun will turn black, the moon will
become as blood, the stars will fall from their places
in the heavens. The physical changes on this earth
will be so momentous and so terrifying that men will
cry out for rocks and mountains to fall on them and
hide them from the wrath of the Lamb of God!

I would point out here that chapter 7 of Revelation
is parenthetical. In this chapter we look away from
the breaking of the seven seals, in order that the Spirit
might enlighten us concerning the sealing of a chosen
group of evangelists to preach the Gospel of the kingdom to the teeming millions who have never heard
the Gospel of the grace of God. The mention of the
sealing of the 144,000 in Revelation chapter 7 does not
mean that they were sealed between the sixth and seventh seals. There is no date or time mentioned. *When*
they were sealed, we do not know, but it was probably
immediately after the Rapture. And just as seven
thousand in Ahab's time would not bow the knee to
Baal (I Kings 19:18), so during the Great Tribulation
there will be 144,000 Israelites who will not bow the
knee to Antichrist. They will be sealed with the im-
print of the Father's name in their foreheads (Rev. 14:1;
22:4). These 144,000 sealed ones will preach the Gospel
of the kingdom throughout every square foot of this
earth during the reign of the Antichrist.

The blood-washed multitude:—

"After this I beheld, and, lo, a great multitude, which no man could number, of all nations, and kindreds, and people, and tongues, stood before the throne, and before the Lamb, clothed with white robes, and palms in their hands; and cried with a loud voice, saying: Salvation to our God which sitteth upon the throne, and unto the Lamb. And all the angels stood round about the throne, and about the elders and the four beasts, and fell before the throne on their faces, and worshipped God, saying, Amen: Blessing, and glory, and wisdom, and thanksgiving, and honour, and power, and might, be unto our God for ever and ever. Amen.

"And one of the elders answered, saying unto me, What are these which are arrayed in white robes? and whence came they? And I said unto him, Sir, thou knowest. And he said to me, These are they which came out of great tribulation, and have washed their robes, and made them white in the blood of the Lamb. Therefore are they before the throne of God, and serve Him day and night in His temple: and He that sitteth on the throne shall dwell among them. They shall hunger no more, neither thirst any more; neither shall the sun light on them, nor any heat. For the Lamb which is in the midst of the throne shall feed them, and shall lead them unto living fountains of waters: and God shall wipe away all tears from their eyes" (Rev. 7:9-17).

In this "great multitude" of which John tells us we see another class of saved people in the end time. We know they are not *the Church*, because they come out of great tribulation. We know they are not *the children of Israel* because (while there will undoubtedly be Jews among them) they are from "all nations, and kindreds, and people, and tongues." They have accepted Christ as Saviour after the Church is caught out of the earth. This great multitude will be saved and will serve God in His heavenly temple. They will never hunger nor thirst any more. These are *the blood-washed multitude!*

The seventh seal removed: —

"And when He had opened the seventh seal, there was silence in heaven about the space of half an hour" (Rev. 8:1).

This period—the time of preparation for greater judgment to follow—is more horrible and terrifying than what has already occurred. Heaven stands silent and aghast for about the space of half an hour. Following this awesome and majestic silence, seven angels in succession will each sound a trumpet.

The first trumpet: —

"The first angel sounded, and there followed hail and fire mingled with blood, and they were cast upon the earth: and the third part of trees was burnt up, and all green grass was burnt up" (Rev. 8:7).

We see here a repetition of the seventh Egyptian plague described in Exodus 9:22-26. The plague in Egypt was *literal* and I see no reason to believe otherwise concerning this judgment of the first trumpet. I believe fire, blood, and ice will fall from heaven, just as the Scripture declares it, and a third part of the trees (and all of the green grass) will be burned up.

This will be the fulfillment of Joel 2:30, 31.

The second trumpet:—

"And the second angel sounded, and as it were a great mountain burning with fire was cast into the sea: and the third part of the sea became blood; and the third part of the creatures which were in the sea, and had life, died; and the third part of the ships were destroyed" (Rev. 8:8, 9).

The "sea" mentioned here is probably the Mediterranean. The burning mountain that falls into it will destroy a third of the *creatures* in the sea and a third of the ships (no doubt fleets which will be assembled there for battle), and the *blood* of the destroyed will stain a third part of the waters of the sea!

The third trumpet:—

"And the third angel sounded, and there fell a great star from heaven, burning as it were a lamp, and it fell upon the third part of the rivers, and upon the fountains of waters: and the name of the star is called Wormwood: and the third part of the waters became wormwood; and many men died of the waters, because they were made bitter" (Rev. 8:10, 11).

The great burning star called Wormwood which falls from the heavens will poison the streams and all fresh water will be made bitter and poisonous. This water will kill many, many people. Jeremiah, the weeping prophet, says of this time, "The Lord saith, Because they have forsaken my law which I set before them, and have not obeyed my voice, neither walked therein; but have walked after the imagination of their own heart, and after Baalim, which their fathers taught

them: therefore thus saith the Lord of hosts, the God
of Israel: Behold, I will feed them, even this people,
with wormwood, and give them *water of gall* to drink"
(Jer. 9:13-15).

The fourth trumpet: —

"And the fourth angel sounded, and the third part of
the sun was smitten, and the third part of the moon,
and the third part of the stars; so as the third part of
them was darkened, and the day shone not for a third
part of it, and the night likewise" (Rev. 8:12).

When the fourth trumpet is sounded the third part
of the sun, moon, and stars will be blacked out and
will not shine. This is one of the signs of which Jesus
spoke in Luke 21:25, 26: "There shall be signs in the
sun, and in the moon, and in the stars; and upon the
earth distress of nations, with perplexity; the sea and
the waves roaring; men's hearts failing them for fear,
and for looking after those things which are coming on
the earth: for the powers of heaven shall be shaken."

After the fourth angel has sounded his trumpet, an
angel will fly through the heavens and announce the
three woes which are to follow the sounding of the
three trumpets which are yet to be heard.

The fifth trumpet: —

"And the fifth angel sounded, and I saw a star fall
from heaven unto the earth: and to him was given the
key of the bottomless pit. And he opened the bottomless pit; and there arose a smoke out of the pit, as the
smoke of a great furnace; and the sun and the air were
darkened by reason of the smoke of the pit.   And there
came out of the smoke locusts upon the earth: and

unto them was given power, as the scorpions of the earth have power. And it was commanded them that they should not hurt the grass of the earth, neither any green thing, neither any tree; but only those men which have not the seal of God in their foreheads. And to them it was given that they should not kill them, but that they should be tormented five months: and their torment was as the torment of a scorpion, when he striketh a man.

"And in those days shall men seek death, and shall not find it; and shall desire to die, and death shall flee from them. And the shapes of the locusts were like unto horses prepared unto battle; and on their heads were as it were crowns like gold, and their faces were as the faces of men. And they had hair as the hair of women, and their teeth were as the teeth of lions. And they had breastplates, as it were breastplates of iron; and the sound of their wings was as the sound of chariots of many horses running to battle.

"And they had tails like unto scorpions, and there were stings in their tails: and their power was to hurt men five months. And they had a king over them, which is the angel of the bottomless pit, whose name in the Hebrew tongue is Abaddon, but in the Greek tongue hath his name Apollyon. One woe is past; and, behold, there come two woes more hereafter" (Rev. 9:1-12).

The first woe:—

The "star" which falls from heaven in this passage is not a literal star, but an angel. Personally I believe this is none other than the Lord Jesus Christ in angelic form.   Some commentators interpret this angel to be Satan, but you will notice he is given the key to the bottomless pit, the key to hell, and certainly God would not trust that key to Satan! Also, in Revelation 1:13-18 John saw the Lord Jesus standing in the midst of the seven candlesticks, declaring, *"I am He that liveth, and was dead; and, behold, I am alive for evermore, Amen; and have THE KEYS OF HELL AND OF DEATH."*   I cannot see this personage as any other than the Christ.

When the Angel takes the key and unlocks the bottomless pit, great billows of smoke rise from the pit, smoke that fills the air and darkens the sun; and from the smoke come forth locusts—but not like the locusts we have on earth today.   These are *demon monstrosities*—a combination of horse, man, woman, lion, and scorpion.   Their size is not mentioned, but the mighty sound of their wings is like the sound of chariots on their way to battle.

The locusts we know today feed on vegetation, but these locust-monstrosities are forbidden to eat grass, trees, or any green thing.   Rather, they are permitted to afflict *men*—"those men which have not the seal of God in their foreheads."   But these men do not *die* under the torment of the locusts.   They *seek* death, they *want* to die to escape the unbearable torture; but death eludes them and for five months they must endure the woeful punishment heaped upon them.

The "king" over this organized army of demon-locusts is called in the Greek "Apollyon," meaning *destroyer*.   This is the angel of the bottomless pit, none other than the devil himself in angelic form.   He will personally lead his army of tormentors.

The sixth trumpet:—

"And the sixth angel sounded, and I heard a voice from the four horns of the golden altar which is before God, saying to the sixth angel which had the trumpet: Loose the four angels which are bound in the great river Euphrates. And the four angels were loosed, which were prepared for an hour, and a day, and a month, and a year, for to slay the third part of men.

"And the number of the army of the horsemen were two hundred thousand thousand: and I heard the number of them. And thus I saw the horses in the vision, and them that sat on them, having breastplates of fire, and of jacinth, and brimstone: and the heads of the horses were as the heads of lions; and out of their mouths issued fire and smoke and brimstone. By these three was the third part of men killed: by the *fire,* and by the *smoke,* and by the *brimstone,* which issued out of their mouths. For their power is in their mouth, and in their tails: for their tails were like unto serpents, and had heads, and with them they do hurt.

"And the rest of the men which were not killed by these plagues yet repented not of the works of their hands, that they should not worship devils, and idols of gold, and silver, and brass, and stone, and of wood: which neither can see, nor hear, nor walk: neither repented they of their murders, nor of their sorceries, nor of their fornication, nor of their thefts" (Rev. 9:13-21).

The second woe:—

At the sound of the sixth trumpet, a voice from the

golden altar will command the trumpeter to free four
angels which are bound in the river Euphrates (and we
know that there is a literal river named Euphrates).
These are *demon angels,* and they lead an army of
"two hundred thousand thousand" — *two hundred mil-
lion!*

But the horses on which this great army is mounted
are not as we know horses today. The horses John
saw had heads "as the heads of lions," their tails were
"like unto serpents," and from their mouths issued fire
and brimstone. The sting of their tails will cause horrible pain, and a third part of the people on earth will
be killed by them. The riders of these horses will wear
breastplates of fire and brimstone, matching the fire
and smoke and brimstone which issue from the horses'
mouths.

I am sure there will be some objection to the idea
that this will be literal, but I would remind you that
supernatural armies are not foreign to the Scriptures.
For example, it was a supernatural army that surrounded Elisha at Dothan. In II Kings 6:13-17 we read of
the hosts of the king of Syria as they came with horses
and chariots, by night, and surrounded the city where
Elisha and his servant were. The servant was gripped
with fear and said to Elisha, "Alas, my master! How
shall we do?" The man of God replied, "Fear not: for
they that be with *us* are more than they that be with
them." Then he prayed that God would open the eyes
(the spiritual eyes) of the young man, "and he saw:
and, behold, *the mountain was full of horses and
chariots of fire round about Elisha!"*

God has no trouble bringing events to pass in a

supernatural way if it pleases Him to do so. When Jesus returns to earth to set up His kingdom He will be followed by the armies of heaven. (Read Revelation 19:11-16.) Satan, too, has armies of demons, and he can call them to fight with him at his command and desire. We learn from the first and second "woes" which occur under the fifth and sixth trumpets that after the Church is raptured from this earth, Satan and his demons will increase in activity and in their power to torment and destroy men.

As there was an interval between the opening of the sixth and seventh seals, there will be an interval between the sounding of the sixth and seventh trumpets. During this interval a Mighty Angel will come down from heaven—and from the description given in Revelation 10:1-7 we know that this Angel is the Lord Jesus Christ Himself. He comes down from heaven, He is clothed with a cloud, He has a rainbow on His head, His face is like the sun, His feet are as pillars of fire. This corresponds with the description of Jesus in Revelation 1:12-15. The fact that His voice is "as when a lion roareth" identifies Him with the Lion of the tribe of Juda (Rev. 5:5). He stands with "His right foot upon the sea, and His left foot on the earth," denoting universal ownership and authority (Psalm 24:1).

This Mighty Angel holds a little book in His hand, and as He stands on the land and on the sea He lifts His hand to heaven and swears that "there should be time no longer." In other words, there will be no longer delay. Time does not end until the close of the perfect age and the beginning of the Age of Ages. Christ will take *formal* possession of the earth at the time of our present Scripture, but He will not take *actual possession* until He stands on the Mount of Olives, as described in Zechariah 14:4.

God's two witnesses:—

In Revelation 11:3-12 we read of *two witnesses* who will prophesy during the last half of Daniel's seventieth week (the last half of the Great Tribulation period). One of these witnesses will have power to shut up heaven so that no rain will fall. The other witness will have power over the waters to turn them to blood, and "to smite the earth with all plagues." There are differences of opinion among Bible scholars of both past and present as to who these two witnesses are. I personally believe they are Moses and Elijah. We know the Prophet Elijah closed up the heavens and it did not rain (I Kings 17:1), and we know Moses turned the water to blood (Ex. 7:20, 21) and brought plagues upon Egypt (Ex. chapters 8—10). However, there is no reason for believers to break fellowship over the identification of these two witnesses. They are God's men, during the days they witness they will have power to destroy their enemies with fire, at the end of their prophecy they will be slain and their bodies will be exposed in the streets of Jerusalem for three and one-half days.

Revelation 11:9 tells us that "they of the people and kindreds and tongues and nations shall see their dead bodies three days and an half, and shall not suffer their dead bodies to be put in graves." A few years ago it would have been impossible to understand how the whole world would see the dead bodies of these prophets as they lie in the streets of Jerusalem; but with the advanced discovery in television, electronics— and with the television satellites today—we know that it is not only possible, but an almost foregone conclusion that such views will be beamed around the world.

After three and one-half days, "the Spirit of life from God" will enter into the prophets and they will stand upon their feet. Great fear will fall upon the people as this takes place, and a voice from heaven will call the witnesses back from whence they came. They will ascend up to heaven in a cloud as their enemies behold them!

The seventh trumpet:—

"And the seventh angel sounded; and there were great voices in heaven, saying: The kingdoms of this world are become the kingdoms of our Lord, and of His Christ; and He shall reign for ever and ever! And the four and twenty elders, which sat before God on their seats, fell upon their faces, and worshipped God, saying: We give thee thanks, O Lord God Almighty, which art, and wast, and art to come; because thou hast taken to thee thy great power, and hast reigned. And the nations were angry, and thy wrath is come, and the time of the dead, that they should be judged, and that thou shouldest give reward unto thy servants the prophets, and to the saints, and them that fear thy name, small and great; and shouldest destroy them which destroy the earth.

"And the temple of God was opened in heaven, and there was seen in His temple the ark of His testament: and there were lightnings, and voices, and thunderings, and an earthquake, and great hail" (Rev. 11:15-19).

The third woe: —

What occurs at the sounding of the seventh trumpet includes all that follows, from this passage to the end of chapter 19. The opening of the seventh *seal* includes the seven trumpets and the seven vials, and the seventh *trumpet* includes the seven vials. We also note that the seventh seal, the seventh trumpet, and the seventh vial all end with voices, thunderings, lightnings, and earthquakes (Rev. 8:5; 11:19; 16:18).

In Revelation chapters 12 and 13, seven persons are mentioned. Time and space will not allow me to describe each of these personages, so let us look at a brief outline of these chapters and then proceed with our study of the tribulation period:

In Revelation 12:1, 2 a woman clothed with the sun appears. This woman is Israel, and she brings forth a man child (v. 5).

In verses 3 and 4 the "great red dragon" (Satan) appears.

In verses 5 and 6 we see the Christ child.

In verses 7 through 12 Michael the archangel appears.

In verses 13 through 16 we again see Satan.

Verse 17 sets forth the Jewish remnant.

Going on into chapter 13, in verses 1 through 10 we see the beast out of the sea.

In verse 11 through the rest of chapter 13 we see the beast out of the earth.

Chapter 14 records John's vision of the angel with the everlasting Gospel (v. 6); the fall of Babylon (v. 8); the announcement of the doom of all who worship the beast (vv. 9-12). Verse 13 proclaims the blessedness of the holy dead and in verses 14 through 20 John records his vision of Armageddon.

Revelation chapter 15 tells of the seven vials of the wrath of God, and of the angels having the seven last plagues. We then go into chapter 16 where the vials of God's wrath are poured out on this earth.

The first vial:—

"And I heard a great voice out of the temple saying to the seven angels, Go your ways, and pour out the vials of the wrath of God upon the earth. And the first went, and poured out his vial upon the earth; and there fell a noisome and grievous sore upon the men which had the mark of the beast, and upon them which worshipped his image" (Rev. 16:1, 2).

Here is a repetition of the sixth Egyptian plague (Ex. 9:8-12), and just as the plague in Egypt was literal, I believe the men who have the mark of the beast and who worship him will be afflicted with literal, running sores.

The second vial:—

"And the second angel poured out his vial upon the sea; and it became as the blood of a dead man: and every living soul died in the sea" (Rev. 16:3).

This is similar to the events that followed the sounding of the second trumpet in chapter 8, verses 8 and 9 when the third part of the sea became blood and the third part of life in the sea died, and the third part of the ships were destroyed.

The third vial:—

"And the third angel poured out his vial upon the

rivers and fountains of waters; and they became blood. And I heard the angel of the waters say, Thou art righteous, O Lord, which art, and wast, and shalt be, because thou hast judged thus. For they have shed the blood of saints and prophets, and thou hast given them blood to drink; for they are worthy. And I heard another out of the altar say, Even so, Lord God Almighty, true and righteous are thy judgments" (Rev. 16:4-7).

When the third vial is poured out, rivers and fountains of fresh water will become as blood. This is a repetition of the first Egyptian plague (Ex. 7:19-24). Can you imagine what it will be like to have no fresh water? When you turn on the water faucet—and only blood will come forth? Or when people living in the country on farms draw from a well and find only blood in the water bucket? The water in streams and rivers will be turned to blood. Yes, I believe this will be literal blood. The angel declares, "They have shed the blood of saints and prophets"—and God will give them blood to drink!

The fourth vial:—

"And the fourth angel poured out his vial upon the sun; and power was given unto him to scorch men with fire. And men were scorched with great heat, and blasphemed the name of God, which hath power over these plagues: and they repented not to give Him glory" (Rev. 16:8, 9).

When the fourth vial of God's wrath is poured out upon the earth God will literally bring the sun so close to earth that the heat from the sun will scorch men's backs! This is the only plague in the seven vials that has no Egyptian parallel. Malachi 4:1 speaks of this plague: "For, behold, the day cometh, that shall burn as an oven; and all the proud, yea, and all that do wickedly, shall be stubble: and the day that cometh shall burn them up, saith the Lord of hosts, and it shall leave them neither root nor branch." It seems that under such torment and anguish men would repent of their sins and turn to God—but these men *blaspheme* the name of God and have no repentance.

The fifth vial:—

"And the fifth angel poured out his vial upon the seat of the beast; and his kingdom was full of darkness; and they gnawed their tongues for pain, and blasphemed the God of heaven because of their pains and their sores, and repented not of their deeds" (Rev. 16:10, 11).

When the fifth vial is poured out there will be darkness over the whole kingdom of the beast, and men will be in such agony and misery that they will literally gnaw their tongues because of the intense pain. This will be a repetition of the ninth Egyptian plague (Ex. 10:21-23).

I personally believe these plagues will follow each other rapidly. In the first plague men will be covered with running sores. In the second plague the sea will become blood and all life in the sea will die. In the third plague the fresh water will be changed to blood and men will be given blood to drink. Under the fourth plague the heat will become so great that men will be scorched and burned; and in the fifth plague darkness will engulf the land. With such suffering as

running sores, blood to drink, and flesh scorched with
fire, these men will blaspheme God and chew their
tongues in their effort to relieve their terrible anguish.

The sixth vial: —

"And the sixth angel poured out his vial upon the
great river Euphrates; and the water thereof was dried
up, that the way of the kings of the east might be
prepared" (Rev. 16:12).

When the sixth vial is poured out on the earth
the river Euphrates will be dried up to allow passage
of "the kings of the east" (probably China, India,
and Japan) and their great armies as they gather for
the battle of Armageddon. This will be a repetition
of the opening of the Red Sea and the river Jordan.
The Prophet Isaiah saw this and prophesied concerning it:

"The Lord shall utterly destroy the tongue of the
Egyptian sea; and with His mighty wind shall He
shake His hand over the river, and shall smite it in
the seven streams, and make men go over dryshod.
And there shall be an highway for the remnant of
His people, which shall be left, from Assyria; like
as it was to Israel in the day that he came up out
of the land of Egypt" (Isa. 11:15, 16).

These nations will be gathered by the three unclean spirits which will proceed out of the mouth
of the dragon (Rev. 16:13, 14). They will be demons,
seducing spirits. In I Timothy 4:1 Paul speaks of "seducing spirits and doctrines of devils." It was such
a spirit that deceived King Ahab and led him to his
death (I Kings 22:20-38).

The seventh vial: —

"And the seventh angel poured out his vial into the air; and there came a great voice out of the temple of heaven, from the throne, saying, It is done. And there were voices, and thunders, and lightnings; and there was a great earthquake, such as was not since men were upon the earth, so mighty an earthquake, and so great.

"And the great city was divided into three parts, and the cities of the nations fell: and great Babylon came in remembrance before God, to give unto her the cup of the wine of the fierceness of His wrath. And every island fled away, and the mountains were not found. And there fell upon men a great hail out of heaven, every stone about the weight of a talent: and men blasphemed God because of the plague of the hail; for the plague thereof was exceeding great" (Rev. 16:17-21).

When the seventh vial of God's wrath is poured out on the earth and the great voice from heaven declares, *"It is DONE!"* there will be a great earthquake such as the world has never known. Great cities of the ten federated kingdoms—cities like London, Rome, Paris—will be destroyed. This earthquake is described in Isaiah 2:17-21. Great hail will fall from heaven, each hailstone weighing from one hundred to three hundred pounds. This will be a repetition of the seventh plague of Egypt (Ex. 9:13-35), except that the hailstones will be much larger and more severe than those which fell on the Egyptians.

Hail has been one of God's tools through the ages. In Joshua 10:11 the Word tells us that more of God's enemies were slain with hailstones than were slain by the children of Israel with the sword. The Mosaic law required that the blasphemer should be stoned (Lev. 24:16). The blasphemers of the end time will be stoned with hail from heaven, and God will do the stoning.

The Battle of Armageddon

"And I saw heaven opened, and behold a white horse; and He that sat upon him was called Faithful and True, and in righteousness He doth judge and make war. His eyes were as a flame of fire, and on His head were many crowns; and He had a name written, that no man knew, but He Himself. And He was clothed with a vesture dipped in blood: and His name is called The Word of God.

"And the armies which were in heaven followed Him upon white horses, clothed in fine linen, white and clean. And out of His mouth goeth a sharp sword, that with it He should smite the nations: and He shall rule them with a rod of iron: and He treadeth the winepress of the fierceness and wrath of Almighty God. And He hath on His vesture and on His thigh a name written, KING OF KINGS, AND LORD OF LORDS.

"And I saw an angel standing in the sun; and he cried with a loud voice, saying to all the fowls that fly in the midst of heaven, Come and gather yourselves together unto the supper of the great God; that ye may eat the flesh of kings, and the flesh of captains, and the flesh of mighty men, and the flesh of horses, and of them that sit on them, and the flesh of all men, both free and bond, both small and great.

"And I saw the beast, and the kings of the earth, and their armies, gathered together to make war against Him that sat on the horse, and against His army. And the beast was taken, and with him the false prophet that wrought miracles before him, with which he deceived them that had received the mark of the beast, and them that worshipped his image. These both were cast alive into a lake of fire burning with brimstone. And the remnant were slain with the sword of Him that sat upon the horse, which sword proceeded out of His mouth: and all the fowls were filled with their flesh" (Rev. 19:11-21).

The demon spirits sent forth from the Satanic trinity (Rev. 16:13, 14) will gather mighty armies to do battle against the Holy City. The place of battle will be the valley of Megiddo in the heart of Palestine, just outside Jerusalem—the same field where great battles of the Old Testament were fought. The forces engaged in the battle will be the allied armies of Antichrist in opposition to Christ and His army. The time of the battle will be when "the harvest of the earth is ripe" (Rev. 14:15).

Zechariah saw this day and this great battle. He declared, "Behold, the day of the Lord cometh, and thy spoil shall be divided in the midst of thee. For I will gather all nations against Jerusalem to battle; and the city shall be taken, and the houses rifled, and the women ravished; and half of the city shall go forth into captivity, and the residue of the people shall not be cut off from the city. Then shall the Lord go forth, and fight against those nations, as when He fought in the day of battle" (Zech. 14:1-3).

The Prophet Isaiah also foresaw the battle of Armageddon, and in Isaiah 63:1-6 we read:

"Who is this that cometh from Edom, with dyed garments from Bozrah? this that is glorious in His apparel, travelling in the greatness of His strength? I that speak in righteousness, mighty to save. Wherefore art thou red in thine apparel, and thy garments like Him that treadeth in the winefat? I have trodden the winepress alone; and of the people there was none with me: for I will tread them in mine anger, and trample them in my fury; and their blood shall be sprinkled upon my garments, and I will stain all my raiment.

"For the day of vengeance is in mine heart, and the year of my redeemed is come. And I looked, and there was none to help; and I wondered that there was none to uphold: therefore mine own arm brought salvation unto me; and my fury, it upheld me. And I will tread down the people in mine anger, and make them drunk in my fury, and I will bring down their strength to the earth."

The "blood" of which Isaiah wrote is not the blood of Jesus, with reference to His atonement on the cross. This is the blood of Christ's enemies, the blood that will stain His garments in His day of vengeance. He says, "The day of vengeance is *in mine heart*," and there certainly was no vengeance in the heart of Jesus when He died on the cross. His heart held nothing but love for those for whom He died. But there will come a day when Christ will take vengeance upon His enemies and redeem His chosen people, Israel.

He will redeem them from the power of Antichrist and will give them their land, and He will fulfill every promise He made to Abraham. In the day of the battle of Armageddon Christ will tread the wine-press of the fierceness of the wrath of Almighty God.

John saw the battle of Armageddon and records a vivid picture of it in Revelation 14:14-20:

"I looked, and behold a white cloud, and upon the cloud One sat like unto the Son of man, having on His head a golden crown, and in His hand a sharp sickle. And another angel came out of the temple, crying with a loud voice to Him that sat on the cloud: Thrust in thy sickle, and reap: for the time is come for thee to reap; for the harvest of the earth is ripe. And He that sat on the cloud thrust in His sickle on the earth; and the earth was reaped.

"And another angel came out of the temple which is in heaven, he also having a sharp sickle. And another angel came out from the altar, which had power over fire; and cried with a loud cry to him that had the sharp sickle, saying: Thrust in thy sharp sickle, and gather the clusters of the vine of the earth; for her grapes are fully ripe.

"And the angel thrust in his sickle into the earth, and gathered the vine of the earth, and cast it into the great winepress of the wrath of God. And the winepress was trodden without the city, and blood came out of the winepress, even unto the horse bridles, by the space of a thousand and six hundred furlongs!"

I believe this will be *a literal battle*, and I believe *blood will flow* to the horses' bridles for the space of sixteen hundred furlongs (approximately two hundred miles) through the valley of Megiddo! It will be the time of which the Prophet Isaiah wrote when he declared that the land will be soaked with blood:

"The indignation of the Lord is upon all nations, and His fury upon all their armies: He hath utterly destroyed them, He hath delivered them to the slaughter. Their slain also shall be cast out, and their stink shall come up out of their carcases, and the mountains shall be melted with their blood. And all the host of heaven shall be dissolved, and the heavens shall be rolled together as a scroll: and all their host shall fall down, as the leaf falleth off from the vine, and as a falling fig from the fig tree. For my sword shall be bathed in heaven: behold, it shall come down upon Idumea, and upon the people of my curse, to judgment.

"The sword of the Lord is filled with blood, it is made fat with fatness, and with the blood of lambs and goats, with the fat of the kidneys of rams: for the Lord hath a sacrifice in Bozrah, and a great slaughter in the land of Idumea. And the unicorns shall come down with them, and the bullocks with the bulls; and their land shall be soaked with blood, and their dust made fat with fatness. For it is the day of the Lord's vengeance, and the year of recompences for the controversy of Zion" (Isa. 34:2-8).

This will be a time of slaughter to exceed any bloodshed known to man. So great will be the destruction that God will prepare in advance to clean up the land, as recorded in the following passages.

The Supper of the Great God

"I saw an angel standing in the sun; and he cried

with a loud voice, saying to all the fowls that fly in the midst of heaven, Come and gather yourselves together unto the supper of the great God; that ye may eat the flesh of kings, and the flesh of captains, and the flesh of mighty men, and the flesh of horses, and of them that sit on them, and the flesh of all men, both free and bond, both small and great. And I saw the beast, and the kings of the earth, and their armies, gathered together to make war against Him that sat on the horse, and against His army" (Rev. 19:17-19).

The supper of the great God when the birds of the air devour the flesh of the slain will be the fulfillment of the words of Jesus in Matthew 24:28: "Wheresoever the carcase is, there will the eagles (birds of prey) be gathered together."

The mighty army of Antichrist will be destroyed by the sword (the Word) which proceeds out of the mouth of Jesus, the Rider of the white horse. All He need do to drain the blood from every soldier and animal of the armies of Antichrist is to speak the Word, "for the Word of God is quick, and powerful, and sharper than any twoedged sword, piercing even to the dividing asunder of soul and spirit, and of the joints and marrow, and is a discerner of the thoughts and intents of the heart" (Heb. 4:12).

Revelation 19:20 tells us that the beast and the false prophet will be cast into the lake of fire and brimstone, proving that the beast and the false prophet are not *systems*, but *actual persons*. They will still be burning in the lake of fire one thousand years later when the devil will be cast alive into the same lake of fire! (Read Revelation 20:7-10.)

If you, dear reader, are born again you have nothing to worry about insofar as the tribulation period is concerned, for the born again people will be taken out of this earth before the tribulation begins. I have already given you the Scriptures which clearly teach this great truth, Scriptures that prove beyond any shadow of doubt that the Church will not enter or go through any part of the Great Tribulation. If you are *NOT born again,* and if the Rapture should occur before you give your heart to Christ, you will find yourself in the reign of the Antichrist which will begin immediately after the Rapture.

You may say, "If that should happen, I will be saved immediately, and that will take care of the situation." But not so! If you have read thus far in this book—or even in this chapter—you have been exposed to the Gospel of the grace of God, you have heard the truth—and before I close this chapter I am going to give you the plan of salvation. If you *refuse* the grace of God and His free salvation, you will be without excuse; and all who have heard and rejected the truth will be damned after the Rapture. Not one person who has heard the Gospel before the Rapture will be born again during the reign of Antichrist. It is true that there will be a great multitude saved during the tribulation period, but they will be people who have never heard the Gospel, they will not have had the *opportunity* to be saved—an opportunity such as *you* have right now. II Thessalonians 2:8-12 tells of those who have rejected the Gospel and then find themselves in the kingdom of Antichrist. You will notice that *because* they rejected salvation "God shall send them strong delusion, that they should believe a lie, *that they all might be damned who believed not the truth,* but had pleasure in unrighteousness."

You, unsaved friend, have heard the truth in this message; and if you reject it, and the Rapture should occur tonight, you will not be saved tomorrow or at any other time in the future. I plead with you to give your heart to Jesus now. Read the following passages from God's Word, and if you will do what they tell you to do you will be saved now, and you need have no fear of the tribulation period:

John 1:12, 13: "As many as received Him, to them gave He power to become the sons of God, even to them that believe on His name: which were born, not of blood, nor of the will of the flesh, nor of the will of man, *but of God.*"

John 3:18: "He that believeth on Him is not condemned: but he that believeth not is condemned already, *because he hath not believed in the name of the only begotten Son of God.*"

John 5:24: "Verily, verily, I say unto you, He that heareth my Word, and believeth on Him that sent me, hath everlasting life, and *shall not* come into condemnation; but *is passed from death unto life.*"

Acts 16:31: "Believe on the Lord Jesus Christ, and *thou shalt be saved,* and thy house."

Ephesians 2:8, 9: "*By grace* are ye saved through faith; and that not of yourselves: *it is the gift of God:* not of works, lest any man should boast."

Romans 10:9, 10: "If thou shalt confess with thy mouth the Lord Jesus, and shalt *believe in thine heart*

that God hath raised Him from the dead, thou shalt
be saved.   For with the heart man believeth unto
righteousness; and with the mouth confession is made
unto salvation."

And finally, *Romans 10:17: "So then FAITH COM-
ETH BY HEARING, and hearing by THE WORD
OF GOD!"*

Chapter VIII

The King of Kings

"For unto us a Child is born, unto us a Son is given: and the government shall be upon His shoulder: and His name shall be called Wonderful, Counsellor, The mighty God, The everlasting Father, The Prince of Peace. Of the increase of His government and peace there shall be no end, upon the throne of David, and upon His kingdom, to order it, and to establish it with judgment and with justice from henceforth even for ever. The zeal of the Lord of hosts will perform this" (Isa. 9:6, 7).

"In the sixth month the angel Gabriel was sent from God unto a city of Galilee, named Nazareth, to a virgin espoused to a man whose name was Joseph, of the house of David; and the virgin's name was Mary. And the angel came in unto her, and said, Hail, thou that art highly favoured, the Lord is with thee: blessed art thou among women.

"And when she saw him, she was troubled at his saying, and cast in her mind what manner of salutation this should be. And the angel said unto her, Fear not, Mary: for thou hast found favour with God. And, behold, thou shalt conceive in thy womb, and bring forth a Son, and shalt call His name JESUS. He shall be great, and shall be called the Son of the Highest: and the Lord God shall give unto Him the

throne of His father David: and He shall reign over
the house of Jacob for ever; and of His kingdom there
shall be no end" (Luke 1:26-33).

More than seven hundred years before the birth of
Jesus, Isaiah prophesied "*a Child IS born . . . a Son
IS given . . .* and His name shall be called Wonderful,
Counsellor, The mighty God, The everlasting Father,
the Prince of Peace." Jesus was *all of this* at His
birth. He was—and is—*Wonderful.* He was—and is—
the Mighty God in flesh. He was—and is—*Counsellor.*
He was—and is—*the everlasting Father.* He was—and
is—*the Prince of Peace.*

But Isaiah also said, "Of the increase of His government and peace there shall be no end, *upon the
throne of David,* and *upon His kingdom,* to order it."
We know that up to this present time Jesus has never
occupied the throne of David, He has never reigned
as King from the city of Jerusalem. From both sacred
and secular history we know the throne of David was
a literal throne as surely as the throne of the Caesars
was literal, as surely as the throne of England today
is a literal throne. Therefore I declare on the basis
of God's Word that just as Jesus was born as prophesied, just as He was all that prophecy had said He
would be, He will also be King of kings and Lord
of lords. He will sit on the throne of David in Jerusalem and reign over this earth.

Gabriel told the Virgin Mary that she would conceive, bring forth a Son, and call His name *Jesus.*
She did conceive, she brought forth a Son, and she
named Him *Jesus.* Gabriel also told Mary that her
Son would be great, that He would be called the Son

of the Highest, and that the Lord God would "give unto Him *the throne of His father David.*" To spiritualize this statement is to wrongly divide the Word of truth. If all the prophecies concerning the *birth* of Jesus were fulfilled literally *(and they were)* then the prophecy of His literal reign on earth will be fulfilled. He will sit on the throne of David and rule over the house of Jacob forever—*"and of His kingdom there shall be no end."* It is true that the *Millennium* will last for only one thousand years (Rev. 20:4-6), but at the end of that period the *millennial* kingdom will merge into the *eternal* kingdom and Jesus will reign *forever.*

At Calvary the Lord Jesus Christ paid in full for the right to reign over a redeemed people in a redeemed creation. He purchased the right to unquestioned sovereignty as King of kings and Lord of lords. First of all He is the sovereign Ruler of the universe because *He is GOD.* In the second place He has the unquestioned right to rule because He is the son of David. In the third place, He has the right to rule because He is the crucified Lord of heaven. These rights He proved at Calvary, and when He returns to this earth with His bride *He will wear "on His vesture and on His thigh" the inscription, "KING OF KINGS, AND LORD OF LORDS"* (Rev. 19:16).

Psalm 2 firmly establishes the sovereign right of Jesus to reign in this universe over a redeemed people and a redeemed creation:

"Why do the heathen rage, and the people imagine a vain thing? The kings of the earth set themselves, and the rulers take counsel together against the Lord,

and against His Anointed, saying: Let us break their
bands asunder, and cast away their cords from us.

"He that sitteth in the heavens shall laugh: the
Lord shall have them in derision. Then shall He
speak unto them in His wrath, and vex them in His
sore displeasure. Yet have I set my King upon my
holy hill of Zion. I will declare the decree: the Lord
hath said unto me, Thou art my Son; this day have
I begotten thee. Ask of me, and I shall give thee
the heathen for thine inheritance, and the uttermost
parts of the earth for thy possession. Thou shalt break
them with a rod of iron; thou shalt dash them in
pieces like a potter's vessel. Be wise now therefore,
O ye kings: be instructed, ye judges of the earth.
Serve the Lord with fear, and rejoice with trembling.
Kiss the Son, lest He be angry, and ye perish from
the way, when His wrath is kindled but a little. Blessed are all they that put their trust in Him."

Nations are raging. People imagine "a vain thing"
—that is, kings and rulers of earth take counsel and
set themselves against Jesus and against Jehovah God.
They scheme and plan and imagine that they will
overthrow God and His Anointed, the Lord Jesus
Christ. They cry out, "Let us break their bonds
asunder, and cast away their cords from us!" In other
words, "Let us *dethrone the Almighty* and take His
place of sovereignty from Him." It was such a plan
and program that caused Lucifer to become the *devil,*
archenemy of God. It was his attempt to overthrow
God that *made* him the devil. But what does God
have to say about all of this? He declares, *"I have
set MY KING upon MY holy hill* of Zion!" It matters

not what the kings and rulers of earth may plan or attempt to do, God *will* carry out His eternal plan and purpose. The unruly, hateful, antagonistic nations cannot successfully oppose God and His anointed King of kings and Lord of lords.

You see, there is a *decree* involved here. *God the eternal Father* said, "*I* will declare the decree." Then the Lord Jesus Christ says, "The Lord hath said to me, *Thou art my Son,* this day have I begotten thee. . . . I shall give thee the heathen for thine inheritance, and the uttermost parts of the earth for thy possession." God further says to His Son, "Thou shalt break them with a rod of iron, thou shalt dash them in pieces like a potter's vessel." So God the Father has given the Son the right to rule, and no power on earth or in hell can keep Jesus from sitting on the throne of David.

Psalm 45:6 also declares the sovereign right of Jesus to rule over the universe: "Thy throne, O God, is for ever and ever: the sceptre of thy kingdom is a right sceptre."

Note here, "*Thy* throne, *O GOD,* is forever" — and which Person of the holy and blessed Trinity is addressed in this verse? The writer of the Hebrew epistle, quoting from Psalm 45, says, "But *of the SON He saith,* THY throne, O God, is for ever and ever" (Heb. 1:8). So when the Psalmist penned the words in Psalm 45:6 he was speaking of *God the SON.* There is ONE GOD manifested in three Persons — Father, Son, and Holy Spirit. The throne of God the Son is established forever *because He IS God.* He is from everlasting to everlasting — the everlasting Son of the everlasting Father (Psalm 90:1, 2).

Micah 5:2 declares, "Thou, Bethlehem Ephratah, though thou be little among the thousands of Judah, yet out of thee shall He come forth unto me that is to be Ruler in Israel; whose goings forth have been from of old, from everlasting."

Of whom is Micah speaking in this passage? Whose *"goings forth"* have been from all eternity? Who alone has eternity in being? Who alone is from everlasting to everlasting? The Babe who was born in Bethlehem and laid in a manger—He is the One who will sit on the throne of David and rule over Israel, God's chosen people.

Now let us look at another Old Testament passage—Psalm 110:

"The Lord said unto my Lord, Sit thou at my right hand, until I make thine enemies thy footstool. The Lord shall send the rod of thy strength out of Zion: rule thou in the midst of thine enemies. Thy people shall be willing in the day of thy power, in the beauties of holiness from the womb of the morning: thou hast the dew of thy youth.

"The Lord hath sworn, and will not repent, Thou art a Priest for ever after the order of Melchizedek. *The Lord at thy right hand shall strike through kings in the day of His wrath. He shall judge among the heathen, He shall fill the places with the dead bodies; He shall wound the heads over many countries.* He shall drink of the brook in the way: therefore shall He lift up the head."

Here the Psalmist declares that God will send forth *the rod of His strength* out of Zion. In other words,

He will send forth His Son, the Lord Jesus Christ, and He will rule in the midst of His enemies. In verse 5 the Psalmist describes the Lord Jesus Christ in His relationship to God the Father—God the Son is *at the right hand* of God the Father, and He will "strike through kings in the day of His wrath."

It is also God the Son who will "judge among the heathen . . . fill the places with the dead bodies" and "wound the heads over many countries." Therefore— according to the Scriptures of the Old Testament—Jesus has the right to rule because He is God—*the everlasting One.* He was in the *beginning* with the Father, and He will be *throughout all eternity* with the Father.

Also, the Lord Jesus Christ has the right to rule on this earth because He is the son of David. Speaking to David through Nathan the prophet, God promised, "Thine house and thy kingdom shall be established *for ever* before thee. *Thy throne shall be established for ever*" (II Sam. 7:16). The Scripture thus makes it clear that someone who was to descend from David would be an everlasting king, one who would have an eternal kingdom. God was saying to David, "Somewhere in your posterity there will be a King who, *because of His relationship to ME,* will sit on your throne—an *everlasting* throne." This son of David by lineage of the flesh is the only begotten Son of God, the Lord Jesus Christ.

Jesus Christ "was made of the seed of David *according to the flesh*" (Rom. 1:3), and the Davidic covenant (upon which Christ's kingdom is to be founded) secures the following:

A Davidic house—that is, posterity, family.

A throne—royal authority.

A kingdom—a sphere of rule.

Perpetuity—forever, unending.

This fourfold covenant has but one condition: Disobedience on the part of the family of David will be visited with judgment and chastisement (Isa. 24:5; II Sam. 7:14)—but not to the *total repealing* of the covenant (II Sam. 7:15; Psalm 89:20-37). God did chasten His people—first in the division of the kingdom under King Rehoboam (I Kings ch. 12), and finally in the captivity recorded in II Kings 25:1-7. Since that time there has been *only one King* of the Davidic family crowned in Jerusalem—*and He was crowned with a crown of thorns!*

The covenant confirmed to David by the oath of God is immutable. It was renewed to Mary by the angel Gabriel (Luke 1:31-33). God will give to His thorn-crowned Son *the throne of His father David* (Acts 2:29-31; 15:14-17). As surely as Jesus was nailed to a cross on Calvary, He is sure to sit on the throne of David and reign over this earth. The covenant God made with David cannot and will not be broken.

That Jesus is of the lineage of David is clearly established in two genealogies—one recorded by Matthew and the other recorded by Luke. (Please study Matthew chapter 1 and Luke chapter 3.) Matthew gives the genealogy of Joseph, husband of Mary. Luke gives the genealogy of Mary and traces her ancestry back to Adam.

Matthew traces the genealogy of Jesus back to David through his son Solomon. Luke traces it back to David through his son Nathan. But why these two lines of descent through *two* sons of David? Why would not Mary's genealogy alone suffice?

Matthew gives the genealogy of the King. *Joseph* was lineally descended from King David through King Solomon. Thus Jesus (born after Mary was married to Joseph) became the legal heir to the throne of David. The blood of Joseph did not flow in the veins of Jesus; yet according to the prophets He was to be the son of David.

Luke also shows this prophecy as fulfilled, for in his genealogy of Mary he traces *her* ancestry through the Davidic line through David's son *Nathan.* Therefore when our Lord was conceived in the womb of the Virgin Mary and born of her, he was not only an actual "son of David," but "THE Son of David." God has been very careful to give us these two genealogies in order to show us that the Lord Jesus is the rightful King. Through Joseph, His foster father, He has a legal right to David's throne, and through His mother, Mary, He is *an actual son of David.*

Furthermore, Jesus has the right to reign as King of kings and Lord of lords *because He is the Crucified One.* What really took place at Calvary? I do not know whether or not John chapter 12 affects you as it affects me, but I *read it with joy unspeakable and full of glory!* In verse 31 of that chapter we read these words of Jesus: "Now is *the judgment of this world.* Now shall the prince of this world be cast out."

Get this picture, beloved: Only hours away from the judgment hall where He would stand before Pilate, the Pharisees, the high priest, and the Roman soldiers to be condemned to die on the cross, our Lord made that statement just quoted. The natural man would say, "Jesus, you are mistaken. It is *your* judgment, not the judgment of this world and the prince of this world that is about to fall." But Jesus was *right*. *Now IS the judgment of this world.* The cross of the Lord Jesus Christ judges the world, and *every person in this world* stands or falls according to his acceptance or rejection of the death of Jesus on Calvary to save sinners!

"NOW is the prince of this world cast out!" The greatest battle of the ages took place when Jesus met Satan and his emissaries in the Garden of Gethsemane. I personally believe the devil marshalled all the forces of the damned and hurled all the powers of hell against Jesus that night; but our Lord marched on to Calvary where He was lifted between heaven and earth on the cross, that you and I might be saved. In His dying hour He cried out, *"It is FINISHED!"*

It was at Calvary that the prince of this world was cast out. Oh, yes—he is still operating, I know. He is still the archenemy of believers. But he is *a defeated foe. This world IS judged,* and one day Jesus will occupy the throne of David and reign in righteousness over this earth.

The Apostle Paul sheds light on the victory won at Calvary. In Colossians 2:14, 15 he tells us that Christ blotted out "the handwriting of ordinances that was against us, which was contrary to us, and took it out of the way, *nailing it to His cross;* and having spoiled principalities and powers, He made a shew of them openly, *triumphing over them in it."*

Revelation chapter 5 tells of the seven-sealed book which contains the redemption terms of this earth, and John wept because "no man was found worthy to open and to read the book, neither to look thereon" (v. 4). Then one of the elders said to John, "Weep not: behold, the Lion of the tribe of Juda, *the Root of David,* hath prevailed to open the book, and to loose the seven seals thereof" (v. 5). John then saw "a Lamb as it had been slain"—and this of course was none other than the Lord Jesus Christ, the Lamb of God. Because of His death, burial, and resurrection, the Lamb of God has the inalienable right to reign over this earth, and over the redeemed people—redeemed because of His shed blood.

Then we read that when the Lamb had taken the book, "the four beasts and four and twenty elders fell down before the Lamb, having every one of them harps, and golden vials full of odours, which are the prayers of saints. And they sung a new song, saying, *Thou art worthy to take the book, and to open the seals thereof: FOR THOU WAST SLAIN, and hast redeemed us to God by thy blood* out of every kindred, and tongue, and people and nation; and hast made us unto our God kings and priests: and we shall reign on the earth. And I beheld, and I heard the voice of many angels round about the throne and the beasts and the elders: and the number of them was ten thousand times ten thousand, and thousands of thousands; saying with a loud voice: *Worthy is the Lamb that was SLAIN to receive power,* and riches, and wisdom, and strength, and honour, and glory, and blessing. And every creature which is in heaven, and

on the earth, and under the earth, and such as are
in the sea, and all that are in them, heard I saying,
Blessing, and honour, and glory, and power, be unto
Him that sitteth upon the throne, and unto the Lamb
for ever and ever.   And the four beasts said, Amen.
And the four and twenty elders fell down and worshipped Him that liveth for ever and ever" (Rev. 5:
8-14).

Isaiah tells us that the Son of God has the right
to divide the spoil with the strong.   Why does He
have this right?   Isaiah 53:12 answers, *"because He
hath poured out His soul UNTO DEATH!"*

In Philippians 2:5-11, Paul declares the same truth
but expresses it in different words.   He speaks of
"Christ Jesus, who, being in the form of God, thought
it not robbery to be equal with God: but made Himself of no reputation, and took upon Him the form
of a servant, and was made in the likeness of men:
and being found in fashion as a man, *He humbled
Himself, and became obedient unto death, even the
death of the cross.   WHEREFORE God also hath
highly exalted Him, and given Him a name which is
above every name:* that at the name of Jesus every
knee should bow, of things in heaven, and things
in earth, and things under the earth; and that every
tongue should confess that Jesus Christ is Lord, to
the glory of God the Father."

As we look around us today it seems that Satan
is winning the victory over the vast majority of people.
They are serving him with the lust of the flesh.   But
one glorious morning Jesus will come, and then as
prophetic events succeed each other (leading to the

glorious reign of Christ) He will come to sit on the throne of David in Jerusalem. *Then* we shall see who is the victor!

The Word of God declares that Jesus "must reign, till He hath put all enemies under His feet" (I Cor. 15:25). The most important question concerning you as an individual is: *Will YOU reign with Him?* If you are born again, you *will.* If you die without Christ you will be hopelessly and eternally *lost.* If you are not saved, I invite you to trust Jesus now. He promised, "Verily, verily, I say unto you, He that heareth my Word, and believeth on Him that sent me, hath everlasting life, and shall not come into condemnation; but is passed from death unto life" (John 5:24).

"If thou shalt confess with thy mouth the Lord Jesus, and shalt believe in thine heart that God hath raised Him from the dead, thou shalt be saved. For with the heart man believeth unto righteousness; and with the mouth confession is made unto salvation" (Rom. 10:9, 10).

Chapter IX

The Visible Kingdom of Christ

"Our Father which art in heaven, Hallowed be thy name. Thy kingdom come. Thy will be done in earth, as it is in heaven. Give us this day our daily bread. And forgive us our debts, as we forgive our debtors. And lead us not into temptation, but deliver us from evil: For thine is the kingdom, and the power, and the glory, for ever. Amen" (Matt. 6:9-13).

"Now is Christ risen from the dead, and become the firstfruits of them that slept. For since by man came death, by man came also the resurrection of the dead. For as in Adam all die, even so in Christ shall all be made alive. But every man in his own order: Christ the firstfruits; afterward they that are Christ's at His coming.

"Then cometh the end, when He shall have delivered up the kingdom to God, even the Father; when He shall have put down all rule and all authority and power. For He must reign, till He hath put all enemies under His feet. The last enemy that shall be destroyed is death. For He hath put all things under His feet. But when He saith all things are put under Him, it is manifest that He is excepted, which did put all things under Him. And when all things shall be subdued unto Him, then shall the Son also Himself be subject unto Him that put all things under Him, *that God may be all in all"* (I Cor. 15:20-28).

The kingly rule of Almighty God in the Son of His love is the final goal of salvation's history, *"that God may be ALL IN ALL."* Therefore the kingdom of God is the real, basic theme of the Word of God. The early believers and the saints of the centuries behind us believed in a visible kingdom of God right here on this earth. Jesus taught His disciples to pray, "Thy kingdom come. Thy will be done in *earth,* as it is in *heaven,"* and one day God's will *shall be* done on earth, even as His will is done in heaven.

The Kingdom of God
Distinguished From the Kingdom of Heaven

"In those days came John the Baptist, preaching in the wilderness of Judaea, and saying, Repent ye: for the *kingdom of heaven* is at hand" (Matt. 3:1,2).

"The kingdom of heaven" is a term found primarily in Matthew's Gospel and it speaks of the messianic reign of Jesus on earth as the son of David. The phrase is derived from the prophecy of Daniel where it is clearly defined. It refers to the rule of the heavens over the earth.

In Daniel 2:34-36, 44 we read: "Thou sawest till that a stone was cut out without hands, which smote the image upon his feet that were of iron and clay, and brake them to pieces. Then was the iron, the clay, the brass, the silver, and the gold, broken to pieces together, and became like the chaff of the summer threshingfloors; and the wind carried them away, that no place was found for them: and the stone that smote the image became a great mountain, and filled the whole earth. . . . And in the days of these kings *shall the God of heaven set up a kingdom, which shall never be destroyed:* and the kingdom shall not be left to other people, but it shall break in pieces and consume all these kingdoms, and *it shall stand for ever."*

In Daniel 7:23-27 we read further of the kingdom of heaven: "The fourth beast shall be the fourth kingdom upon earth, which shall be diverse from all kingdoms, and shall devour the whole earth, and shall tread it down, and break it in pieces. And the ten horns out of this kingdom are ten kings that shall arise: and another shall rise after them; and he shall be diverse from the first and he shall subdue three kings.

"And he shall speak great words against the most High, and shall wear out the saints of the most High, and think to change times and laws: and they shall be given into his hand until a time and times and the dividing of time. But the judgment shall sit, and they shall take away his dominion, to consume and to destroy it unto the end. *And the kingdom and dominion, and the greatness of the kingdom under the whole heaven, shall be given to the people of the saints of the most High, whose kingdom is AN EVERLASTING KINGDOM, and all dominions shall serve and obey Him."*

Daniel makes it clear that *the kingdom of heaven* is the kingdom which *the God of heaven* will set up here on earth after the destruction of the enemies of God by the stone "cut out without hands." This speaks of the Gentile world systems (of which the devil is the prince and ruler) and the "Stone" is the Lord Jesus Christ. The kingdom which the God of heaven will set up is the kingdom promised to David's posterity.

The kingdom of heaven as described by the Old Testament prophets was confirmed to Jesus through the Annunciation (Luke 1:32, 33), and when John the Baptist came on the scene as the forerunner of Jesus he preached, *"Repent! . . . for the kingdom of heaven is AT HAND!"* This message of the kingdom was preached until Israel rejected her King and demanded His death. It was when the Jews rejected and crucified their King that God turned to the Gentiles; and since the Day of Pentecost God has been calling out a people for His name—i. e., the Gentile bride of Christ. When the bride, the New Testament Church, is complete, Christ will catch away His own—and then God will again deal with the nation Israel, as declared in Acts 15:13-18 when James preached before the council at Jerusalem:

"After they had held their peace, James answered, saying, Men and brethren, hearken unto me: Simeon hath declared how God at the first did visit the Gentiles, to take out of them a people for His name. And to this agree the words of the prophets; as it is written:

"After this I will return, and will build again the tabernacle of David, which is fallen down; and I will build again the ruins thereof, and I will set it up: that the residue of men might seek after the Lord, and all the Gentiles, upon whom my name is called, saith the Lord, who doeth all these things. Known unto God are all His works from the beginning of the world."

The kingdom of heaven will be set up after the return of the King in His glory, with His bride and all of the holy angels. In connection with this please read Matthew 24:29 through Matthew 25:46. Also read Luke 19:12-27.

However, the kingdom of *heaven* is not to be confused with the kingdom of *God*. The two are to be distinguished from each other in the following ways:

1. The *kingdom of GOD* is universal and spiritual. It includes all believers of the past, present, or future (Luke 13:28, 29). We can enter the kingdom of God only by the miracle of the new birth (John 3:3-7), and all who are truly born of the Spirit belong to the kingdom of God.

The kingdom of *heaven* is messianic, mediatorial, and Davidic. It has for its object the establishment of God's kingdom here on earth, at which time God's Son will sit on the throne of David and reign in righteousness.

2. The *kingdom of GOD* comes not with outward show. It is inward and spiritual. Jesus said to the Pharisees, "The kingdom of God cometh not with observation: . . . The kingdom of God is within you" (Luke 17:20, 21). Romans 14:17 declares, "The kingdom of God is not meat and drink; but righteousness, and peace, and joy in the Holy Ghost."

The kingdom of *heaven* is organic and will have its full manifestation (in glory) right here on earth. The kingdom of heaven will merge into the eternal kingdom of God when Christ the Son has reigned until He has put all enemies under His feet. At that time, the kingdom of heaven will be delivered up to God the Father, and the kingdom of heaven (the millennial reign of Christ) will *merge into* the eternal, unending kingdom of God.

The kingdom of God promised to David and his seed (as described by the prophets—see II Samuel 7:8-17 and Zechariah 12:8 for example) enters the New Testament account *unchanged.* In Luke 1:31-33 the angel Gabriel instructed Mary that she would be the mother of the King who would sit on the throne of David and reign over the house of Jacob forever. The King was born of the Virgin Mary, He was born in Bethlehem, just as prophesied (Micah 5:2; Isa. 7:14; Matt. 1:18-25; 2:1).

The *forerunner* of the King announced the kingdom at hand (Matt. 3:1-12). The *King* Himself announced the kingdom at hand, and the twelve *apostles* preached the kingdom at hand; but both the King and the kingdom were rejected by the Jews. They first rejected the kingdom *morally* (Matt. 11:20-24) and later they rejected it *officially* (Matt. 21:42, 43). They crowned their King with thorns and crucified Him.

In Matthew 16:18 the King announced that He would build His Church—a mystery hidden from eternity but revealed to the Apostle Paul by the Holy Ghost through the inspiration of God. In Ephesians 3:8-11 Paul explains:

"Unto me, who am less than the least of all saints, is this grace given, that I should preach among the Gentiles the unsearchable riches of Christ; and to make all men see what is the fellowship of *the mystery which from the beginning of the world hath been HID IN GOD*, who created all things by Jesus Christ: to the intent that now unto the principalities and powers in heavenly places might be known by the Church the manifold wisdom of God, according to the eternal purpose which He purposed in Christ Jesus our Lord."

The mystery of the New Testament Church is being *fulfilled NOW*—that is, in this present age, from Pentecost until the Rapture. The Church, the bride of Christ, will be caught up in the Rapture to meet Jesus in the air, as described in I Thessalonians 4:14-17.

When the King returns with His bride He will restore the Davidic monarchy in His own Person. He will regather Israel from the ends of the earth, He will sit on the throne of David, He will establish His power over all the earth, and He will reign for one thousand glorious years (Matt. 24:27-31; Luke 1:31-33; Acts 15:14-17; Rev. 20:1-6).

The kingdom of heaven, *when established* under the rule of David's Divine Son, will have as its objective the restoration of divine authority on earth. Creation will be delivered from the curse and the knowledge of the Lord will cover the earth as the waters now cover the sea. The earth can be described now as a *province* of the kingdom of God, a province which has revolted against Him but which will be reinstated when Jesus delivers the kingdom up to the Father. The eternal throne is that *of God and of the Lamb* (Rev. 22:1).

The kingdom age—the thousand-year reign of Christ —constitutes the seventh dispensation, "the dispensation of the fulness of times" (Eph. 1:10). That will be the last dispensation having to do with human life here on this earth and is identical with the kingdom God promised to David and his seed. The time of oppression and misrule will come to an end when Jesus takes over the throne of David in His kingdom (Isa. 11:1-5); but just *before* Jesus comes to set up His king-

dom the earth will be engulfed in judgment such as
has never before been known (Matt. 25:31-46; Acts
17:31).

Then the time of toil and weariness will come to an
end and give over to rest and reward (II Thess. 1:7).
"There remaineth therefore a rest to the people of God"
(Heb. 4:9). Since Adam sinned, the whole creation has
groaned and travailed in pain even until now, waiting
for the promised morning of deliverance (Rom. 8:18-23).
The time of Israel's blindness and chastisement will
come to an end. Christ will gather His people from
the ends of the earth, they will be restored to their
own land, and they will be converted (Rom. ch. 11;
Ezek. ch. 39). "Who hath heard such a thing? Who
hath seen such things? Shall the earth be made to
bring forth in one day? or shall a nation be born at
once? for as soon as Zion travailed, she brought forth
her children" (Isa. 66:8).

The "times of the Gentiles" will end in the smiting
of the great image and the setting up of the kingdom
of the heavens as described in Daniel 2:34, 35 and Revelation 19:15-21. Then will be the glorious day when
the King of kings and Lord of lords puts down all
iniquity and ungodliness. The earth is filled with
righteousness and holiness, creation will be delivered
from the curse of Genesis 3:16-19 and the sons of God
will be made manifest (Isa. 11:6-9; Rom. 8:19-21); *for*
"God, who is rich in mercy, for His great love where-
with He loved us, even when we were dead in sins,
hath quickened us together with Christ, (by grace ye
are saved;) and hath raised us up together, and made
us sit together in heavenly places in Christ Jesus:

That in the ages to come He might shew the exceeding riches of His grace in His kindness toward us through Christ Jesus" (Eph. 2:4-7).

The Visible Kingdom Confirms God's Faithfulness

The visible kingdom of Christ is the only adequate confirmation of the faithfulness of God to His promises. God cannot lie (Tit. 1:2; Heb. 6:18). "Yea, let God be true, but every man a liar!" (Rom. 3:4).

The visible kingdom of Christ is *a divine "must"* in order for God to keep His promises to Abraham and his descendants. To the believing natural descendants of faithful Abraham God promised the land that is clearly marked out in Genesis chapter 15:

"And He (God) brought (Abraham) forth abroad, and said: *Look now toward heaven, and tell the stars, if thou be able to number them.* And He said unto him, *So shall thy seed be.* And (Abraham) believed in the Lord; and He counted it to him for righteousness. And He said unto him, *I am the Lord that brought thee out of Ur of the Chaldees, to give thee this land to inherit it.* . . . In the same day the Lord made a covenant with Abram, saying, *Unto thy seed have I given this land, from the river of Egypt unto the great river, the river Euphrates"* (Gen. 15:5-7, 18).

God's promise to Abraham was made before the law was given; therefore it was not founded on law, but *grace.* In Genesis 12:1-3 God said to Abraham, "Get thee out of thy country, and from thy kindred, and from thy father's house, unto a land that I will shew thee: and *I will* make of thee a great nation, and *I will* bless thee, and make thy name great; and thou shalt be a blessing: and *I will* bless them that bless thee, and curse him that curseth thee: *and in thee shall all families of the earth be blessed."*

Paul also declares that God's promise to Abraham was of grace: "What saith the Scripture? *Abraham believed God,* and it was counted unto him for righteousness. . . . For the promise, that he should be the heir of the world, was not to Abraham, or to his seed, through *the LAW,* but through *the righteousness of FAITH.*   For if they which are of the law be heirs, faith is made void, and the promise made of none effect. . . . *Therefore it is of faith, that it might be BY GRACE;* to the end the promise might be sure to all the seed; not to that only which is of the law, but to that also which is of the faith of Abraham; who is the father of us all" (Rom. 4:3, 13-16).

Since God's promise to Abraham was not by law but by grace, it cannot be annulled because of Israel's failure.   The promise abides unchanged for the sake of God's honor and truthfulness, and for the sake of Abraham, the friend of God.   "Therefore say unto the house of Israel, Thus saith the Lord God: *I do not this for YOUR sakes, O house of Israel, but FOR MINE HOLY NAME'S SAKE,* which ye have profaned among the heathen, whither ye went" (Ezek. 36:22).   Please also read Genesis 26:2-5, Leviticus 26:42, and Romans 15:8.

God's promises are as sure as God Himself, and the Scriptures make it clear that God's promise to Abraham and his descendants cannot be broken.   "For the mountains shall depart, and the hills be removed; but *my kindness shall NOT depart from thee, neither shall the covenant of my peace be removed,* saith the Lord that hath mercy on thee" (Isa. 54:10).

God's promises are as positive as the course of day and night: *"Thus saith the Lord:* If ye can break my covenant of the day, and my covenant of the night, and that there should not be day and night in their season; then may also my covenant be broken with David my servant, that he should not have a son to reign upon his throne; and with the Levites the priests, my ministers. . . . *Thus saith the Lord:* If my covenant be not with day and night, and if I have not appointed the ordinances of heaven and earth; then will I cast away the seed of Jacob, and David my servant, so that I will not take any of his seed to be rulers over the seed of Abraham, Isaac, and Jacob . . ." (Jer. 33:20-26 in part).

God's promises are as secure as the laws of the sun and the stars: "Thus saith the Lord, which giveth the sun for a light by day, and the ordinances of the moon and of the stars for a light by night, which divideth the sea when the waves thereof roar—the Lord of hosts is His name: *If those ordinances depart from before me . . . then the seed of Israel also shall cease from being a nation before me for ever.* Thus saith the Lord: *If heaven above can be measured, and the foundations of the earth searched out beneath, I will also cast off all the seed of Israel for all that they have done"* (Jer. 31:35-37).

God's promise to Israel is as everlasting as the new heavens and the new earth: "For as the new heavens and the new earth, which I will make, shall remain before me, saith the Lord, so shall your seed and your name remain" (Isa. 66:22).

Concerning God's promise of the visible kingdom
we read in Psalm 89:3, 34-37: "I have made a covenant
with my chosen. I have sworn unto David my servant,
. . . *My covenant will I not break, nor alter the thing
that is gone out of my lips.* Once have I sworn by
my holiness that I will not lie unto David. His seed
shall endure for ever, and his throne as the sun before
me. It shall be established for ever as the moon, and
as a faithful witness in heaven."

These prophecies of the visible kingdom of Christ
were intended to be taken literally, they were never
meant to be spiritualized. *The kingdom of GOD* is
spiritual, it is within the born again people of God;
but the kingdom of heaven will be right here on earth,
a literal kingdom with a literal throne, and King Jesus
will reign from that throne for one thousand glorious
years. God cannot break His Word. He will fulfill
every promise He made to Abraham and Abraham's
descendants.

The Visible Kingdom Interprets
Messianic Prophecies of the Old Testament

The visible kingdom of Christ is really *the only
logical and reasonable* interpretation of the messianic
prophecies recorded by the prophets in the Old Testament.

In Isaiah 9:6 we read, "Unto us a Child is born,
unto us a Son is given: and the government shall be
upon His shoulder: and His name shall be called
Wonderful, Counsellor, The mighty God, The everlasting Father, The Prince of Peace." We accept that
prophecy as being *fulfilled literally* in the birth of

Jesus; but the next verse tells us, "Of the increase of His government and peace there shall be no end, upon the throne of David, and upon His kingdom, to order it, and to establish it with judgment and with justice from henceforth even for ever. The zeal of the Lord of hosts will perform this" (Isa. 9:7). *This* verse which speaks of the government, the throne, and the kingdom is often spiritualized—but why? Why should we accept the *birth* of a literal Child and then *spiritualize* His throne, His kingdom, and His government? This is wrongly dividing the Word of truth.

The promises of Christ's first coming were fulfilled in every detail. The prophecies of His second coming often appear in the same verse with the prophecies of His first coming, so why should we not believe that these, too, will be literally fulfilled? Who can justify their being taken *spiritually?* Gabriel plainly told Mary that the Son she was to bring forth would be the Son of the Highest—the Son of God; and that He would sit on the throne of David and reign over the house of Jacob (Luke 1:31-33). Jesus was *literally born* —why should we not believe that He will also literally *reign?*

Micah 5:2 declared that Christ would come from the little town of Bethlehem, and his prophecy was literally fulfilled (Matt. 2:1; Luke 2:15).

Zechariah 9:9 declared that the King of kings would enter Jerusalem "riding upon an ass, and upon a colt the foal of an ass." This prophecy, too, was literally fulfilled. Read Matthew 21:1-11.

Zechariah 11:12 prophesied the Lord's betrayal for thirty pieces of silver. Matthew 26:15 records the exact fulfillment of this prophecy, as Judas sold Jesus into the hands of His enemies for thirty pieces of silver— the price of a slave!

Psalm 22:16 declared that the hands and feet of Jesus would be pierced. The Gospels—as well as many other passages in the New Testament—tell of the fulfillment of this prophecy. Jesus was literally crucified, with literal nails piercing His hands and His feet!

Psalm 34:20 tells us, "He keepeth all His bones: not one of them is broken." This is a literal fact, so stated in John 19:31-33. When the soldiers came to break the legs of the men who hung on the crosses, they broke the legs of the two thieves who were crucified with Jesus—"but when they came to Jesus, and saw that He was dead already, *they brake not His legs.*"

Zechariah 12:10 prophesied that Jesus would be pierced, and this was literally fulfilled. John 19:34 tells us, "One of the soldiers with a spear *pierced His side,* and forthwith came there out blood and water."

In Isaiah 53:8, 9, 12 we read the prophecy of the death of Jesus. In John 19:38-42 we read of the literal fulfillment of that prophecy as Joseph of Arimathaea and Nicodemus came to Pilate to ask for the body of Jesus. They took His body from the cross, prepared it for burial, and laid it in Joseph's new tomb "wherein was never man yet laid."

It was prophesied that Jesus would rise from the dead (Psalm 16:10). His literal, bodily resurrection is recorded in the Gospels and throughout the New Testament.

We have not the time or space here to quote the

text of the following prophecies concerning the first coming of Jesus, but I do urge you to take your Bible and read the following passages from the Old Testament, and then compare them with the New Testament passages which record their literal fulfillment:

Compare: —
    Psalm 41:9 with John 13:18.
    Zechariah 13:7 with Matthew 26:31.
    Psalm 35:11 with Matthew 26:60.
    Isaiah 50:6 with Matthew 26:67.
    Zechariah 11:13 with Matthew 27:7-10.

I am sure you will find these comparisons most interesting. And now I ask you, since the prophecies concerning the first coming of Christ were literally and minutely fulfilled, why should we not believe with heart, soul, and mind that the prophecies concerning His *second coming* will also be literally fulfilled? Why should these prophecies be spiritualized? Why should we spiritualize the promised kingdom on earth and the reign of Christ from the throne of David?

Did Jesus drink "spiritual" *vinegar?* (You will find the prophecy in Psalm 69:21, its fulfillment in Matthew 27:48, Mark 15:36, John 19:29.)

Did the soldiers around the foot of the cross gamble for "spiritual" *garments?* (Prophesied in Psalm 22:18, fulfilled in Matthew 27:35, John 19:23, 24.)

Did God *figuratively* scatter the nation Israel to the ends of the earth, as declared in Deuteronomy 4:27, and is that nation even now only *figuratively* "without a king, and without a prince, and without a sacrifice, and without an image, and without an ephod, and

without teraphim"? (Hos. 3:4). Both sacred and secular history record the fulfillment, *literally,* of that
prophecy. *All* prophecy concerning Israel and the first
coming of Christ came to pass literally and actually,
not figuratively or spiritually. Therefore we have every
reason to believe that the second coming will be literal,
the kingdom will be literal, the throne will be literal,
and the reign of Jesus on earth will be literal. It is
wrongly interpreting the Word to spiritualize what
God through the prophets declared to be literal.

Some people teach that God is finished with the
nation Israel—but such teaching is error, as Romans
chapter 11 plainly declares. God *has not* cast aside
His people, and no one has the right to take what
God promised to the Jews and give those promises to
the Church, the bride of Christ. The throne of David
did not stand in heaven, but upon this earth. The
land where God will regather Israel has never been
anywhere except right here on earth—in a specific
location, *Palestine.*

Please study the following Scriptures in connection
with God's promise to bring Israel to the land promised to Abraham and his seed: Jeremiah 16:14, 15; Zechariah 10:8, 9; Isaiah 27:12, 13; Ezekiel 11:17; 28:25.

The Visible Kingdom
Explains the History of the End

The visible kingdom of Christ on earth is the only
reasonable and logical explanation of the history of
the end, a history which agrees with the words of Jesus
while He tabernacled on earth, and with the words
penned by the apostles under inspiration of the Holy

Spirit.

In Matthew 23:37-39 Jesus wept over Jerusalem and lamented, "O Jerusalem, Jerusalem! Thou that killest the prophets, and stonest them which are sent unto thee, how often would I have gathered thy children together, even as a hen gathereth her chickens under her wings, *and ye would not!* Behold, your house is left unto you *desolate.* For I say unto you, Ye shall not see me henceforth, till ye shall say, *Blessed is He that cometh in the name of the Lord.*"

From these words of Jesus we know that the house of Israel will not always *remain* desolate. Israel will not forever be under the judgment of God. In the fulness of time in the eternal program of God, the people of Israel will *recognize* their Messiah and receive Him with joy and gladness. When they see the scars in His hands and side as He stands again on the Mount of Olives (the place from which He spoke these words) they will recognize Him and receive Him, they will honor Him and will crown Him King of kings and Lord of lords. Thus being converted they will surrender themselves wholly to Him, and from the throne of David He will reign over the house of Israel. There will then be peace on earth, good will toward men. (Please study Zechariah 13:6,7 and all of Zechariah chapter 14.)

In *origin and character* the kingdom of the Lord Jesus Christ is not *OF this present world* (John 18:36), but it is certainly *FOR this present world* (Matt. 19:28). After His resurrection the disciples asked Jesus, "Lord, wilt thou at this time restore again the kingdom to Israel?" (Acts 1:6). You will notice the Lord did not

rebuke the disciples for asking this question, nor did
He say, "You have *fleshly conceptions* of the kingdom." In other words, He did not deny the coming
of the kingdom in *the visible sense* to which they had
reference. They were asking Him if He would set up
a literal kingdom *at that TIME.* His reply was, "It is
not for you to *know* the times or the seasons, which
the Father hath put in His own power" (Acts 1:7).

The mention of *"times or seasons"* proves beyond
any shadow of doubt that the kingdom of Christ *will
come* some day, *visibly,* and will be set up right here
on earth. As Jesus explained in Matthew 8:11, "Many
shall come from the east and west, and shall sit down
with Abraham, and Isaac, and Jacob, in *the kingdom
of heaven."* Then at the institution of the Lord's Supper Jesus said of the cup, "This is my blood of the
new testament, which is shed for many for the remission of sins. But I say unto you, I will not drink
henceforth of this fruit of the vine, *until that day when
I drink it new with you IN MY FATHER'S KING-
DOM"* (Matt. 26:28, 29).

In II Corinthians 3:14-16 the Apostle Paul compares
the glory of the old covenant with the glory of the
new covenant, and in this comparison he speaks of the
unbelief of Israel in the time of that nation's blindness:

"Their minds were blinded: for until this day remaineth the same vail untaken away in the reading of
the Old Testament; which vail is done away in Christ.
But even unto this day, when Moses is read, the vail
is upon their heart. Nevertheless when it shall turn to
the Lord, the vail shall be taken away."

Now compare these words with the words of Exodus 34:34: "When Moses went in before the Lord to speak with Him, he took the vail off, until he came out. And he came out, and spake unto the children of Israel that which he was commanded."

Paul was looking at a time when Israel as a nation will turn to their Messiah, when the veil will be removed from their hearts and they will attain glory and true freedom promised them in the covenant God made with Abraham. This passage in II Corinthians is a clear testimony that the Apostle Paul expected a future salvation of the nation Israel and a *visible* future kingdom. Moses removed the veil from his face every time he turned to God. In like manner, when the people of Israel turn to God, when they are converted to Jesus their true Messiah, the veil will be taken away from them and they will understand that the glory of Moses is not to be compared with the glory of the only begotten Son of God who came into this world "full of grace and truth . . . for the law was given by *Moses*, but *grace and truth came by Jesus Christ*" (John 1:14, 17).

In I Corinthians 15:20-24 Paul speaks of the bodily resurrection of the dead and specifically points out the *order* of the resurrection:

"Christ the firstfruits," then

"those that are Christ's at His coming" (in the Rapture).

"Then cometh the end," when Christ gives over the kingdom to God the Father.

Even though Israel is now scattered to the ends of the earth and is living in the hour of judgment, God has not cast away His people. He has only set them aside for a time (Rom. 11:1). Even during the dispersion, Israel still retains its hope. In Leviticus 26:44, 45 God declared:

"Yet for all that, when they be in the land of their enemies, *I will not cast them away, neither will I abhor them, to destroy them utterly,* and to break my covenant with them: for I am the Lord their God. But *I will for their sakes remember the covenant of their ancestors,* whom I brought forth out of the land of Egypt in the sight of the heathen, that I might be their God: *I am the LORD.*"

God's dealings with His chosen nation brings blessings for mankind in general; because *through the judgment of God upon Israel,* the Gospel has been proclaimed *for all the world* (Rom. 11:1-15). And when Israel is at last spiritually renewed, that nation will be received and blessed according to God's promises (Rom. 11:16-32). The blindness that has come upon Israel happened only *"in part . . . until the fulness of the Gentiles be come in"* (v. 25). At that time, the natural branches which were broken off the olive tree of God's kingdom shall be "graffed in" again, *and so all Israel shall be SAVED.*

A careful study of Romans chapter 11, comparing Scripture with Scripture and spiritual things with spiritual, will reveal the solution of the apparent conflict between God's calling of *Israel* and His calling of the bride of Christ (the New Testament Church) from among the peoples of the whole world. It is only by the future that the past can be reconciled with the present. Only by the end is the intermediate period justified. Paul's message of the grace of God stands or falls with the acknowledgement of these clear propositions. Therefore to deny the prophecies concerning the nation Israel is to deny the basis of the New Testament Church.

The question of the visible kingdom of Christ right here on earth (the millennial kingdom) is not only a question of vital history, but a question which at the same time touches the very heart of the Gospel of the grace of God, *free from law*—the Gospel that offers the gift of God to all the world. To deny the Millennium, the visible kingdom of Christ on earth, is to make God a liar in relation to His prophets, or make Paul a false witness in relation to believers in this Dispensation of Grace. Romans chapters 9 through 11 contains not only the message that justifies *God* in *His* actions, but also the message that justifies *Paul's doctrine* of justification by faith in the finished work of the Lamb of God.

According to the Gospel penned by Paul under the inspiration of the Holy Ghost, the reviving of the nation Israel and the re-gathering of God's elect people from the ends of the earth will have a definite effect on the Gentile world. It will amount to a widespread rebirth in the kingdom of the risen Christ. Jesus said to His disciples, ". . . Ye which have followed me, in the regeneration when the Son of man shall sit in the throne of His glory, ye also shall sit upon twelve thrones, judging the twelve tribes of Israel" (Matt. 19:28).

Now hear the inspired words of Paul as he penned them in Romans 11:12-15: "Now if the fall of (Israel) be the riches of the world, and the diminishing of them the riches of the Gentiles; how much more their fulness? For I speak to you Gentiles, inasmuch as I am the apostle of the Gentiles, I magnify mine office: if by any means I may provoke to emulation them which are my flesh, and might save some of them. For if the casting away of them be the reconciling of the world, what shall the receiving of them be, but life from the dead?"

Paul here confessed that he believed in *the full conversion* of the nation Israel, and explained that *from* that conversion *the most blessed effects* will flow out to mankind. In comparison with these blessings and gifts of God, all former national life will appear as lifeless, and all former riches will seem as poverty. All former national well-being (yes, even the present "poverty program" and the giving away of millions upon millions of dollars by the governments of the world) will seem as abject misery in comparison with the glorious reign of righteousness here on earth when King Jesus rules from the throne of David in Jerusalem!

Paul not only declares his belief in a future spiritual and national salvation of Israel, but at the same time shows the significance of this momentous event as including national affairs affecting the entire world and the history of salvation. Remember, "God sent not His Son into the world to condemn the world; but that the world through Him might be saved" (John 3:17), "and He is the propitiation for our sins—and not for our's only, but also for the sins of the whole world" (I John 2:2).

To What Purpose
Is the Visible Kingdom of Christ?

In Genesis chapters 1 through 3 we read the account of the creation and of the fall of man. For centuries the devil has been showing the world how he can lie and deceive, corrupt and damn souls. Does it not seem reasonable, therefore, that God should show the world how *He*, in Christ, can save and bless, and give peace—and do these things right here on the soil of this old earth which He created?

Indeed God *will* show the world that there can be peace on earth and good will toward men. He will show the world that there can be blessing and honor and glory instead of shame and disgrace and damnation. God the Father is obligated to give to His anointed King, His only begotten Son, the opportunity to prove that He is the best Judge, the best world Ruler, the greatest King ever to live on earth.

There is a minority of people in this world who love and honor Christ. There has always been such a minority, and there always *will be*. But the mass of mankind has always ignored Christ—His suffering, His death, His shame, and even His sacrifice. But one day His glory will be displayed to all creation. That glory will be displayed in the Church, the "pearl of great price," in the Pearly White City when God fulfills the promise of a new heaven, a new earth, and a new Jerusalem. But during the reign of Christ on earth, God will prove to mankind, to Satan, and to all hell that there *can be* peace even on this earth where Adam sold out to the devil. The *last* Adam (Christ) will regain all that the first Adam lost. God's

righteousness demands that Jesus be crowned King
right here on this earth where Satan has reigned as
the prince of the power of the air and the god of
this age.   It was here that Christ declared Himself
victor over the world, the flesh, and the devil, death,
hell, and the grave; and all the combined powers
of the underworld cannot keep Him from occupying
the throne of David and reigning in righteousness!
The only complete conclusion of divine self-justifica-
tion in the history of salvation will be displayed in
the visible kingdom of the Lord Jesus Christ.

Now what about the visible kingdom of Christ
on earth with reference to *mankind?* Until this present
hour man has not known how happy and glorious
life on earth could be if the Lord personally dwelt
here and occupied the throne of David to reign in
the affairs of men.   It is difficult for the mind of
man to realize that the millennial reign of Christ will
be free from prejudice, free from hatred, malice, strife,
envy, stealing, and all other species of sin so much
in evidence today.   This poor earth has had six thousand years of burdens and heartaches—but there is
coming a day of rest.

"One day is with the Lord as a thousand years,
and a thousand years as one day" (II Pet. 3:8).   So
for six days man has labored and suffered, and the
Sabbath of rest is sure to come.   This divinely revealed fact is the great world-transfiguring idea of
the revelation that the visible kingdom of God is to
be right here on earth; and by that visible kingdom
God will prove that it was not the fault of circumstance or elementary powers that men could not live

in peace with one another.   It was the fault of the sin of man, and corruption through man's archenemy, the devil.

But notice: *After* the thousand years of glorious peace and blessing with the King of kings reigning in righteousness, *what does man do?*   When the millennial kingdom comes to an end, we see *how hopelessly lost* man is by nature, for after a thousand years under a perfect, divine government—*what happens?*   The account is given in Revelation 20:7-10:

"And when the thousand years are expired, Satan shall be loosed out of his prison, and shall go out to deceive the nations which are in the four quarters of the earth, Gog and Magog, to gather them together to battle: the number of whom is as the sand of the sea.   And they went up on the breadth of the earth, and compassed the camp of the saints about, and the beloved city: and fire came down from God out of heaven, and devoured them.

"And the devil that deceived them was cast into the lake of fire and brimstone, where the beast and the false prophet are, and shall be tormented day and night for ever and ever."

Yes, even after one thousand years of perfect government, man rebels against God and an army of untold millions will surround the Holy City in a last all-out, diabolical attempt to destroy Christ! So man's last testing proves that the natural man is hopelessly lost, desperately wicked, and doomed to an eternal hell far from the grace of God provided through His Son at Calvary.

In the millennial kingdom, under the most ideal

economic and political conditions, ruled by King Jesus
in righteousness and peace, the nations of earth learn
so little!   And at the end of the Millennium seduced
by the devil, they will unite in the most fearful of
all human wars—which will end, of course, in victory
for Christ, and Satan will meet his final doom.   The
visible kingdom of Christ gives irrefutable proof that
man is not only unable to *create* ideal conditions, but
even when ideal conditions exist and man *lives under
those conditions* he remains by nature totally de-
praved.

Because of the sin of Adam, conditions cannot
improve man.   So the glorious period in history known
as the Millennium will be sad proof that God was
right when in the matter of human redemption He
completely excluded man's ability, wisdom, strength,
and power.   *God* provided salvation—"Salvation is
of the Lord" (Jonah 2:9).   This will be proved publicly,
before all creation, at the close of the Millennium
when Satan gathers the armies of Gog and the last
fearful battle is fought—when fire from heaven will
destroy the armies of Gog.   There is—there *can* be—
ONLY ONE WAY through which man can find peace,
peace with God and peace with himself, and that
one way is by the grace of God alone.   There has
never been but one way of salvation—the way of the
cross of the Lord Jesus Christ.   To Thomas He said,
"I am the WAY, the TRUTH, and the LIFE. No
man cometh unto the Father but by me" (John 14:6).

The visible kingdom of Christ is the necessary
means of carrying human history forward from this
present hour to its goal in the eternal kingdom of

God. It is true that the kingdom of God today is within the hearts of believers. Christ is the second Person of the Godhead. He is the brightness of God's glory (Heb. 1:3), "the image of the invisible God" (Col. 1:15), and He abides in the heart of every born again believer—"Christ in you, the hope of glory" (Col. 1:27). Therefore the kingdom of God is within man, and there are millions on earth today who are citizens of the kingdom of God through the new birth, the miracle of God's grace. But out of this present *hidden character* the kingdom of God will one day step forth into world-wide display, when all things are delivered unto the Father *that He may be all in all* (I Cor. 15:28).

Then in the glorious twenty-first chapter of Revelation, John the Beloved records the revelation of the new heavens, the new earth, and the Pearly White City, "the holy Jerusalem, descending out of heaven from God." John saw the new temple, and in Revelation chapter 22 he saw the new paradise and the river of the water of life. Then in chapter 22, verses 8 through 10, we read these words:

"I John saw these things, and heard them. And when I had heard and seen, I fell down to worship before the feet of the angel which shewed me these things. Then saith he unto me, See thou do it not: for I am thy fellowservant, and of thy brethren the prophets, and of them which keep the sayings of this book: worship God.

"And he saith unto me, *Seal not the sayings of the prophecy of this book: for THE TIME IS AT HAND!*"

Chapter X

The Visible Kingdom of Christ on Earth Will Be a Glorious Kingdom

"Behold, the days come, saith the Lord, that the plowman shall overtake the reaper, and the treader of grapes him that soweth seed; and the mountains shall drop sweet wine, and all the hills shall melt. And I will bring again the captivity of my people of Israel, and they shall build the waste cities, and inhabit them; and they shall plant vineyards, and drink the wine thereof; they shall also make gardens, and eat the fruit of them. And I will plant them upon their land, and they shall no more be pulled up out of their land which I have given them, saith the Lord thy God" (Amos 9:13-15).

"Then answered Peter and said unto Him, Behold, we have forsaken all, and followed thee; what shall we have therefore? And Jesus said unto them, Verily I say unto you, That ye which have followed me, in the regeneration when the Son of man shall sit in the throne of His glory, ye also shall sit upon twelve thrones, judging the twelve tribes of Israel. And every one that hath forsaken houses, or brethren, or sisters, or father, or mother, or wife, or children, or lands, for my name's sake, shall receive an hundredfold, and shall inherit everlasting life" (Matt. 19:27-29).

All creation—Israel, the Gentile nations, nature—

will have part in the visible glory of God's kingdom on earth. In that glorious day the glory of the Lord which departed from the temple (Ezek. 10:18; 11:23) will suddenly come again to His temple:

"Behold, I will send my messenger, and he shall prepare the way before me: and the Lord, whom ye seek, shall suddenly come to His temple, even the messenger of the covenant, whom ye delight in: behold, He shall come, saith the Lord of hosts" (Mal. 3:1).

Ezekiel 43:2-5 declares, "Behold, the glory of the God of Israel came from the way of the east: and His voice was like a noise of many waters: and the earth shined with His glory. . . . And the glory of the Lord came into the house by the way of the gate whose prospect is toward the east. So the Spirit took me up, and brought me into the inner court; *and, behold, THE GLORY OF THE LORD FILLED THE HOUSE!*"

Since "the times of the Gentiles" began, the city of Jerusalem has been ruled by Gentile powers:

In May of 1948 Palestine returned to the Jews and the new state of Israel was recognized. When King Jesus suddenly appears in the temple, *the glory of the Lord* will return to Jerusalem and the times of the Gentiles will come to an end:

"When ye shall see Jerusalem compassed with armies, then know that the desolation thereof is nigh. Then let them which are in Judaea flee to the mountains; and let them which are in the midst of it depart out; and let not them that are in the countries enter thereinto. For these be the days of vengeance, that all things which are written may be fulfilled. But woe unto them that are with child, and to them that give suck, in those days! for there shall be great distress in the land, and wrath upon this people. And they shall fall by the edge of the sword, and shall be led away captive into all nations: and *Jerusalem shall be trodden down of the Gentiles, until the TIMES OF THE GENTILES BE FULFILLED"* (Luke 21:20-24).

John the Beloved describes the glorious reign of Christ in these words: "The tabernacle of God is with men" (Rev. 21:3).

Christ the Glorious, Divine King

Christ will reign in GLORY:

Christ's *personal* glory will be displayed to all creation. II Samuel 23:3, 4 describes the glorious King:

"The God of Israel said, the Rock of Israel spake to me, He that ruleth over men must be just, ruling in the fear of God. And He shall be as the light of the morning, when the sun riseth, even a morning without clouds; as the tender grass springing out of the earth by clear shining after rain!"

This glorious King is IMMANUEL:

"Therefore the Lord Himself shall give you a sign: Behold, a virgin shall conceive, and bear a Son, and shall call His name Immanuel" (Isa. 7:14).

"Behold, a virgin shall be with child, and shall bring forth a Son, and they shall call His name Emmanuel, which being interpreted is, God with us" (Matt. 1:23).

This glorious King is the VICTORIOUS ONE:

"That every tongue should confess that Jesus Christ

is Lord, to the glory of God the Father" (Phil. 2:11).

This glorious King is the VICTORIOUS HERO:

"The Lord thy God in the midst of thee is mighty. He will save, He will rejoice over thee with joy. He will rest in His love, He will joy over thee with singing" (Zeph. 3:17).

This glorious King is the ONE HEAD over all:

"That in the dispensation of the fulness of times He might gather together in one all things in Christ, both which are in heaven, and which are on earth; even in Him" (Eph. 1:10).

"And the Lord shall be King over all the earth. In that day shall there be one Lord, and His name one" (Zech. 14:9).

"Then shall the children of Judah and the children of Israel be gathered together, and appoint themselves one head, and they shall come up out of the land: for great shall be the day of Jezreel" (Hosea 1:11).

This glorious King will UNITE HIS PEOPLE
as King David did:

"And I will make them one nation in the land upon the mountains of Israel; and one King shall be king to them all: and they shall be no more two nations, neither shall they be divided into two kingdoms any more at all" (Ezek. 37:22).

"And I will set up one shepherd over them, and he shall feed them, even my servant David. He shall feed them, and he shall be their shepherd. And I the Lord will be their God, and my servant David a prince among them. I the Lord have spoken it" (Ezek.

34:23, 24).

"Afterward shall the children of Israel return, and seek the Lord their God, and David their king; and shall fear the Lord and His goodness in the latter days" (Hosea 3:5).

This glorious King is THE PRINCE OF PEACE:

This earth has not known peace since the fall of man, but when Jesus reigns there *will be* peace:

"For unto us a Child is born, unto us a Son is given: and the government shall be upon His shoulder; and His name shall be called Wonderful, Counsellor, The mighty God, The everlasting Father, *THE PRINCE OF PEACE.*   Of the increase of His government and peace there shall be no end, upon the throne of David, and upon His kingdom, to order it, and to establish it with judgment and with justice from henceforth even for ever.   The zeal of the Lord of hosts will perform this" (Isa. 9:6, 7).

"He shall judge among the nations, and shall rebuke many people: and they shall beat their swords into plowshares, and their spears into pruninghooks: nation shall not lift up sword against nation, neither shall they learn war any more" (Isa. 2:4).

This glorious King will give glorious REST:

"In that day there shall be a root of Jesse, which shall stand for an ensign of the people; to it shall the Gentiles seek: and His rest shall be glorious" (Isa. 11:10).

This glorious King will be permeated with
the sevenfold Spirit of God:

"The Spirit of the Lord shall rest upon Him, the

spirit of wisdom and understanding, the spirit of counsel and might, the spirit of knowledge and of the fear of the Lord" (Isa. 11:2).

"I beheld, and, lo, in the midst of the throne and of the four beasts, and in the midst of the elders, stood a Lamb as it had been slain, having seven horns and seven eyes, which are the seven Spirits of God sent forth into all the earth" (Rev. 5:6).

"And out of the throne proceeded lightnings and thunderings and voices: and there were seven lamps of fire burning before the throne, which are the seven Spirits of God" (Rev. 4:5).

This glorious King will be the PRIEST-KING:

The Priest-King, "the Branch" of the Lord, will wear the gold and silver crown:

"Then take silver and gold, and make crowns, and set them upon the head of Joshua the son of Josedech, the high priest; and speak unto him, saying, Thus speaketh the Lord of hosts, saying, Behold the Man whose name is The BRANCH; and He shall grow up out of His place, and He shall build the temple of the Lord: Even He shall build the temple of the Lord; and He shall bear the glory, and shall sit and rule upon His throne; and He shall be a Priest upon His throne: and the counsel of peace shall be between them both" (Zech. 6:11-13).

The judgments that will come upon this earth during the tribulation period and at the close of the tribulation are symbolized in the horse-chariots of Zechariah 6:1-8.

Then immediately (vv. 9-15) Zechariah describes the

manifestation of Christ in His glorious kingdom. According to the Scriptures in both the Old and the New Testaments, this is the prophetic order—first the judgments of the Day of the Lord (the Day of the Lord is darkness and not light) and then the glorious kingdom set up immediately following these horrible judgments. (Please read Isaiah 2:10-22; 10:33, 34; 11:1-10; Revelation 19:19-21; 20:4-6.)

This is all set forth *in type* by the crowning of "Joshua the son of Josedech, the high priest" in Zechariah 6:11. (This was not a vision. Joshua was actually crowned.)

The fulfillment in The Branch will infinitely transcend the symbol. The Branch (Christ) "shall bear the glory" as the Priest-King sitting on His own throne (Zech. 6:13; Heb. 7:1-3). Christ has not yet taken His own throne, He is now seated at the right hand of God *as Priest* (Heb. 1:3; Rev. 3:21), but He is still the Holiest within the veil. The crowns that were made for the *typical* crowning of Joshua were to be laid up in the temple as a memorial, pointing to the glorious hope of Israel and keeping alive in their hearts the larger hope of the nation, namely the visible reign of their King right here on earth.

"The Branch of Jehovah" is a name of Christ and is used in the Scriptures in a fourfold way:

1. As the Son of God: "In that day shall the Branch of the Lord be beautiful and glorious, and the fruit of the earth shall be excellent and comely for them that are escaped of Israel" (Isa. 4:2). This presents the character of Christ as *Immanuel* (Isa. 7:14), "beautiful and glorious . . . *God with us*" (Matt. 1:23). This will be fully manifest to Israel when that nation is converted and restored to their own land after the return of Jesus in divine glory to regather them from the ends of the earth.

2. *As the Son of man, the last Adam:* "The first man Adam was made a living soul; the last Adam was made a quickening spirit. Howbeit that was not first which is spiritual, but that which is natural; and afterward that which is spiritual. The first man is of the earth, earthy: the second Man is the Lord from heaven" (I Cor. 15:45-47). Christ will reign as Priest-King over this earth, in the dominion given to Adam and lost by him in the Garden of Eden. Jesus the last Adam will redeem all that the first Adam lost.

3. *As Servant:* "Hear now, O Joshua the high priest, thou, and thy fellows that sit before thee: for they are men wondered at: for, behold, I will bring forth *my Servant the BRANCH*" (Zech. 3:8). This speaks of the Messiah's humiliation, His obedience "unto death, even the death of the cross" (Phil. 2:5-8). Read also Isaiah 52:13-15; 53:1-12.

4. *As King:* "Behold, the days come, saith the Lord, that I will raise unto David a righteous Branch, and a King shall reign and prosper, and shall execute judgment and justice in the earth" (Jer. 23:5). This speaks of Christ the Messiah "of the seed of David according to the flesh" (Rom. 1:3). He was truly God in flesh, but He was also very man, and as the seed of David He will be revealed in His earthly glory as King of kings and Lord of lords when He sits on the throne of David in Jerusalem.

The Gospel of Matthew is the Gospel of "the Branch

of *David.*"

The Gospel of Mark is the Gospel of *"Jehovah's Servant,* the Branch."

The Gospel of Luke is the Gospel of "the *Man* whose name is the Branch."

The Gospel of John is the Gospel of "the Branch of *Jehovah.*"

Christ, the glorious King of kings and Lord of lords, is the promise and fulfillment in one. He is *the bright and morning star* in the darkest night. He is the *dawn of the new day,* the *herald of the eternal sunrise.*

The Temple of God Rebuilt

The glorious King of kings and Lord of lords will be worshipped by all mankind during the Millennium:

"For from the rising of the sun even unto the going down of the same my name shall be great among the Gentiles; and in every place incense shall be offered unto my name, and a pure offering: for my name shall be great among the heathen, saith the Lord of hosts" (Mal. 1:11).

In the prophecy of Ezekiel, beginning with chapter 40 and continuing through chapter 44, it is plain that the events there recorded take place during the millennial reign of Christ. For a picture of the future service of offerings with so many detailed appointments, please notice Ezekiel 45:23-25; 46:4-15. Then read the account of the detailed measurements in Ezekiel 40:6-15, 41:1-4, and 43:13-18. However, it is impossible to understand these prophecies if we spiritualize them or consider them figuratively. They are *not* spiritual or figurative, but *literal and real.*

The temple will be literally built again in the city of Jerusalem:

"Moreover I will make a covenant of peace with them; it shall be an everlasting covenant with them: and I will place them, and multiply them, and will set my sanctuary in the midst of them for evermore. My tabernacle also shall be with them: yea, I will be their God, and they shall be my people. And the heathen shall know that I the Lord do sanctify Israel, when my sanctuary shall be in the midst of them for evermore" (Ezek. 37:26-28).

"And He said unto me, Son of man, the place of my throne, and the place of the soles of my feet, where I will dwell in the midst of the children of Israel for ever, and my holy name shall the house of Israel no more defile, neither they, nor their kings, by their whoredom, nor by the carcases of their kings in their high places" (Ezek. 43:7).

A careful study of Ezekiel 43:18-27; 44:11-15, 27-29; Zechariah 14:20, 21 will clearly reveal that all the chief kinds of offerings—the burnt offering, the meal offering, the thanksgiving offering, the sin offering—will be offered in the temple when it is rebuilt in Jerusalem.

Certain feasts will be solemnized—the feast of the Passover (Ezek. 45:21), the feast of tabernacles (Zech. 14:16).

The sabbaths will be kept (Ezek. 44:24; 45:17; 46:3).

In that glorious kingdom the priesthood will be in the hands of the sons of Zadok the righteous (Ezek. 40:46; 43:19; 44:15).

In Ezekiel chapters 40 through 48 the general theme is *Israel in the promised land during the Kingdom Age.*

Chapters 40 through 44 give the account of the rebuilding of the temple of the tabernacle of God.

The Scriptures mention all *eight* temples of God:

1. The tabernacle of Moses—1500 to 1000 B. C.
2. The temple of Solomon—1000 to 586 B. C.
3. The temple of Zerubbabel—516 B. C. to 70 A. D. (This temple was destroyed by Titus the Roman and was rebuilt by Herod—John 2:20.)
4. The temple of the body of Jesus (John 2:21).
5. The spiritual temple—the New Testament Church (Eph. 2:21, 22). The local church is mentioned as the temple in I Corinthians 3:16, 17, and in I Corinthians 6:19 the individual Christian is the temple.
6. The temple of the end-days (Rev. 11:1, 2).
7. The temple described by Ezekiel in chapters 40 through 44 of his prophecy.
8. The eternal temple, the New Jerusalem, described in Revelation chapter 21. It is true that John tells us, *"I saw no temple therein"*—but then he adds, *"for the LORD GOD ALMIGHTY and the LAMB are the temple of it"* (Rev. 21:22).

I know there will be some objections offered, some declarations to the effect that after the cross there will never be a service of offerings again. These objections and declarations are based on Hebrews 7:18, 8:13, and 10:10-14. I personally believe that the offerings in the Millennium will be to that time as the Lord's Supper and the rite of baptism are to this Dispensation of Grace. They will be memorial tokens representing the completed work of redemption. The services, feasts, and offerings will *look backward* to Calvary, even as the Old Testament offerings *looked forward* to Calvary

and were done away with by the cross. The Old Testament offerings look forward to the still-to-be-com-
pleted work of redemption, and even though Jesus
declared from the cross, "It is finished!" there is no
reason why Israel will not observe the feasts and offerings, pointing back to and remembering the sufferings
of the Lord that all creation might be delivered from
the curse.

The temple in the Millennium will be quite different
from the temple of Solomon. There will be no ark of
the covenant in the millennial temple: "And it shall
come to pass, when ye be multiplied and increased in
the land, in those days, saith the Lord, they shall say
no more, The ark of the covenant of the Lord: neither
shall it come to mind: neither shall they remember it;
neither shall they visit it; neither shall that be done
any more. At that time they shall call Jerusalem the
throne of the Lord; and all the nations shall be gathered unto it, to the name of the Lord, to Jerusalem:
neither shall they walk any more after the imagination
of their evil heart" (Jer. 3:16, 17).

In the temple in the Millennium there will be no
ark of the covenant (Jer. 3:16, 17), no lampstand, no
table of shewbread, no veil between the holy place
and the holy of holies. (Compare Hebrews 9:8 and
Matthew 27:51.)

Since the destruction of Jerusalem by Nebuchadnezzar, Israel has had no ark of the covenant. This
was a tremendous loss for Israel and for the temple of
Zerubbabel (516 B. C. – 70 A. D.) for without the ark
the temple was but a shell. The ark of the covenant
was the throne of the Lord, the symbol of Jehovah's

presence, the most holy object in the most holy place in the temple (Ex. 25:22). However, the absence of the ark in the Millennium will be great gain, for instead of the ark of the covenant *the Lord Himself will be present.* Jerusalem is His throne, and the presence of God is the cloud of Shekinah glory; so that the symbol (being fulfilled) now gives way to reality:

"At that time they shall call Jerusalem the throne of the Lord; and all the nations shall be gathered unto it, to the name of the Lord, to Jerusalem: neither shall they walk any more after the imagination of their evil heart" (Jer. 3:17).

"And the Lord will create upon every dwelling place of Mount Zion, and upon her assemblies, a cloud and smoke by day, and the shining of a flaming fire by night: for upon all the glory shall be a defence" (Isa. 4:5).

"Then a cloud covered the tent of the congregation, and the glory of the Lord filled the tabernacle. And Moses was not able to enter into the tent of the congregation, because the cloud abode thereon, and the glory of the Lord filled the tabernacle. And when the cloud was taken up from over the tabernacle, the children of Israel went onward in all their journeys: but if the cloud were not taken up, then they journeyed not till the day that it was taken up. For the cloud of the Lord was upon the tabernacle by day, and fire was on it by night, in the sight of all the house of Israel, throughout all their journeys" (Ex. 40:34-38).

The absence of the ark of the covenant in the millennial temple signifies the nature of the millennial kingdom. The Millennium is the transitional period of salvation into the ages of ages, the eternity of eternities. In the heavenly Jerusalem there will be no literal building. Christ will fill all things, He is the temple (Rev. 21:22).

Although in the millennial kingdom the chief part of the temple (the ark of the covenant) disappears, the shell of the temple remains throughout the Millennium. The millennial kingdom has the germ of divine perfection, the visible presence of Christ; but the shell, the old world, has not yet been done away with. All things have not yet been made new. Therefore the Millennium is at the same time the fulfillment of prophecy and the introduction to the consummation. It is the conclusion of this temple condition and also the dawn of the eternal, unending day.

Although the visible kingdom of Christ is a most perfect type of the Divine glory, that kingdom is not really the chief matter. The chief matter is *the eternal kingdom,* when all will be perfected, when all things will be delivered unto God and all creation will be made new. Glorious as the Millennium will be, the *most glorious* time will be the eternity when all things have been made new, when all things head up in the Father, the Son, and the Holy Spirit. The essence of the kingdom of Christ is the new world.

The Millennium and the kingdom of God (which will continue throughout the eternal day) are separated by the new creation. At the close of the millennial kingdom Satan will be loosed for a little season. There will be world destruction, world judgment, and then after the world has been renovated by fire and literally melted with fervent heat, there will be world transfiguration. (Study Revelation 20:1 through Revelation 21:1.)

The Old Testament prophets did not see as we see from this side of Calvary. They saw time and eternity as one, the earthly Jerusalem and the heavenly Jerusalem as one. Thus the Prophet Isaiah, speaking of the new heaven and the new earth (Isa. 65:17; 66:22), speaks of a new earth in which there will be sin and death— even though these are the exception rather than the rule: "There shall be no more thence an infant of days, nor an old man that hath not filled his days: for the child shall die an hundred years old; but the sinner being an hundred years old shall be accursed" (Isa. 65:20).

Certainly Isaiah was not speaking of the kingdom of God which will begin with the ages of ages when time is no more. He was referring to the *earthly* kingdom mentioned in Revelation 21:4. Speaking of the Jerusalem of the end-times Isaiah declares that the city has no need of the sun or the moon, because "the Lord shall be thine everlasting light" (Isa. 60:20). In this statement the prophet speaks of the kingdom of God which will continue throughout eternity.

Daniel clearly confessed that he did not understand what he had written after God had given him the twelve chapters of the prophecy that bears his name. The Old Testament writers did not understand all that they penned down under the inspiration of the Holy Spirit, but we have no such excuse today! We have the perfect law of liberty, the complete Scriptures; and the New Testament draws a clear line which divides eternity from time. There is no reason for us to spiritualize things that are definitely literal, so declared in Scriptures that cannot be misunderstood if they are studied and rightly divided as the Holy Ghost sheds light. The most glorious era this world will ever know —yea, even beyond the Garden of Eden—will be the visible kingdom of glory in the visible kingdom of Christ here on this earth!

Israel In the Glorious Kingdom

Prophetic truth in the Old Testament clearly reveals that God will one day gather His people from the ends of the earth and plant them in their own land, the land promised to Abraham, never to be plucked up again:

"It shall come to pass in that day, that the Lord shall beat off from the channel of the river unto the stream of Egypt, and *ye shall be gathered one by one, O ye children of Israel.* And it shall come to pass in that day, that the great trumpet shall be blown, and they shall come which were ready to perish in the land of Assyria, and the outcasts in the land of Egypt, and shall worship the Lord in the holy mount at Jerusalem" (Isa. 27:12, 13).

"Lift up thine eyes round about, and see: *all they gather themselves together,* they come to thee: thy sons shall come from far, and thy daughters shall be nursed at thy side" (Isa. 60:4).

"They shall walk after the Lord. He shall roar like a lion. When He shall roar, then the children shall tremble from the west. They shall tremble as a bird out of Egypt, and as a dove out of the land of Assyria: and I will place them in their houses, saith the Lord" (Hosea 11:10, 11).

"If any of thine be driven out unto the outmost parts of heaven, from thence will the Lord thy God gather thee, and from thence will He fetch thee" (Deut. 30:4).

God will use various methods to return His people from the ends of the earth to Palestine:

Through nations and kings:

Isaiah speaks of *nations* and *kings* as having to do with the return of Israel to the promised land:

"Thus saith the Lord God, Behold, I will lift up mine hand to the *Gentiles,* and set up my standard to the people: and they shall bring thy sons in their arms, and thy daughters shall be carried upon their shoulders. And *kings* shall be thy nursing fathers, and their queens thy nursing mothers. They shall bow down to thee with their face toward the earth, and lick up the dust of thy feet; and thou shalt know that I am the Lord: for they shall not be ashamed that wait for me" (Isa. 49:22, 23).

"Surely the isles shall wait for me, and the ships of Tarshish first, to bring thy sons from far, their silver and their gold with them, unto the name of the Lord thy God, and to the Holy One of Israel, because He hath glorified thee. *And the sons of strangers shall build up thy walls, and their kings shall minister unto thee:* for in my wrath I smote thee, but in my favour have I had mercy on thee" (Isa. 60:9, 10).

"And they shall bring all your brethren for an offering unto the Lord out of *all nations* upon horses, and in chariots, and in litters, and upon mules, and upon swift beasts, to my holy mountain Jerusalem, saith the Lord, as the children of Israel bring an offering in a clean vessel into the house of the Lord" (Isa. 66:20).

Through visible signs and wonders:

"And the Lord shall utterly destroy the tongue of the Egyptian sea; and with His mighty wind shall He shake His hand over the river, and shall smite it in the seven streams, and make men go over dryshod. And there shall be an highway for the remnant of His people, which shall be left, from Assyria; like as it was to Israel in the day that he came up out of the land of Egypt" (Isa. 11:15, 16).

"According to the days of thy coming out of the land of Egypt will I shew unto him marvellous things" (Mic. 7:15).

"And he shall pass through the sea with affliction, and shall smite the waves in the sea, and all the deeps of the river shall dry up: and the pride of Assyria shall be brought down, and the sceptre of Egypt shall depart away" (Zech. 10:11).

Through the personal leadership
of the Lord Jesus Christ:

"Ye shall not go out with haste, nor go by flight: for the Lord will go before you; and the God of Israel will be your rereward" (Isa. 52:12).

"The breaker is come up before them: they have broken up, and have passed through the gate, and are gone out by it: and their King shall pass before them, and the Lord on the head of them" (Mic. 2:13).

"Then shall the children of Judah and the children

of Israel be gathered together, and appoint themselves *one head,* and they shall come up out of the land: for great shall be the day of Jezreel" (Hosea 1:11).

"They shall come with weeping, and with supplications will I lead them: I will cause them to walk by the rivers of waters in a straight way, wherein they shall not stumble: for I am a father to Israel, and Ephraim is my firstborn" (Jer. 31:9).

The return of Israel from the Babylonian captivity is a TYPE of their future return to the promised land:

In Jeremiah 23:5-8 we read: "Behold, the days come, saith the Lord, that I will raise unto David a righteous Branch, and a King shall reign and prosper, and shall execute judgment and justice in the earth. In His days Judah shall be saved, and Israel shall dwell safely: and this is His name whereby He shall be called, THE LORD OUR RIGHTEOUSNESS. Therefore, behold, the days come, saith the Lord, that they shall no more say, The Lord liveth, which brought up the children of Israel out of the land of Egypt; but, The Lord liveth, which brought up and which led the seed of the house of Israel out of the north country, and from all countries whither I had driven them; and they shall dwell in their own land."

The future return of Israel to their own land will be much greater and more outstanding in every respect than their return from Babylon. In Isaiah 11:11, 12 we read:

"It shall come to pass in that day, that the Lord shall set His hand again the second time to recover the remnant of His people, which shall be left, from Assyria, and from Egypt, and from Pathros, and from

Cush, and from Elam, and from Shinar, and from Hamath, and from the islands of the sea. And He shall set up an ensign for the nations, and shall assemble the outcasts of Israel, and gather together the dispersed of Judah from the four corners of the earth."

When Israel returned from the Babylonian captivity they returned from only ONE PLACE of captivity— BABYLON. Their return at the beginning of the Millennium will be out of ALL PEOPLES, and from THE ENDS OF THE EARTH:

"Then the Lord thy God will turn thy captivity, and have compassion upon thee, and will return and gather thee *from all the nations,* whither the Lord thy God hath scattered thee" (Deut. 30:3).

"Fear not: for I am with thee: I will bring thy seed from the east, and gather thee from the west. I will say to the north, Give up; and to the south, Keep not back. Bring my sons from far, and my daughters from the ends of the earth" (Isa. 43:5, 6).

"The Lord liveth, which brought up and which led the seed of the house of Israel out of the north country, and from all countries whither I had driven them; and they shall dwell in their own land" (Jer. 23:8).

"I will be found of you, saith the Lord: and I will turn away your captivity, and I will gather you from all the nations, and from all the places whither I have driven you, saith the Lord; and I will bring you again into the place whence I caused you to be carried away captive" (Jer. 29:14).

"Behold, I will gather them out of all countries, whither I have driven them in mine anger, and in my fury, and in great wrath; and I will bring them again unto this place, and I will cause them to dwell safely: and they shall be my people, and I will be their God" (Jer. 32:37, 38).

"For thus saith the Lord God: Behold, I, even I, will both search my sheep, and seek them out. As a shepherd seeketh out his flock in the day that he is among his sheep that are scattered; so will I seek out my sheep, and will deliver them out of all places where they have been scattered in the cloudy and dark day" (Ezek. 34:11, 12).

The return of Israel from the Babylonian captivity was experienced primarily by TWO TRIBES — the kingdom of Judah united with Benjamin. (Study Ezra chapter 2.) *But the return from the present dispersement will include all twelve tribes — THE ENTIRE KINGDOM OF ISRAEL:*

"In those days the house of Judah shall walk with the house of Israel, and they shall come together out of the land of the north to the land that I have given for an inheritance unto your fathers" (Jer. 3:18).

"For, lo, the days come, saith the Lord, that I will bring again the captivity of my people Israel and Judah, saith the Lord: and I will cause them to return to the land that I gave to their fathers, and they shall possess it" (Jer. 30:3).

"At the same time, saith the Lord, will I be the God of all the families of Israel, and they shall be my people" (Jer. 31:1).

"I will cause the captivity of Judah and the captivity of Israel to return, and will build them, as at the first" (Jer. 33:7).

"I will strengthen the house of Judah, and I will

save the house of Joseph, and I will bring them again
to place them; for I have mercy upon them: and they
shall be as though I had not cast them off: for I am
the Lord their God, and will hear them" (Zech. 10:6).

"Then shall the children of Judah and the children
of Israel be gathered together, and appoint themselves
one head, and they shall come up out of the land: for
great shall be the day of Jezreel" (Hosea 1:11).

*The return from Babylon came to an end when Jeru-
salem was destroyed by Titus the Roman in 70 A. D.,
but when God's chosen people return to their homeland in the future, they will remain in that land FOR-
EVER.*   The people of Israel, renewed spiritually, will
dwell in Jerusalem in safety:

"And men shall dwell in it, and there shall be no
more utter destruction; but Jerusalem shall be safely
inhabited" (Zech. 14:11).

"For I will set mine eyes upon them for good, and
I will bring them again to this land: and I will build
them, and not pull them down; and I will plant them,
and not pluck them up" (Jer. 24:6).

"I will betroth thee unto me for ever; yea, I will
betroth thee unto me in righteousness, and in judgment, and in lovingkindness, and in mercies.   I will
even betroth thee unto me in faithfulness: and thou
shalt know the Lord" (Hosea 2:19, 20).

*After Israel is settled in their own land in the Mil-
lennium, they will never again be driven from the land:*

"I will plant them upon their land, and they shall
no more be pulled up out of their land which I have
given them, saith the Lord thy God" (Amos 9:15).

Jerusalem, city of the temple, city of the great King,

has been destroyed and rebuilt more than twenty times in the course of history; but when King Jesus sits on the throne and Israel is gathered again into their own land, that city will be no more destroyed as long as the earth remains:

"Behold, the days come, saith the Lord, that the city shall be built to the Lord from the tower of Hananeel unto the gate of the corner. And the measuring line shall yet go forth over against it upon the hill Gareb, and shall compass about to Goath. And the whole valley of the dead bodies, and of the ashes, and all the fields unto the brook of Kidron, unto the corner of the horse gate toward the east, shall be holy unto the Lord. It shall not be plucked up, nor thrown down any more for ever" (Jer. 31:38-40).

"Awake, awake; put on thy strength, O Zion; put on thy beautiful garments, O Jerusalem, the holy city: for henceforth there shall no more come into thee the uncircumcised and the unclean" (Isa. 52:1).

"My people shall dwell in a peaceable habitation, and in sure dwellings, and in quiet resting places" (Isa. 32:18).

"All thy children shall be taught of the Lord; and great shall be the peace of thy children. In righteousness shalt thou be established: thou shalt be far from oppression; for thou shalt not fear: and from terror; for it shall not come near thee" (Isa. 54:13, 14).

"So shall ye know that I am the Lord your God dwelling in Zion, my holy mountain: then shall Jerusalem be holy, and there shall no strangers pass through her any more" (Joel 3:17).

The return of Israel from the Babylonian captivity

was connected with an awakening. From that time forward that nation never again fell into idolatry. But the future return will be connected with *the full messianic salvation* (Isa. 49:8-13).

The first awakening degenerated into dead orthodoxy, a dead mental belief which was almost as subtle and deadly as idolatry. But when God calls the Israelites from the ends of the earth and puts them back in their own land at the Millennium there will be a true *heart-faith* and real spiritual life. No idolatry will be left anywhere on the face of the earth (Hos. 2:17).

When Israel is again called into their own land, when King Jesus rules from the throne of David, God will put His Word into the hearts of His chosen people, they will be truly converted, and their hearts will be filled with faith and true spiritual life.

Some teachers and commentators declare that the Scriptures which speak of the gathering of Israel into the land of Palestine were fulfilled in the return from the Babylonian captivity in 536 B. C., but the references I have given show conclusively that it is impossible for *all* of these prophecies to be applied to the return of Israel from Babylon. Isaiah speaks specifically of a *second* gathering of Israel from the nations of the whole world and from the islands of the sea (Isa. 11:11).

About 520 B. C. (and therefore after the return from Babylon) Zechariah spoke of a return that was still in the future, and he spoke of the return of *the entire nation of Israel* from a *world-wide* dispersion (Zech. 10:8-10).

Furthermore, the extent, duration, and content of

the prophecies having to do with the captivity and return of Israel from Babylon and the later dispersement and return from all the earth do not agree in many ways, proving that the *second gathering* is yet to be fulfilled.   It is true that *some* of the prophecies speak of both events as one, and certainly the return from Babylon is a *type* of the last great gathering of Israel into their own land; but many other prophecies speak, principally or entirely, of the gathering at the beginning of the Millennium when Jesus, from the throne of David, will reign over the house of Israel.

It is a historical fact that since May of 1948, when the new state of Israel was recognized by the United Nations, millions of Jews have returned to Palestine— and many more will return to that land before the coming of Antichrist.   (It is in Judaea that Antichrist will so severely oppress the people of Israel during the tribulation period.)   But the Jews in Palestine now are still in unbelief and they will not become believers until they see Jesus standing on the Mount of Olives (Zech. 14:4).   When they see the scars in His hands and feet they will recognize Him as their Messiah and will receive Him; but until that time, they will remain in unbelief.   Their return to Palestine will not be as much for spiritual matters as for political reasons.

In Ezekiel's vision of the valley of dry bones (recorded in Ezekiel 37:1-14) he saw the bones come together before the breath of life came into them.   The bones signify the nation Israel and the breath of life is the Spirit of God.   It is when the Spirit of God enters the dry bones that Israel as a nation will come to life, spiritually speaking.   When they see Jesus standing on the Mount of Olives they will know Him—and then will be a time of terrible mourning:

"I will pour upon the house of David, and upon the inhabitants of Jerusalem, the Spirit of grace and of supplications: and they shall look upon me whom they have pierced, and they shall mourn for Him, as one mourneth for his only son, and shall be in bitterness for Him, as one that is in bitterness for his firstborn.

"In that day shall there be a great mourning in Jerusalem, as the mourning of Hadadrimmon in the valley of Megiddon. And the land shall mourn, every family apart; the family of the house of David apart, and their wives apart; the family of the house of Nathan apart, and their wives apart; the family of the house of Levi apart, and their wives apart; the family of Shimei apart, and their wives apart; all the families that remain, every family apart, and their wives apart" (Zech. 12:10-14).

When the people of Israel recognize Jesus they will weep and mourn because of their sins—and especially because they crucified their Messiah. They will realize their crime against the Lord of heaven—against Him whose name they "profaned among the heathen, whither they went" (Ezek. 36:21). Because of their sins and their demanding the death of their Messiah these people were loathsome to God; but they will now loathe *themselves* because of their iniquity and their evil ways:

"I will destroy your high places, and cut down your images, and cast your carcases upon the carcases of your idols, *and my soul shall abhor you!*" Thus did

God speak through Moses in Leviticus 26:30.

But hear this from Ezekiel 20:41-43: "I will accept you with your sweet savour, when I bring you out from the people, and gather you out of the countries wherein ye have been scattered; and I will be sanctified in you before the heathen. And ye shall know that I am the Lord, when I shall bring you into the land of Israel, into the country for the which I lifted up mine hand to give it to your fathers. *And there shall ye remember your ways, and all your doings, wherein ye have been defiled; and YE SHALL LOTHE YOURSELVES IN YOUR OWN SIGHT for all your evils that ye have committed!"*

Then in Ezekiel 36:31 we read, "Then shall ye remember your own evil ways, and your doings that were not good, *and shall LOTHE YOURSELVES IN YOUR OWN SIGHT for your iniquities and for your abominations.*"

Thus will the people of Israel be melted and broken, and in continual weeping, seeking God: "They shall come with weeping, and with supplications will I lead them. I will cause them to walk by the rivers of waters in a straight way, wherein they shall not stumble: for I am a Father to Israel, and Ephraim is my firstborn" (Jer. 31:9).

"In those days, and in that time, saith the Lord, the children of Israel shall come, they and the children of Judah together, going and weeping: they shall go, and seek the Lord their God. They shall ask the way to Zion with their faces thitherward, saying, Come, and let us join ourselves to the Lord in a perpetual covenant that shall not be forgotten" (Jer. 50:4, 5).

When Israel shall recognize and acknowledge their
Messiah they will literally confess the truth declared in
Isaiah chapter 53, and on that glorious morning the
fountain of life will be opened to the house of David
and to the people of Israel.   God will forgive their
sins, cover their iniquity, and heal their apostasy—and
a nation will be born in a day:

"In that day there shall be a fountain opened to the
house of David and to the inhabitants of Jerusalem for
sin and for uncleanness" (Zech. 13:1).

"And I will cleanse them from all their iniquity,
whereby they have sinned against me; and I will par-
don all their iniquities, whereby they have sinned, and
whereby they have transgressed against me" (Jer. 33:8).

"I will heal their backsliding, I will love them freely: for mine anger is turned away from him.   I will
be as the dew unto Israel: he shall grow as the lily,
and cast forth his roots as Lebanon.   His branches
shall spread, and his beauty shall be as the olive tree,
and his smell as Lebanon.   They that dwell under his
shadow shall return; they shall revive as the corn, and
grow as the vine: the scent thereof shall be as the
wine of Lebanon" (Hos. 14:4-7).

In that glorious day God will take away the stony
heart of Israel (Ezek. 11:19; 36:26).

He will take away their wrong spirit (Zech. 12:10;
Ezek. 11:19).

He will cleanse them from blood-guiltiness (Isa.
4:3, 4).

The "dry bones" of that nation will be quickened,
revived, and will receive life (Ezek. 37:9; Hos. 6:2).

God will sprinkle them with clean, pure water to

cleanse them from filthiness and from idols (Ezek. 36:25).

Israel's Spiritual Rebirth

"Who hath heard such a thing? Who hath seen such things? Shall the earth be made to bring forth in one day? or shall a nation be born at once? For as soon as Zion travailed, she brought forth her children" (Isa. 66:8).

Of the day of the spiritual rebirth of Israel, Hosea says, "I will sow her unto me in the earth; and I will have mercy upon her that had not obtained mercy; and I will say to them which were not my people, Thou art my people; and they shall say, Thou art my God" (Hosea 2:23).

Spiritually reborn, Israel will enter into the new covenant with God: "And they shall teach no more every man his neighbour, and every man his brother, saying, Know the Lord: for they shall all know me, from the least of them unto the greatest of them, saith the Lord: for I will forgive their iniquity, and I will remember their sin no more. . . . And I will make an everlasting covenant with them, that I will not turn away from them, to do them good: but I will put my fear in their hearts, that they shall not depart from me" (Jer. 31:34; 32:40).

Spiritually renewed, reborn Israel will enter into the blessings God promised Abraham, they will enter into happy betrothal and marriage to Jehovah:

"In that day will I make a covenant for them with the beasts of the field, and with the fowls of heaven, and with the creeping things of the ground: and I will break the bow and the sword and the battle out of the earth, and will make them to lie down safely. And I will betroth thee unto me for ever; yea, I will betroth thee unto me in righteousness, and in judgment, and in lovingkindness, and in mercies. I will even betroth thee unto me in faithfulness: and thou shalt know the Lord" (Hosea 2:18-20).

"Thou shalt no more be termed Forsaken; neither shall thy land any more be termed Desolate: but thou shalt be called Hephzi-bah, and thy land Beulah: for the Lord delighteth in thee, and thy land shall be married. For as a young man marrieth a virgin, so shall thy sons marry thee: and as the bridegroom rejoiceth over the bride, so shall thy God rejoice over thee" (Isa. 62:4, 5).

All this will take place in Israel's own land, the land God gave to Abraham. There will be a great day in the land of Palestine—"great is the day of Jezreel." The Lord will speedily carry out His work of new creation: "A little one shall become a thousand, and a small one a strong nation: I the Lord will hasten it in his time" (Isa. 60:22).

In one day the whole land will be brought into being, at one time the nation shall be born:

"Thy watchmen shall lift up the voice; with the voice together shall they sing: for they shall see eye to eye, when the Lord shall bring again Zion" (Isa. 52:8).

"Before she travailed, she brought forth; before her pain came, she was delivered of a man child. Who hath heard such a thing? Who hath seen such things? Shall the earth be made to bring forth in one day? or shall a nation be born at once? for as soon as Zion travailed, she brought forth her children. Shall I bring to the birth, and not cause to bring forth? saith the Lord. Shall I cause to bring forth, and shut the womb? saith thy God" (Isa. 66:7-9).

From that day forward, Israel will be a holy people:

"It shall come to pass, that he that is left in Zion, and he that remaineth in Jerusalem, shall be called holy, even every one that is written among the living in Jerusalem" (Isa. 4:3).

The nation will not commit evil in the holy mountain of God:

"They shall not hurt nor destroy in all my holy mountain: for the earth shall be full of the knowledge of the Lord, as the waters cover the sea" (Isa. 11:9).

In that day, Israel's righteousness will be perfect— her salvation will be as a burning lamp:

"For Zion's sake will I not hold my peace, and for Jerusalem's sake I will not rest, until the righteousness thereof go forth as brightness, and the salvation thereof as a lamp that burneth" (Isa. 62:1).

The beauty of Israel will be as a royal diadem in the hand of Almighty God:

"Thou shalt also be a crown of glory in the hand of the Lord, and a royal diadem in the hand of thy God" (Isa. 62:3).

Jerusalem will be the capital city of the millennial earth:

"So shall ye know that I am the Lord your God dwelling in Zion, my holy mountain: then shall Jerusalem be holy, and there shall no strangers pass through her any more" (Joel 3:17).

"Awake, awake; put on thy strength, O Zion; put on thy beautiful garments, O Jerusalem, the holy city: for henceforth there shall no more come into thee the uncircumcised and the unclean" (Isa. 52:1).

The people who occupy the holy city will be the righteous nation of Israel:

"Open ye the gates, that the righteous nation which keepeth the truth may enter in" (Isa. 26:2).

Palestine is God's ornament of the whole world:

"But I said, How shall I put thee among the children, and give thee a pleasant land, a goodly heritage of the hosts of nations? and I said, Thou shalt call me, My father; and shalt not turn away from me" (Jer. 3:19).

The individual Israelites are spoken of as jewels that sparkle on the soil of their own land:

"And the Lord their God shall save them in that day as the flock of His people: for they shall be as the stones of a crown, lifted up as an ensign upon His land" (Zech. 9:16).

Jerusalem is called the city of truth:

"Thus saith the Lord: I am returned unto Zion, and will dwell in the midst of Jerusalem: and Jerusalem shall be called a city of truth; and the mountain of the Lord of hosts the holy mountain" (Zech. 8:3).

The walls of the holy city are called salvation:

"In that day shall this song be sung in the land of Judah: We have a strong city; salvation will God appoint for walls and bulwarks" (Isa. 26:1).

"Violence shall no more be heard in thy land, wasting nor destruction within thy borders; but thou shalt call thy walls Salvation, and thy gates Praise" (Isa.

60:18).

The King of kings and Lord of lords who will occupy the throne in the city of Jerusalem is the Lord, the Mighty One, the Everlasting One—the Rock of Ages:

"Trust ye in the Lord for ever: for in the Lord JEHOVAH is *everlasting strength*" (Isa. 26:4). The Hebrew word here translated "everlasting strength" can just as truly be rendered *"Rock of Ages."*

Since Israel rejected their King and cried out, "Crucify Him! Let His blood be upon us and upon our children," that nation has been filled with sorrow, misery, and woe. *But a day of blessedness lies ahead for the people of Israel:*

"And the ransomed of the Lord shall return, and come to Zion with songs and everlasting joy upon their heads: they shall obtain joy and gladness, and sorrow and sighing shall flee away" (Isa. 35:10).

"Therefore the redeemed of the Lord shall return, and come with singing unto Zion; and everlasting joy shall be upon their head: they shall obtain gladness and joy; and sorrow and mourning shall flee away" (Isa. 51:11).

"Afterward shall the children of Israel return, and seek the Lord their God, and David their king; and shall fear the Lord and His goodness in the latter days" (Hosea 3:5).

"Thus saith the Lord: Again there shall be heard in this place, which ye say shall be desolate without man and without beast, even in the cities of Judah, and in the streets of Jerusalem, that are desolate, without man, and without inhabitant, and without beast, the

voice of joy, and the voice of gladness, the voice of
the bridegroom, and the voice of the bride, the voice
of them that shall say, Praise the Lord of hosts: for
the Lord is good; for His mercy endureth for ever: and
of them that shall bring the sacrifice of praise into the
house of the Lord. For I will cause to return the captivity of the land, as at the first, saith the Lord"
(Jer. 33:10, 11).

"O thou afflicted, tossed with tempest, and not
comforted, behold, I will lay thy stones with fair
colours, and lay thy foundations with sapphires. And
I will make thy windows of agates, and thy gates of
carbuncles, and all thy borders of pleasant stones"
(Isa. 54:11, 12). It is true that Isaiah's description here
fits the splendor of the *heavenly Jerusalem* described in
Revelation chapter 21; but here the prophet can only
be speaking of the *earthly* city, for the heavenly Jerusalem will never be afflicted and without comfort.

Certainly the earthly Jerusalem will be "the city of
the great King" (Matt. 5:35; Psalm 48:2).

The earthly Jerusalem will be "*the city of the Lord,
the Zion of the Holy One of Israel*" (Isa. 60:14).

Jerusalem "shall be trodden down of the Gentiles
until the times of the Gentiles be fulfilled" (Luke
21:24), *but God will build again the earthly city:* "And
they that shall be of thee shall build the old waste
places: thou shalt raise up the foundations of many
generations; and thou shalt be called, The repairer of
the breach, The restorer of paths to dwell in" (Isa.
58:12).

In that glorious day, Jerusalem will not only be a
city of blessedness, it will also be *a city of safety:*

"And men shall dwell in it, and there shall be no more utter destruction; but Jerusalem shall be safely inhabited" (Zech. 14:11), "and they shall dwell safely therein, and shall build houses, and plant vineyards. Yea, they shall dwell with confidence, when I have executed judgments upon all those that despise them round about them; and they shall know that I am the Lord their God" (Ezek. 28:26).

In that city there will be *no destruction of homes and property, no sickness to destroy the body:*

"There shall be no more thence an infant of days, nor an old man that hath not filled his days: for the child shall die an hundred years old; but the sinner being an hundred years old shall be accursed. And they shall build houses, and inhabit them; and they shall plant vineyards, and eat the fruit of them. They shall not build, and another inhabit; they shall not plant, and another eat: for as the days of a tree are the days of my people, and mine elect shall long enjoy the work of their hands. They shall not labour in vain, nor bring forth for trouble; for they are the seed of the blessed of the Lord, and their offspring with them" (Isa. 65:20-23).

"Violence shall no more be heard in thy land, wasting nor destruction within thy borders; but thou shalt call thy walls Salvation, and thy gates Praise" (Isa. 60:18).

The temple in that glorious city of blessedness and safety will rise above all other mountains and hills:

"And it shall come to pass in the last days, that the mountain of the Lord's house shall be established in the top of the mountains, and shall be exalted above the hills; and all nations shall flow unto it" (Isa. 2:2).

In the temple will be the throne of David, the throne of the King of kings and Lord of lords (Luke 1:32, 33), and His throne will be surrounded by the thrones of the twelve apostles (Matt. 19:28). The apostles will be at the head of a wide circle of subordinate princes, and will, in the name of the King of kings, rule in righteousness over the people of Israel (Isa. 1:26; 32:1; Jer. 23:4; Obad. 21).

In that hour Israel will reach the fulness of the salvation promised to Abraham and his seed—praise and fame in the lands of their reproach:

"Behold, at that time I will undo all that afflict thee: and I will save her that halteth, and gather her that was driven out; and I will get them praise and fame in every land where they have been put to shame. At that time will I bring you again, even in the time that I gather you: for I will make you a name and a praise among all people of the earth, when I turn back your captivity before your eyes, saith the Lord" (Zeph. 3:19, 20).

"And their seed shall be known among the Gentiles, and their offspring among the people: all that see them shall acknowledge them, that they are the seed which the Lord hath blessed" (Isa. 61:9).

When God dispersed Israel to the ends of the earth, this is what He said concerning them:

"I will deliver them to be removed into all the kingdoms of the earth for their hurt, to be a reproach and a proverb, a taunt and a curse, in all places whither I shall drive them" (Jer. 24:9).

Just as the Jew has been a reproach he will one day

be a benediction to all peoples of the earth:

"It shall come to pass, that as ye were a curse among the heathen, O house of Judah, and house of Israel; so will I save you, and ye shall be a blessing: fear not, but let your hands be strong" (Zech. 8:13).

All this is the wonderful work of Almighty God. It is certainly not the work of human ability or national strength on the part of Israel. When God first chose that nation, it was the smallest of all people. In Deuteronomy 7:7 Moses said to his people, "The Lord did not set His love upon you, nor choose you, because ye were more in number than any people; for ye were the fewest of all people."

Israel in rebellion against God was a thorn-bush (Mic. 7:4), an abomination to God (Lev. 26:30). Therefore the glorious blessings that are in store for that nation in the future can come only through the miracle of Almighty God. Their spiritual transformation at the beginning of the new era of salvation for Israel will be God's miracle, and He will perform it to the glory of His own name, to display His new creating power. In Jeremiah 33:9 God declares, "It shall be to me a name of joy, a praise and an honour before all the nations of the earth, which shall hear all the good that I do unto them: and they shall fear and tremble for all the goodness and for all the prosperity that I procure unto it."

Therefore we see—not the glory of *Israel*, but the power and glory of the God who brought that nation into being and who will bless them as they have never been blessed before. This is made very plain in Ezekiel 36:22, 23:

"Therefore say unto the house of Israel, *Thus saith
the Lord God:* I do not this for *your* sakes, O house
of Israel, *but FOR MINE HOLY NAME'S SAKE,
which ye have profaned among the heathen, whither
ye went.* And I will sanctify my great name, which
was profaned among the heathen, which ye have profaned in the midst of them; *and the heathen shall
know that I AM THE LORD,* saith the Lord God,
when I shall be sanctified in you before their eyes."

Then again in Ezekiel 36:32 we read, "Not for *your*
sakes do I do this, saith the Lord God, be it known
unto you: be ashamed and confounded for your own
ways, O house of Israel."

The transformation of Israel will be wholly *for the
Lord's sake.* It is for the Lord God Almighty that
Zion will be built: "Behold, the days come, saith the
Lord, that the city shall be built to the Lord from
the tower of Hananeel unto the gate of the corner"
(Jer. 31:38). And God's blessings will be seen in everything having to do with the glorious era that is ahead
for Israel: "And their seed shall be known among
the Gentiles, and their offspring among the people:
all that see them shall acknowledge them, that they
are the seed which the Lord hath blessed" (Isa. 61:9).

God's glorious deeds will be proclaimed in Jerusalem: "The multitude of camels shall cover thee, the
dromedaries of Midian and Ephah; all they from Sheba
shall come: they shall bring gold and incense; and
they shall shew forth the praises of the Lord" (Isa.
60:6). The people will come together and worship God
(Jer. 3:17). God's name will be honored, revered, and
hallowed through the healing of the nation Israel (Isa.

29:23). God's glory will be displayed before the eyes
of all the nations of earth (Ezek. 39:21).

Since God was in the beginning, since all things
were created by Him and for His glory, it is His own
divine privilege in everything to glorify Himself: "Sing,
O ye heavens; for the Lord hath done it. Shout, ye
lower parts of the earth: break forth into singing, ye
mountains, O forest, and every tree therein: for the
Lord hath redeemed Jacob, and glorified Himself in
Israel" (Isa. 44:23). "I will say to the north, Give up;
and to the south, Keep not back: bring my sons from
far, and my daughters from the ends of the earth; even
every one that is called by my name: for I have created him for my glory, I have formed him; yea, I have
made him" (Isa. 43:6, 7).

It is only through the grace of God that Israel will
be re-gathered, re-accepted, and through God's re-
acceptance of Israel that nation will become a glory
to God and display God's glory here on earth during
the Millennium: "Thy people also shall be all righteous: they shall inherit the land for ever, the branch
of my planting, the work of my hands, *that I may be
glorified*" (Isa. 60:21).

Since the day Israel demanded the crucifixion of
their King and cried out, "Let His blood be upon us,
and upon our children!" they have been "a reproach
and a proverb, a taunt and a curse" in all places
where they have been driven (Jer. 24:9). But in that
glorious day the re-gathered, renewed, and re-accepted
Israel will become a bearer of the good news of the
kingdom: "This Gospel of the kingdom shall be
preached in all the world for a witness unto all na-

tions; and then shall the end come" (Matt. 24:14). Isaiah declares this truth in these words: "Arise, shine; for thy light is come, and the glory of the Lord is risen upon thee" (Isa. 60:1).

The saved of the nations of earth during the Millennium will also declare the message to distant peoples throughout the ends of the earth: ". . . It shall come, that I will gather all nations and tongues; and they shall come, and see my glory. And I will set a sign among them, and I will send those that escape of them unto the nations . . . that have not heard my fame, neither have seen my glory; and they shall declare my glory among the Gentiles" (Isa. 66:18, 19).

We might compare millennial Israel with the Apostle Paul—in the early days of the Church, and then after his conversion. At first he persecuted the Church, hated believers, and did his utmost to stamp out Christianity (Acts 7:58; 8:1, 3; 9:1, 2). Then one day on the road to Damascus he met Jesus face to face (Acts 9:3-20) and became the greatest missionary ever to carry the Gospel of God's saving grace.

In like manner, *Israel* persecuted the name of Jesus, rejected and crucified Him, and despised all who taught in His name; but one day they, too, will see and recognize their Messiah, and a nation will be born in a day. And just as Paul became the missionary to the Gentiles, so will Israel become the greatest missionary *nation* ever to exist on this earth. They will have their "Damascus hour" when they see Jesus standing on the Mount of Olives, and from that time forward Israel will become God's witness to all mankind, and will be a blessing to the entire earth (Isa. 19:24).

Always, in the history of Israel, a faithful remnant is seen—a spiritual Israel within national Israel. It was for the sake of a very small remnant that God spared Israel in the days of Isaiah (Isa. 1:9). During the captivities the remnant (spiritual Israel) is seen in men like Ezekiel, Daniel, Shadrach, Meshach, Abednego, and others. At the end of the seventy years of Babylonian captivity, it was the *remnant* which returned to Jerusalem under the leadership of Ezra and Nehemiah, to rebuild the temple. When the Lord Jesus came, the remnant consisted of Simeon, Anna, and "them that looked for redemption in Jerusalem" (Luke 2:25-38); and in this Day of Grace the remnant is made up of all born again, believing Jews—"a remnant according to the election of grace" (Rom. 11:5).

However, the chief interest in *spiritual* Israel is prophetic. During the Great Tribulation, under the reign of Antichrist, a remnant out of Israel will turn to Jesus and accept Him as Messiah. They will become His witnesses to the ends of the earth and many of those who believe their message will be martyred by Antichrist and his henchmen (Rev. 6:9-11). Many of the Psalms express prophetically the glorious days and joys of Israel, and also the time of tribulation and sorrows that lie ahead for that nation during the reign of Antichrist. But I repeat—the greatest and most glorious era for Israel is still in the future.

The Nations In the Visible Kingdom

"I the Lord have called thee in righteousness, and will hold thine hand, and will keep thee, and give thee for a covenant of the people, for a light of the

Gentiles; to open the blind eyes, to bring out the
prisoners from the prison, and them that sit in darkness out of the prison house" (Isa. 42:6, 7).

"And He said, It is a light thing that thou shouldest
be my servant to raise up the tribes of Jacob, and to
restore the preserved of Israel: I will also give thee
for a light to the Gentiles, that thou mayest be my
salvation unto the end of the earth" (Isa. 49:6).

"Mine eyes have seen thy salvation, which thou
hast prepared before the face of all people; a light to
lighten the Gentiles, and the glory of thy people Israel" (Luke 2:30-32).

Not only is the most glorious era ahead for Israel,
but also for the nations who will receive the Lord
Jesus Christ as King of kings through the preaching
of the Gospel of the kingdom:

"And many nations shall come, and say, Come,
and let us go up to the mountain of the Lord, and
to the house of the God of Jacob; and He will teach
us of His ways, and we will walk in His paths: for
the law shall go forth of Zion, and the Word of the
Lord from Jerusalem" (Micah 4:2).

The nations evangelized through the message of
God's kingdom will submit themselves to Christ as
their King: "For I know their works and their thoughts:
it shall come, that I will gather all nations and tongues;
and they shall come, and see my glory" (Isa. 66:18).

All idols God will put down, and all human religions will vanish (Zech. 13:2; Jer. 16:20, 21).

In that glorious day, King Jesus will sit on the
throne of David in *Jerusalem,* but He will be King
over the entire earth:

"Say among the heathen (nations) that the Lord reigneth: *the world* also shall be established that it shall not be moved. He shall judge the people righteously" (Psalm 96:10).

"Let the floods clap their hands: let the hills be joyful together before the Lord; for He cometh to judge *the earth:* with righteousness shall He judge *the world,* and the people with equity" (Psalm 98:8, 9).

"*The earth* is the Lord's, and the fulness thereof; *the world,* and they that dwell therein" (Psalm 24:1).

"*The Lord shall be King OVER ALL THE EARTH! In that day shall there be ONE LORD, and His name one*" (Zech. 14:9).

In that glorious day when Christ is King over all the earth we will have the answer to the prayer of Matthew 6:9, 10: "Our Father which art in heaven, Hallowed be thy name. *Thy kingdom come. Thy will be done in EARTH, as it is in heaven.*"

Hear these marvelous words from the inspired pen of the Prophet Isaiah:

"The Lord shall be known to Egypt, and the Egyptians shall know the Lord in that day, and shall do sacrifice and oblation; yea, they shall vow a vow unto the Lord, and perform it. And the Lord shall smite Egypt: He shall smite and heal it: and they shall return even to the Lord, and He shall be intreated of them, and shall heal them. In that day shall there be a highway out of Egypt to Assyria, and the Assyrian shall come into Egypt, and the Egyptian into Assyria, and the Egyptians shall serve with the Assyrians. In that day shall Israel be the third with Egypt and with Assyria, even a blessing in the midst of the land:

whom the Lord of hosts shall bless, saying, Blessed
be Egypt my people, and Assyria the work of my
hands, and Israel mine inheritance" (Isa. 19:21-25).

These words seem strange, but they will be *literally
fulfilled* in that glorious day when Jesus rules as King
of the entire earth and the knowledge of the Lord will
cover the earth as the waters now cover the sea. The
Lord will receive all of these nations, just as Isaiah
prophesied. They will see Him, they will believe on
Him and trust Him—and He will bless them, each of
His people, *His inheritance.*

In that glorious day Israel will be in their own
land, the land God promised Abraham. He will bring
them "out of the land of Egypt, and gather them out
of Assyria, and . . . bring them into the land of Gilead
and Lebanon . . ." (Zech. 10:10). The people who
make up the other nations will dwell in their lands,
but they will experience a spiritual birth, a divine
new birth (Psalm 87:4-6; Zech. 14:9; Rev. 21:24).

As King of kings and Lord of lords, Jesus will rule
over all mankind in righteousness and peace. "Yea,
many people and strong nations shall come to seek
the Lord of hosts in Jerusalem, and to pray before
the Lord" (Zech. 8:22), "and many nations shall be
joined to the Lord in that day, and shall be my people: and I will dwell in the midst of thee, and thou
shalt know that the Lord of hosts hath sent me unto
thee" (Zech. 2:11).

The result of this will be the universal subjection
of the world and all creation to Christ: "For the
kingdom is the Lord's, and He is the governor among
the nations. . . . For *God is the King of all the earth.*

Sing ye praises with understanding. God reigneth over the heathen: God sitteth upon the throne of His holiness. The princes of the people are gathered together, even the people of the God of Abraham: for the shields of the earth belong unto God: He is greatly exalted" (Psalms 22:28; 47:7-9). (Please study Psalms 50:1, 2; 72:8-11; 86:9; and 99:1-3.)

The reign of the righteous King of kings is a mission to mankind under the sceptre of the Almighty. The proclamation of the kingdom will turn all peoples to Jehovah God. This will be the most important and most real missionary era known to history. For the first time this earth will be filled with the knowledge of the Lord (Isa. 11:9), and the association of peoples will be as God in the beginning intended it should be. In Isaiah 45:22-25 we read:

"Look unto me, and be ye saved, all the ends of the earth: for I am God, and there is none else. I have sworn by myself, the Word is gone out of my mouth in righteousness, and shall not return, That unto me every knee shall bow, every tongue shall swear. Surely, shall one say, in the Lord have I righteousness and strength: even to Him shall men come; and all that are incensed against Him shall be ashamed. In the Lord shall all the seed of Israel be justified, and shall glory."

The peoples of the nations who harden their hearts against God and rebel against Him will be killed in the battle of Armageddon, and during the Millennium the devil will be bound and will not be operating to mislead the people (Rev. 20:1, 2). Therefore "at that time they shall call Jerusalem the throne of the Lord;

and all the nations shall be gathered unto it, to the name of the Lord, to Jerusalem: neither shall they walk any more after the imagination of their evil heart'' (Jer. 3:17).

Zephaniah 3:9 tells us that the people will ''call upon the name of the Lord, to serve Him with one consent.'' ''And many nations shall come, and say, Come, and let us go up to the mountain of the Lord, and to the house of the God of Jacob; and He will teach us of His ways, and we will walk in His paths: for the law shall go forth of Zion, and the Word of the Lord from Jerusalem'' (Mic. 4:2).

During this glorious era there will be no more war among the nations, for ''they shall beat their swords into plowshares, and their spears into pruninghooks. Nation shall not lift up sword against nation, neither shall they learn war any more'' (Isa. 2:4). Thus there will be no more striving after power, no nation seeking to enslave the peoples of other nations, no plundering or oppression. There will be mutual and peaceful exchange of food, clothing, and other necessities. There will be harmony instead of discord—an age of unselfishness when people will be concerned about the welfare of their fellowman, for *Christ will be on the throne and righteousness will reign supreme.*

Isaiah chapter 35 describes the blessings of the kingdom in that glorious era:

''The wilderness and the solitary place shall be glad for them; and the desert shall rejoice, and blossom as the rose. It shall blossom abundantly, and rejoice even with joy and singing: the glory of Lebanon shall be given unto it, the excellency of Carmel and Sharon, they shall see the glory of the Lord, and the excellency of our God.

"Strengthen ye the weak hands, and confirm the feeble knees. Say to them that are of a fearful heart, Be strong, fear not: behold, your God will come with vengeance, even God with a recompence; He will come and save you. Then the eyes of the blind shall be opened, and the ears of the deaf shall be unstopped. Then shall the lame man leap as an hart, and the tongue of the dumb sing: for in the wilderness shall waters break out, and streams in the desert.

"And the parched ground shall become a pool, and the thirsty land springs of water: in the habitation of dragons, where each lay, shall be grass with reeds and rushes. And an highway shall be there, and a way, and it shall be called *The way of holiness*. The unclean shall not pass over it; but it shall be for those: the wayfaring men, though fools, shall not err therein.

"No lion shall be there, nor any ravenous beast shall go up thereon, it shall not be found there; but the redeemed shall walk there: and the ransomed of the Lord shall return, and come to Zion with songs and everlasting joy upon their heads: they shall obtain joy and gladness, and sorrow and sighing shall flee away" (Isa. 35:1-10).

As seen in verses 5 and 6 of this passage, the people in the glorious kingdom will enjoy perfect health. (See also Isaiah 65:20.)

Labor will be profitable and men will be rewarded for their labors—they shall "enjoy the work of their hands" (Isa. 65:21-23).

There will be social justice and righteousness (Isa.

11:3-5).

There will be mutual assistance within the community—people will be concerned about each other in that glorious era (Isa. 58:7).

There will be an avoidance of great cities: "In that day, saith the Lord of hosts, shall ye call every man his neighbour under the vine and under the fig tree" (Zech. 3:10). "They shall sit every man under his vine and under his fig tree; and none shall make them afraid: for the mouth of the Lord of hosts hath spoken it" (Mic. 4:4).

During the kingdom age, there will be God-determined equality of rights for all, for the King "shall judge among many people, and rebuke strong nations afar off; and they shall beat their swords into plowshares, and their spears into pruninghooks: nation shall not lift up a sword against nation, neither shall they learn war any more" (Mic. 4:3).

In that glorious kingdom, people will continue their national life and yet work together as a harmonious organism, as the members of one body. Mutual well-being will be promoted by all. Like one big family, there will be much variety and yet there will be perfect unity.

Only GOD can bring about such an era, and it will come only when "the earth shall be filled with the knowledge of the glory of the Lord, as the waters cover the sea" (Hab. 2:14). From sunrise to sunset His name shall be great among the Gentiles; "and in every place incense shall be offered" to His name, for His name "shall be great among the heathen" (Mal. 1:11). "And it shall come to pass, that from one new moon to another, and from one sabbath to another, shall all flesh come to worship before me, saith the Lord" (Isa. 66:23), "for as the earth bringeth forth her bud, and as the garden causeth the things that are sown in it to spring forth; so the Lord God will cause righteousness and praise to spring forth before all the nations" (Isa. 61:11).

The Church In the Millennium

"For the Lord Himself shall descend from heaven with a shout, with the voice of the archangel, and with the trump of God: and the dead in Christ shall rise first: then we which are alive and remain shall be caught up together with them in the clouds, *to meet the Lord in the air: AND SO SHALL WE EVER BE WITH THE LORD"* (I Thess. 4:16, 17).

Where is the Church during the thousand-year reign of Christ on earth? The answer is found in these words: ". . . so shall we ever be *with the Lord.*"

Personally I do not believe Jesus will remain on the earth throughout the Millennium. I believe He will have access to heaven and earth, and so do I believe that *the Church* will have access to heaven and earth. I do not believe the Church will be on the earth always, nor do I believe that it will remain in heaven throughout the thousand years. We know that Jesus is the head of the Church and *"we are members of His body, of His flesh, and of His bones"* (Eph. 5:23, 30). Therefore we share in the sovereignty and glory of Christ: "Whereunto He called you by our Gospel, to the obtaining of the glory of our Lord Jesus Christ" (II Thess. 2:14), and "when Christ, who is our life, shall appear, then shall ye also appear with Him in glory" (Col. 3:4).

The Church will *reign* with Christ during the Millennium: "It is a faithful saying: For if we be dead with Him, we shall also *live* with Him. If we suffer, we shall also *reign* with Him. If we deny Him, He also will deny us" (II Tim. 2:11, 12).

"And I saw *thrones,* and they sat upon them, and judgment was given unto them: and I saw the souls of them that were beheaded for the witness of Jesus, and for the Word of God, and which had not worshipped the beast, neither his image, neither had received his mark upon their foreheads, or in their hands; *and they lived and reigned with Christ a thousand years.* But the rest of the dead lived not again until the thousand years were finished. This is the first resurrection. Blessed and holy is he that hath part in the first resurrection: on such the second death hath no power, but *they shall be priests of God and of Christ, and shall reign with Him a thousand years*" (Rev. 20:4-6).

"Do ye not know that *the saints shall judge the world?* and if the world shall be judged by you, are ye unworthy to judge the smallest matters? Know ye not that *we shall judge angels?* How much more things that pertain to this life?" (I Cor. 6:2, 3).

Believers, members of the body of Christ, have the promise of Jesus Himself, "To him that overcometh will I grant *to sit with me in my throne,* even as I also overcame, and am set down with my Father in His throne" (Rev. 3:21).

In Matthew 19:28 Jesus said to His disciples, "Verily

I say unto you, That ye which have followed me, in the regeneration when the Son of man shall sit in the throne of His glory, *ye also shall sit upon twelve thrones*, judging the twelve tribes of Israel."

In the Millennium, believers will be in their glorified bodies. Christ will "change our vile body, that it may be fashioned *like unto His glorious body*, according to the working whereby He is able even to subdue all things unto Himself" (Phil. 3:21). (Please also read I Corinthians 15:40-49.)

Spiritually embodied believers will be definitely distinguished from Israel and the nations which will occupy the earth at that time—that is, believers will appear as glorified persons with spiritual bodies, similar to the appearance of the Lord Jesus after His resurrection. Believers will belong to the heavenly world, but even in spiritual bodies we can take part in earthly life as Jesus did after His resurrection.

It is of course *impossible to fathom or explain* the minute details of the glory that will belong to the Church in that glorious day, the glory we will share with Christ; but the details of that glory we can confidently leave with God who knoweth all things.

In the Millennium the Church will stand far above Israel. The Israelites will be *subjects* of Christ's kingdom, while the members of the Church will be His *co-regents* (II Tim. 2:12; Matt. 19:28). The people of Israel will belong to the kingdom, but the Church is the bride of Christ. The Israelites are God's *earthly* people: "Thy people also shall be all righteous: they shall inherit the land for ever, the branch of my planting, the work of my hands, that I may be glorified"

(Isa. 60:21). *The Church* is God's heavenly people: "Blessed be the God and Father of our Lord Jesus Christ, who hath blessed us with all spiritual blessings in heavenly places in Christ" (Eph. 1:3).

Therefore, as the heaven is higher than the earth, so the New Testament Church is higher than the earthly blessings of the converted nation Israel in the millennial kingdom. From the heavenly Jerusalem the Lord will cause His marvelous grace and peace to stream out over the earthly Jerusalem — and to the ends of the earth, blessing all peoples of the earth: "And many people shall go and say, Come ye, and let us go up to the mountain of the Lord, to the house of the God of Jacob; and He will teach us of His ways, and we will walk in His paths: for out of Zion shall go forth the law, and the Word of the Lord from Jerusalem" (Isa. 2:3).

The Earth During the Millennium

The whole earth will share in the glory of Christ's millennial reign, for when the sons of God are redeemed the whole creation will be set free from the bondage of corruption:

"For the earnest expectation of the creature waiteth for the manifestation of the sons of God. For the creature was made subject to vanity, not willingly, but by reason of Him who hath subjected the same in hope. Because the creature itself also shall be delivered from the bondage of corruption into the glorious liberty of the children of God. For we know that the whole creation groaneth and travaileth in pain together until now. And not only they, but ourselves also, which have the firstfruits of the Spirit, even we ourselves groan within ourselves, waiting for the adoption, to wit, the redemption of our body" (Rom. 8:19-23).

Canaan will indeed be the land that flows with milk and honey: "And it shall come to pass in that day, that the mountains shall drop down new wine, and the hills shall flow with milk, and all the rivers of Judah shall flow with waters, and a fountain shall come forth of the house of the Lord, and shall water the valley of Shittim" (Joel 3:18).

"A land flowing with milk and honey" (Jer. 11:5) means a *fruitful* land, and the earth in the Millennium will be as a magnificent paradise: "For the Lord shall comfort Zion: He will comfort all her waste places; and *He will make her wilderness like Eden, and her desert like the garden of the Lord.* Joy and gladness shall be found therein, thanksgiving, and the voice of melody" (Isa. 51:3). "And they shall say, This land that was desolate is become *like the garden of Eden;* and the waste and desolate and ruined cities are become fenced, and are inhabited" (Ezek. 36:35).

The Prophet Amos tells us that the earth will be filled with flowering, fruitful gardens: "I will bring again the captivity of my people of Israel, and they shall build the waste cities, and inhabit them; and they shall plant vineyards, and drink the wine thereof; they shall also make gardens, and eat the fruit of them" (Amos 9:14).

This earth will be a place where the fields are *exceedingly fruitful:* ". . . I will call for the corn, and will increase it, and lay no famine upon you. And I will multiply the fruit of the tree, and the increase of the field, that ye shall receive no more reproach of famine among the heathen" (Ezek. 36:29, 30). "And the tree of the field shall yield her fruit, and the earth shall yield her increase, and they shall be safe in their land, and shall know that I am the Lord, when I have broken the bands of their yoke, and delivered them out of the hand of those that served themselves of them" (Ezek. 34:27).

The mountains will flow with oil, and corn, and new wine: ". . . Behold, I will send you corn, and wine, and oil, and ye shall be satisfied therewith: and I will no more make you a reproach among the heathen" (Joel 2:19).

The earth will be blessed as before the curse: "I will make them and the places round about my hill a blessing; and I will cause the shower to come down in his season; there shall be showers of blessing" (Ezek. 34:26).

The harvest will be abundant: "Your threshing shall reach unto the vintage, and the vintage shall reach unto the sowing time: and ye shall eat your bread to the full, and dwell in your land safely" (Lev. 26:5). "The floors shall be full of wheat, and the fats shall overflow with wine and oil" (Joel 2:24). "Behold, the days come, saith the Lord, that the plowman shall overtake the reaper, and the treader of grapes him that soweth seed; and the mountains shall drop sweet wine, and all the hills shall melt" (Amos 9:13).

The earth will be filled with *joy and happiness in field, forest, and plain:* "Ye shall go out with joy, and be led forth with peace: the mountains and the hills shall break forth before you into singing, and all the trees of the field shall clap their hands. Instead of the thorn shall come up the fir tree, and instead of the brier shall come up the myrtle tree: and it shall be to the Lord for a name, for an everlasting sign that shall not be cut off" (Isa. 55:12, 13).

The *animal kingdom* will be delivered from the curse and there will be peace between beast and beast: "The wolf also shall dwell with the lamb, and the leopard shall lie down with the kid; and the calf and the young lion and the fatling together; and a little child shall lead them. And the cow and the bear shall feed; their young ones shall lie down together: and the lion shall eat straw like the ox" (Isa. 11:6, 7).

During the Millennium there will also be peace *between the beasts and man:* "In that day I will make a covenant for them with the beasts of the field, and with the fowls of heaven, and with the creeping things of the ground: and I will break the bow and the sword and the battle out of the earth, and will make them to lie down safely" (Hos. 2:18). "And I will make with them a covenant of peace, and will cause the evil beasts to cease out of the land: and they shall dwell safely in the wilderness, and sleep in the woods" (Ezek. 34:25). "And I will give peace in the land, and ye shall lie down, and none shall make you afraid: and I will rid evil beasts out of the land, neither shall the sword go through your land" (Lev. 26:6).

The serpent is the only creature that will not be totally delivered from the curse—but even the serpent will no longer be poisonous. The serpent beguiled

Adam and Eve, and God said, "Because thou hast done this, thou art cursed above all cattle, and above every beast of the field. Upon thy belly shalt thou go, and dust shalt thou eat *all the days of thy life!* And I will put enmity between thee and the woman, and between thy seed and her seed; it shall bruise thy head, and thou shalt bruise His heel" (Gen. 3:14,15). The curse will not be wholly lifted from the serpent, for in Isaiah 65:25 we read, "The wolf and the lamb shall feed together, and the lion shall eat straw like the bullock: *and DUST shall be THE SERPENT'S MEAT* . . . ." But even though the serpent will carry the curse in the Millennium, the *poison* will be removed from it: "The sucking child shall play on the hole of the *asp* (the deadly serpent), and the weaned child shall put his hand on the *cockatrice'* den" (Isa. 11:8).

The atmospheric and starry *heavens* will also be delivered from the curse. Before Adam sinned there were no storms, no thunder, lightning, tornadoes, or hurricanes. Until the judgment of the flood came upon the earth it had never rained, but *a mist came up* each night to water the ground (Gen. 2:5,6). However, there will be no storms in the Millennium. There will be no thunder, lightning, or tempests. This earth will again be watered with a mist from the ground, as before the curse. There will be no hot days or nights, no cold days or nights. We might say that the earth will be "air conditioned" throughout the year. The temperature will be perfect all the time. Isaiah 30:26 tells us, "Moreover the light of the moon shall be as the light of the sun, and the light of the sun shall be sevenfold, as the light of seven days, in the day that the Lord bindeth up the breach of His people, and healeth the stroke of their wound."

When Almighty God delivers man from the curse and the Millennium begins, His redemption will be world-wide. The whole world will be set free from the bondage of corruption: "The creature itself also shall be delivered from the bondage of corruption into the glorious liberty of the children of God" (Rom. 8:21).

"Repent ye therefore, and be converted, that your sins may be blotted out, when *the times of refreshing* shall come from the presence of the Lord . . . whom the heaven must receive until *the times of restitution of all things*, which God hath spoken by the mouth of all His holy prophets since the world began" (Acts 3:19, 21).

I close this chapter with the words of the Psalmist:

"Let the HEAVENS rejoice, and let the EARTH be glad. Let the sea roar, and the fulness thereof. Let the field be joyful, and all that is therein. Then shall all the trees of the wood rejoice before the Lord: for He cometh, for He cometh to judge the earth. HE SHALL JUDGE THE WORLD WITH RIGHTEOUS-NESS, AND THE PEOPLE WITH HIS TRUTH" (Psalm 96:11-13).

Chapter XI

The Future of the Nation Israel

"Shall a nation be born at once?"
(Isaiah 66:8)

There has been—and is—much discussion among Bible scholars, teachers, and ministers concerning the nation Israel. Some say that God has finished with Israel and that the promises made to Abraham and his seed are now inherited by the New Testament Church. Others teach that the British are the present day Israelites. Therefore in our study of the future of the nation Israel we will look into the Word of God and "let God be true, but every man a liar" (Rom. 3:4).

There were people in Paul's day who thought that God had finished with Israel because the Jews had rejected Messiah and demanded His death. Therefore Paul was led to deal with that question, and in Romans 11:1-25 he explained:

"I say then, *Hath God cast away His people?* God forbid! For I also am an Israelite, of the seed of Abraham, of the tribe of Benjamin. *God HATH NOT cast away His people which He foreknew.* Wot ye not what the Scripture saith of Elias? how he maketh intercession to God against Israel, saying, Lord, they have killed thy prophets, and digged down thine altars; and I am left alone, and they seek my life.

"But what saith the answer of God unto him? I

have reserved to myself seven thousand men, who
have not bowed the knee to the image of Baal. *Even
so then at this present time also there is a remnant
according to the election of grace.* And if by grace,
then is it no more of works: otherwise grace is no
more grace. But if it be of works, then is it no more
grace: otherwise work is no more work.

"What then? Israel hath not obtained that which
he seeketh for; but the election hath obtained it, and
the rest were blinded (according as it is written, God
hath given them the spirit of slumber, eyes that they
should not see, and ears that they should not hear;)
unto this day. And David saith, Let their table be
made a snare, and a trap, and a stumblingblock, and
a recompence unto them. Let their eyes be darkened,
that they may not see, and bow down their back
alway.

"I say then, Have they stumbled that they should
fall? God forbid! but rather through their fall salvation
is come unto the Gentiles, for to provoke them to
jealousy. Now if the fall of them be the riches of the
world, and the diminishing of them the riches of the
Gentiles; how much more their fulness? For I speak
to you Gentiles, inasmuch as I am the apostle of the
Gentiles, I magnify mine office: if by any means I
may provoke to emulation them which are my flesh,
and might save some of them.

"For if the casting away of them be the reconciling
of the world, what shall the receiving of them be, but
life from the dead? For if the firstfruit be holy, the
lump is also holy: and if the root be holy, so are
the branches. And if some of the branches be broken

off, and thou, being a wild olive tree, wert graffed in among them, and with them partakest of the root and fatness of the olive tree; boast not against the branches. But if thou boast, thou bearest not the root, but the root thee.

"Thou wilt say then, The branches were broken off, that I might be graffed in. Well; because of unbelief they were broken off, and thou standest by faith. Be not highminded, but fear: for if God spared not the natural branches, take heed lest He also spare not thee.

"Behold therefore the goodness and severity of God: on them which fell, severity; but toward thee, goodness, if thou continue in His goodness: otherwise thou also shalt be cut off. And they also, if they abide not still in unbelief, shall be graffed in: for God is able to graff them in again. For if thou wert cut out of the olive tree which is wild by nature, and wert graffed contrary to nature into a good olive tree: how much more shall these, which be the natural branches, be graffed into their own olive tree?

"For I would not, brethren, that ye should be ignorant of this mystery, lest ye should be wise in your own conceits; that *blindness IN PART is happened to Israel, until the fulness of the Gentiles be come in.*"

God is eternal—from everlasting to everlasting (Psalm 90:2); but God also sets His own time to work out His purposes, in His own way and by His own will. In the Garden of Eden He promised Adam and Eve the seed of the woman, the seed who would be victorious over the devil and bruise the serpent's head (Gen. 3:15). Centuries later, "when the fulness of the

time was come, *God sent forth His Son,* made of a
woman, made under the law, to redeem them that were
under the law, that we might receive the adoption of
sons" (Gal. 4:4, 5). Yes, when the fulness of the time
was come—*the fulness of God's OWN time.*

Again, in Romans 5:6 we read, "For when we were
yet without strength, *in DUE TIME Christ died for
the ungodly.*" In due time, *at GOD'S APPOINTED
time,* Christ died for poor, ungodly sinners. You see,
God has a program, a blueprint, and He runs His
affairs according to His purpose and by His own will.
There are no accidents with God. *All* things are *ordained* of God, *allowed* of God, in the *program* of
God. *"Known unto God are ALL HIS WORKS from
the beginning of the world"* (Acts 15:18). I repeat—
God sets His own time to accomplish His own purpose
according to His own will and in His own way.

However, God has placed Himself under certain
limitations in the declarations of His holy Word regarding His elect nation Israel. It is true that Israel
is God's peculiar treasure, "for the Lord hath chosen
Jacob unto Himself, and Israel for His peculiar treasure" (Psalm 135:4). It is also true that Israel is God's
chosen nation, and in Isaiah 45:4 He said, "For Jacob
my servant's sake, and Israel mine elect, I have even
called thee by thy name: I have surnamed thee,
though thou hast not known me." God declares Israel
is "as the apple of His eye" (Deut. 32:10), and in
Zechariah 2:8 He declared of that nation, "He that
toucheth you toucheth the apple of His eye." But in
spite of this, God has placed Himself under certain
limitations regarding that nation.

One of these limitations is expressed in the word *"until,"* a word used many times in the Old Testament prophecies in connection with the nation Israel. For example, regarding Israel's *punishment* the Prophet Isaiah asked, *"Lord, how long?"* and God replied:

"UNTIL the cities be wasted without inhabitant, and the houses without man, and the land be utterly desolate, and the Lord have removed men far away, and there be a great forsaking in the midst of the land. But yet in it shall be a tenth, and it shall return, and shall be eaten: as a teil tree, and as an oak, whose substance is in them, when they cast their leaves: so the holy seed shall be the substance thereof" (Isa. 6:11-13).

The holy city Jerusalem and the land of Palestine certainly have been wasted. The nation Israel has been wasted and scattered to the ends of the earth. It is true that many millions of Jews have returned to Palestine in recent years, but there are millions more still scattered among other nations and the islands of the sea. However, the Lord will not allow His chosen people to be wasted to complete extermination.

Seven "Until's"

The Scriptures record seven other instances where the word "until" is used in relation to Israel and the second coming of Jesus. We can discuss them but briefly in this message, but I would like to at least point them out:

The "until" of treading down: —
"And they shall fall by the edge of the sword, and

shall be led away captive into all nations: and Jerusalem shall be *trodden down* of the Gentiles until the times of the Gentiles be fulfilled" (Luke 21:24).

The "times of the Gentiles" began in the days of Nebuchadnezzar and will continue until the time when Jesus will turn again to the nation Israel and a nation will be born in a day. God will then deal again with Israel in the covenant blessings promised to father Abraham.

The "until" of suspension: —

"I would not, brethren, that ye should be ignorant of this mystery, lest ye should be wise in your own conceits; that *blindness in part is happened to Israel,* until the fulness of the Gentiles be come in" (Rom. 11:25).

The "fulness of the Gentiles" is the completion of the purpose and program of God in this dispensation, the calling out from among the Gentiles a people for His name—the New Testament Church which is the body of Christ (Eph. 1:22, 23; Acts 15:14). As soon as the Church is completed, Israel will come into God's blessing again. The natural branches (which were broken off that the wild olive branch might be grafted in) will be grafted in again and God will again deal with Israel as His elect nation.

The "until" of restoration: —

"Repent ye therefore, and be converted, that your sins may be blotted out, when the *times of refreshing* shall come from the presence of the Lord; and He shall send Jesus Christ, which before was preached unto you:

whom the heaven must receive until *the times of restitution of all things,* which God hath spoken by the
mouth of all His holy prophets since the world began"
(Acts 3:19-21).

The "times of restitution" (or restoration) of which
Peter spoke here are the times Jehovah God promised
through His prophets, the promises made to Abraham
and to the faithful prophets in the Old Testament.

The "until" of tribulation:—

". . . The fourth beast shall be the fourth kingdom
upon earth, which shall be diverse from all kingdoms,
and shall *devour the whole earth, and shall tread it
down, and break it in pieces.* And the ten horns out
of this kingdom are ten kings that shall arise: and
another shall rise after them; and he shall be diverse
from the first, and he shall subdue three kings. And
he shall speak great words against the most High, and
shall wear out the saints of the most High, and think
to change times and laws: and they shall be given
into his hand until a time and times and the dividing
of time" (Dan. 7:23-25).

The last world ruler will be the Antichrist and he
will seek to "wear out the saints of the most High"—
that is, he will seek to destroy the saints of God until
he and his armies will finally be destroyed by the
coming of the Lord Jesus Christ in glory. The same
period of three and one-half years (and the actions of
the same person) is also described in Revelation. Daniel chapter 9 tells us that this person will bring peace
for three and one-half years, followed by approximately
three and one-half years of terror. He will make a

covenant with the Jews, but in the midst of the week
of years he will break the covenant and "shall cause
the sacrifice and the oblation to cease, and for the
overspreading of abominations he shall make it desolate, even until the consummation, and that determined shall be poured upon the desolate" (Dan. 9:27).

The "until" of protection:—

During the Great Tribulation that shall come upon
the whole earth, especially under the fifth, sixth, and
seventh seals described in Revelation, God will protect
a third part of His people in the land. Isaiah also
speaks of this protection as God invites, "Come, my
people, enter thou into thy chambers, and shut thy
doors about thee. Hide thyself as it were for a little
moment, *until the indignation be overpast*" (Isa. 26:20).

"And *I will bring the third part through the fire,*
and will refine them as silver is refined, and will try
them as gold is tried: they shall call on my name,
and I will hear them: I will say, It is my people:
and they shall say, The Lord is my God" (Zech. 13:9).

The "until" of punishment:—

"The fierce anger of the Lord shall not return, until
He have done it, and until He have performed the
intents of His heart: in the latter days ye shall consider it" (Jer. 30:24).

The fury and judgment poured out upon the wicked
does not speak of the wicked in general, but of *the
wicked one,* Antichrist, the devil incarnate. The fierce
judgment of God will not return until He has executed
it, until He has performed "the intents of His heart."

And please notice this will be *in the latter days,* just before God turns again to the nation Israel.

The "until" of accomplishment:—

"I will overturn, overturn, overturn, it: and it shall be no more, *until He come whose right it is;* and I will give it Him" (Ezek. 21:27).

In the verses given in these seven "until's" we have seen Israel as God's elect nation, His peculiar treasure. We have seen a time of trial, great tribulation, and distress through which that nation must pass, and we have seen God's gracious, tender care concerning His people. We have seen a terrible, indescribable punishment which will come upon the Antichrist, the devil in flesh. All these things focus in, lead up to, and are consummated by the second coming of Christ in glory, when every eye shall see Him and the people who pierced Him will recognize Him by the prints of the nails in His hands.

The Nation of Israel— The Object of God's Special Attention

There are many reasons why God will quicken the nation Israel and bless His people again as they were blessed during the Old Testament economy—and with even greater blessings. I would like to point out at least seven reasons *why* He will redeem Israel, quicken that nation, and place them back in their own land:

1. Because He chose them in a special covenant of grace:—

"When Abram was ninety years old and nine, the

Lord appeared to Abram, and said unto him: I am the Almighty God; walk before me, and be thou perfect. And I will make my covenant between me and thee, and will multiply thee exceedingly. And Abram fell on his face: and God talked with him, saying:

"As for me, behold, my covenant is with thee, and thou shalt be a father of many nations. Neither shall thy name any more be called Abram, but thy name shall be Abraham; for a father of many nations have I made thee. And I will make thee exceeding fruitful, and I will make nations of thee, and kings shall come out of thee. And I will establish my covenant between me and thee and thy seed after thee in their generations for an everlasting covenant, to be a God unto thee, and to thy seed after thee. And I will give unto thee, and to thy seed after thee, the land wherein thou art a stranger, all the land of Canaan, for an everlasting possession; and I will be their God" (Gen. 17:1-8).

This covenant of grace with the nation Israel was made between God and Abraham, a covenant with a striking peculiarity: *The Lord Himself undertook to carry through all the conditions of the covenant.* We see this in the seven "I will's" in the passage just given from Genesis 17. The only obligation that rested on Abraham and his seed was that they observe the rite of circumcision:

"And God said unto Abraham, Thou shalt keep my covenant therefore, thou, and thy seed after thee in their generations. This is my covenant, which ye shall keep, between me and you and thy seed after thee: *Every man child among you shall be circumcised.* And ye shall circumcise the flesh of your foreskin; and it shall be a token of the covenant betwixt me and you" (Gen. 17:9-11).

Paul speaks of this covenant in Romans 4:9-12: "Cometh this blessedness then upon the circumcision only, or upon the uncircumcision also? for we say that faith was reckoned to Abraham for righteousness. How was it then reckoned? when he was in circumcision, or in uncircumcision? Not in circumcision, but in uncircumcision. And he received the sign of circumcision, a seal of the righteousness of the faith which he had yet being uncircumcised: that he might be the father of all them that believe, though they be not circumcised; that righteousness might be imputed unto them also: and the father of circumcision to them who are not of the circumcision only, but who also walk in the steps of that faith of our father Abraham, which he had being yet uncircumcised."

It was because of His covenant with Abraham that God redeemed Israel from the Egyptian bondage: "God heard their groaning, and God remembered His covenant with Abraham, with Isaac, and with Jacob. And God looked upon the children of Israel, and God had respect unto them" (Ex. 2:24, 25).

Centuries later, because of the covenant between God and Abraham, God sent His only Son to be the Saviour of Israel. Luke 1:68-75 declares:

"Blessed be the Lord God of Israel; for He hath visited and redeemed His people, and hath raised up an horn of salvation for us in the house of His servant David; as He spake by the mouth of His holy prophets, which have been since the world began: that we

should be saved from our enemies, and from the hand
of all that hate us; to perform the mercy promised to
our fathers, and to remember His holy covenant—the
oath which He sware to our father Abraham, that He
would grant unto us, that we being delivered out of
the hand of our enemies might serve Him without fear,
in holiness and righteousness before Him, all the days
of our life."

Not only did God send Christ to be the Saviour of
Israel, but to be the Saviour of all who believe on
Him:

"Christ hath redeemed us from the curse of the law,
being made a curse for us: for it is written, Cursed
is every one that hangeth on a tree: *that the blessing
of Abraham might come on the Gentiles through Jesus
Christ;* that we might receive the promise of the Spirit
through faith.

"Brethren, I speak after the manner of men: Though
it be but a man's covenant, yet if it be confirmed, no
man disannulleth, or addeth thereto. Now to Abraham
and his seed were the promises made. He saith not,
And to SEEDS, as of *many;* but as of *one,* And to
thy SEED, which is Christ. And this I say, that the
covenant, that was confirmed before of God in Christ,
the law, which was four hundred and thirty years after,
cannot disannul, that it should make the promise of
none effect. For if the inheritance be of the law, it is
no more of promise: but *God gave it to Abraham by
PROMISE*" (Gal. 3:13-18).

Because of His covenant with Abraham, God will
restore the nation Israel to national and spiritual blessing as He promised to do. Going back to the passage

quoted from Genesis 17:1-8 we find seven *"I will's"* in God's covenant with Abraham. These are the keys to the grace of God in Christ to Israel—and through Israel to the whole world:

(1) the "I will" of *obligation*—"I will make my *covenant* between me and thee" (v. 2).

(2) the "I will" of *multiplication*—"I will *multiply thee* exceedingly" (v. 2).

(3) the "I will" of *abundance*—"I will make thee exceeding fruitful" (v. 6).

(4) the "I will" of *greatness*—"I will make *nations* of thee, and *kings* shall come out of thee" (v. 6).

(5) the "I will" of *perpetuity*—"I will establish my covenant between me and thee and *thy seed* after thee in their generations for an *EVERLASTING covenant*" (v. 7).

(6) the "I will" of *possession*—"I will *give* unto thee, and to thy seed after thee, the land wherein thou art a stranger, all the land of Canaan, for an *everlasting possession*" (v. 8).

(7) the "I will" of *relationship*—"I will be *their GOD*" (v. 8).

You may rest assured that God has kept, is keeping, and will keep each of these "I will's" spoken to faithful Abraham.

2. Because He loved Israel with a very special love:—

The second reason God will quicken and redeem Israel is because of His very special love for that nation. It is unmistakeably clear in the Old Testament Scriptures that God chose Israel to be His elect people, and He then loved His people with unfailing, unending, love. Therefore He was, is, and will be faithful to His promise to that nation. He has never lost sight of the fact that He placed Himself under obligation to bless Abraham and his seed, and God cannot break His Word, it is impossible for Him to lie (Heb. 6:18; Tit. 1:2).

Ezekiel tells of Israel's rebellion against God—how they worshipped idols and broke every law God had given them; but Ezekiel also tells of how God loved and delivered His people *for His name's sake:*

"But I wrought *for my name's sake,* that it should not be polluted before the heathen, among whom they were, in whose sight I made myself known unto them, in bringing them forth out of the land of Egypt. . . . But I wrought *for my name's sake,* that it should not be polluted before the heathen, in whose sight I brought them out. . . . Nevertheless I withdrew mine hand, and wrought *for my name's sake,* that it should not be polluted in the sight of the heathen, in whose sight I brought them forth. . . . And ye shall know that I am the Lord, when I have wrought with you *for my name's sake,* not according to your wicked ways, nor according to your corrupt doings, O ye house of Israel, saith the Lord God" (Ezek. 20:9, 14, 22, 44).

Also in Ezekiel 36:16-18 we read, "Moreover the Word of the Lord came unto me, saying: Son of man, when the house of Israel dwelt in their own land, *they defiled it by their own way and by their doings.* Their way was before me as the uncleanness of a removed woman. *WHEREFORE I poured my fury upon them* for the blood that they had shed upon the land, and for their idols wherewith they had polluted it!"

So God scattered His people among the heathen—and even in the lands where they were dispersed they profaned the holy name of Jehovah God. Then in Ezekiel 36:21-32 we read:

"But I had pity for MINE HOLY NAME, which the house of Israel had profaned among the heathen, whither they went. Therefore say unto the house of Israel, Thus saith the Lord God: I do not this for *your* sakes, O house of Israel, but *for mine holy name's sake,* which ye have profaned among the heathen, whither ye went. And I will sanctify my great name, which was profaned among the heathen, which ye have profaned in the midst of them; and the heathen shall know that I am the Lord, saith the Lord God, when I shall be sanctified in you before their eyes. For I will take you from among the heathen, and gather you out of all countries, and will bring you into your own land.

"Then will I sprinkle clean water upon you, and ye shall be clean: from all your filthiness, and from all your idols, will I cleanse you. . . . And ye shall dwell in the land that I gave to your fathers; and ye shall be my people, and I will be your God. . . .

"Not for YOUR sakes do I this, saith the Lord God, *be it known unto you: be ashamed and confounded for your own ways, O house of Israel."*

In connection with these enlightening words from the Prophet Ezekiel, hear these words given through Moses in Deuteronomy 9:5, 6:

"Not for thy righteousness, or for the uprightness of thine heart, dost thou go to possess their land: but for the wickedness of these nations the Lord thy God doth drive them out from before thee, and that He may perform the word which the Lord sware unto thy fathers, Abraham, Isaac, and Jacob. *Understand therefore, that the Lord thy God giveth thee not this good land to possess it for THY righteousness; for THOU ART A STIFFNECKED PEOPLE!"*

So we see that God spared and delivered Israel—not for their own sake nor because of their righteousness, but for His holy name's sake and because of His peculiar love for His elect nation.

The book of Deuteronomy places unmistakeable emphasis on God's love for Israel, and the *reason* He loved them is found *in Himself:*

"Because He loved thy fathers, therefore He chose their seed after them, and brought thee out in His sight with His mighty power out of Egypt" (Deut. 4:37).

Again in Deuteronomy 7:7, 8 Moses said to Israel, "The Lord did not set His love upon you, nor choose you, because ye were more in number than any people; for ye were the *fewest* of all people: but because the Lord loved you, and because He would keep the oath which He had sworn unto your fathers, hath the Lord brought you out with a mighty hand, and redeemed you out of the house of bondmen, from the hand of Pharaoh king of Egypt."

In Deuteronomy 10:15 Moses told the people, "Only the Lord had a *delight* in thy fathers to love them, and He chose their seed after them, even *you above all people*, as it is this day."

The hireling prophet Balaam was used in the hire of Balak to curse God's people, but God overruled the curse and turned it into a blessing—not because Israel *deserved* the blessing, but because of God's love for and delight in that nation. (Read Numbers chapters 22 and 23.) "Nevertheless the Lord thy God would not hearken unto Balaam; but the Lord thy God turned the curse into a blessing unto thee, because the Lord thy God loved thee" (Deut. 23:5). God loved Israel in spite of their unfaithfulness. He made a covenant with Abraham, and because of God's own love and faithfulness He will not, yea, He *cannot* break His covenant with Abraham.

3. *Because Israel is God's peculiar treasure, His special people:—*

God will quicken and redeem Israel because they are holy unto Him. He chose Israel as the nation through which His Son would be born, therefore He chose them "to be *a special people* unto Himself, above all people that are upon the face of the earth" (Deut. 7:6). "The Lord hath chosen Jacob unto Himself, and Israel for His *peculiar treasure*" (Psalm 135:4).

The book of Deuteronomy consists of the parting counsels Moses delivered to the nation Israel in view of their impending entrance upon their covenanted possession. Also in Deuteronomy we find a summary of Israel's wilderness wanderings. This is important as unfolding the moral judgment of God upon those events, for Moses was relating the events to a generation which had grown up in the wilderness. At the same time, he was giving instruction as to the conduct of Israel in the promised land.

Deuteronomy 30:1-9 also sets forth the Palestinian

Covenant.   We must remember that even though the
land of promise was *unconditionally* given to Abraham
and to his seed in the Abrahamic Covenant of Genesis
13:14-17 and 15:1-18, the land was given to the generation which had grown up in the wilderness under the
conditional terms of the Palestinian Covenant. (Read
Deuteronomy chapters 28 through 30:9.) They entered
the land under the leadership of Joshua, and under
the conditional Palestinian Covenant. They *violated*
the conditions of the covenant, and as a result of their
disobedience the nation was first disrupted, and then
cast out of the land (I Kings ch. 12; II Kings 17:1-18;
24:1 − 25:11).

But Israel's violation of the conditions of the Palestinian Covenant did not annul God's covenant with
Abraham.   That same covenant *unconditionally promises* a national regathering and restoration of the nation, a promise yet to be fulfilled. "In the same day
the Lord made a covenant with Abram, saying, *Unto
thy seed have I given this land,* from the river of Egypt
unto the great river, the river Euphrates" (Gen. 15:18).
So regardless of Israel's rebellion against God in the
Old Testament era—and even in the days of Jesus—
that nation is still holy unto God, a special people
which He has chosen for Himself above all other nations on earth.

In Malachi 3:16-18 we read, "Then they that feared
the Lord spake often one to another: and the Lord
hearkened, and heard it, and a book of remembrance
was written before Him for them that feared the Lord,
and that thought upon His name. And they shall be
mine, saith the Lord of hosts, in that day when I make

up my jewels; and I will spare them, as a man spareth his own son that serveth him. Then shall ye return, and discern between the righteous and the wicked, between him that serveth God and him that serveth Him not."

Malachi was speaking of that glorious day when Israel will be quickened and God will remember His covenant with Abraham, Isaac, and Jacob, and will grant unto IIis people, His "jewels," all that He promised to Abraham.

4. Because of His promise concerning the land: —

God promised Abraham a land, a specific parcel of ground, for *an ETERNAL possession* (Gen. 15:18; 17:8). The land possessed by Israel in the Old Testament economy did not extend to the limit spelled out in the Scriptures—i. e., "from the river of Egypt unto the great river . . . Euphrates." In fact, the land actually possessed by them came to be commonly spoken of as "from Dan to Beersheba" (I Sam. 3:20; II Sam. 17:11; 24:2, 15; I Chron. 21:2).

The land "from Dan to Beersheba" occupied only about 30,000 square miles, but when the Lord Jesus returns to this earth and Israel takes possession of the land promised to Abraham, that nation will occupy a much greater territory than ever before. According to the Prophet Ezekiel, the land promised to Abraham will extend far beyond the boundaries of the land possessed by the nation Israel up to this present time:

"Thus saith the Lord God: This shall be the border, whereby ye shall inherit the land according to the twelve tribes of Israel: Joseph shall have two portions.

And ye shall inherit it, one as well as another: concerning the which I lifted up mine hand to give it unto your fathers: and this land shall fall unto you for inheritance.

"And this shall be the border of the land toward the *north* side, from the great sea, the way of Hethlon, as men go to Zedad; Hamath, Berothah, Sibraim, which is between the border of Damascus and the border of Hamath; Hazar-hatticon, which is by the coast of Hauran. And the border from the sea shall be Hazar-enan, the border of Damascus, and the north northward, and the border of Hamath. And this is the north side.

"And the *east* side ye shall measure from Hauran, and from Damascus, and from Gilead, and from the land of Israel by Jordan, from the border unto the east sea. And this is the east side.

"And the *south* side southward, from Tamar even to the waters of strife in Kadesh, the river to the great sea. And this is the south side southward.

"The *west* side also shall be the great sea from the border, till a man come over against Hamath. This is the west side" (Ezek. 47:13-20).

Great Bible scholars of the past who have made a thorough study of the area promised to Abraham and have estimated the boundaries of that area according to Scripture, declare that the promised land will cover approximately 300,000 square miles. By comparison, this is two and one-half times as large as Great Britain and Ireland combined—an area of great magnitude, many times larger than the territory occupied by the present state of Israel. Abraham's people have never possessed this land, but *God will give it to them* as promised.

5. *Because God made a pledge to David:—*

God will quicken and restore the nation Israel because He made a promise to David that one of his seed would one day occupy his throne and *from* that throne would rule forever.

More than seven centuries before Jesus was born, Isaiah penned these inspired words: "For unto us a Child is born, unto us a Son is given: and the government shall be upon His shoulder: and His name shall be called Wonderful, Counsellor, The mighty God, The everlasting Father, The Prince of Peace" (Isa. 9:6).

Since the *first* part of this prophecy has been literally fulfilled, why should we not expect the *second* part to be literally fulfilled? The Son was given as promised, the Child was born of the Virgin Mary. He was—and is—Wonderful, Counsellor, God in flesh, the Prince of Peace. But the government has never been upon His shoulders and He has never occupied the throne of David. That part of the promise is yet to be fulfilled—and it *will be,* just as God declares in His infallible Word.

God's promise to David is recorded in II Samuel 7:10-17: "Moreover I will appoint a place for my people Israel, and will plant them, that they may dwell in a place of their own, and move no more; neither shall the children of wickedness afflict them any more, as beforetime, and as since the time that I commanded judges to be over my people Israel, and have caused thee to rest from all thine enemies. Also the Lord telleth thee that He will make thee an house. And when thy days be fulfilled, and thou shalt sleep with thy fathers, I will set up thy seed after thee, which shall proceed out of thy bowels, and I will establish His kingdom. He shall build an house for my name, and I will establish the throne of His kingdom for ever. I will be His Father, and He shall be my Son. If He commit iniquity, I will chasten Him with the rod of men, and with the stripes of the children of men: but my mercy shall not depart away from Him, as I took it from Saul, whom I put away before thee. *And thine house and thy kingdom shall be established for ever before thee: thy throne shall be established for ever.* According to all these words, and according to all this vision, so did Nathan speak unto David."

I realize that this passage speaks of David's son King Solomon; but its *ultimate fulfillment* ("thy throne shall be established *forever*") is in the Lord Jesus Christ.

Also in these verses we see eight emphatic *"I WILL'S"*:

(1) the "I will" of *appointment*—"I will appoint *a place* for my people Israel" (v. 10).

Until May 1948 when the state of Israel was set up and recognized by other nations, Israel *had* no appointed place, they were scattered to the ends of the earth. But there is a nucleus of people in the state of Israel now, and others will return until their regathering is complete.

(2) the "I will" of *permanence*—"I will . . . plant them, that they may dwell in a place of their own,

and *move no more"* (v. 10).

Israel will be regathered and appointed a place for a permanent habitation, never again to be driven out. They will then possess all of the land promised to Abraham.

(3) the "I will" of *rest*—". . . rest from *all thine enemies"* (v. 11).

There has been no rest for Israel since they were first driven from their land in judgment. Even those who have returned to Palestine since 1948 have had no rest and no peace. They have lived in constant fear, knowing that they are hated by other peoples, knowing that their enemies would annihilate them from the face of the earth if it were possible for them to *be* annihilated. But when Jesus rules from the throne of David *there will be rest* for the people of Israel.

(4) the "I will" of *setting up*—"I will set up *thy seed* after thee" (v. 12).

The seed of David is not reigning today, but when that glorious day arrives, the seed of David in the Person of the Lord Jesus Christ will sit on David's throne and reign in righteousness and peace.

(5) the "I will" of *establishment*—"I will *establish* His kingdom" (v. 12).

When Jesus stands on the Mount of Olives and the Jews see and recognize Him as Messiah, they will accept Him, a nation will be born in a day, and the kingdom will be established to remain forever.

(6) the "I will" of *perpetuity*—"I will establish the throne of His kingdom *for ever"* (v. 13).

This, of course, speaks of the kingdom over which King Jesus will reign, the time when the knowledge of the Lord will cover the earth as the waters cover the sea.

(7) the "I will" of *relationship*—"I will be His Father . . . He shall be my Son" (v. 14).

God's Son has never yet occupied the throne of David, but we have a definite promise that *He will* occupy that throne at the appointed hour, and will reign as King of kings and Lord of lords, the Son of God.

(8) the "I will" of *chastisement*—"If He commit iniquity, I will *chasten* Him with the rod . . ." (v. 14).

Jesus will be the righteous Ruler. There was no guile in Him when He was *born* King of the Jews, He *lived* apart from sin, and He challenged His enemies, "Which of you convinceth me of sin?" (John 8:46). When He reigns from the throne of David in Jerusalem, righteousness will engulf the earth, for His reign will be in righteousness, holiness, justice, and peace.

Also, in the passage just discussed from II Samuel 7:10-17 we notice *four things* distinctly and definitely having to do with the throne of David: (1) It will be occupied by a descendant of David. (2) It will be perpetual and unending in its rule. (3) It will be associated with a specific people, God's people Israel. (4) It is to be in a certain place—Israel's own place—Jerusalem in the land of Palestine. I would call your attention to the scriptural fact that not one of these four things was fulfilled in David's son, Solomon; therefore if we rightly divide the Word of Truth we know that there is a future Ruler who will occupy the throne of David, and *in HIM* these four things will be fulfilled.

They will be fulfilled by David's *greater* Son, *Son of God*, Son of David *according to the flesh.*

Jesus was God incarnate, the fulness of the Godhead bodily; but He was just as truly the Son of man. The Gospels emphasize His manhood. He was the God-Man—Son of God, Son of man.

In the Annunciation, the angel Gabriel emphatically told Mary that she would be the mother of the Son of Almighty God:

"The angel said unto her, Fear not, Mary: for thou hast found favour with God. And, behold, thou shalt conceive in thy womb, and bring forth a Son, and shalt call His name JESUS. He shall be great, and shall be called *the Son of the HIGHEST:* and the Lord God shall give unto Him the throne of His father David: and He shall reign over the house of Jacob for ever; and of His kingdom there shall be no end" (Luke 1:30-33).

In this announcement we see seven *"shall's"*—or *"shalt's"*:

(1) *"Thou SHALT conceive in thy womb,* and bring forth a Son" (v. 31).

(2) *". . . and SHALT call His name JESUS"* (v. 31).

The name *Jesus* means "Saviour." So the Son of God was named on purpose. He was to save His people from their sins.

(3) *"He SHALL be great"* (v. 32).

Jesus was to be great in character—and He *was* great. He was the greatest *Teacher* who ever lived, the greatest *Preacher* who ever lived. Even His enemies confessed, "Never man spake like THIS Man!" (John 7:46). He was the greatest *Healer* who ever

lived—He defied all the laws of medicine and science.
He touched the leper and cleansed him. He spoke a
word and raised the dead. He made the blind to see—
and "since the world began was it not heard that any
man opened the eyes of one that was born blind" (John
9:32).   He was great *in every aspect* of His earthly life.

(4) ". . . *and SHALL be called the Son of the High-est*" (v. 32).

Mary was to bring forth no ordinary son. He would
be noble in His title—He was called *the Son of God.*
Even the demons recognized Him and cried out, "What
have we to do with thee, *Jesus, thou Son of God?*   Art
thou come hither to torment us before the time?"
(Matt. 8:29).   But while *demons* believed and trembled
at His presence, many *men* refused to recognize Him
as the Son of God.

(5) ". . . *the Lord God SHALL give unto Him the throne of His father David*" (v. 32).

The *Son* Mary was to bring forth would be royal
in His position—He was to be a King. He has not yet
occupied the promised throne of David, but God's
Word cannot fail. He will one day see that His Son
reigns as King of kings and Lord of lords.

(6) *"He SHALL reign over the house of Jacob for ever"* (v. 33).

The Son of God would be specific in His rule, He
was to reign over a specific people—the house of Jacob.
And at that time He will quicken the nation Israel
and give them the land God promised to Abraham.

(7) ". . . *and of His kingdom there SHALL be no end*" (v. 33).

The Son Mary was to bring forth would have an

unending rule. He will reign over the entire earth, and His kingship will be eternal.

6. *Because of His unfailing Word:*—

God will regather and quicken Israel because of the infallibility of His Word. Prophecies associated with the nation Israel were not all fulfilled at the restoration of Judah from Babylon, nor were they all fulfilled at the first coming of Christ. Therefore if God did not regather His people as He promised, His Word would fail—and that cannot be.

In Isaiah 11:11 we read: "And it shall come to pass in that day, that the Lord shall set His hand again the second time to recover the remnant of His people, which shall be left, from Assyria, and from Egypt, and from Pathros, and from Cush, and from Elam, and from Shinar, and from Hamath, and from the islands of the sea."

I would like to point out three things in this verse of Scripture:

(1) The title which the Lord gives Himself signifies proprietary rights.

(2) The Lord will recover His people. The Hebrew points out that He will *purchase* His people, the same statement used in Exodus 15:16 which speaks of the people (Israel) whom God has *purchased.* The Lord God will acquire His elect people again, He "shall set His hand again *the SECOND time* to recover the remnant of His people."

(3) The *time* when God will return His people to the land the second time is specified as "*in THAT DAY.*" In prophecy, this expression when used concerning the

nation Israel always speaks of the Millennium, the one thousand years when Jesus will sit on the throne of David and rule over this earth.

Notice the words of Jeremiah, the weeping prophet, concerning the gathering again of the children of Israel and Judah:

"It shall come to pass, when ye be multiplied and increased in the land, in those days, saith the Lord, they shall say no more, The ark of the covenant of the Lord: neither shall it come to mind: neither shall they remember it; neither shall they visit it; neither shall that be done any more. At that time they shall call Jerusalem the throne of the Lord; and all the nations shall be gathered unto it, to the name of the Lord, to Jerusalem: neither shall they walk any more after the imagination of their evil heart. In those days the house of Judah shall walk with the house of Israel, and they shall come together out of the land of the north to the land that I have given for an inheritance unto your fathers" (Jer. 3:16-18).

Also in Jeremiah 16:14-16 we read concerning the return of Israel to the land:

"Therefore, behold, the days come, saith the Lord, that it shall no more be said, The Lord liveth, that brought up the children of Israel out of the land of Egypt; but, The Lord liveth, that brought up the children of Israel from the land of the north, and from all the lands whither He had driven them: and I will bring them again into their land that I gave unto their fathers. Behold, I will send for many fishers, saith the Lord, and they shall fish them; and after will I send for many hunters, and they shall hunt them from every mountain, and from every hill, and out of the holes of the rocks."

In Jeremiah 23:5-8 the weeping prophet again speaks of Judah and all Israel as returning from the ends of the earth where they have been driven:

"Behold, the days come, saith the Lord, that I will raise unto David a righteous Branch, and a King shall reign and prosper, and shall execute judgment and justice in the earth. In His days Judah shall be saved, and Israel shall dwell safely: and this is His name whereby He shall be called, THE LORD OUR RIGHTEOUSNESS. Therefore, behold, the days come, saith the Lord, that they shall no more say, The Lord liveth, which brought up the children of Israel out of the land of Egypt; but, The Lord liveth, which brought up and which led the seed of the house of Israel out of the north country, and from all countries whither I had driven them; and they shall dwell in their own land."

In Jeremiah 30:3-11 we read not only of the *regathering* of Israel from the ends of the earth, but also of the destruction of the nations who through many centuries have *enslaved* God's chosen people:

"For, lo, the days come, saith the Lord, that I will bring again the captivity of my people Israel and Judah, saith the Lord: and I will cause them to return to the land that I gave to their fathers, and they shall possess it. And these are the words that the Lord spake concerning Israel and concerning Judah. For thus saith the Lord: We have heard a voice of trembling, of fear, and not of peace. Ask ye now, and see whether a man doth travail with child? Wherefore do

I see every man with his hands on his loins, as a woman in travail, and all faces are turned into paleness? Alas! for that day is great, so that none is like it: it is even the time of Jacob's trouble, but he shall be saved out of it.

"For it shall come to pass in that day, saith the Lord of hosts, that I will break his yoke from off thy neck, and will burst thy bonds, and strangers shall no more serve themselves of him: but they shall serve the Lord their God, and David their king, whom I will raise up unto them. Therefore fear thou not, O my servant Jacob, saith the Lord; neither be dismayed, O Israel: for, lo, I will save thee from afar, and thy seed from the land of their captivity; and Jacob shall return, and shall be in rest, and be quiet, and none shall make him afraid. For I am with thee, saith the Lord, to save thee: though I make a full end of all nations whither I have scattered thee, yet will I not make a full end of thee: but I will correct thee in measure, and will not leave thee altogether unpunished."

Through Jeremiah God declared that He will one day make a new covenant with Israel, a covenant of spiritual blessing, when He will put His law in the inner man:

"Behold, the days come, saith the Lord, that I will make a new covenant with the house of Israel, and with the house of Judah: Not according to the covenant that I made with their fathers in the day that I took them by the hand to bring them out of the land of Egypt; which my covenant they brake, although I was an husband unto them, saith the Lord: but this shall be the covenant that I will make with the house of Israel: After those days, saith the Lord, I will put my law in their inward parts, and write it in their hearts; and will be their God, and they shall be my people" (Jer. 31:31-33).

Here we see the new covenant contrasted with the covenant God made with Israel in the wilderness.

In Zechariah 10:6-12 we read: "I will strengthen the house of Judah, and I will save the house of Joseph, and I will bring them again to place them; for I have mercy upon them: and they shall be as though I had not cast them off: for I am the Lord their God, and will hear them. And they of Ephraim shall be like a mighty man, and their heart shall rejoice as through wine: yea, their children shall see it, and be glad; their heart shall rejoice in the Lord.

"I will hiss for them, and gather them; for I have redeemed them: and they shall increase as they have increased. And I will sow them among the people: and they shall remember me in far countries; and they shall live with their children, and turn again.

"I will bring them again also out of the land of Egypt, and gather them out of Assyria; and I will bring them into the land of Gilead and Lebanon; and place shall not be found for them. And he shall pass through the sea with affliction, and shall smite the waves in the sea, and all the deeps of the river shall dry up: and the pride of Assyria shall be brought down, and the sceptre of Egypt shall depart away. And I will strengthen them in the Lord; and they shall walk up and down in His name, saith the Lord."

In these verses from the post-exile writings of the

Prophet Zechariah we see nine *"I will's"* which do not
speak of the restoration of the Jews from Babylon:

(1) "I will strengthen the house of Judah" (v. 6).

(2) "I will save the house of Joseph" (v. 6).

(3) "I will bring them again to place them; for I
have mercy upon them" (v. 6).

(4) "I will hear them" (v. 6).

(5) "I will hiss for them and gather them; for I have
redeemed them" (v. 8).

(6) "I will sow them among the people" (v. 9).

(7) "I will bring them again also out of the land
of Egypt" (v. 10).

(8) "I will bring them into the land of Gilead and
Lebanon" (v. 10).

(9) "I will strengthen them in the Lord, and they
shall walk up and down in His name, saith the Lord"
(v. 12).

Isaiah 14:1,2 is another outstanding prophecy concerning the nation Israel which *was not fulfilled* when
the remnant of Jews (Judah) returned from *Babylon,*
nor was it fulfilled *at Christ's first advent:*

"For the Lord will have mercy on Jacob, and will
yet choose Israel, and set them in their own land: and
the strangers shall be joined with them, and they shall
cleave to the house of Jacob. And the people shall
take them, and bring them to their place: and the
house of Israel shall possess them in the land of the
Lord for servants and handmaids: and they shall take
them captives, whose captives they were; and they
shall rule over their oppressors."

We know the Jews *did not* rule over their oppressors
as is definitely prophesied in this passage from the pen

of Isaiah. (Throughout this study please keep in mind the following facts: The kingdom of Israel was divided [I Kings 12:16-20]. Judah and Benjamin [the southern kingdom] were dispersed into Babylon [II Kings 24 and 25]. The other ten tribes [the northern kingdom] were dispersed [II Kings 17:6-23] and have not returned as yet.)

Jeremiah also speaks of the time when Israel will rule over her enemies:

"For, lo, the days come, saith the Lord, that I will bring again the captivity of my people *Israel and Judah,* saith the Lord: and I will cause them to return to the land that I gave to their fathers, and they shall possess it. And these are the words that the Lord spake concerning Israel and concerning Judah. For thus saith the Lord:

"We have heard a voice of trembling, of fear, and not of peace. Ask ye now, and see whether a man doth travail with child? Wherefore do I see every man with his hands on his loins, as a woman in travail, and all faces are turned into paleness? Alas! for that day is great, so that none is like it: it is even the time of Jacob's trouble, but he shall be saved out of it.

"For it shall come to pass in that day, saith the Lord of hosts, that I will break his yoke from off thy neck, and will burst thy bonds, and strangers shall no more serve themselves of him: but they shall serve the Lord their God, and David their king, whom I will raise up unto them. Therefore fear thou not, O my servant Jacob, saith the Lord; neither be dismayed, O Israel: for, lo, I will save thee from afar, and thy seed from the land of their captivity; and Jacob shall return, and shall be in rest, and be quiet, and none shall make him afraid. For I am with thee, saith the Lord, to save thee: though I make a full end of all nations whither I have scattered thee, yet will I not make a full end of thee: but I will correct thee in measure, and will not leave thee altogether unpunished.

"For thus saith the Lord, Thy bruise is incurable, and thy wound is grievous. There is none to plead thy cause, that thou mayest be bound up: thou hast no healing medicines. All thy lovers have forgotten thee; they seek thee not; for I have wounded thee with the wound of an enemy, with the chastisement of a cruel one, for the multitude of thine iniquity; because thy sins were increased.

"Why criest thou for thine affliction? Thy sorrow is incurable for the multitude of thine iniquity: because thy sins were increased, I have done these things unto thee. Therefore all they that devour thee shall be devoured; and all thine adversaries, every one of them, shall go into captivity; and they that spoil thee shall be a spoil, and all that prey upon thee will I give for a prey" (Jer. 30:3-16).

God promised Israel complete deliverance from their enemies and He will keep His promise. Ezekiel gives a minute description of the victory Israel will have over the great northern army which will sweep down on them in an attempt to completely annihilate that nation. Ezekiel chapters 38 and 39 clearly tell us that Israel will be the victor.

Not only did God promise to give His chosen people victory over and deliverance from their oppressors and enemies, He also promised that their deliverance would be everlasting—they would never again be oppressed:

"I will plant them upon their land, and *they shall NO MORE be pulled up out of their land which I have given them,* saith the Lord thy God" (Amos 9:15).

"For as the new heavens and the new earth, which I will make, shall remain before me, saith the Lord, *so shall your seed and your name remain*" (Isa. 66:22).

"Then will I cause you to dwell in this place, in the land that I gave to your fathers, *for ever and ever*" (Jer. 7:7).

"Sing, O daughter of Zion. Shout, O Israel. Be glad and rejoice with all the heart, O daughter of Jerusalem. The Lord hath taken away thy judgments, He hath cast out thine enemy: the King of Israel, even the Lord, is in the midst of thee: thou shalt not see evil any more.

"In that day it shall be said to Jerusalem, Fear thou not: and to Zion, Let not thine hands be slack. The Lord thy God in the midst of thee is mighty; He will save, He will rejoice over thee with joy; He will rest in His love, He will joy over thee with singing.

"I will gather them that are sorrowful for the solemn assembly, who are of thee, to whom the reproach of it was a burden. Behold, at that time I will undo all that afflict thee: and I will save her that halteth, and gather her that was driven out; and I will get them praise and fame in every land where they have been put to shame. At that time will I bring you again, even in the time that I gather you: for I will make you a name and a praise among all people of the earth, when I turn back your captivity before your eyes, saith the Lord" (Zeph. 3:14-20).

Anyone who would suggest that these prophecies were fulfilled—either upon Judah's return from the Babylonian captivity or at the first coming of Jesus— is certainly wrongly dividing the Word of Truth.

Zechariah also tells of a day yet to come, when the Lord returns in glory:

"Behold, the day of the Lord cometh, and thy spoil shall be divided in the midst of thee. For I will gather all nations against Jerusalem to battle; and the city shall be taken, and the houses rifled, and the women ravished; and half of the city shall go forth into captivity, and the residue of the people shall not be cut off from the city.

"Then shall the Lord go forth, and fight against those nations, as when He fought in the day of battle. And His feet shall stand in that day upon the Mount of Olives, which is before Jerusalem on the east, and the Mount of Olives shall cleave in the midst thereof toward the east and toward the west, and there shall be a very great valley; and half of the mountain shall remove toward the north, and half of it toward the south" (Zech. 14:1-4).

Certainly these prophecies were not fulfilled when a remnant of Israel returned from the Babylonian captivity nor when Jesus came the first time. When He came as a Babe in a manger the Jews demanded His death; but when He comes the second time they will mourn because of their sins and they will accept Him as Messiah and Deliverer. The salvation of Israel, deliverance from their enemies, and their holiness to God will be brought about when Jesus returns to this earth and stands on the Mount of Olives.

7. Because of the vision God gave Ezekiel: —

God will quicken the nation Israel because He gave the Prophet Ezekiel a special vision of His *intention* to restore that nation and bring them back to life; and that vision is recorded in Ezekiel chapter 37:

The vision of the valley of dry bones: —"The hand of the Lord was upon me, and carried me out in the Spirit of the Lord, and set me down in the midst of the valley which was full of bones, and caused me to pass by them round about: and, behold, there were very many in the open valley; and, lo, they were very dry. And He said unto me, Son of man, can these bones live? And I answered, O Lord God, thou knowest. . . ."

The vision explained: —"Then He said unto me, Son of man, these bones are the whole house of Israel: behold, they say, Our bones are dried, and our hope is lost: we are cut off for our parts. Therefore prophesy and say unto them, Thus saith the Lord God: Behold, O my people, I will open your graves, and cause you to come up out of your graves, and bring you into the land of Israel. And ye shall know that I am the Lord, when I have opened your graves, O my people, and brought you up out of your graves, and shall put my Spirit in you, and ye shall live, and I shall place you in your own land. Then shall ye know that I the Lord have spoken it, and performed it, saith the Lord."

The sign of the two sticks: —"The word of the Lord came again unto me, saying: Moreover, thou son of man, take thee one stick, and write upon it, For Judah, and for the children of Israel his companions. Then take another stick, and write upon it, For Joseph, the stick of Ephraim, and for all the house of Israel his companions: and join them one to another into one stick; and they shall become one in thine hand. . . .

"And say unto them, Thus saith the Lord God: Behold, I will take the children of Israel from among the heathen, whither they be gone, and will gather them on every side, and bring them into their own land: and I will make them one nation in the land upon the mountains of Israel; and one King shall be king to them all: and they shall be no more two nations, neither shall they be divided into two kingdoms any more at all: neither shall they defile themselves any more with their idols, nor with their detestable things, nor with any of their transgressions: but I will save them out of all their dwellingplaces, wherein they have sinned, and will cleanse them: so shall they be my people, and I will be their God.

"And David my servant shall be king over them; and they all shall have one shepherd: they shall also walk in my judgments, and observe my statutes, and do them. And they shall dwell in the land that I have given unto Jacob my servant, wherein your fathers have dwelt; and they shall dwell therein, even they, and their children, and their children's children for ever: and my servant David shall be their prince for ever. Moreover I will make a covenant of peace with them; it shall be an everlasting covenant with them: and I will place them, and multiply them, and will set my sanctuary in the midst of them for evermore. My tabernacle also shall be with them: yea, I will be their God, and they shall be my people. And the heathen shall know that I the Lord do sanctify Israel, when my sanctuary shall be in the midst of them for evermore" (Ezek. 37:1-28).

In this chapter from Ezekiel's prophecy we find God's divine declaration emphatically declared in seventeen *"I will's"*:

(1) "I will cause breath to enter into you, and ye shall live" (v. 5).

(2) "I will lay sinews upon you" (v. 6).

(3) "I will . . . bring up flesh upon you" (v. 6).

(4) "I will open your graves, and cause you to come up out of your graves" (v. 12). *"Graves"* as used here speaks of the nations where the children of Israel have been driven.

(5) "I will place you in your own land" (v. 14).

(6) "I will take the stick of Joseph, which is in the hand of Ephraim" (v. 19).

(7) "I will put them with him, even with the stick of Judah, and make them one stick, and they shall be one in mine hand" (v. 19).

(8) "I will take the children of Israel from among the heathen, whither they be gone" (v. 21).

(9) "I will . . . gather them on every side, and bring them into their own land" (v. 21).

(10) "I will make them one nation in the land upon the mountains of Israel; and one King shall be king to them all" (v. 22).

(11) "I will save them out of all their dwelling-places, wherein they have sinned" (v. 23).

(12) "I will . . . cleanse them: so shall they be my people" (v. 23).

(13) "I will be their God" (v. 23).

(14) "I will make a covenant of peace with them . . .

an everlasting covenant" (v. 26).

(15) "I will place them, and multiply them" (v. 26).

(16) "I will . . . set my sanctuary in the midst of them for evermore" (v. 26).

(17) "I will be their God, and they shall be my people" (v. 27).

Then in verse 28, God makes it clear that He will do these marvelous things for the nation Israel in order that *"the heathen shall KNOW that I the Lord do sanctify Israel, when my sanctuary shall be in the midst of them for evermore!"*

Throughout the book of Ezekiel there are prophetic foregleams and emphatic prophecies having to do with God's future plans for the nation Israel. A singular thing about the prophecies recorded in Ezekiel is the certainty of their utterance—there are more than three hundred *"I will's"* in Ezekiel's prophecy. Some of these "I will's" have been fulfilled, but the majority of them are yet future. I want us to study nine of the seventeen "I will's" listed above, and the entire seventeen can be summarized from the nine to be discussed:

(1) the "I will" of *regeneration:—*

"I will cause breath to enter into you, and ye shall live" (v. 5).

The Hebrew word used for *"breath"* is found no less than ten times in chapter 37 of the prophecy of Ezekiel (just quoted in part). Five times it is trans-lated "breath" (vv. 5, 6, 8, 10). Three times in verse 9 it is translated *"wind."* Twice it is translated *"spirit"* (vv. 1 and 14). In each instance the word would be better rendered *"spirit"*—speaking of the Holy Spirit, the Life-giver, He who quickens or makes alive.

When the bones are first united and covered with sinews and flesh there is a great shaking, then a uniform covering—but at this point there is no life. All the shaking and coming together is in unbelief; yet God declares, *"I WILL put my Spirit in you"* (vv. 5, 6, 10, 14). And at the appointed time God will quicken the nation Israel and give them life.

(2) the "I will" of *resurrection:*—

"I will open your graves, and cause you to come up out of your graves" (v. 12).

What is the *meaning* of this statement? Some teach that this speaks of the national resurrection of Jewish bodies, but there are many reasons why such an interpretation cannot be true. In the first place, the land promised Abraham would not be large enough to hold and sustain such a multitude of people. Furthermore, this is not a picture of *physical* resurrection, but *the spiritual resurrection of a nation.* The cry of the bones in verse 11 is, *"Our bones are dried, and our hope is lost! We are cut off for our parts."* This is not the cry of physically dead individual Israelites. It is the cry of a spiritually dead nation, a nation cut off from its own land.

Also, *"graves"* here does not speak of literal graves or burying places. The bones were not *interred* when Ezekiel saw them, but scattered over the valley. The meaning of the passage is simply that God is going to bring back His people who are buried in captivity in the graveyards of other nations. Nothing is said here about opening graves *in the land of Israel.* The graves will be opened in other lands and God's chosen people will be brought back to the land of Israel. Therefore we see that this could not refer to a general resurrection of physically dead Jews, but rather to the bringing back of the Israelites from the nations whither they have been scattered, to establish them again in their own land, Palestine.

(3) the "I will" of *restoration:* —

"I will bring you into the land of Israel. . . . I will place you in your own land" (vv. 12, 14).

I believe the greatest fulfillment of prophecy since the birth of Jesus was the birth of the state of Israel in 1948. For twenty-five centuries they were without a kingdom and without a temple. Today they have their own government and their worship, the stage is set for the restoration of the nation from the ends of the earth; but what has taken place in that country since May 1948 is not the regathering spoken of by the prophets in the Old Testament Scriptures, the time when Israel will be judged and converted as a nation.

As the Jews return to Palestine there is much speculating concerning the ten lost tribes. No one knows who—or where—these tribes are today, but at the appointed time they will hear of God's blessings poured out upon the tribe of Judah, and hearing what God has done for Judah they, too, will come into the land and shall share in the blessings. At the appointed time God will find them.

Hosea tells us clearly that the lost ten tribes will share in the blessings at that appointed hour:

"Yet the number of the children of Israel shall be as the sand of the sea, which cannot be measured nor numbered; and it shall come to pass, that in the place where it was said unto them, Ye are not my people, there it shall be said unto them, Ye are the sons of the living God. Then shall the children of Judah and the children of Israel be gathered together, and appoint themselves one head, and they shall come up out of the land: for great shall be the day of Jezreel" (Hosea 1:10, 11).

"Come, and let us return unto the Lord: for He hath torn, and He will heal us; He hath smitten, and He will bind us up. After two days will He revive us: in the third day He will raise us up, and we shall live in His sight. Then shall we know, if we follow on to know the Lord: His going forth is prepared as the morning; and He shall come unto us as the rain, as the latter and former rain unto the earth" (Hosea 6:1-3).

"O Israel, return unto the Lord thy God; for thou hast fallen by thine iniquity. . . . I will heal their backsliding, I will love them freely: for mine anger is turned away from him. I will be as the dew unto Israel: he shall grow as the lily, and cast forth his roots as Lebanon. His branches shall spread, and his beauty shall be as the olive tree, and his smell as Lebanon.

"They that dwell under his shadow shall return; they shall revive as the corn, and grow as the vine: the scent thereof shall be as the wine of Lebanon. Ephraim shall say, What have I to do any more with idols? I have heard him, and observed him: I am like a green fir tree. From me is thy fruit found. Who is wise, and he shall understand these things? Prudent, and he shall know them? For the ways of the Lord are right, and the just shall walk in them: but the transgressors shall fall therein" (Hosea 14:1, 4-9).

(4) the "I will" of *recognition:* —

". . . and shall put my Spirit in you, and ye shall live, and I shall place you in your own land: then shall ye know that I the Lord have spoken it, and performed it, saith the Lord" (Ezek. 37:14).

The quickening power of the Holy Spirit will open the spiritual eyes of the nation Israel — eyes which have been veiled in unbelief. They will realize what God has done for them, they will recognize Jesus as the Man of Sorrows of Isaiah chapter 53, and they will receive Him as their true Messiah.

(5) the "I will" of *reunion:* —

"Thus saith the Lord God: Behold, I will take the stick of Joseph, which is in the hand of Ephraim, and the tribes of Israel his fellows, and will put them with him, even with the stick of Judah, and make them one stick, and they shall be one in mine hand. And the sticks whereon thou writest shall be in thine hand before their eyes. And say unto them, Thus saith the Lord God: Behold, I will take the children of Israel from among the heathen, whither they be gone, and will gather them on every side, and bring them into their own land: and I will make them one nation in the land upon the mountains of Israel; and one King shall be king to them all: and they shall be no more two nations, neither shall they be divided into two kingdoms any more at all" (Ezek. 37:19-22).

The twelve tribes of Israel have not been unified in one nation since the days of King David and his son Solomon. The revolt which took place during the reign of Rehoboam ended in the division of the nation, with the ten tribes separated from Judah. (Study II Chronicles chapter 10.) This division had been prophesied by Ahijah to Jeroboam (I Kings 11:29-35). Then because of Israel's practice of the terrible sin of idolatry, that nation was taken captive by the Assyrians. (Study II Kings chapter 17.)

Judah—also because of the sin of idolatry—was taken captive by Babylon. (Study II Kings chapter 25.) Since then the two sections of the twelve tribes, Judah and Israel, have not been under one ruler, nor will they be under one ruler until their King, the Lord Jesus Christ, returns to this earth to reign from the throne of David. That will be the time when all Israel shall be saved (Rom. 11:26). This does not mean that every Jew will be saved individually. It means that all the nation will be resurrected from their graves among other nations and all twelve tribes will be brought back into the promised land.

(6) the "I will" of *regathering:* —

"Thus saith the Lord God: Behold, I will take the children of Israel from among the heathen, whither they be gone, and will gather them on every side, and bring them into their own land" (Ezek. 37:21).

The statement here clearly indicates that the entire nation of Israel will be gathered back into the land God promised Abraham. At the appointed time, the God who scattered them to the ends of the earth will gather them again into their own land: "Hear the word of the Lord, O ye nations, and declare it in the isles afar off, and say, He that scattered Israel will gather him, and keep him, as a shepherd doth his flock" (Jer. 31:10).

The Lord God is the Good Shepherd of the sheep, and as a good shepherd seeketh out his flock, then the Lord God in that day will seek out His sheep, that are scattered to the ends of the earth: "For thus saith the Lord God: Behold, I, even I, will both search my sheep, and seek them out. As a shepherd seeketh out his flock in the day that he is among his sheep that are scattered; so will I seek out my sheep, and will deliver them out of all places where they have been scattered in the cloudy and dark day" (Ezek. 34:11, 12).

(7) the "I will" of *redemption:*—

"Neither shall they defile themselves any more with their idols, nor with their detestable things, nor with any of their transgressions: but I will save them out of all their dwellingplaces, wherein they have sinned, and will cleanse them: so shall they be my people, and I will be their God" (Ezek. 37:23).

In this verse, the word *"save"* means "to be open, free, or rescued." So Israel will be *set free,* and made safe in their own land. The same word is used in Exodus 14:30 in connection with God's redemption of Israel from Egypt: "Thus the Lord *SAVED Israel."* Notice also the statement "I will *cleanse* them." The word "cleanse" means that which is "pure, uncontaminated, bright." In Proverbs 20:9 the same word is translated "pure." Twenty-four times in Leviticus chapter 14 it is found in a double connection (namely, being pronounced clean through atonement by the blood) rendered *"clean, cleansed, pronounced clean."*

In Psalm 51:2 and Ezekiel 36:25 the same word is

translated "to be cleansed from sin and wickedness." Therefore the "I will" of redemption speaks of the salvation of Israel and the cleansing of the people from contamination and pollution, setting them free from sin—and certainly no other nation has sinned against God as grievously as has His elect nation Israel, the apple of His eye.   But He will completely cleanse them and set them free from all sin in that glorious day when they put their faith in their Messiah.

(8) the "I will of *relationship:* —

". . . so shall they be my people, and I will be their God" (Ezek. 37:23).

The Author of redemption frees from the shackles of sin which bind, that He may cleanse from the power that bound, and take the redeemed one unto Himself, *for* Himself.   Redemption is *by* the Lord God, and we are redeemed *unto* the Lord God.

We read further, "My tabernacle also shall be with them: yea, I will be their God, and they shall be my people" (Ezek. 37:27).   God makes His dwelling place among His people in order that they may have a continual and constant supply of redeeming grace and keeping grace—the grace that supplies every need.

(9) the "I will" of *regard* (or promise): —

God made a threefold promise to Israel:

"I will make a covenant of peace with them . . .

I will place them, and multiply them . . .

I will set my sanctuary in the midst of them for evermore" (Ezek. 37:26).

Israel's night of persecution has been long and dark and dreary.   Even today that nation is held in the shackles of unbelief and sin. But there is a day coming

when Israel's Messiah will come as the mighty Deliverer. He will cause the bondage of Israel to cease,
He will cause the night of darkness to pass away. He
will take away the veil of unbelief, and the promised
land will be given to Israel. Then will be the most
glorious era that nation has ever known. In spite of
all false doctrines and false teachers, God will keep
His promise to Abraham and his seed.

History records the literal fulfillment of God's Word.
The people of Israel have been scattered—but never
destroyed. For centuries they have been absorbed
among other nations of the earth—but they have never
lost their identity. God has preserved them for the
fulfillment of His promise to gather them again in the
end time and make the nation Israel His kingdom on
this earth. Today we stand at the very threshhold of
the fulfillment of the prophecy of Israel's being re-
gathered into their own land.

Few people realize the tremendous importance of
what is going on in the land of Palestine in this hour.
The most outstanding and significant fulfillment of
prophecy is the recognition of Israel as a state, a nation, in what is at least a *part* of the land promised
to Abraham. We have recognized the existence of
Israel as a nation for the first time in more than 2,500
years, and as the fig tree buds we witness the increase
of wickedness, moral decay, war, earthquakes, race
hatred, and many other outstanding signs which are
fulfillments of the Word of God. All of these things
were foretold by the prophets, and their fulfillment
tells us that Jesus is surely at the door.

However, nothing else compares with the significance of the revival of the state of Israel, established with their own president, their own constitution, their own flag, their own currency, their own armed forces, and with the recognition of other nations. For centuries the Jews have had no national existence; but the "dry bones" are beginning to come together in unity, sinews and flesh are forming on the skeleton of the nation of Israel. There remains to be fulfilled the prophecy of the breath of God—His Spirit—entering into that nation and bringing spiritual revival to them.

There are many figures in prophecy which give a picture of Israel. For instance, *the burning bush* in the desert represented Israel and the fires of affliction and persecution through which the people would pass— but would not be consumed. *The vine* in Isaiah chapter 5 is a picture of Israel—the vineyard of the Lord given over to enemies but someday to be restored. *The fig tree* which Jesus cursed is a picture of Israel— withered from the roots but some day to once again blossom, bud, and bear fruit. Paul expressed the same truth in Romans chapter 11, speaking of the olive tree whose branches have been broken off temporarily, while God deals with the wild branches (the Gentiles). Some day the natural branches will be grafted in, and it seems that the grafting is going on this very moment.

The fulfillment of Ezekiel's vision of the valley of dry bones is also beginning to take shape right before our eyes. Today Israel is a democracy, not a kingdom; and for this reason that nation has a president, not a king. But soon King Jesus will return to His people,

His peculiar treasure, His elect nation; and that nation
will settle in their own land forever. As we witness
these things occurring at this very moment, surely
we can lift our eyes toward heaven and raise our
voices with John the Beloved as he prayed:

"Even so, COME, Lord Jesus!"

Chapter XII

Peace On Earth —
Good Will Toward Men

"And there were in the same country shepherds abiding in the field, keeping watch over their flock by night. And, lo, the angel of the Lord came upon them, and the glory of the Lord shone round about them: and they were sore afraid. And the angel said unto them, Fear not: for, behold, I bring you good tidings of great joy, which shall be to all people. For unto you is born this day in the city of David a Saviour, which is Christ the Lord. And this shall be a sign unto you: Ye shall find the Babe wrapped in swaddling clothes, lying in a manger.

"And suddenly there was with the angel a multitude of the heavenly host praising God, and saying, Glory to God in the highest, and on earth peace, good will toward men. And it came to pass, as the angels were gone away from them into heaven, the shepherds said one to another, Let us now go even unto Bethlehem, and see this thing which is come to pass, which the Lord hath made known unto us.

"And they came with haste, and found Mary, and Joseph, and the Babe lying in a manger. And when they had seen it, they made known abroad the saying which was told them concerning this Child. And all they that heard it wondered at those things which were told them by the shepherds. But Mary kept all these things, and pondered them in her heart. And the shepherds returned, glorifying and praising God for all the things that they had heard and seen, as it was told unto them" (Luke 2:8-20).

This present generation, for one particular reason, may well go down in history as the most *paradoxical* age of all time. The world talks of peace, security, and deliverance from fear and poverty—at the same time preparing for exactly the opposite. Man contradicts himself at every turn. There is more talk about peace today than ever before in the history of man. Yet, paradoxically, there has never been a time when men were so dedicated to thinking, planning, and preparing for the destruction of the human race!

Considering the potentialities of modern weapons and methods of warfare, it is common knowledge that another war could well mean the end of civilization. Yet there are more men under arms today than at any other time in history when the world was nominally at peace. There are wars and rumors of wars around the globe, and billions upon billions of dollars are being spent for the development and manufacture of powerful weapons of war, weapons more deadly than previous generations dreamed of! During the past few years there have been skirmishes and "little wars" throughout the world—which is in accordance with the prophecy of Matthew 24:6, 7.

In spite of peace conferences, promises of peace, and programs to wipe out poverty, our newspapers, magazines, and newscasts by radio and television cause us to wonder if there really *is* any hope for this poor, blood-soaked world! Will we continue to fight and destroy each other until finally mankind destroys *himself?* The Word of God holds the answer to this question. Yes, there is hope—a *sure* hope—of peace on earth and good will among men—but not through the *efforts* of men. Peace and good will will come only through the personal return of the Prince of Peace, the Lord Jesus Christ. War and bloodshed will cease and universal justice and love will prevail on this earth—but only when the King of kings reigns in righteousness from the throne of David.

The only true peace in the world today is in the hearts of individuals who are born again believers, born again through faith in the Lord Jesus Christ, and who follow in His steps. World peace—politically, socially, and nationally—can never be known until the Prince of Peace returns to this earth. *Then,* as Isaiah declared, "of the increase of His government and peace there shall be no end, upon the throne of David, and upon His kingdom, to order it, and to establish it with judgment and with justice from henceforth even for ever. . ." (Isa. 9:7).

God Knows What He Is Doing

"Known unto God are all His works from the beginning of the world" (Acts 15:18).

God is eternal. From everlasting to everlasting *He is GOD* (Psalm 90:2). He is *the great I AM.* He is omniscient, omnipotent, omnipresent. God loves, lives, and works in the eternal present, but He has a program and plan for the ages; and *when time shall be no more* His kingdom will be everlasting—through the ages of ages unending.

"In the beginning *God CREATED . . .*" (Gen. 1:1), and in the process of creation He formed man of the dust of the ground, breathed into his nostrils the breath of life, and man became a living soul (Gen. 2:7). But man disobeyed God and fell into sin (Gen. 3:1-19)—and through the disobedience of Adam all men became sinners.

God condemned the attempted atoning work of Adam's hands and Himself provided coats of skins to clothe Adam and Eve. Then in the process of instructions to the parents of the human race He promised the Deliverer, the One who would deliver man—and eventually all creation—from the curse of sin (Gen. 3:15).

Centuries later, the Seed of the woman, the Prince of Peace, was born (Gal. 4:4, 5), and although there were centuries between the promise and its fulfillment, God knew what was going on all the time. The devil did everything in his power to destroy the Seed of the woman. He brought about the murder of Abel, the righteous son of Adam (Gen. 4:1-15). He caused the terrible wickedness of man which demanded the judgment of the flood (Gen. 6:5-7). He filled Abraham with fear and caused him to lie about Sarah, his wife (Gen. 12:10-20). And so the battle raged, until at one point the devil had managed to destroy the seed of the royal line except for one little boy, Joash, who was hidden in the house of the Lord until it was time for him to reign (II Kings 11:1-3).

But in spite of all Satan and his forces of hell could do, in the fulness of time God kept His promise and (through the Virgin Mary) the Son of God, Saviour of the world, came. Still Satan did not give up. After the birth of Jesus, he did everything he *could* do in his efforts to destroy the Babe who was born King of the Jews. He caused Herod to issue a decree that all babies under two years of age should be slain—"all the children that were in Bethlehem, and in all the coasts thereof" (Matt. 2:16).

Then immediately following the baptism of Jesus, as He entered His public ministry, the devil approached Him in the wilderness and tried to entice Him to sell out and take a detour around Calvary and the cross (Matt. 4:1-11).

On one occasion, as Jesus spoke in the synagogue at Nazareth, the people became so angry they took Him outside the city and attempted to push Him over a precipice and kill Him. "But He passing through the midst of them went His way" (Luke 4:28-30).

On another occasion the Jews attempted to stone Him—"but Jesus hid Himself, and went out of the temple, going through the midst of them, and so passed by" (John 8:59).

But in spite of all the forces of the devil and hell combined, at the appointed time Christ died on the cruel cross exactly as was determined before the foundation of the world. "For when we were yet without strength, *IN DUE TIME Christ died for the ungodly*" (Rom. 5:6).

The heavenly host made no mistake in announcing from the sky over Bethlehem, "Glory to God in the highest, and *on earth PEACE, good will toward men!*" (Luke 2:14). To His disciples Jesus said, *"Peace I leave with you, MY peace I give unto you. Not as*

the world giveth, give I unto you. Let not your heart
be troubled, neither let it be afraid" (John 14:27).

Jesus was speaking of peace to individual hearts.
In the Word of God peace is spoken of in three ways:

(1) *peace WITH God:*

"Therefore being justified by faith, we have *peace
with God* through our Lord Jesus Christ" (Rom. 5:1).
Peace with God is the work of Christ, and the individual finds peace with God by faith in the shed
blood and finished work of God's only begotten Son.

(2) *the peace OF God:*

"And the *peace of God,* which passeth all understanding, shall keep your hearts and minds through
Christ Jesus" (Phil. 4:7). This is the inward peace of
the believer who has entered into peace *with* God
through faith in the finished work of Jesus and who,
through prayer, complete surrender, and supplication
with thanksgiving, has committed to God all of his
anxieties and fears. Such a believer experiences the
indwelling peace of God. We are admonished, "Be
careful for nothing; but in every thing by prayer and
supplication with thanksgiving let your requests be
made known unto God" (Phil. 4:6).

(3) *peace on EARTH:*

"Glory to God in the highest, and *on earth PEACE,*
good will toward men" (Luke 2:14).

"In His days shall the righteous flourish; and *abundance of PEACE* so long as the moon endureth" (Psalm
72:7).

"Mercy and truth are met together; *righteousness
and PEACE* have kissed each other" (Psalm 85:10).

There will be peace on earth, *universal peace,* when

the Prince of Peace occupies the throne of David and reigns in righteousness over the whole earth. Christ's first coming did not bring peace, but conflict—as He declared in Matthew 10:34-36 when He said to His disciples, "Think not that I am come to send peace on earth: *I came NOT to send peace, but a sword.* For I am come to set a man at variance against his father, and the daughter against her mother, and the daughter in law against her mother in law. And a man's foes shall be they of his own household!" We who are nineteen centuries this side of Calvary know that His words are true.

That God foreknew "all His works from the beginning of the world" is also clearly declared in Peter's second sermon—recorded in Acts 3:12-26—showing that even the evil intent of wicked men was made to carry out the divine purpose of Almighty God:

"Ye men of Israel, . . . The God of Abraham, and of Isaac, and of Jacob, the God of our fathers, hath glorified His Son Jesus; *whom ye delivered up, and denied Him in the presence of Pilate,* when he was determined to let Him go. But *ye denied the Holy One and the Just,* and desired a murderer to be granted unto you; *and killed the Prince of Life,* whom God hath raised from the dead; whereof we are witnesses. . . . And now, brethren, I wot that *through ignorance ye did it,* as did also your rulers. *But THOSE THINGS, WHICH GOD BEFORE HAD SHEWED BY THE MOUTH OF ALL HIS PROPHETS, that Christ should suffer, He hath so FULFILLED.*

"Repent ye therefore, and be converted, that your sins may be blotted out, *when the times of REFRESH-*

ING shall come from the presence of the Lord; and
He shall send Jesus Christ, which before was preached
unto you: *whom the heaven must receive UNTIL
THE TIMES OF RESTITUTION OF ALL THINGS,
which God hath spoken by the mouth of all His holy
prophets since the world began"* (Acts 3:12-21 in part).

Notice the twofold *"times"* referred to in these
verses:

(1) the times of *refreshing:*—

This is the result of conversion and points to the
blessing which comes upon the converted one. The
sinner is dead in sin, dry and barren. After conversion,
there is within the inner man a well of living water,
springing up into everlasting life, refreshing the saved
one.

(2) the times of *restitution of all things:*—

This speaks of the return of the Lord Jesus Christ,
when everything in this earth will be as God intended
it to be, before man sinned and sold the entire human
race (and all creation) into suffering and slavery under
sin. But the *restitution of all things* does not mean
universal salvation; it is restricted to that "which God
hath spoken by the mouth of all His holy prophets."
Peter's words were addressed primarily to Israel, and
not to man *universally.*

Wicked, evil men smote the Rock of Ages, the Lord
Jesus Christ; yet from the smitten Rock gushed forth
the water of life. The wicked hand of man thrust the
spear into the heart of Jesus; yet that spear brought
forth blood, and the blood shed on Calvary cleanses
from all sin—*"WITHOUT shedding of blood is no
remission"* (Heb. 9:22).

"Repent ye THEREFORE . . . ." The cross demands that we take God's side against ourselves in condemning the sin that caused Him to suffer as no mortal man ever suffered. The power of the cross of Jesus is the power that breaks the sinner's heart and then breaks away the shackles of sin. True repentance, moved by the Holy Spirit, brings salvation through faith in the shed blood and finished work of the Son of God, and unites the believer to Christ. We thus become members of His body, bone of His bone and flesh of His flesh. "For by one Spirit are we all baptized into one body, whether we be Jews or Gentiles, whether we be bond or free; and have been all made to drink into one Spirit" (I Cor. 12:13).

"Repent ye therefore, and be converted, *that your sins may be BLOTTED OUT . . . ."* The Greek word translated *"blotted out"* means "to wipe out." In Colossians 2:14 the same word is rendered "blotting out"—speaking of Christ's having blotted out "the handwriting of ordinances that was against us, which was contrary to us, and took it out of the way, nailing it to His cross." The same word is used in Revelation 7:17 and 21:4 where it is translated "wipe away"— "God shall *wipe away* all tears from their eyes."

When the unbeliever repents and exercises faith in God, God removes all sin from the heart and conscience. He wipes them away—thoroughly and completely. The blood of Jesus leaves no trace of sin or uncleanness. It is when sins are blotted out, washed away, that the forgiven one enjoys "the times of refreshing." This is the result of the removal of sins. When the sin that separates us from God is removed, the refreshing stream of living water (the fountain of life) fills and refreshes us.

You see, the Jews were expecting a Messiah who would deliver them from the tyranny of Rome and set up a glorious kingdom on earth; but Peter reminded them that they rejected their Messiah, demanded His death, and chose a robber in His stead. Therefore heaven received Him "until the times of restitution of all things."

It is important that we fully understand the meaning of the Greek word here translated *"restitution."* This is the only place in the New Testament where this particular Greek word is used, but there is a kindred verb which occurs in seven other passages and in each instance is translated either *"restore"* or *"restored"*:

In Matthew 12:13, when the man with the withered hand came to Jesus, the Lord said to him, *"Stretch forth thine hand.* And he stretched it forth: *and it was RESTORED whole,* like as the other." The same word, with the same translation, is also found in Mark 3:5 and Luke 6:10.

In Mark 8:25 the same word is also rendered *restored*—Jesus put His hands on the eyes of the blind man, *"and made him look up: and he was RESTORED, and saw every man clearly."*

The same word is used in Hebrews 13:19 where Paul asked the Hebrew believers to pray for him *that he might be RESTORED to them.*

The same word is used in Mark 9:12 where Jesus said, "Elias verily cometh first, *and RESTORETH all things . . . ."*

Then in Acts 1:6, after Christ's resurrection, the disciples asked Him, "Lord, wilt thou at this time *RESTORE again the kingdom to Israel?*"

From these verses the meaning of *"restitution"* is very clear, and I believe its usage here indicates some of the glorious things that will occur at "the time of the restitution of all things." For example, the man with the withered hand was healed, restored, delivered. In Isaiah 35:6 we read concerning the kingdom blessings, "Then shall the *lame man* leap as an hart, and the tongue of the *dumb* sing: for in the wilderness shall waters break out, and streams in the desert."

The blind man's sight was gloriously restored; and during that glorious day when Jesus reigns from the throne of David there will be no blindness: "In that day shall the deaf hear the words of the book, and the eyes of the blind shall see out of obscurity, and out of darkness" (Isa. 29:18). "Then the eyes of the blind shall be opened, and the ears of the deaf shall be unstopped" (Isa. 35:5).

The *restitution of all things* speaks not of the heavenly order of things, but of the *earthly* order of things. Let us face it, beloved—if *Satan's deception* goes further than *Christ's redemption and restoration,* then Christ failed! It was through Adam's sin in the Garden of Eden that Paradise was lost. The earth became a place of thorns and thistles. The animal kingdom no longer lived in perfect harmony and peace, but became a suffering, groaning, travailing, devouring kingdom. However, the earth, the animal kingdom— the whole creation—will be restored and delivered from the curse of sin, because if the redemption purchased at the tremendous price of the blood of Jesus did not go as far as the consequences of sin, redemption would be a failure. It matters not how many *individuals* are saved, if *all things* are not redeemed, redemption would not be a full success. Therefore we can rest assured that "the restitution of all things" is as certain as God.

The Time Is Coming When Death
Will Be the Exception Instead of the Rule

"We know that the whole creation groaneth and travaileth in pain together until now" (Rom. 8:22).

Since the day Adam sinned, all creation has groaned and travailed in pain because of sin. "Wherefore, as by one man (Adam) sin entered into the world, and death by sin; and so death passed upon all men, for that all have sinned" (Rom. 5:12).

Because of Adam's sin, God cursed the serpent, the tool of Satan, and changed him from a beautiful, subtle creature to a loathsome reptile, consigned to eat dust all of his days—even in the Millennium. Then to the woman God said, "I will greatly multiply thy sorrow and thy conception. In sorrow thou shalt bring forth children; and thy desire shall be to thy husband, and he shall rule over thee."

To Adam, God said, "Because thou hast hearkened unto the voice of thy wife, and hast eaten of the tree, of which I commanded thee, saying, Thou shalt not eat of it: cursed is the ground for thy sake; in sorrow shalt thou eat of it all the days of thy life; thorns also and thistles shall it bring forth to thee; and thou shalt eat the herb of the field. In the sweat of thy face shalt thou eat bread, till thou return unto the ground; for out of it wast thou taken: for dust thou art, and unto dust shalt thou return" (Gen. 3:14-19).

All we need do to see the fulfillment of this Scripture is simply to look around us. On every hand we see suffering, sorrow, pain, anguish, misery and death. But this will not always be. In the coming days of Christ's millennial glory, life will be greatly prolonged. Hear what the Lord says in Isaiah 65:19-22:

"I will rejoice in Jerusalem, and joy in my people: and the voice of weeping shall be no more heard in her, nor the voice of crying. There shall be no more thence an infant of days, nor an old man that hath not filled his days: for the child shall die an hundred years old; but the sinner being an hundred years old shall be accursed. And they shall build houses, and inhabit them; and they shall plant vineyards, and eat the fruit of them. They shall not build, and another inhabit; they shall not plant, and another eat: for as the days of a tree are the days of my people, and mine elect shall long enjoy the work of their hands."

Then the time is coming in the eternal ages when there will *be* no more sorrow, sickness, pain, or death— yes, even *death* will be destroyed (I Cor. 15:26): "And God shall wipe away all tears from their eyes; and there shall be no more death, neither sorrow, nor crying, neither shall there be any more pain: for the former things are passed away" (Rev. 21:4).

Then in Revelation 22:1-3 we read of the New Paradise, with its "river of water of life, clear as crystal, proceeding out of the throne of God and of the Lamb. In the midst of the street of it, and on either side of

the river, was there the tree of life, which bare twelve
manner of fruits, and yielded her fruit every month:
and the leaves of the tree were for the healing of the
nations. *And there shall be NO MORE CURSE:* but
the throne of God and of the Lamb shall be in it; and
His servants shall serve Him!"

The Time Is Coming
When There Will Be Universal Peace

"Suddenly there was with the angel a multitude of
the heavenly host praising God, and saying, *Glory to
God in the highest, and ON EARTH PEACE, GOOD
WILL TOWARD MEN"* (Luke 2:13, 14).

To *listen* is to hear the rumbling of the volcano of
distress under *everything* in this hour in which we
live—labor against capital, race against race, man
against man. There is division, confusion, misunderstanding, hatred, malice, and strife. The storm of
world conditions causes every phase of life on this
earth to tremble. But there is a day coming when the
Lord Jesus Christ will step on the scene and once
again command, "Peace! be still!" and there will be a
great calm. The fires of hatred will be extinguished
and love will prevail. The knowledge of God will
engulf the earth as the waters now cover the sea and
there will be world-wide peace and good will.

The Word of God contains many passages with
descriptions of this glorious coming age of peace, prosperity, and universal tranquility. It would be impossible to give all of those descriptions in this message,
but we will look at just a few of them:

Isaiah 2:2-4: "It shall come to pass in the last days,

that the mountain of the Lord's house shall be established in the top of the mountains, and shall be exalted above the hills; and all nations shall flow unto it. And many people shall go and say, Come ye, and let us go up to the mountain of the Lord, to the house of the God of Jacob; and He will teach us of His ways, and we will walk in His paths: for out of Zion shall go forth the law, and the word of the Lord from Jerusalem. And He shall judge among the nations, and shall rebuke many people: and they shall beat their swords into plowshares, and their spears into pruning-hooks: nation shall not lift up sword against nation, neither shall they learn war any more.''

Isaiah's message is unmistakeable: *"Thus saith the LORD!"* God, upon the authority of His own Word, declares that there will come a time when wars will cease and men will no longer manufacture guns and implements of destruction. Weapons of war will be turned into implements of peace and prosperity and will join in the blessings of mankind. There will be no more military camps, no factories turning out guns and ammunition, no young men in uniform. *"Neither shall they learn war any more."*

Isaiah speaks again concerning a kingdom whose Ruler will govern in righteousness and peace, a kingdom where there will be security and prosperity:

"There shall come forth a rod out of the stem of Jesse, and a Branch shall grow out of his roots: and the Spirit of the Lord shall rest upon Him, the Spirit of wisdom and understanding, the Spirit of counsel and might, the Spirit of knowledge and of the fear of the Lord; and shall make Him of quick understanding in the fear of the Lord: and He shall not judge after the sight of His eyes, neither reprove after the hearing of His ears: but with righteousness shall He judge the poor, and reprove with equity for the meek of the earth: and He shall smite the earth with the rod of His mouth, and with the breath of His lips shall He slay the wicked. And righteousness shall be the girdle of His loins, and faithfulness the girdle of His reins.

"The wolf also shall dwell with the lamb, and the leopard shall lie down with the kid; and the calf and the young lion and the fatling together; and a little child shall lead them. And the cow and the bear shall feed; their young ones shall lie down together: and the lion shall eat straw like the ox. And the sucking child shall play on the hole of the asp, and the weaned child shall put his hand on the cockatrice' den. They shall not hurt nor destroy in all my holy mountain: for the earth shall be full of the knowledge of the Lord, as the waters cover the sea. And in that day there shall be a root of Jesse, which shall stand for an ensign of the people; to it shall the Gentiles seek: and His rest shall be glorious" (Isa. 11:1-10).

Search history—both sacred and secular—and you will find that there has never been such a time upon this earth since the fall of man. So this kingdom is yet future—and please note that this is not to be *spiritualized*. The glorious era described in the verses just quoted will take place literally, right here on earth. Isaiah declares that *the EARTH*, not heaven, shall be full of the knowledge of the Lord. He was not describing the Pearly White City, nor was he describing heaven. He was speaking of the millennial earth during the reign of the King of kings and Lord of lords.

Jeremiah, "the weeping prophet," also speaks of this glorious time. In Jeremiah 23:5 we read:

"Behold, the days come, saith the Lord, that I will raise unto David a righteous Branch, and a King shall reign and prosper, and shall execute judgment and justice in the earth."

The Prophet Amos declares, "Behold, the days come, saith the Lord, that the plowman shall overtake the reaper, and the treader of grapes him that soweth seed; and the mountains shall drop sweet wine, and all the hills shall melt. And I will bring again the captivity of my people of Israel, and they shall build the waste cities, and inhabit them; and they shall plant vineyards, and drink the wine thereof; they shall also make gardens, and eat the fruit of them. And I will plant them upon their land, and they shall no more be pulled up out of their land which I have given them, saith the Lord thy God" (Amos 9:13-15).

The Psalmist declares, "He maketh wars to cease unto the end of the earth; He breaketh the bow, and cutteth the spear in sunder; He burneth the chariot in the fire" (Psalm 46:9).

The Prophet Zechariah declares that there is a day coming when the Lord will be King, not only over Jerusalem, but over the entire earth. In Zechariah 14:9 we read, "The Lord shall be King *over all the earth:* in that day shall there be one Lord, and His name one."

We live in a day of violence, strife, and hatred between races and classes of people. But the day is coming when violence will cease and class strife and hatred will be no more:

"Violence shall no more be heard in thy land, wasting nor destruction within thy borders; but thou shalt call thy walls Salvation, and thy gates Praise. The sun shall be no more thy light by day; neither for brightness shall the moon give light unto thee: but the Lord shall be unto thee an everlasting light, and thy God thy glory" (Isa. 60:18, 19).

Through centuries past—even until this present hour —man has tried to deal with discrimination, with national and racial lines, but there has been very little progress. The world is filled with hatred and strife, but one day God will "set up an ensign for the nations, and shall assemble the outcasts of Israel, and gather together the dispersed of Judah from the four corners of the earth. The envy also of Ephraim shall depart, and the adversaries of Judah shall be cut off. Ephraim shall not envy Judah, and Judah shall not vex Ephraim" (Isa. 11:12, 13).

There will be no hatred between nations and races when Jesus reigns in righteousness and the knowledge of the Lord covers the earth, as the waters now cover the sea.

The Time Is Coming
When Wrong Will Be Replaced With Right

"He shall judge the poor of the people, He shall save the children of the needy, and shall break in pieces the oppressor. . . . For He shall deliver the needy when he crieth, the poor also, and him that hath no helper. He shall spare the poor and needy, and shall save the souls of the needy" (Psalm 72:4, 12, 13).

These verses are from the millennial Psalm which describes Christ's glorious and bountiful reign on earth. We hear much talk today, both politically and socially, concerning the equality of man; but it is clearly evident on every hand that racial and social equality are as yet non-existent on this earth. Nor will such a condition come to pass until Christ comes in glory and sets up His kingdom! Evil will not be *erased or remedied* by legislation or social reform. The only cure for evil and oppression is "the restitution (or regeneration) of all things." When the Lord Jesus Christ takes the reins of government, when the government is "upon His shoulder," He will see that there is no partiality, no evil or wrong-doing among mankind. All of earth's inhabitants will live in peace and security. The meek shall inherit the earth and shall dwell in the abundance of peace.

Political leaders today preach social equality, racial equality, and all men living on the same level. Such men do not know the teaching of the Word of God; and as long as the devil is out of the pit there will *be* no "peace on earth," no "good will toward men." There will be no social, racial, or monetary equality. On the contrary, the Scriptures clearly teach that the nearer we come to the end of this Day of Grace, the more perilous the times will be. The Apostle Paul emphatically points out this fact in his second letter to young Timothy:

"This know also, that in the last days perilous times shall come. For men shall be lovers of their own selves, covetous, boasters, proud, blasphemers, disobedient to parents, unthankful, unholy, without natural affection, trucebreakers, false accusers, incontinent, fierce, despisers of those that are good, traitors, heady, highminded, lovers of pleasures more than lovers of God; having a form of godliness, but denying the power thereof: from such turn away. . . . But evil men and seducers shall wax worse and worse, deceiving, and being deceived" (II Tim. 3:1-5, 13).

"Perilous times" means *dangerous* times. The human race will not get better, but worse and worse. Man will be selfish, covetous, proud. Evil men and seducers will wax worse and worse until the end of time; but when Jesus comes to reign on earth, evil men and seducers will be destroyed and their spirits consigned to the lake of fire. Wrong will be made right. The Lord Jesus Christ will deal with all men in righteousness and divine justice, and we will live with Him in a land where there will be no wrong, a land where evil will be completely stamped out.

"Then cometh the end, when He shall have delivered up the kingdom to God, even the Father; when He shall have put down all rule and all authority and power. For He must reign, till He hath put all enemies under His feet. The last enemy that shall be destroyed is death" (I Cor. 15:24-26).

Jesus *will* put all enemies under His feet, and when the devil, the beast, and the false prophet are in the lake of fire and brimstone, all social evils and injustices will be wiped out, erased from the face of the earth. There has never been a time in the history of man when people have had so little respect for their bodies and for each other as in this day and hour! Even many church members seem to have no conscience regarding their dress and habits of life. Drunkenness, dope addiction, immorality, lust—*all manner of evil*—pervade society today—and those evils are growing by leaps and bounds.

Only the return of the Lord Jesus Christ will save this civilization from total decay. As it was in the days of Noah, as it was in the days of Lot, so shall it be in the days when Jesus appears the second time. Are the days of Noah, the days of Lot, with us today? Surely anyone who takes time to read current newspapers and magazines, anyone who is familiar with the magazine and book racks in stores where all types of sex and sadist literature are sold, must agree that the sin of Sodom is with us today. The sins that brought the judgment of the flood in Noah's day are with us wholesale in this day in which we live.

But make no mistake, beloved. *"The earth is the LORD'S, and the fulness thereof!"* and one glorious day He will claim it. He will purify it and it will be inhabited by people who will live in righteousness and peace. The Prince of Peace will calm every disturbing element, erase every scar caused by sin, put down every wrong, and replace all evil with righteousness. The sinner "being an hundred years old" (Isa. 65:20) shows that there will be sin—and sinners—but Jesus will cut them off! He will touch and heal every inflamed, running sore of this sick society and end the torture of suffering humanity. He will adjust every difference between men by His rule of equity and truth. He will harmonize all conflicting claims in the melting power of His great love!

So in the words of John the Beloved I pray, "Even so, COME, Lord Jesus!"

Chapter XIII

All Creation Will Be Delivered From the Curse

"For we know that the whole creation groaneth and travaileth in pain together until now" (Rom. 8:22).

In II Timothy 2:15 we are admonished, "Study to shew thyself approved unto God, a workman that needeth not to be ashamed, rightly dividing the word of truth." There are laws of Bible interpretation which must be observed if we hope to understand the truth. Scripture *must* be studied in the light of other Scriptures. We cannot take a passage or verse out of its setting and use it to prove or disprove a point.

Paul explained that God reveals His truth to us "by His Spirit: for the Spirit searcheth all things, yea, the deep things of God. For what man knoweth the things of a man, save the spirit of man which is in him? Even so the things of God knoweth no man, but the Spirit of God. Now we have received, not the spirit of the world, but the Spirit which is of God; that we might know the things that are freely given to us of God. Which things also we speak, not in the words which man's wisdom teacheth, but which the Holy Ghost teacheth; comparing spiritual things with spiritual" (I Cor. 2:10-13).

One of the laws of Biblical interpretation is the law of "full mention." This is especially applicable in the

study of prophetic truth.   There are passages of Scripture which contain a full revelation on a given truth
or Bible doctrine.   Let us look at just a few such
passages which give a full revelation on a given truth:

John chapter 3 reveals the divine necessity, and the
nature, of the new birth.

Romans chapter 3 records the full revelation of the
condition and character of the unbeliever.

I Corinthians chapter 13 reveals the traits of true
love.

Hebrews chapter 10 tells of the nature and outcome
of the atoning work of the Lord Jesus Christ, the only
begotten Son of God.

Hebrews chapter 11 makes known what faith in God
accomplishes—and it is emphatically declared that
without faith it is impossible to please God.

Luke chapter 15 paints a beautiful picture of a father's love for a lost son.

Psalm 119 reveals the power and perfection of God's
Word.

The same principle is illustrated in *Romans 8:18-23,*
which reveals the cause of creation's bondage—the
present moaning and groaning of all creation—and the
sure emancipation and total deliverance of all creation
from the curse:

"For I reckon that the sufferings of this present time
are not worthy to be compared with the glory which
shall be revealed in us. For the earnest expectation of
the creature waiteth for the manifestation of the sons
of God.   For the creature was made subject to vanity,
not willingly, but by reason of Him who hath subjected the same in hope.   Because the creature itself also

shall be delivered from the bondage of corruption into the glorious liberty of the children of God.

"For we know that the whole creation groaneth and travaileth in pain together until now. And not only they, but ourselves also, which have the firstfruits of the Spirit, even we ourselves groan within ourselves, waiting for the adoption, to wit, the redemption of our body."

Creation Made Subject to Vanity

Creation was subjected to vanity when sin entered the earth—*and the curse BECAUSE of sin.* But creation was not subjected to vanity of its own will. In the beginning, God created the heaven and the earth, and He did not create anything vain, "without form, and void." When God created the earth it was a *perfect* creation. A perfect God could create nothing less. It was when sin entered the earth (through the temptation of Satan in the form of the serpent), when Adam yielded and lost his innocence and state of perfection before God, that God cursed Adam; and *the whole creation* was subjected to vanity *because* of the curse.

The *animal* creation was cursed also. The serpent (which seems to have been a beautiful, erect creature when he entered the garden) was cursed and made to crawl upon his belly, "cursed above all cattle," and dust will be the serpent's meat all the days of his life (Gen. 3:14; Isa. 65:25).

I believe that when the animals entered the ark, God temporarily lifted the curse from the animal kingdom and they lived together in the ark in perfect

harmony. There was no killing among the animals in
the ark. In Isaiah chapter 11, the Word of God clearly
teaches that the animal kingdom will be delivered
from the curse during the Millennium. I believe there
will be many kinds of animals in the new earth, and
they will not be under the curse because there will be
no sin, therefore no curse. This is borne out in Isaiah
11:6-9:

"The wolf also shall dwell with the lamb, and the
leopard shall lie down with the kid; and the calf and
the young lion and the fatling together; and a little
child shall lead them. And the cow and the bear shall
feed; their young ones shall lie down together: and
the lion shall eat straw like the ox. And the sucking
child shall play on the hole of the asp, and the weaned
child shall put his hand on the cockatrice' den. They
shall not hurt nor destroy in all my holy mountain: for
the earth shall be full of the knowledge of the Lord,
as the waters cover the sea."

Sin placed creation under vanity, instead of under
blessing as God intended it to be. There would never
have been thorns, briars, weeds, and thistles if Adam
had not sinned. There would never have been a storm
if sin had not entered the earth. It had not even
rained upon the earth until the flood. Instead of rain,
a mist went up from the earth and watered the ground
(Gen. 2:5, 6). Storms are a result of the curse.

"To *subject*" means "to put under, to subordinate."
Creation was subjected to *"vanity"*—meaning *useless
or profitless.* We need but look across the fields and
countryside to see weeds, thorns, and thistles. The
animal kingdom is vicious and cruel, the animals

killing and devouring one another. Certainly God did not intend His creation to be as we know it today, and one glorious day all creation will be *delivered* from the curse.

All Creation Is Groaning

But—"we know that the whole creation groaneth and travaileth in pain together until now" (Rom. 8:22). The meaning of *"groan"* is "to sigh, to pray, to be moved with inward feeling." All creation is burdened under the curse in the manner of a man groaning under a load too heavy for him to bear. Creation is bearing a burden God did not intend it should bear—and which it would not have borne if sin had not entered the world. It matters not where we travel nor where we look, our eyes meet misery, pain, tears, woe, death and decay! As we look upon the fields and the mountains, we see the scourge of barrenness. We behold the fury of the elements in mighty storms. We see the destructive and murderous instinct of the animal kingdom. The very laws which govern vegetation spell out death and decay. A tree grows, it dies, it decays and returns to dust. An animal is born, it grows, and even if it is not killed and devoured by another animal, its life span is short. It dies in a very few years or months and returns to the ground. Death, decay, and groaning are everywhere—in the air, on the land, in the sea. We need but *listen* in order to hear the cry of universal suffering, the woeful sigh and groaning which perpetually ascend from the entire creation.

I was reared on a farm. I lived close to nature and I heard many groans not heard by the city dweller.

I have heard the screams of a little kitty-cat as it was devoured by a dog. I have heard the yelp of a little dog as it was being brutally chewed to bits by a *larger* dog. I have heard the shriek of little animals as they were being taken captive in the clutches and claws of larger, more powerful animals. I have heard the cry of the vultures as they circled overhead in search of prey. In the jungles of Africa, while traveling with a missionary, I have heard the roar of a lion seeking other animals which he would kill for food.

Even in *nature* we see and hear evidences of the curse. Beyond the white sands of the seashore we hear the continual moaning and groaning of the sea. We hear the moaning of the storm as it rushes onward. We feel the tremor of the earth as it groans in the travail of an earthquake. Surely we must admit, with Paul, that all creation is groaning and travailing in pain. But in a glorious day yet to come, Jesus will say, "Peace! Be still!" and all creation will be delivered from the curse—"and not only they, but ourselves also, which have the firstfruits of the Spirit, even we ourselves groan within ourselves, waiting for the adoption, to wit, the redemption of our body" (Rom. 8:23).

Jesus groaned with indignation as He beheld the ravages of death at the tomb of His friend Lazarus. When He saw Mary weeping, "and the Jews also weeping which came with her, *He groaned in the spirit,* and was troubled." As He approached the grave wherein Lazarus' body lay, He *groaned "in Himself"* (John 11:33, 38).

In Psalm 38:9, a prophetic Psalm, Jesus cried out,

"Lord . . . my *groaning* is not hid from thee!"

The Psalmist, burdened with grief and sorrow, weary with pain and woe, cried out, "I am weary with my groaning" (Psalm 6:6). In Psalm 102:5 he cried out, "By reason of the voice of my *groaning* my bones cleave to my skin!"

Yes, even the dearest saints, with those who possess "the firstfruits of the Spirit," groan and suffer; but one day we will be delivered from this body of suffering and pain and we will have a body like unto the glorious body of Jesus:

"Beloved, *now* are we the sons of God, and it doth not yet appear what we shall be: but we know that, when He shall appear, *we shall be like Him;* for we shall see Him as He is" (I John 3:2).

The true believer *longs* for that glorious house from heaven. Paul speaks of this in his second letter to the Corinthian believers:

"For we know that if our earthly house of this tabernacle were dissolved, we have a building of God, an house not made with hands, eternal in the heavens. For in this we groan, earnestly desiring to be clothed upon with our house which is from heaven: if so be that being clothed we shall not be found naked. For we that are in this tabernacle do groan, being burdened; not for that we would be unclothed, but clothed upon, that mortality might be swallowed up of life. Now He that hath wrought us for the selfsame thing is God, who also hath given unto us the earnest of the Spirit. Therefore we are always confident, knowing that, whilst we are at home in the body, we are absent from the Lord" (II Cor. 5:1-6).

Paul also declares that the Holy Spirit which dwells within the heart of every believer makes *intercession* for us "with *groanings which cannot be uttered*" (Rom. 8:26).

As we look upon creation and listen to its groaning we realize that present conditions are certainly not ideal. The earth is *not* covered with the knowledge of the Lord as the waters cover the sea. This is *not* the time when there is no hurt or destruction in the holy mountain of God. But the day is coming, that glorious day, when there will be peace on earth and good will among men, as well as peace in the atmosphere and in the animal kingdom!

All Creation Is Travailing

"For we know that the whole creation *groaneth and TRAVAILETH* in pain together until now" (Rom. 8:22).

The compound Greek word translated "travailing in pain together" means to have birth pains in company with another, jointly travailing in the throes of birth. The same word is used in Galatians 4:19 and in Revelation 12:2.

There is a common groaning among the creatures of all creation—but there is more: There is *travail*—the struggling of birth pangs as a woman travails in childbirth. Thus it seems as if nature is striving to bring forth new creation, and the day is coming when nature *will* bring forth, and the old creation, so long under the curse, will pass away and give over to the *new* creation.

"Because the creature itself also shall be delivered from the bondage of corruption into the glorious liberty of the children of God" (Rom. 8:21). The *"bondage of corruption"* means more than just being bound. It means *servitude,* it means *slavery.* "Corruption" as used here also signifies ruin, decay, death. The same word, used in Colossians 2:22, is rendered "perish."

The Greek word here translated *"bondage"* is also used in Titus 3:3 where it is rendered *"serving."* Therefore because of the curse nature is prevented from putting forth her powers and manifesting her real beauty and grandeur. Creation is gravely handicapped and marred because of the curse, and all that nature *produces* is doomed to death. Because of the curse, nature is compelled to slay her own offspring. For example, the forked lightning in the storm flashes toward the beautiful tree, makes contact—and the tree dies. The cold blasts of winter kill the beautiful green foliage and flowers of spring and summer. Animals devour each other in order to maintain life. But one day this will no longer be. The curse will be lifted, and all creation will be delivered from the bondage of corruption and from the slavery of the curse.

Creation Is Longing and Expecting

"For the earnest expectation of the creature waiteth for the manifestation of the sons of God" (Rom. 8:19).

The longing which God implanted in all creation will surely be met and satisfied by the God who implanted it. It is a known fact in nature that God has never put an intuition *within* without meeting that intuition. By way of illustration, the young eagle has had no experience in flying; yet the "flying" intuition within him causes him to flap his wings. Thus, in the flapping of his wings, the young eagle finds that *the air responds* to the movement of his wings and bears him up as he soars aloft.

The Greek word here translated *"expectation"* is made up from *apo-kara-doika. Apo* signifies *"from,"* or *"from afar." Kara* means *"the head." Doika* means *"to wait for"*—not casual waiting, but looking with intense expectation. The compound Greek word suggests a person who, with raised head, looks intently toward the distant horizon, deep longing in his eyes, expecting to receive something from another.

The Greek word here translated "waiteth" is *apeka-dkomai.* This word is composed of a verb and two prepositions. *Dkomai* means "to receive." This same word is used in Acts 7:59 where Stephen, the first martyr, prayed, "Lord Jesus, *receive* my spirit." The two prepositions are *ek* (meaning "out of") and *apo* (meaning "from"). Again we see a suggestive statement. The compound word speaks of one waiting to receive something from the hands of another who extends a gift from afar.

This same Greek word (*apekadkomai*) is found seven times in the New Testament, and in all seven instances it is identified with the second coming of the Lord Jesus Christ. In Romans 8:23 and I Corinthians 1:7 it is translated "waiting." In Romans 8:25 and Galatians 5:5 the same word is translated "wait for." In Philippians 3:20 and Hebrews 9:28 it is rendered "look for," and in Romans 8:19 it is translated "waiteth."

Even though all creation is in bondage and slavery, groaning and travailing in pain, it is not in despair, for creation is earnestly expecting something from

Someone. Creation is waiting for and looking forward with intense expectation to that glorious day when the saints will be translated, the dead in Christ will be raised incorruptible, and Jesus will return to deliver all creation from the curse.

The Holy Spirit reveals that for which creation is waiting—it "waiteth for the manifestation of the sons of God" (Rom. 8:19).

The Holy Spirit also reveals that which creation is expecting—it is expecting to be "delivered from the bondage of corruption into the glorious liberty of the children of God" (Rom. 8:21).

Three things are clearly revealed here: (1) for *whom* creation is waiting, (2) for *what* creation is waiting, (3) to what creation is *destined*.

Creation is waiting for the sons of God. *(Believers are waiting for the appearing of THE SON of God.)* The day is coming when creation will be delivered from the bondage of corruption and will be given the glorious liberty of the children of God.

In the Greek language there is one word which is translated "sons" and another word which is translated "children," but the words are not identical in meaning. It is remarkable how the Holy Spirit, in dictating the Word of God to holy men, guarded these cardinal truths. Greek scholars tell us that the Greek word *teknon* denotes, without exception, one who is a descendant. That word is never used concerning Christ as a Son of God, nor is it used in connection with Christ as the Son of man. Christ is not a *descendant* of God, He IS God, very God in flesh. He is not said to be a *teknon* (son) of man because He was begotten by the Holy Spirit.

The Greek word *whyos* is used of Christ because it is the adoptive title which He assumed when He took a body of humiliation and came into this world. Both Greek words (*teknon* and *whyos*) are used in Romans chapter 8. *Whyos* is used twice in relation to believers (vv. 14 and 19), *teknon* is used three times (vv. 16, 17, and 21). Thus we see that the word translated "children" speaks of those who are descendants of their parents, denoting kinship; whereas "sons" speaks of adoption. Born again believers have all of the rights which belong to our position as *children* of God *now*, but we do not have all of our rights as *sons* as having to do with adoption. We are "*waiting* for the adoption, to wit, *the redemption of our body.*" When we as believers are manifest in all of the rights in the fulness of our adoption, then all creation will come into privilege and deliverance from corruption, from slavery, and the curse. Therefore we see how important it is to recognize the fact that when the "sons of God" have come into their adoption and have obtained what they are waiting for (the redemption of their bodies), then creation will be blessed *next* in the order of events.

All creation is waiting for the manifestation (the revealing) of the *sons of God*. The Greek word here is *apokalupsis*, translated "manifestation," meaning "*unveiling.*" In Luke 2:32 the same word is translated "to lighten." In II Thessalonians 1:7 it is translated "revealed." In I Peter 1:7 it is translated "appearing," and in I Corinthians 1:7 the same word is rendered "coming."

All creation is longing for and earnestly expecting that glorious day when the sons of God will appear in glorified bodies, unveiled in all the glory Christ will give to His own. When Christ who is our life shall be made manifest, then shall we also be made manifest with Him in glory. When we see Him we will be like Him. We will have a body like unto His glorious body, and we will be delivered from this body of humiliation and weakness. When the sons of God appear with Christ in glory, all creation will be liberated and delivered from the curse.

All born again believers are children of God, "and if children, then heirs; heirs of God, and joint-heirs with Christ; if so be that we suffer with Him, that we may be also glorified together" (Rom. 8:17). The question then arises, *"Heirs to WHAT?"* We are heirs to the glory of the likeness of our Saviour. We are heirs to the glory of Christ in His body of glory. Grace has determined that we are to be conformed to His image. We will enjoy the liberty of His glory, and creation, too, will enjoy liberty—freedom from the bondage of corruption, misery, pain, and woe under which creation has labored and travailed since the curse. In this present hour, creation is bathed in tears and blood, engulfed in misery and pain, but when the sons of God are made manifest, all creation will enjoy total deliverance from the curse of sin.

Points of Identity
Concerning the Children of God and Creation

In the verses we have been studying from Romans chapter 8, there are seven statements which reveal the identity between the children of God and creation:

1. Suffering and glory: Oneness with Christ not only means identification with Him in position and privilege, but also in suffering and shame. So creation was identified with the first Adam, not only in the perfect condition before Adam fell, but also in the suffering and shame after his fall.

So all creation is suffering, even those who have the firstfruits of the Spirit. But one glorious day, suffering will give way to glory—for creation, as well as for the children of God. "For I reckon that the sufferings of this present time are not worthy to be compared with the glory which shall be revealed in us" (Rom. 8:18).

2. Expectation and revelation: "For the earnest expectation of the creature waiteth for the manifestation of the sons of God" (Rom. 8:19). Revelation of the sons of God will mean deliverance for all creation.

3. Subjection and Subjector: "For the creature was made subject to vanity, not willingly, but by reason of Him who hath subjected the same in hope" (Rom. 8:20).   According to the Scriptures, it was the Lord who subjected all creation to vanity, and we dare not question the doings of the Lord. He knew the end in the beginning, He doeth all things well, and one glorious day He will make known to us the secret things that belong unto Him.

4. Creation and children: "Because the creature itself also shall be delivered from the bondage of corruption into the glorious liberty of the children of God" (Rom. 8:21).   The Holy Spirit clearly reveals that the whole creation will be delivered from the curse of sin, into the freedom of the glory of God's children.

The birthright of the believer, the child of God, secures for him the glories of God. One day we will share in God's glory, for we are heirs of God and joint-heirs with Christ. Heirship is founded upon relationship, and we are God's sons by birth and by adoption.

Man's fall brought the *curse* upon all creation, therefore man's *redemption* will bring blessing and deliverance for all creation. Glory for the sons of God means liberty for all creation. The living waters that will flow from the sanctuary of God will bring blessing to the children of God and to all creation (Ezek. 47:1-9).

5. *Groaning and travailing:* "For we know that the whole creation groaneth and travaileth in pain together until now" (Rom. 8:22). The whole creation—believers included—groans and travails in pain. We groan *within* ourselves. Even those of us who are *born of the Spirit* and possess the *firstfruits* of the Spirit are not yet delivered from groaning and pain. But in that glorious resurrection morning we *will be* delivered.

6. *Firstfruits and redemption:* "And not only they, but ourselves also, which have the firstfruits of the Spirit, even we ourselves groan within ourselves, waiting for the adoption, to wit, the redemption of our body" (Rom. 8:23). Born again believers have the Holy Spirit as the firstfruits, therefore we have the pledge of the harvest of redemption. Believers are also the firstfruits of God's creatures. "Of His own will begat He us with the Word of truth, that we should be a kind of firstfruits of His creatures" (James 1:18). The Holy Spirit is the pledge of our full redemption, for He (the Holy Spirit) who "borns" us into the family of God will also quicken our mortal bodies. Believers

are the firstfruits of creation's freedom, and when believers are made manifest as the sons of God, all creation will be set free.

7. *Hope and fulfillment:*   "For we are saved by hope: but hope that is seen is not hope: for what a man seeth, why doth he yet hope for? But if we hope for that we see not, then do we with patience wait for it" (Rom. 8:24, 25).   Born again believers are sons of God now—heirs of God and joint-heirs with Christ; but our salvation will not be full and complete until we receive our glorified bodies. We look for "that blessed hope, and the glorious appearing of the great God and our Saviour Jesus Christ" (Tit. 2:13).   Christ is our hope; and since we know that He lives, seated at the right hand of the Father, we have a LIVING hope:

"Blessed be the God and Father of our Lord Jesus Christ, which according to His abundant mercy hath begotten us again unto a LIVELY (living) hope by the resurrection of Jesus Christ from the dead" (I Pet. 1:3). We *look for* that Blessed Hope—and when we see Him we will be fully satisfied, and we will then see all creation delivered from the curse.

Creation's Greatest Era Just Ahead

"And there shall be no more curse: but the throne of God and of the Lamb shall be in it; and His servants shall serve Him" (Rev. 22:3).

When Jesus comes in the Rapture for His own, believers will experience and enjoy full redemption—soul, spirit, and body. We are redeemed from the curse of the law now. We are sons of God now. But only when we see Him as He is will we be like Him (I John 3:2).

Creation's total deliverance from the curse will occur when Jesus returns to this earth with His saints. The curse will be lifted, thorns and thistles will disappear. The animal kingdom will be delivered from bondage and the strong will no longer prey upon the weak. Isaiah gives a moving description of the animal kingdom during the glorious Millennium, and I personally believe this glorious era for the animal kingdom will merge into the eternal kingdom of God:

"The wolf also shall dwell with the lamb, and the leopard shall lie down with the kid; and the calf and the young lion and the fatling together; and a little child shall lead them. And the cow and the bear shall feed; their young ones shall lie down together: and the lion shall eat straw like the ox. And the sucking child shall play on the hole of the asp, and the weaned child shall put his hand on the cockatrice' den" (Isa. 11:6-8).

Yes, I take these words literally. This is not a parable, nor is it an allegory. I believe the animal kingdom will be literally delivered from the curse, and the wolf, the lion, the leopard, the lamb, the kid, the serpent, and a little child will all dwell together in perfect peace and harmony in that millennial day. In Genesis 1:24, 25 we read:

"God said, Let the earth bring forth the living creature after his kind, cattle, and creeping thing, and beast of the earth after his kind: and it was so. And God made the beast of the earth after his kind, and cattle after their kind, and every thing that creepeth upon the earth after his kind: and God saw that it was good." In the Garden of Eden the animal kingdom lived in peace and harmony one with another. Adam had dominion over all creation. So shall it be in the millennial earth and the new earth. Jesus will be King over the whole earth, but man will be the ruler over all creation under the Lord Jesus Christ, King of kings and Lord of lords.

Chapter XIV

The New Earth

"O sing unto the Lord a new song: *sing unto the Lord, all the EARTH.* Sing unto the Lord, bless His name; shew forth His salvation from day to day. Declare His glory among the heathen, His wonders among all people. For the Lord is great, and greatly to be praised: He is to be feared above all gods. For all the gods of the nations are idols: but the Lord made the heavens. Honour and majesty are before Him: strength and beauty are in His sanctuary.

"Give unto the Lord, O ye kindreds of the people, give unto the Lord glory and strength. Give unto the Lord the glory due unto His name: bring an offering, and come into His courts. O worship the Lord in the beauty of holiness: fear before Him, *all the EARTH.* Say among the heathen that *the Lord REIGNETH: the WORLD also shall be established that it shall not be moved.* He shall judge the people righteously.

"Let the heavens rejoice, and let the EARTH be glad; let the sea roar, and the fulness thereof. *Let the FIELD be joyful, and all that is therein. Then shall all the trees of the wood REJOICE BEFORE THE LORD:* for He cometh, for *He cometh to judge the EARTH.* He shall judge *the WORLD* with righteousness, and the people with His truth" (Psalm 96: 1-13).

"The Lord REIGNETH! Let the EARTH rejoice; let the multitude of the isles be GLAD thereof" (Psalm 97:1).

"He hath remembered His mercy and His truth toward the house of Israel. *All the ends of the EARTH* have seen the salvation of our God" (Psalm 98:3).

"God be merciful unto us, and bless us; and cause His face to shine upon us . . . *that thy way may be known upon EARTH*, thy saving health among *all NATIONS.* Let the people praise thee, O God. Let all the people praise thee. *O let the NATIONS be glad and sing for joy:* for thou shalt judge the people righteously, *and govern the NATIONS upon EARTH.* . . . Let the people praise thee, O God. Let all the people praise thee. Then shall *the EARTH* yield her increase; and God, even our own God, shall bless us. God shall bless us; and *all the ends of the EARTH shall fear Him"* (Psalm 67:1-7).

There are scores of verses in the Psalms which speak of the earth as continuing forever. In Psalm 78:69 we read, "He built His sanctuary like high palaces, *like the EARTH which He hath established FOR EVER."*

In Psalm 104:5 we are told that *God "laid the foundations of the EARTH that it should not be removed FOR EVER."*

Zechariah 14:9 tells us that "the Lord shall be King *over all the EARTH:* in that day shall there be one Lord, and His name one."

II Peter 3:1-14 tells us clearly why the Holy Spirit gave Peter his second epistle:

"This second epistle, beloved, I now write unto you; in both which I stir up your pure minds by way of remembrance: that ye may be mindful of the words which were spoken before by the holy prophets, and of the commandment of us the apostles of the Lord and Saviour:

"Knowing this first, that there shall come in the last days scoffers, walking after their own lusts, and saying, Where is the promise of His coming? for since the fathers fell asleep, all things continue as they were from the beginning of the creation. For this they willingly are ignorant of, that by the Word of God the heavens were of old, and the earth standing out of the water and in the water: whereby the world that then was, being overflowed with water, perished: But the heavens and the earth, which are now, by the same word are kept in store, reserved unto fire against the day of judgment and perdition of ungodly men.

"But, beloved, be not ignorant of this one thing, that one day is with the Lord as a thousand years, and a thousand years as one day. The Lord is not slack concerning His promise, as some men count slackness; but is longsuffering to us-ward, not willing that any should perish, but that all should come to repentance.

"But the day of the Lord will come as a thief in the night; in the which the heavens shall pass away with a great noise, and the elements shall melt with fervent heat, the earth also and the works that are therein shall be burned up. Seeing then that *all these things shall be dissolved,* what manner of persons ought ye to be in all holy conversation and godliness, looking for and hasting unto the coming of the day of God, *wherein the HEAVENS being on fire shall be DISSOLVED, and the ELEMENTS shall melt with fervent heat?*

"*NEVERTHELESS we, according to His promise, look for NEW HEAVENS and a NEW EARTH, wherein dwelleth righteousness.* Wherefore, beloved, seeing that ye look for such things, be diligent that ye may be found of Him in peace, without spot, and blameless.*"

In this passage the Holy Spirit clearly points out three things concerning the earth:

1. The *past history* of the earth, before man was created and placed upon it.

2. The *present* history of man up to this hour, including the first Adam and the last Adam.

3. The *future* of the earth as it *will be*—a place wherein dwelleth righteousness. The earth will then be in its eternal state, full of the knowledge of the Lord and the glory of God.

History of the Earth Before the Creation of Man

In verse 5 of the passage just quoted, Peter speaks of the heavens which were "*of old,* and the earth standing *out* of the water and *in* the water." This refers back to the earth as described in Genesis 1:1, 2:

"*In the BEGINNING God created* the heaven and the earth. And the earth was *without form, and void;* and *darkness* was upon the face of the deep . . . ." In the *beginning* God created the heaven and the earth, *but when the beginning WAS,* we do not know. It could have been millions—or even *billions*—of years ago. We *do* know, however, that approximately six thousand years ago God brought order out of chaos and created Adam from the dust of the ground.

The same verse in II Peter chapter 3 also tells us that creation was *"by the Word of God"*—that is, *God spoke* and the earth *was*. He created the earth beautiful and perfect. (Any reasonable person must confess that God could not create anything that was *not* perfect.) God is entirely righteous, sinless, and perfect. Therefore He *could not* have created the earth *"without form and void,"* an empty nothingness. We do not know exactly what happened, but we do know that *judgment* struck this earth at some time after God's perfect creation, and the formless emptiness was the result of that judgment. The Hebrew verb translated "was" should have been rendered *"became."* Thus, the earth, *"became* without form and void." The same Hebrew word is used in Genesis 19:26 speaking of Lot's wife who *"BECAME a pillar of salt"* when she looked back at the burning city of Sodom. She was not a pillar of salt to begin with, she was a woman of flesh, blood, and bones. It was because of her disobedience that she *"became"* a pillar of salt.

God did not create this earth in vanity, but in beauty: "For thus saith the Lord that created the heavens, God Himself that formed the earth, and made it; He hath established it, *He created it not in vain, He formed it to be inhabited:* I AM THE LORD; and there is none else" (Isa. 45:18). But some form of judgment struck the earth and brought about chaos. Many Bible scholars believe this occurred when God cast Lucifer out of heaven—*and this might be.* I do not say it is not true. Although we do not know positively *when* or *why* judgment struck, we do know that the earth *became* without form, void, waste, empty, and darkness moved upon the face of the deep. *"And the Spirit of God moved upon the face of the waters."* (This earth has been completely covered by water at least two times—before the creation of Adam, and in the days of the flood when only Noah and his family were saved.) "And God said, Let there be a firmament in the midst of the waters, and let it divide the waters from the waters. . . . And God said, Let the waters under the heaven be gathered together unto one place, and let the dry land appear—AND IT WAS SO" (Gen. 1:6, 9).

Present History of the Earth

"But the heavens and the earth, *which are NOW*, by the same Word are kept in store, reserved unto fire against the day of judgment and perdition of ungodly men" (II Pet. 3:7).

Peter here contrasts *the earth which now IS* ("reserved unto fire"—or *stored with fire*) and *the earth that then WAS* ("being overflowed with water"). It has been suggested that this speaks of the flood of Noah's day, but it seems to me that this statement points back to the time before the creation of Adam when judgment struck the earth and it became empty, void, and completely covered with water.

The earth as we know it today has not been altered in its order of things since God created Adam. After the flood in Noah's day the earth was not spoken of as being "without form and void." When Noah came out of the ark he did not find chaos which required God's creative acts, such as those recorded in Genesis chapters 1 and 2. As soon as the flood waters abated, the dove Noah had sent out returned to the ark, bearing an olive leaf, proclaiming the earth's fertility and fruitfulness. Therefore it would seem reasonable that the statement in our passage from II Peter points back to the judgment that struck the earth before the creation of man.

The Earth In the Future

"Nevertheless we, *according to His promise,* look for *NEW heavens and a NEW EARTH,* wherein dwelleth righteousness" (II Pet. 3:13).

The new heavens and the new earth reach beyond the Millennium. It is true that there are certain *corresponding conditions* in the millennial earth and in the new earth:

In Isaiah 65:17-25 we read: "For, behold, I create new heavens and a new earth: and the former shall not be remembered, nor come into mind. But be ye glad and rejoice for ever in that which I create: for, behold, I create Jerusalem a rejoicing, and her people a joy. And I will rejoice in Jerusalem, and joy in my people: and the voice of weeping shall be no more heard in her, nor the voice of crying.

"There shall be no more thence an infant of days, nor an old man that hath not filled his days: for the child shall die an hundred years old; but the sinner being an hundred years old shall be accursed. And they shall build houses, and inhabit them; and they shall plant vineyards, and eat the fruit of them. They shall not build, and another inhabit; they shall not plant, and another eat: for as the days of a tree are the days of my people, and mine elect shall long enjoy the work of their hands. They shall not labour in vain, nor bring forth for trouble; for they are the seed of the blessed of the Lord, and their offspring with them.

"And it shall come to pass, that before they call, I will answer; and while they are yet speaking, I will hear. The wolf and the lamb shall feed together, and the lion shall eat straw like the bullock: and dust shall be the serpent's meat. They shall not hurt nor destroy in all my holy mountain, saith the Lord."

There are also conditions in the new earth which do not apply to the Millennium. For example, in Isaiah 32:1, speaking of the millennial reign of Christ, we read, "Behold, *a King shall reign IN RIGHT-EOUSNESS*, and princes shall rule in judgment," whereas II Peter 3:13 tells us that in the *new earth* righteousness will *dwell*. This will not be the result of the righteousness which will cover the earth when Christ the righteous King sits on the throne. In other words, righteousness will not *abide* in the earth as the result of the strong hand of righteousness belonging to the righteous King. Such will be true in the Millennium, but in the *new earth* righteousness is an *inherent quality* which pervades and acts.

Will This Earth Ever Be Annihilated?

". . . the heavens shall pass away with a great noise, and the elements shall melt with fervent heat, the earth also and the works that are therein shall be burned up. Seeing then that all these things shall be dissolved, what manner of persons ought ye to be in all holy conversation and godliness" (II Pet. 3:10, 11).

Some people believe that this earth will one day cease to exist. They speak of "the end of the world." In our present Scripture, Peter tells us that the heavens will *"pass away,"* the elements will *"melt,"* and the earth will be *"burned up."* Does this mean that our present earth will cease to be? Will it be completely erased from the universe? No, Peter is not telling us that this earth will be annihilated. Let us study the true meaning of the language used in our Scripture.

In the New Testament we find four different words translated *"world"*:

1. *Cosmos*—the opposite of chaos—denotes the present ordered universe. We find it used in I Peter 1:20 where we are told that Christ's sacrificial death was "foreordained before the foundation of *the world . . . .*" In I Peter 3:3 the same word is translated "adorning." So we see that there are instances when *cosmos* signifies the earth *on which man lives,* and other instances where it speaks of men who *live on the earth.*

2. *Gee* is another word which signifies the earth in contrast to the sea and the heavens. It is so used in Acts 4:24 where the believers praised God "with one accord, and said, Lord, thou art God, which hast made *heaven, and EARTH, and the sea,* and all that in them is."

3. *Oikoumene* is the word used in referring to the inhabited or civilized world. It is used in Luke 2:1, where Caesar Augustus sent out a decree "that *ALL THE WORLD should be taxed."*

4. *Aion* is the Greek word which means *"age"*—a period of time. Sometimes it speaks of eternity, the

ages of ages. In Hebrews 9:26 it is used in speaking
of Christ's suffering—"now once in the end of the
world (or *age*) hath He appeared to put away sin by
the sacrifice of Himself." In Galatians 1:4 the same
word is used with reference to believers being delivered
"from this present evil *world* (or *age*) according to the
will of God and our Father." In Hebrews 6:5 the same
word, translated "world," speaks of *the ages to come.*
In Matthew 13:39, 40, 49; 24:3; and 28:20 the same word
is used, speaking of *"the end of the WORLD"*—or
the end of this *age.*

Therefore, when we study these passages of Scripture
we see that the annihilation of the earth is not the
meaning at all, but simply the end of a particular
period of time.

The same is true of the expression "to pass away."
It does not mean *extinction,* but *transition.* For example, in Revelation 21:4 we read that *"the former
things are PASSED AWAY."* The Greek word here
(*aperkomai*) is used in a variety of ways, but *never*
denoting extinction. In Mark 1:35 it is translated *"departed,"* speaking of the Lord Jesus going from one
place to another. In John 4:8 the same word is rendered "gone away," speaking of the disciples who had
gone into the city to buy bread. In Acts 4:15 we find
the same word translated "to go aside," when the
disciples were asked to leave the council room.

"Dissolve," as used in II Peter 3:11, 12, does not
mean annihilation, but *liberation.* The same Greek
word (*luo*) is used in Mark 11:2-5 and translated "loose"
—speaking of the Lord's instructions to His disciples:
"Go your way into the village . . . ye shall find a colt

tied. . . . *Loose* him, and bring him." In Luke 3:16 the same word is translated "unloose," when John the Baptist spoke of being unworthy to "unloose" the shoes of Jesus. In John 2:19 the same word is translated "destroy"—Jesus said to the Jews, *"Destroy* this temple, and in three days I will raise it up." In John 5:18 the same word is translated "broken," where the Jews accused Jesus of having *"broken* the Sabbath" by healing on that day. In II Peter 3:10 the same word is translated *"melt,"* speaking of the elements *melting "with fervent heat."* In John 11:44 it is again translated "loose" when Jesus called Lazarus forth from the grave and said to the people around him, *"LOOSE him, and let him go!"* The dissolution of the earth signifies what, in other places, the Scriptures call "the restitution of all things" (Acts 3:21).

In Hebrews 1:11, speaking of the heavens and the earth, Paul said, *"They shall PERISH"*—but he did not mean that the heavens and earth would be annihilated. The same Greek word is used eight times in the fifteenth chapter of Luke, and is translated "perish . . . lose . . . lost." (Please read Luke 15:4, 6, 8, 9, 17, 24, 32.) In these verses the word refers to the lost sheep, the lost coin, and the lost son; yet we know that neither the sheep, the coin, nor the son were annihilated—or they could not have been found!

In II Peter 3:6, speaking of this present earth, we read, "Whereby the world that then was, being overflowed with water, *perished"*—but what was it that perished? It was not the planet *earth,* but *the CONDITION of things* that existed on the earth.

The Greek word *apollumi,* sometimes translated

"perish," is used by the high priest in John 18:14 when (speaking of Jesus) he said it was *"expedient that one man DIE for the people."* The word is used speaking of the people of Noah's day who were *destroyed* in the flood (Luke 17:27)—and yet we read that these people were visited by Christ centuries later. Luke 17:27 tells us that they ate, drank, married, and were given in marriage "until the day that Noe entered into the ark, and the flood came, *and DESTROYED them all."* Then in I Peter 3:18,19 we are told that Christ, "put to death in the flesh but quickened by the Spirit . . . went and preached unto *the spirits in prison."* Therefore by comparing Scripture with Scripture we see that these people who are referred to as being "destroyed" were not annihilated, they did not cease to be. Their *bodies* were destroyed—but *their spirits live on,* even today!

You may search the Scriptures from Genesis through Revelation, but you will find no scriptural evidence that this earth will ever be *completely erased* from God's creation! The Lord Jesus Christ consecrated this earth by His presence. It was on earth that He shed His precious blood for the remission of sins. It was on this earth that the only begotten Son of God was born, grew to manhood, taught, preached, suffered, died, rose again, and for forty days after His resurrection appeared to His disciples and others of the saints of God. This earth is the place where God in His divine love and mercy poured out the costliest sacrifice known to heaven or earth! This earth is the stage upon which the most momentous deeds ever performed took place, as men and angels looked on! I personally believe that one of the outstanding reasons this earth will not be destroyed is the fact that it was here that the Son of God was bruised, and it will be here that He will one day crush the head of Satan forever when He puts him into the lake of fire.

The Word of God settles it: *"THE EARTH IS THE LORD'S, AND THE FULNESS THEREOF; THE WORLD, AND THEY THAT DWELL THEREIN. For He hath founded it upon the seas, and established it upon the floods.* Who shall ascend into the hill of the Lord? or who shall stand in His holy place? He that hath clean hands, and a pure heart; who hath not lifted up his soul unto vanity, nor sworn deceitfully. He shall receive the blessing from the Lord, and righteousness from the God of his salvation.

"This is the generation of them that seek Him, that seek thy face, O Jacob. Selah. Lift up your heads, O ye gates; and be ye lift up, ye everlasting doors; and the King of glory shall come in. *Who is this King of glory? The Lord strong and mighty, the Lord mighty in battle.* Lift up your heads, O ye gates; even lift them up, ye everlasting doors; and the King of glory shall come in. *Who is this King of glory? The Lord of hosts, He is the King of glory.* Selah" (Psalm 24: 1-10).

God will never deliver this earth over to everlasting nothingness! This earth will never cease to be one of the most cherished planets in God's great creation. It will one day be made new, *renovated* but *never annihilated!*

In Psalm 90:1, 2 we read, "Lord, thou hast been our dwelling place in all generations. Before the mountains

were brought forth, or ever thou hadst formed the
earth and the world, even *from everlasting to everlasting,* thou art God."

In Exodus 3:15 God said to Moses, "Thus shalt thou
say unto the children of Israel: The Lord God of your
fathers, the God of Abraham, the God of Isaac, and
the God of Jacob, hath sent me unto you: *this is my
name FOR EVER,* and this is my memorial unto all
generations."

In Hebrews 13:8 Paul wrote to the Hebrew believers,
"Jesus Christ, the same yesterday, and to day, *and
FOR EVER."*   In other words, Paul was telling the
Hebrew Christians that Jesus was the same as the God
of their fathers.   Christ was God in flesh—the same
yesterday, today, *and FOREVER.*

The same terms are used in connection with this
earth.   Speaking of the land God gave to Israel in His
perpetual covenant with Abraham, Deuteronomy 4:40
declares, "Thou shalt keep therefore His statutes, and
His commandments, which I command thee this day,
that it may go well with thee, and with thy children
after thee, and that thou mayest prolong thy days upon
*the EARTH, which the Lord thy God giveth thee,
FOR EVER."*

Also in Joshua 14:9 we read, "Moses sware on that
day, saying, Surely the land whereon thy feet have
trodden shall be *thine inheritance, and thy children's
FOR EVER,* because thou hast wholly followed the
Lord my God."

God's promise to David concerning his throne declares, "Thine house and thy kingdom shall be *established FOR EVER* before thee: thy throne shall be

established FOR EVER" (II Sam. 7:16). In this same chapter of II Samuel, verses 13-29, the word *"forever"* occurs over and over again in connection with the reign of David over his people *in their land.* Then in Luke 1:33 we read, *"He shall reign over the house of Jacob FOR EVER; and of His kingdom there shall be NO END."*

Exodus 32:13 declares, "Remember Abraham, Isaac, and Israel, thy servants, to whom thou swarest by thine own self, and saidst unto them, I will multiply your seed as the stars of heaven, and *all this land that I have spoken of* will I give unto your seed, and they shall *inherit it FOR EVER."*

Jeremiah is even more emphatic. He declares, "Then will I cause you to dwell in this place, *in the land that I gave to your fathers, FOR EVER AND EVER!"* (Jer. 7:7). The same promise is made in Jeremiah 25:5— "the land that the Lord hath given *unto you and to your fathers FOR EVER AND EVER."*

Ezekiel 37:25 declares the same thing: "They shall dwell in the land that I have given unto Jacob my servant, wherein your fathers have dwelt; and they shall dwell therein, even *they, and their children, and their children's children FOR EVER . . . ."*

God gave Daniel a prophetic vision of the kingdoms of this world associated with the chosen nation Israel during the Millennium, when this earth will be possessed by the saints of God and Christ will reign from the throne of David for one thousand years. Daniel speaks of the kingdom as continuing forever and ever. In Daniel 7:18 we read, "The saints of the most High shall take the kingdom, *and possess the kingdom FOR*

EVER, even FOR EVER AND EVER." In verse 27
of that same chapter we read, "And the kingdom and
dominion, and the greatness of the kingdom under the
whole heaven, shall be given to the people of the saints
of the most High, whose kingdom is *an EVERLAST-
ING kingdom,* and all dominions shall serve and obey
Him!"

God cannot lie (Heb. 6:18; Tit. 1:2). He definitely
promised a portion of this earth to Israel for an *everlasting possession* (Gen. 48:4). And since God promised
a *portion* of the earth to Israel forever, it stands to
reason that the *rest* of the earth will be eternal. Certainly it will not be annihilated! It is true that the
earth as we know it now will melt with fervent heat,
the works thereof will be burned up, and we will have
a new heaven and a new earth wherein dwelleth righteousness. The earth will be *made NEW,* not annihilated. It will be renovated, purified, delivered from
the curse and will be a glorious Paradise. There will
be no more storms, no more winter, no more summer,
no more thorns and thistles. The earth will be perfect,
the climate will be perfect. Everything will be as God
intended things to be in the beginning before sin
brought the curse upon creation.

The New Heaven — The New Earth —
The Pearly White City

"And I saw a new heaven and a new earth: for
the first heaven and the first earth were passed away;
and there was no more sea. And I John saw the holy
city, new Jerusalem, coming down from God out of
heaven, prepared as a bride adorned for her husband.

And I heard a great voice out of heaven saying, Behold, the tabernacle of God is with men, and He will dwell with them, and they shall be His people, and God Himself shall be with them, and be their God. And God shall wipe away all tears from their eyes; and there shall be no more death, neither sorrow, nor crying, neither shall there be any more pain: for the former things are passed away.

"And He that sat upon the throne said, Behold, I make all things new. And He said unto me, Write: for these words are true and faithful. And He said unto me, It is done. I am Alpha and Omega, the beginning and the end. I will give unto him that is athirst of the fountain of the water of life freely. He that overcometh shall inherit all things; and I will be his God, and he shall be my son. But the fearful, and unbelieving, and the abominable, and murderers, and whoremongers, and sorcerers, and idolaters, and all liars, shall have their part in the lake which burneth with fire and brimstone: which is the second death.

"And there came unto me one of the seven angels which had the seven vials full of the seven last plagues, and talked with me, saying, Come hither, I will shew thee the bride, the Lamb's wife. And he carried me away in the Spirit to a great and high mountain, and shewed me that great city, the holy Jerusalem, descending out of heaven from God, having the glory of God: and her light was like unto a stone most precious, even like a jasper stone, clear as crystal; and had a wall great and high, and had twelve gates, and at the gates twelve angels, and names written thereon, which are the names of the twelve tribes of the children of Israel: On the east three gates; on the north three gates; on the south three gates; and on the west three gates.   And the wall of the city had twelve foundations, and in them the names of the twelve apostles of the Lamb.

"And he that talked with me had a golden reed to measure the city, and the gates thereof, and the wall thereof.   And the city lieth foursquare, and the length is as large as the breadth: and he measured the city with the reed, twelve thousand furlongs.   The length and the breadth and the height of it are equal.   And he measured the wall thereof, an hundred and forty and four cubits, according to the measure of a man, that is, of the angel.

"And the building of the wall of it was of jasper: and the city was pure gold, like unto clear glass.   And the foundations of the wall of the city were garnished with all manner of precious stones.   The first foundation was jasper; the second, sapphire; the third, a chalcedony; the fourth, an emerald; the fifth, sardonyx; the sixth, sardius; the seventh, chrysolyte; the eighth, beryl; the ninth, a topaz; the tenth, a chrysoprasus; the eleventh, a jacinth; the twelfth, an amethyst. And the twelve gates were twelve pearls; every several gate was of one pearl: and the street of the city was pure gold, as it were transparent glass.

"And I saw no temple therein: for the Lord God Almighty and the Lamb are the temple of it.   And the city had no need of the sun, neither of the moon, to shine in it: for the glory of God did lighten it, and the Lamb is the light thereof. And the nations of them which are saved shall walk in the light of it: and the kings of the earth do bring their glory and honour into it. And the gates of it shall not be shut at all by day: for there shall be no night there. And they shall bring the glory and honour of the nations into it. And there shall in no wise enter into it any thing that defileth, neither whatsoever worketh abomination, or maketh a lie: but they which are written in the Lamb's book of life.

"And he shewed me a pure river of water of life, clear as crystal, proceeding out of the throne of God and of the Lamb. In the midst of the street of it, and on either side of the river, was there the tree of life, which bare twelve manner of fruits, and yielded her fruit every month: and the leaves of the tree were for the healing of the nations.

"And there shall be no more curse: but the throne of God and of the Lamb shall be in it; and His servants shall serve Him: and they shall see His face; and His name shall be in their foreheads. And there shall be no night there; and they need no candle, neither light of the sun; for the Lord God giveth them light: and they shall reign for ever and ever.

"And he said unto me, These sayings are faithful and true: and the Lord God of the holy prophets sent His angel to shew unto His servants the things which must shortly be done. Behold, I come quickly: blessed is he that keepeth the sayings of the prophecy of this book" (Rev. 21:1 — 22:7).

"He that sat upon the throne said, *Behold, I make ALL THINGS NEW!*" This statement means exactly what it says. God *will* make *ALL things NEW,* and the new earth will be all that our great God can make

it to be for our joy and pleasure. Everything hurtful
or annoying will be removed from the new earth. There
will be many new species of plants, birds, animals.
Whatever will afford help and pleasure to God's children will be created and placed in the new earth.
Some of the animals which we know today will remain
—i. e., the Bible speaks of the lion, the leopard, the
wolf, the bear, and cow. These will be delivered from
the curse and their present characteristics will be
changed.

John says, *"I saw a new HEAVEN."* This does not
refer to the *third* heaven, God's house, but the *atmospheric heavens* just above us, where Satan's kingdom is today.   Satan is "the prince of the power of
the air" (Eph. 2:2), but he will be burned out. The
atmospheric heavens will pass away with a great noise
and the elements will melt with fervent heat. And
then there will be *new* heavens just above the earth—
all demons and evil spirits removed and placed in the
lake of fire; no more storms or clouds. The atmospheric heavens will be just as they were before the
curse.

"And I John saw *the holy city,* new Jerusalem,
coming down from God out of heaven, prepared as a
bride adorned for her husband." John saw a magnificent city, decked out in all kinds of precious jewels,
with more beauty and brilliance than the mind of man
can conceive. Moreover, *the city will be HOLY.* Nothing that defiles or mars shall ever enter there. In the
new creation there will be no recurrence of what happened in the Garden of Eden when Satan entered. The
Holy City will sparkle and shine with unmarred beauty,

and the God of holiness will cause it to shine with His own glory. Yes, the glory of God will illumine all of the new creation. Satan reigns in this present world, he is the god of this world (II Cor. 4:4); but *when all things are created new,* Satan will be in the pit and God's glory will fill all of His new creation. "The city had no need of the sun, neither of the moon, to shine in it: for the glory of God did lighten it, and the Lamb is the light thereof" (Rev. 21:23).

This magnificent Holy City which John saw descending from God out of heaven will be the home of the bride of Christ, the New Testament Church, although the bride will have access to all of God's new creation. Paul tells us that even when we were dead in sins, God "hath quickened us together with Christ . . . and hath raised us up together, and made us sit together in heavenly places in Christ Jesus: that in the ages to come He might *shew the EXCEEDING RICHES OF HIS GRACE in His kindness toward us* through Christ Jesus" (Eph. 2:5-7).

God will display the exceeding riches of His grace when He displays the Church, the bride of Christ, in the Pearly White City—probably suspended between heaven and earth but much nearer to the earth than to any of the other planets of the solar system. However, since we will then have a body like the glorified body of Jesus (I John 3:2), we will have access to any and all of the new creation. Jesus traveled from the Father's house to the earth in a matter of seconds, and we will be able to travel in like manner. The risen Christ, in His glorified body, appeared in the upper room where the disciples were gathered behind

closed doors (John 20:19, 26).   So will *we* be able to
move about, in our resurrection bodies.

God With Man

"And I heard a great voice out of heaven saying,
*Behold, the tabernacle of God is with men, and He will
DWELL with them,* and they shall be His people, and
God Himself will be with them, and be their God"
(Rev. 21:3).

In the Old Testament era, God abode with Israel as
long as that nation obeyed and served Him: *"If ye
walk in my statutes, and keep my commandments, and
do them* . . . I will set my tabernacle among you: and
my soul shall not abhor you. And I will walk among
you, and will be your God, and ye shall be my people" (Lev. 26:3, 11, 12).   During the Millennium God
will bless Israel in a peculiar manner.   Other nations
will be blessed in connection with Israel, but the Millennium is the Utopia promised to Abraham and to
his seed.

In the *new* earth, God will *dwell* with men because
there will be no wicked people at that time.   The earth
will be populated by men who worship God, and God
will abide with them.   In this era, this Dispensation of
Grace, God abides in the heart of the believer in the
Person of the Holy Spirit; but in the new creation He
will dwell with men, they will be His people, and He
will be their God.

No More Tears

"*And God shall wipe away all tears from their eyes
. . .*" (Rev. 21:4).

In the Garden of Eden, God made it very clear to
Adam and Eve that they would suffer for their sin—
and mankind has suffered ever since that day because
of Adam's disobedience to God. Rivers of tears have
been shed as a result of the curse—but in the new
earth there will be no more weeping. God Himself will
wipe away all tears. Job 14:1 tells us, "Man that is
born of a woman is of few days, and full of trouble."
Romans 8:23 tells us that even we who possess "the
firstfruits of the Spirit" groan and travail in pain in
this body of humiliation and death. How wonderful to
know that in the new creation there will be no reason
for tears because all men will worship God and will
live in peace and harmony, apart from disease, heartache, or misery.

No More Death

"... *and there shall be no more death* ..." (Rev.
21:4). Death is the rule in this world. *ALL men
DIE*. It is appointed unto men once to die (Heb. 9:27).
When sin is finished, it brings forth death (James 1:15).
We know that this earthly house, this tabernacle of
flesh, will be dissolved (II Cor. 5:1). Yes, death is the
rule now, rather than the exception; but in the new
earth there will be no more death. There will be no
graves in the new creation, no undertakers, no funeral
wreaths. Think of the *billions of dollars* death has
cost!—hospital bills, funerals, undertaker's expense,
gravediggers, a plot of earth in a cemetery or a crypt
in a mausoleum. Think of the heartache and sorrow
when a loved one dies. Think of the man-hours lost
by people attending funerals. Truly, death is an *enemy*

—but praise God! one day that enemy will be destroyed (I Cor. 15:26).

No More Sorrow

". . . there shall be . . . neither *sorrow,* nor *crying,* neither shall there be *any more pain . . .*" (Rev. 21:4). Three things are mentioned here that will be *no more* in God's new creation: (1) sorrow, (2) crying, (3) pain. This poor, tear-stained civilization knows sorrow and pain such as has not heretofore been known by man. Think of the sorrow and mourning caused by the ever-increasing drug traffic! Think of the grief and pain caused by strong drink—broken homes, hungry children, and many other evils. All of this will be forever removed when God renovates the earth by fire and creates all things new. There will be no more sorrow, grief, or pain. What a glorious day that will be—eternal day with joy such as has never been known by man since the beginning of time!

No Night

"And the gates of it shall not be shut at all by day: *for there shall be NO NIGHT there*" (Rev. 21:25). As the earth rotates on its axis today, we have day and night; but the *new earth* will not be able to turn from the light, for the radiance of God will illumine all creation all the time. In that glorious day, the prophecy of Zechariah 14:6, 7 will be literally fulfilled: "And it shall come to pass in that day, that the light shall not be clear, nor dark: but it shall be *ONE (uninterrupted) DAY* which shall be known to the Lord, not day, nor night: but it shall come to pass, that *at evening time it shall be light."*

In the new earth there will be one eternal day of light—no darkness, no weeping, no sorrow, no pain, no death. ONE ETERNAL DAY of light, joy, and glory with God!

The New Paradise

"And he shewed me *a pure river of water of life,* clear as crystal, proceeding out of the throne of God and of the Lamb" (Rev. 22:1). The *"water* of life" and the tree of life will be in the new Paradise of God, and the people of God will drink from the river of the water of life and feast on the fruit from the *tree of life,* which will bear twelve kinds of fruit, with a different harvest every month.

The *leaves* of the tree of life will be "for the healing of the nations" (Rev. 22:2). In other words, the fruit and leaves of the tree of life will guarantee health; they will be imparters of longevity. It was in God's mercy that He drove Adam and Eve from the Garden of Eden, because if they had remained there and had eaten of the fruit of the tree of life, they would have lived forever in their sinful bodies! Therefore God did not allow them to partake of the fruit of that tree. He drove them from the Garden and made sure they did not return and eat of the fruit that would have given them eternal life in mortal bodies.

How I thank God that I will not live forever in this body of pain and sorrow! I will one day have a new body—incorruptible, glorified, like the glorious body of Jesus. When we enter the new Paradise we will be holy, righteous—and it will be impossible for us to sin. God will therefore allow us to partake of the tree of life.

No More Curse

"And there shall be *no more curse:* but the throne of God and of the Lamb shall be in it; and His servants shall serve Him" (Rev. 22:3). The Greek word here translated "curse" means *"cursed thing"*—as in Romans 9:3. In the new earth, the Paradise of God, there will be nothing accursed, nothing that brings a curse. "There shall in no wise enter into it *any thing that defileth,* neither whatsoever worketh abomination, or maketh a lie . . ." (Rev. 21:27). God has made sure that there will be no repetition of the Garden of Eden.

The Eternal Blessing of Israel In the New Earth

In Isaiah 65:17 we find these words: "Behold, I create new heavens and a new earth: and the former shall not be remembered, nor come into mind." This statement certainly looks beyond the Millennium. The Holy Spirit, through Isaiah, definitely speaks of the new heavens and the new earth. Then in the same chapter, in verses 18 through 25, we find the description of Israel in the Millennium, and of the earth during that period:

"But be ye glad and rejoice for ever in that which I create: for, behold, I create Jerusalem a rejoicing, and her people a joy. And I will rejoice in Jerusalem, and joy in my people: and the voice of weeping shall be no more heard in her, nor the voice of crying.

"There shall be no more thence an infant of days, nor an old man that hath not filled his days: for the child shall die an hundred years old; but the sinner being an hundred years old shall be accursed. And they shall build houses, and inhabit them; and they shall plant vineyards, and eat the fruit of them. They shall not build, and another inhabit; they shall not plant, and another eat: for as the days of a tree are the days of my people, and mine elect shall long enjoy the work of their hands. They shall not labour in vain, nor bring forth for trouble; for they are the seed of the blessed of the Lord, and their offspring with them. And it shall come to pass, that before they call, I will answer; and while they are yet speaking, I will hear. The wolf and the lamb shall feed together, and the lion shall eat straw like the bullock: and dust shall be the serpent's meat. They shall not hurt nor destroy in all my holy mountain, saith the Lord."

These verses tell us that Jerusalem will be a city of rejoicing, its people filled with joy. This has not been true since the crucifixion of Jesus. Yet the Word proclaims, "I will rejoice in Jerusalem" — and He will have joy in His people. There will be no weeping then in the streets of that Holy City. People will again live to be hundreds of years old. There will be no such thing as "an infant of days" — that is, the person who is a hundred years old will still be a child. Longevity will be the common rule.

We also are told that the people of Israel will build houses — and live in them. They will plant vineyards — and drink the fruit of the vine. When Jesus instituted the Lord's Supper He said to His disciples, "I will not drink henceforth of this fruit of the vine, until that day when I drink it new with you *in my Father's kingdom"* (Matt. 26:29). He was speaking of the Millennium, the time when God will bless the labor of the hands of His people.

History bears out the statement that wherever the Jew has gone since the dispersion, there has been trouble; but during the Millennium there will be perfect peace for that nation. Their labor will not be in vain, their homes and vineyards will not be taken away by their enemies. God promises that even before they call, He will answer; and while they are still speaking He will hear their cry. Then in verse 25 we see the curse lifted from the animal kingdom—the wolf and the lamb will feed together, the lion will eat straw like the bullock, and there will be no killing or destruction in God's holy mountain. This speaks very definitely of the Millennium.

Then in Isaiah 66:22 we read, "For as the new heavens and the new earth, which I will make, shall remain before me, saith the Lord, *so shall your seed and your name remain!"* So we see that the nation Israel and the seed of David are an eternal people. They will remain as long as the new heavens and the new earth remain—and that will be throughout eternity.

There are Scriptures in both the Old and the New Testaments which speak of the Millennium—the reign of Christ on earth; and *in the same passage* we read of the new heaven and the new earth, speaking of His *eternal* reign. The Word of God clearly teaches that there will be a period of one thousand years when Jesus will sit on the throne of David in Jerusalem and reign over this earth *as it is now*—except for the lifting of the curse. Then at the close of the Millennium

the devil will be loosed and will go out through the
entire earth to test and try all who have been born
during the Millennium and have never known temptation.

Those who *follow* Satan will make up the armies
of Gog and Magog, and will completely compass the
Holy City Jerusalem to do battle against God's people.
At that moment it will seem that Satan is about to
win a great victory—but fire will come down from God
out of heaven and devour the armies which in number
will be as the sands of the seashore. Then immediately following the battle of Gog and Magog the kingdom
of Christ will merge into the eternal kingdom of God,
and Christ will reign with the Father throughout all
eternity.

One passage which illustrates this is Isaiah 9:6,7:
"Unto us a Child is born, unto us a Son is given:
and the government shall be upon His shoulder: and
His name shall be called Wonderful, Counsellor, The
mighty God, The everlasting Father, The Prince of
Peace. Of the increase of His government and peace
there shall be no end, upon the throne of David, and
upon His kingdom, to order it, and to establish it with
judgment and with justice from henceforth even for
ever. The zeal of the Lord of hosts will perform this."

In verse 6 we are told that a Child is born—and
in the next verse we are told that the Child will sit
on the throne of David and will reign—not only for
one thousand years, but forever. *Of His government
and peace there shall be no end.* Certainly this does
not speak of the millennial reign, because that reign
will come to an end at the time when Satan is loosed

from his prison to go to the four corners of the earth to tempt the multiplied millions of people who will be born during the Millennium. However, when fire from heaven destroys the armies of Gog and Magog, the kingdom of Christ on earth will merge into the eternal kingdom. (Please study Revelation 20:1-10.)

Hear these Scriptures again, as divine proof that this earth will never be annihilated, but will continue throughout eternity, created anew along with the new heaven and the Pearly White City, eternal home of the redeemed:

In II Samuel 7:16 God promised David, "Thine house and thy kingdom shall be established *for ever* before thee. Thy throne shall be established *for ever.*"

This promise God later confirmed with an oath: "I have made a covenant with my chosen. I have sworn unto David my servant, Thy seed will I establish *for ever,* and build up thy throne to all generations. . . . Once have I *sworn by my holiness* that I will not lie unto David. His seed shall endure *for ever,* and his throne as the sun before me. It shall be established *for ever* as the moon, and as a faithful witness in heaven" (Psalm 89:3, 4, 35-37).

God's covenant with David was unconditional, and it was reaffirmed to Israel through the Prophet Jeremiah many years after David died:

"For thus saith the Lord: David shall never want a man to sit upon the throne of the house of Israel; neither shall the priests the Levites want a man before me to offer burnt-offerings, and to kindle meat-offerings, and to do sacrifice continually.

"And the Word of the Lord came unto Jeremiah,

saying, Thus saith the Lord: *If ye can break my covenant of the DAY, and my covenant of the NIGHT, and that there should not be day and night in their season; then may also my covenant be broken with David my servant,* that he should not have a son to reign upon his throne; and with the Levites the priests, my ministers. As the host of heaven cannot be numbered, neither the sand of the sea measured: so will I multiply the seed of David my servant, and the Levites that minister unto me.

"Moreover the Word of the Lord came to Jeremiah, saying: Considerest thou not what this people have spoken, saying, The two families which the Lord hath chosen, He hath even cast them off? Thus they have despised my people, that they should be no more a nation before them.

"Thus saith the Lord: If my covenant be not with day and night, and if I have not appointed the ordinances of heaven and earth; then will I cast away the seed of Jacob, and David my servant, so that I will not take any of his seed to be rulers over the seed of Abraham, Isaac, and Jacob: for I will cause their captivity to return, and have mercy on them" (Jer. 33:17-26).

At the time of Jeremiah's writing, Israel had lapsed into gross idolatry; but in spite of their idolatry, in spite of all the devil had done and was doing to discredit God's people and take His promise from them, God reaffirmed His promise that David would never lack a son to sit upon his throne. These promises did not mean that David would be followed by an *unbroken* line of successors to his throne. This is

clear from the fact that after Solomon's reign the kingdom was divided, and about 587 B. C. the last king
of Judah was carried captive into Babylon. The passage just given from Jeremiah is speaking of *a future
King* whom God will raise up to sit on the throne of
David and reign *forever,* and this future King will be
none other than the Lord Jesus Christ, the Son of
God:

"Behold, the days come, saith the Lord, that I
will raise unto David *a righteous BRANCH,* and a
King shall reign and prosper, and shall execute *judgment and justice in the EARTH.* In His days Judah
shall be saved, and Israel shall dwell safely: *and this
is His name whereby He shall be called: THE LORD
OUR RIGHTEOUSNESS"* (Jer. 23:5, 6).

The key that unlocks the prophecy of Isaiah 9:6, 7
is found in Luke 1:26-33: "And in the sixth month the
angel Gabriel was sent from God unto a city of Galilee, named Nazareth, to a virgin espoused to a man
whose name was Joseph, *of the house of DAVID;* and
the virgin's name was Mary. . . . And the angel said
unto her, Fear not, Mary: for thou hast found favour
with God.   And, behold, thou shalt conceive in thy
womb, and bring forth a Son, and shalt call His name
JESUS.   He shall be great, and shall be called the
Son of the Highest: and the Lord God shall give unto
Him *the THRONE of His father DAVID: and He
shall REIGN over the house of Jacob FOR EVER;
and of His kingdom THERE SHALL BE NO END."*

So the Scriptures clearly teach that Jesus will reign—
not only for the thousand-year period of the Millennium, but after the battle of Gog and Magog the earth

will be renovated by fire, there will be a new earth wherein dwelleth righteousness, *and the kingdom of God will continue on throughout eternity.* *"Of His kingdom there shall be NO END!"*

On the Isle of Patmos, God showed John the Beloved the new heaven, the new earth, and the Pearly White City. The *new earth,* completely delivered from the curse, will be occupied by Israel and the saved nations. The *Pearly White City* will be the home of the bride of Christ, the New Testament Church. The *third heaven* will be the home of God the Father and the angels—and I personally believe that God's house will eternally remain as it is. It is the heavens just above us that will be delivered from the curse, freed from Satan and all of his evil spirits, and made new.

The greatest minds of the ages have attempted to interpret creation, redemption, and the consummation of the world. Their answers have been varied, contradictory, and often completely incomprehensible. Master minds have brought about system after system which, one after another, have been discarded. Upon the ruins of one system, another has been devised; and today men continue to wrestle with these three great truths—creation, redemption, and the end of the world.

Yet all we need to know about these subjects is found in the Word of God. He gives the answers Himself. His *thoughts* are by no means "ideas," but *creative deeds*—deeds that only Almighty God could perform, but which directly incorporate themselves within all history. The history of the ages is the history of mankind, and the history of mankind is the history of God. God's answer concerning creation, redemption, and the consummation of all things *is simply HIMSELF.* Even before the foundation of the world, the Holy Trinity—*Father, Son, and Holy Spirit*—planned, programmed, and finished all things from the beginning to the end.

God (as *the Eternal Word*) was manifested in His Son, and the Son of God is the center of all Divine revelation. All things proceed from God, "for *BY HIM were all things created,* that are in heaven, and that are in earth, visible and invisible, whether they be thrones, or dominions, or principalities, or powers: *all things were created by Him, and for Him*" (Col. 1:16). "All things were made by Him; and without Him was not any thing made that was made" (John 1:3).

All things are *completed* by Almighty God. In this we have the explanation and the answer to the question of the present process of world redemption that is definitely proceeding according to God's schedule, *"for OF Him, and THROUGH Him, and TO Him, are all things: to whom be glory for ever. Amen"* (Rom. 11:36).

All things *move back* to Almighty God, and in this is revealed the goal of the future—the essential character of all world consummation. "Therefore, my beloved brethren, be ye stedfast, unmoveable, always abounding in the work of the Lord, forasmuch as ye know that your labour is not in vain in the Lord" (I Cor. 15:58).

Everything God *has* done, *is* doing, or ever *will do* has Himself eternally as its goal. Whatsoever *has* come to pass, everything that ever *will* come to pass, is *"for His name's sake"* (Psalm 23:3). We are *saved* "for Christ's sake" (Eph. 4:32; I John 2:12). We are added to the body of Christ, "of His flesh, and of His bones" (Eph. 5:30). We are members of the New Testament Church of which Jesus is the head, for the glory of God and for His sake, that He might present the Church to Himself, "a glorious Church, not having spot, or wrinkle, or any such thing; but that it should be holy and without blemish" (Eph. 5:27).

For almost twenty centuries God has been calling out a people for His name, and as each individual receives the Lord Jesus Christ as Saviour, that individual is added to the body of Christ. This will continue until the bride of Christ is complete, the time when Christ will catch away His Church in the Rapture. Then in the ages of ages the bride will occupy the Pearly White City, and throughout all eternity God will display in that city the exceeding riches of His grace in Christ Jesus—to the eternal glory of Himself, "to the praise of the glory of His grace, wherein He hath made us accepted in the Beloved . . . that we should be to the praise of His glory, who first trusted in Christ" (Eph. 1:6, 12).

God is the Creator of all things, the Author and Finisher of salvation. All things consist because of Him and all of this is true that God may be all in all: "And when all things shall be subdued unto Him, then shall the Son also Himself be subject unto Him that put all things under Him, *that God may be ALL IN ALL*" (I Cor. 15:28).

Since God is holy, righteous, and perfect, He must

always wish the highest; and since God by virtue of His deity *is* the highest, He must always have as the goal of His own will that which is within His own nature. Therefore He must *work* all things and *order* all things, that in the end *all things may lead to Him.* All things *begin* in God, all things must *end* in God. He is the Alpha and the Omega.

Thus the purpose of the creation in the beginning, thus the deliverance of the world from its watery grave when order was brought out of chaos and man was created. Thus the creation of the new heavens and the new earth just before the beginning of the ages of ages, when God will have put down all evil. Therefore the purpose of all that He *has* done, *is doing,* and *will do* must consist in the unfolding, the setting forth, and the display of the glory of God.

"Known unto God are all His works from the beginning of the world" (Acts 15:18). God has a plan, a program; and all hell cannot frustrate the fulfillment of that plan. One day, time will be no more. Eternity will begin—and then Almighty God will have put down all enemies, all sin, all evil; and will have made sure that there will never be a repetition of the Garden of Eden! He will dwell with His people in the new heaven and in the new earth—and in the Pearly White City. What a glorious time the ages of ages beyond ending time will be!